Yours
FOR
Humanity

Yours
FOR
Humanity

New Essays on

PAULINE

ELIZABETH

HOPKINS

EDITED BY

JoAnn Pavletich

The University of Georgia Press

ATHENS

© 2022 by the University of Georgia Press
Athens, Georgia 30602
www.ugapress.org
All rights reserved
Designed by Kaelin Chappell Broaddus
Set in 10.75/13.5 Corundum Text Book by Kaelin Chappell Broaddus

Most University of Georgia Press titles are
available from popular e-book vendors.

Printed digitally

Library of Congress Cataloging-in-Publication Data

Names: Pavletich, JoAnn, 1954– editor.
Title: Yours for humanity : new essays on Pauline Elizabeth Hopkins /
edited by JoAnn Pavletich.
Description: Athens : The University of Georgia Press, [2022]
| Includes bibliographical references and index.
Identifiers: LCCN 2022025156 | ISBN 9780820363141 (hardback) |
ISBN 9780820363134 (paperback) | ISBN 9780820363158 (ebook)
Subjects: LCSH: Hopkins, Pauline E. (Pauline Elizabeth)—Criticism and interpretation. |
African Americans in literature. | Race in literature. | LCGFT: Literary criticism. | Essays.
Classification: LCC PS1999.H4226 Z97 2022 | DDC 813/.4—dc23/eng/20220722
LC record available at https://lccn.loc.gov/2022025156

This book is dedicated to the extraordinary life of
PAULINE ELIZABETH HOPKINS
*and to the many African American women who,
like her, have led extraordinary lives that for too long
have gone unappreciated and unsung.*

CONTENTS

PART 3. TEXTUAL PRACTICES

"Coming Unalone"
REFLECTIONS ON TEACHING PAULINE HOPKINS
Geoffrey Sanborn

The Serial Pleasures of Reading
Pauline Elizabeth Hopkins
Cherene Sherrard-Johnson

AFTERWORD
"I Sing of the Wrongs of a Race"
PAULINE E. HOPKINS AS EDITOR AND AUTHOR
Edlie L. Wong

CONTRIBUTORS

INDEX

FOREWORD

Imagining Pauline Hopkins
across Time
John Cullen Gruesser

In 1972 Ann Allen Shockley, a librarian at Fisk University, published a short essay subtitled "A Biographical Excursion into Obscurity" about an all-but--forgotten Black woman writer named Pauline E. Hopkins (1859–1930). Six years later, Southern Illinois University Press reprinted Hopkins's little-known 1900 novel, *Contending Forces: A Romance Illustrative of Negro Life North and South,* in its Lost American Fiction series. Started in 1972 and edited by Matthew J. Bruccoli, the book series had reprinted twenty-two works of fiction in hardcover by 1978, some of which (but not *Contending Forces*) were also brought out in paper by the Popular Library. According to Bruccoli, he and his colleagues were looking for two qualities in the books to be included: "'life': does the work live?—does it have a voice of its own—does it present human nature convincingly? . . . [and] historical value: does it illuminate the literary or social history of its time?" ("Lost Fiction Series" 415). Acknowledging that some of the titles "will vanish again: We cannot claim that all of the volumes are lost masterpieces," he nevertheless contends that "some of them are" (Bruccoli, "Lost American Fiction" 416).[1] Either Bruccoli or Southern Illinois University Press recruited perhaps the best-known and certainly the most lauded Black woman writer of the day to write the afterword to Hopkins's book: poet and novelist Gwendolyn Brooks, the first African American to win the Pulitzer Prize. At the time, Brooks was fifty-one and had more than twenty years of life ahead of her; meanwhile, Hopkins had been dead for nearly half a century, and a rediscovery of her career as a prolific, multitalented author and a pioneering editor could not have been imagined by anyone.

Especially but by no means exclusively because of what has happened to Hopkins studies since then, Brooks's piece is remarkable. When I first read it roughly thirty years ago, I did so defensively, wincing at or being incensed by its assertions about Hopkins. Richard Yarborough, who wrote about Hopkins in his groundbreaking dissertation and edited the game-changing 1988 Schomburg Library of Nineteenth-Century Black Women Writers edition of *Contending Forces*, has recently characterized Brooks's assessment of the novel a "brutal judgment."[2] As Yarborough aptly states, the afterword "reflects the all-too-common lack at the time of a nuanced, informed engagement with much post-Reconstruction African American literature broadly and with that produced by African American women in particular."

Brooks begins, "No, it is not *Native Son, Invisible Man, Jubilee, Roots*. Pauline Hopkins is not Richard Wright, Ralph Ellison, Margaret Walker, Alex Haley" (403). She asserts that Hopkins is "often indignant, but not indignant enough" (403) and terms her or her writing "quaint," "brainwashed," "querulous," "assimilationist," "crippled," and even "inarticulate." Moreover, Brooks implies that Hopkins was naive or uninformed about (1) racism (were Hopkins alive in the late 1970s, she "would look about her and discover that cruelty, once at least to some degree impulsive or random or spasmodic, is now deliberate, massively and cleverly organized, steady, fundamental, *national*" [407]); (2) Africa ("our author would see, certainly, . . . that what is happening to the 'weak' on the Afrikan continent can by all means be called rape and slave-driving and lynching" [407]); (3) imperialism ("she would question, would investigate that word *weak*. So many millions of the 'weak'—in the grip of the comparative handful of the 'strong'! I believe she would have cared to predict that the 'weak' would, finally, perceive the impressiveness of their numbers, perceive the quality and legitimacy of their essence, and take a *sufficiency* of indicated steps toward their definition, clarification, and indisputable salvation" [408]); and (4) the need for political action ("Hopkins would take note of the glitterings of promise on the horizon. She would note that many of the 'weak'—not all—are raising their voices and their fists, fists in which often may be found 'means necessary'" [408]). These were the contentions about Hopkins that rankled me on first reading Brooks's afterword.

Now I see so much that I missed. The piece unquestionably and understandably reveals far more about Brooks and her own tumultuous time than about Hopkins and hers, and in this way, it to some extent resembles that portion of Alice Walker's justly famous 1972 essay, "In Search of Our Mothers' Gardens," in which she asks "How could she?" in response to Phillis Wheatley's depiction of a blond-haired goddess of Liberty in her poem dedicated to George Washington. As a result of attending the Second Black Writers' Conference at Fisk University in 1967, Brooks became a fervent advocate of Black Power and in

1971 visited East Africa, a journey she recounted in the autobiographical *Report from Part One* the following year. Her afterword also vividly illustrates how far scholarship on Hopkins has come since not only the 1970s but also the early 1990s, when more than a thousand pages of her fiction was back in print as a result of the publication of three Schomburg Library volumes. Yet little was known of her life, and only a handful of scholars had published essays, reference book entries, or book chapter sections about her or her texts.

Before sitting down several months ago to reexamine the afterword, my idea was to imagine, What if Brooks had read Hopkins's serial novels published between 1901 and 1903 in the *Colored American Magazine*—*Hagar's Daughter: A Story of Southern Caste Prejudice* (discussed by Valerie Sirenko and Cherene Sherrard-Johnson in this volume), *Winona: A Tale of the South and Southwest* (the subject of this volume's essay by Colleen O'Brien), and *Of One Blood; or, The Hidden Self* (the focus of this volume's contributions by Courtney Novosat and Geoffrey Sanborn); what if she had had a thorough familiarity with the writings that Hopkins was responding to and could see how she often signified on them (as illustrated in the essays by Hanna Wallinger and Sabine Engwer in this collection); what if she had been fully informed about Hopkins's role in the Booker T. Washington versus W. E. B. Du Bois and William Monroe Trotter struggle and about her firing from the *Colored American Magazine*; and, finally, what if she had known about Hopkins the editor not only making literature by Black writers, especially women, a top priority (as documented by Elizabeth J. Cali in this volume) but also strategically including articles on Africa, Cuba, and the Philippines—in other words, what if Brooks had known that Hopkins was fully engaged in debates about relations between "weak" and "strong" peoples or nations, that is, imperialism?

However, whereas I had remembered my knee-jerk response to Brooks's reading of Hopkins, I had forgotten key things about it, such as how poetic it is at times, featuring four distinctively Brooksian alliterative trios reminiscent of "Sadie and Maud" and "We Real Cool"—"wheedle, whip, whine"; "sing, sass, singe"; "churn, check, channelize"; "trust, try, traipse"—and that the afterword itself imagines the two women meeting. This is something, by the way, that could have happened: Brooks was born in 1917, and Hopkins died in 1930; the former could have encountered the latter as a teenager, just as Hopkins likely met William Wells Brown when she was young. But Brooks, anticipating to some extent Afrofuturism (a subject touched on by both Novosat and Cherene Sherrard-Johnson in this volume), also imagines Hopkins somehow being brought to life in the late 1970s and responding to the conditions at that time: "And what conclusions would Pauline Hopkins draw, if she were alive today. It is to be supposed that most of the agitation she suffered during the composition of *Contending Forces* would be distinct in her today. I believe she would be angrier. I believe she would scream to herself and to whatever listeners she could muster: 'What! This is all that has been achieved in the minds and morals of men and women?'" (408).

Of course, this opens the door for us to imagine Brooks still alive today or time traveling to our moment and seeing what has become of Pauline Hopkins: the copious, incisive scholarship on her, including two full-length biographies, Hanna Wallinger's *Pauline Elizabeth Hopkins: A Literary Biography* (2005) and Lois Brown's *Pauline Elizabeth Hopkins: Black Daughter of the Revolution* (2008); the anthology *Daughter of the Revolution: The Major Nonfiction Works of Pauline E. Hopkins* (2007), edited by Ira Dworkin; the book-length critical studies *Pauline Hopkins and the American Dream*, by Alisha R. Knight (2011), and *The Motherless Child in the Novels of Pauline Hopkins*, by Jill Bergman (2012); countless articles and chapters in monographs and dissertations; Broadview critical editions of *Hagar's Daughter* (2021) and *Of One Blood* (2022); and, with the publication of this volume, two collections of literary critical essays, as well as her consistent appearance in anthologies of African American and, more recently, American literature. In sum, today there is nothing to be defensive about when it comes to Hopkins, as she, along with Harriet Jacobs, Charles Chesnutt, Zora Neale Hurston, and others, has joined Brooks in the canon. What's more, were she somehow alive today, Brooks would be confronted with the existence of the Pauline Elizabeth Hopkins Society, an international organization that in May 2019 celebrated its tenth anniversary by sponsoring a staged reading of *Peculiar Sam; or, The Underground Railroad*, Hopkins's 1879 musical, which is widely regarded as the first true African American drama, and by conferring its scholarship award that year on Greg Laski's 2018 monograph *Untimely Democracy: The Politics of Progress after Slavery*, in which he examines late nineteenth- and early twentieth-century literary productions by writers including Hopkins, Du Bois, Chesnutt, Frederick Douglass, Stephen Crane, and Sutton Griggs that elaborate and wrestle with the persistence of slavery and white racial prejudice in a self-proclaimed democratic nation during a supposedly progressive era, and he extols and explicates *Contending Forces* as the supreme and most penetrating example among these texts.

Both Gwendolyn Brooks and Pauline Hopkins are, of course, long gone—the former, after decades of acclaim, passing in 2000; the latter, a figure that few people remembered, dying (under tragic circumstances) seventy years earlier. However, thanks to the kind of contextualizing scholarship exemplified by this volume, these Black women authors, their writings, and their eras have not been forgotten. Were Brooks with us now, she might see that Hopkins, rather than being out of tune with the times, was, as the essays that follow confirm, a leading figure in her own time, someone who meditated profoundly about time, a thinker far ahead of her time, and, perhaps (only time will tell), a writer for all time.

NOTES

1. At the time it was republished, Hopkins's novel was the earliest text in the Lost American Fiction series and the only one by an African American. The twenty-one titles published before *Contending Forces* were *Weeds* and *The Devil's Hand*, by the Canadian-- born Edith Summer Kelley; *The Professors Like Vodka*, by Harold Loeb (who was the inspiration for Ernest Hemingway's Robert Cohn); John Thomas's *Dry Martini: A Gentleman Turns to Love* (the basis of a 1928 film starring Mary Astor); Stephen French Whitman's *Predestined: A Novel of New York Life*; *The Cubical City*, by Janet Flanner (longtime Paris correspondent for the *New Yorker*); the southern noir novel *They Don't Dance Much*, by James Ross; Robert M. Coates's *Yesterday's Burdens*; Donald Ogden Stewart's comic novel *Mr. and Mrs. Haddock Abroad*; *Flesh Is Heir*, by Lincoln Kirstein (cofounder of the New York City Ballet); *The Wedding*, by the proletarian writer Grace Lumpkin; Floyd Gibbons's political novel *The Red Napoleon*; the screenwriter John Monk Saunders's *Single Lady*; Carroll Graham and Garrett Graham's Hollywood novel, *Queer People*; Robert McAlmon's *A Hasty Bunch*; David Graham Phillips's *Susan Lenox: Her Fall and Rise* (adapted as a film starring Greta Garbo and Clark Gable in 1931); Emerson Price's *Inn of That Journey*; Peter Martin's *The Landsmen*; the war novels *Through the Wheat*, by Thomas Boyd, and *Delilah*, by Marcus Goodrich; and Paul Cain's hard-boiled fiction *Fast One* (Bruccoli, "Lost Fiction Series").

2. A specific "brutal judgment" by Brooks that Yarborough singles out is "Oft doth the brainwashed slave revere the modes and idolatries of the master. And Pauline Hopkins consistently proves herself a continuing slave" (404–05).

WORKS CITED

Brooks, Gwendolyn. Afterword. *Contending Forces: A Romance Illustrative of Negro Life North and South*, by Pauline Hopkins, Southern Illinois University Press, 1978, pp. 403–09.

Bruccoli, Matthew J. "Lost American Fiction." *Contending Forces: A Romance Illustrative of Negro Life North and South*, by Pauline Hopkins, Southern Illinois University Press, 1978, pp. 416–17.

———. "Lost Fiction Series." *Contending Forces: A Romance Illustrative of Negro Life North and South*, by Pauline Hopkins, Southern Illinois University Press, 1978, pp. 413–15.

Walker, Alice. "In Search of Our Mothers' Gardens." *In Search of Our Mothers' Gardens: Womanist Prose*, by Alice Walker, Harcourt, Brace, Jovanovich, 1983, pp. 231–43.

Yarborough, Richard. Introduction. "Rethinking Pauline Hopkins: Plagiarism, Appropriation, and African American Literary Cultural Production," by Richard Yarborough, JoAnn Pavletich, Ira Dworkin, and Lauren Dembowitz. *American Literary History*, vol. 30, no. 4, Winter 2018, https://academic.oup.com/alh/article/30/4/e3/5099108?login=true.

ACKNOWLEDGMENTS

These acknowledgments must begin with the scholars who make up this collection. It was an honor to play a part in their creative and scholarly process. I've learned a tremendous amount witnessing the development of their ideas and dedication to their craft. I have much respect and a deep appreciation for all who appear in these pages.

In 2015, when I first joined the Pauline Elizabeth Hopkins Society, I did not fully understand the energizing role groups such as PEHS could play in the recovery of a marginalized author, as well as in a scholar's life. However, participating in the life of the society has made Hopkins's recovery more palpable and more urgent. The organization did not literally underwrite this project; however, its very existence made the book more possible, just as its existence has supported and will support other scholars in the future. I am grateful to PEHS for its commitments to a full exploration of the life, work, and times of Pauline Elizabeth Hopkins and its collegiality. I urge others to consider supporting this organization (http://www.paulinehopkinssociety .org/) or other author or special interest organizations. They enliven and broaden one's scholarly life as much as they contribute to their field.

Another institution I wish to acknowledge with sincere thanks is the William I. Dykes Library at the University of Houston–Downtown. The positive impact of the staff's expert and cheerful support cannot be underestimated. Additionally, in 2015 I received a UHD Faculty Leave Award that changed my life. Having one full semester to research and write began the journey that eventually led to this collection. I will always be profoundly grateful to the University of Houston–Downtown for that award and the opportunities it made possible. The University of Georgia Press has been helpful, patient, and kind. The three anonymous reviewers of this collection provided important suggestions for strengthening it, as well as much-valued support.

Many individuals have been generous with time, expertise, and wisdom. Karin Hooks and Mari LaRoche provided invaluable technical support: smart, attentive, and timely. They make a great team. John Gruesser's experience and insight made legible problems that were otherwise amorphous. I am incredibly fortunate to have many supportive friends and family members who have contributed to making this book a reality simply by being who they are. I am grateful to each of them for that. Very special thanks to Sara Farris and Margot Backus for too much to even begin listing. I am grateful to my sister, Pauline Vargo, who, in a sweet coincidence shares her first name, a career in a stenographic practice, and her own undeniable power and presence with Pauline Hopkins. Life often seems to be a series of "inspired borrowings," and one page of acknowledgments will not cover all the people and institutions who converged in the creation of this book. My deep gratitude to all.

Yours
FOR
Humanity

INTRODUCTION

The Expansive Vision of Pauline Elizabeth Hopkins

JoAnn Pavletich

Pauline Elizabeth Hopkins's artistic and professional versatility and multidimensional political commitments place her, according to the late Nellie McKay, alongside such celebrated "warriors" as Ida B. Wells-Barnett, Sojourner Truth, Harriet Jacobs, and Harriet Tubman (2). Even in such exalted company, however, Hopkins's oeuvre is distinguished by both its volume and its dazzling variety. Over the course of her career, she was a playwright, singer, novelist, prominent activist, powerful editor of an important journal of culture and politics, and, we must not forget, full-time stenographer for many years when the profession was male dominated and few Black women held professional positions of any kind. By many measures, Pauline Hopkins was an extraordinary woman who was also "the single most productive black woman writer at the turn of the century" (Yarborough xxviii). Above all, hers was a life steeped in language. She lived immersed in the spoken, sung, written, and read word.

It is not only the volume and variety of work that distinguishes her, however; it is the astonishing complexity of that work. After more than thirty years of recovery we continue to discover new and important approaches to understanding Hopkins's oeuvre that provide a surplus of evidence for her dense and complicated creativity.[1] This surfeit of creativity appears to have been a part of Hopkins's life from an early age. Hopkins was born in 1859 in Portland, Maine, and she and her mother and stepfather soon moved to Boston, where Hopkins attended the legendary Girls' High School. As Lois Brown puts it in her biography of Hopkins, "She grew up in a loving and large extended family that linked her to freedom in the colonial North and to bondage in the antebellum South. Her first mentors were drawn from her family; these influential figures recognized and nurtured her creative genius and flair for performance. By the early 1870s, Hopkins was breaking new ground as an African American play-wright, and by her early twenties she had become the first woman of color to write and star in her own dramatic work" (1). That work, *Peculiar Sam; or, The Underground Railroad*, had much success, and in the 1880s Hopkins trav-eled the Northeast and Midwest as part of the Hopkins Colored Troubadours. In the 1890s she supported herself as an orator and stenographer. By the late 1890s, Hopkins had joined the staff of the *Colored American Magazine* (*CAM*), initiating the phase of life that we know best from her journalism and novels.[2] Hopkins shaped her mature public persona, according to Brown, stressing the political commitments that she understood as her inheritance from the long line of free people of color from whom she descended. Her oeuvre honors this in-heritance of African American action, creativity, and perseverance: "for hu-manity," as the signature line on her photo in *Contending Forces* asserts.

Considered from the broadest of perspectives, Hopkins's life work occupies itself with the critique and creation of epistemologies that control racialized knowledge and experience. Whether they are representations of a critical con-temporary problem such as lynching, imperialism, or Pan-African unity or they are representations of African American women's voices, Hopkins's texts create new knowledge and new frames for understanding this knowledge. I am cer-tainly not the first to discuss Hopkins or African American literature in these terms. In this collection alone, Colleen O'Brien, John Cyril Barton, Valerie Si-renko, and Courtney Novosat point to Hopkins's critique of existing epistemol-ogies (Sirenko and Novosat) or her creation of new structures of knowledge (O'Brien and Barton) that offer alternatives to the anti-Black ways of know-ing that underpin her era's social and political thought. Hopkins's preoccupa-tion with the epistemological lens that produces collective understanding is par-ticularly noteworthy in her depictions and articulations of African American women.

The 1988 republication of Hopkins's four novels and resulting scholarly in-terest have led to a broad critical acceptance of the liberatory potential of Hop-kins's compelling female figures. As embodiments of gendered and racialized knowledge, Hopkins's female characters have served as mentors, teaching our generation of scholars how to understand them. This is not to make claims of verisimilitude or even comprehensiveness but rather to observe that Hop-kins's representational strategies for these figures—from Ma Smith and Sappho Clark in *Contending Forces* to "Famous Women of the Negro Race" in *CAM*—have, over time, made legible and describable complex layers of racism, racial-ized gender norms, the impact of racist norms and discourses, and resistance to them. This legibility has increased as the critical work has grown, and in turn, this critical progress has been influenced by and contributed to a better understanding of the post-Reconstruction period generally, a period that has received more focused attention in the last decade than in the previous three.[3] As Brittany Cooper argues in her important book (itself an example of the growth of post-Reconstruction studies), *Beyond Respectability: The Intellectual Thought of Race Women*, Hopkins was one of a number of "race women" who deliberately created an intellectual tradition and a body of knowledge that "maps" how "Black women chose to take up and transform intellectual and physical spaces in service of their racial uplift projects" (22). Hopkins's representation of racialized and gendered figures is part of her map.[4]

Hopkins's composing process, including her extensive appropriation of language, plot structures, and characters originating with other authors, is another arena that offers insights to her episteme-crafting efforts.[5] Ira Dworkin has argued that Hopkins's textual appropriations result in "her own voice and her own language" (e20). I agree, and the essays in this collection all substantiate that claim, even if they do so in different registers. Nevertheless, Hopkins's creation of this unique voice and language appears to have been less motivated by her own individualism than by her desire to voice a Black intellectual tradition that challenges conventional notions of authorship and ownership as it raises complex questions of voice. In other words, the composing process in Hopkins's hands is, broadly, an epistemological enterprise of deconstructing printed texts and circulating discourses in order to create new windows through which we can see more clearly.

While I am convinced that Hopkins's writing practice points directly to the importance of her voice, knowledge of the practice raises critical and practical challenges. Above all, it is wise to ask ourselves how the critical attention we devote to Hopkins's intertextualities might detract from her continued recovery if they are perceived as what we today call plagiarism. Indeed, the history of plagiarism accusations is littered with claims of illegitimate appropriation leveled by cultural gatekeepers. Hopkins may have quasi-canonical status, but that would not necessarily prevent the taint of plagiarism in an academy shaped by a long history of excluding Black writers and a profound commitment to individual authorship, individualism, and notions of text as property from once again relegating Hopkins to the status of minor historical figure.[6] Perceptions of individual property rights from enslavement through copyrights could easily marginalize the life and work of one more African American woman, exerting a "hidden hand" in decisions.[7] It is not hard to see the responsibility we have to continue a thorough and rigorously antiracist recovery of Pauline Hopkins that accounts for the double binds and distortions complicating Black cultural intellectual production in her period and our own.

We must also recognize how important Hopkins's goals had to have been to her in order for her to risk all that she did. Her practices would have been considered plagiarism by many if not most gatekeepers at a time when the term was solidifying into the shape most commonly recognized today.[8] Hopkins's notoriously strained relationship with Booker T. Washington and his followers would have been further strained, and it is unlikely that the Boston Literary and Historical Society, an African American organization with commitments to burgeoning twentieth-century notions of "great literature," would have appreciated Hopkins's composing practice. Hopkins risked her employment and her reputation in the name of her multivocal composing process.

Marilyn Randall and others who examine the history of plagiarism insist that plagiarism is a relation of power. For Hopkins, her composing process *is* a manifestation of her power, as her palimpsestic texts teach us, perhaps force us, to look at them through layers of discursive connecting, colliding, and correcting. There is no shortage of euphemisms for her practice, and each of them, from "inspired borrowings" through "textual suturing" to "appropriations," offers a valuable perspective on this deeply complex practice. John Gruesser and Geoffrey Sanborn have independently suggested the pluralized "plagiarisms," to describe the results of her practice, that is, varieties of plagiarism defined differently in different communities and circumstances.[9] Hopkins's intertextualities are not only plagiarism, however. Whatever else Hopkins's practice may be, it is one of the most important avenues of research today. Questions of voice and authorship have been a fundamental part of the African American literary tradition since the earliest slave narrative and have changed literary history while making it. These critical interrogations of voice and authorship will most certainly continue to build a better comprehension of Hopkins's process and oeuvre. While we may better understand Hopkins today than we did in 1988, there is still much to probe and unravel.

Whereas Hopkins's novels have been the primary focus of this research, her journalism and editorial work have remained largely critically neglected. Elizabeth J. Cali and Edlie L. Wong make major contributions in this collection. Additionally, Wong's recent essay, "An Unexpected Direction: Pauline Hopkins, S. E. F. C. C. Hamedoe and 'The Darker Races of the Twentieth Century,'" charts how Hopkins's five-part ethnological series, published in *Voice of the Negro* in 1905, "seized on imperial expansion's utopian possibilities to imagine new, international solidarities to bring about global resistance to racial cap-

italism" (726). Wong also speculates that S. E. F. C. C. Hamedoe, a contributor to *CAM* while Hopkins was editor, may have been a Hopkins pseudonym.
This additional shapeshifting is not an enormous surprise, as we have known
for a long time about some of her pseudonyms. However, it does indicate that
the extent of Hopkins's shapeshifting is still not thoroughly known. Regardless
of the number of pseudonyms or texts Hopkins appropriated, the meaning behind her choices remains for our interrogation, and it may be from her journalism and editorial efforts that we gain the greatest clarity about her political convictions, visions, and composing practice. In the case of "The Darker Races of
the Twentieth Century," Wong argues that the series "allowed Hopkins to experiment with various epistemologies of racial and historical knowledge in her
efforts to formulate an understanding of Blackness that, like the episodic serial
form, was open-ended, accretive, and noncohesive" (727). Whether in fiction
or journalism, Hopkins's intellectual efforts stemmed from an extremely broad
perspective that experimented with manifold versions of Blackness from Professor Hamedoe to Venus Johnson in *Hagar's Daughter* and with discursive
structures from the trope of the tragic mulatta through Pan-Africanism.

This collection of essays constitutes a new phase in the full historical and literary recovery of Pauline Elizabeth Hopkins. Essays in part 1, "Texts and Contexts," examine the complicated and volatile post-Reconstruction context both
in Boston, where Hopkins lived and worked, and nationally. Part 2, "Intertexts," addresses Hopkins's unattributed appropriation of texts in her novels.
Part 3, "Textual Practices," reflects on two of the least explored areas of Hopkins studies: pedagogy and Hopkins's relevance to twenty-first-century popular culture. Hopkins's life and work are typically contextualized in terms of late
nineteenth-century conditions in the United States and the complexities of the
post-Reconstruction period, a period that witnessed an explosive growth of formal and informal structures of racism, including mob violence, Black exclusion
from the legal system, and the discursive justification of those actions. This period also saw a lightning-swift rise in Black literacy rates; the continued growth
of a Black bourgeoisie; an explosion of Black churches, schools, publications,
and associations; and, importantly, organized resistance to white supremacy.
These aspects of Hopkins's historical context are examined in part 1.

John Cyril Barton's essay, "'Strun 'Em Up fer a Eggsample to the Res'":
Lynch Law's Rhetoric of Exemplarity and Pauline E. Hopkins's *Contending
Forces*," focuses on one of the most horrific manifestations of human subjuga-
tion: widespread lynching. Barton discusses Hopkins's first novel, *Contending
Forces*, in terms of lynching and a "rhetoric of exemplarity," defined as "dra-
matic representations of mob violence that not only self-consciously call upon

the judgment of readers but overtly thematize the idea of 'example' as pattern, punishment, or model." Barton identifies this rhetoric in William Wells Brown's *Clotel* and in the work of other important Black writers, arguing that Hopkins's representation of lynching demonstrates how she "draws from and criticizes the general conventions for representing lynching; . . . however, [she] pushes the critique much further by making lynching the example par excellence of an ideology of white supremacy rather than one example among others expressing that ideology." Employing a comparative-critical strategy, Barton joins recent studies that emphasize Hopkins's connections to Herman Melville, W. E. B. Du Bois, James Weldon Johnson, Edith Wharton, Frances Harper, and Alfred, Lord Tennyson (see Barnes; Hack; Paulin; Randall; and Wooley). These fruitful comparisons amplify our understanding of Hopkins's cultural inheritance while illuminating the specific issues that preoccupied her.

Pauline Hopkins's role in shaping the *Colored American Magazine* is, perhaps, the least studied aspect of her oeuvre. Elizabeth J. Cali's essay, "Pauline E. Hopkins's Editorial Rise and Radical Racial Uplift in Fiction Publishing at the *Colored American Magazine*," breaks important ground, as Cali, using a "dataset representing the volume and demographics of fiction publications in *CAM* from May 1900 to March 1904," charts Hopkins's rise and fall at *CAM* through its publication of literary texts. The essay parallels the inclusion of literature by African American women with the growth of Hopkins's influence and control at *CAM*, demonstrating that as Hopkins became more central to each issue of *CAM*, more literature in general and more literature by Black women appeared. The essay demonstrates how, in spite of much argument within *CAM* on the role of literature in a magazine for African Americans, Hopkins persevered in making it central to the journal. Moreover, when Hopkins was forced out of *CAM*, the literature went with her, and so, it seems, did readers. This essay offers a valuable model in addition to the indispensable information it provides, exemplifying the treasure trove of knowledge available from studies grounded in demographics or other specific and quantifiable categories. Cali's claims about Hopkins's editorial practices as part of a conscious effort to establish an African American literary tradition open new possibilities for understanding her motivations and choices during her too-short career at that journal.

Valerie Sirenko's essay, "Literary and Legal Genres in Pauline Hopkins's *Hagar's Daughter*: Black Testimony, the Production of Truth, and the Regulation of Property," follows with a contextual emphasis on legal discourse and rhetoric. Sirenko critically refocuses Hopkins's important genre experimentation in her argument that Hopkins "manipulates the conventions of popular literary genres to unpack the function of legal genres." She persuasively discusses courtroom testimony, forensic discourse, and legal documents as legal genres with conventions liable to predictability and disruption. These legal genres, according to Sirenko, function to control and shape the supposed "truths" of a racist legal system. It is at the moment of generic disruption, signified in *Hagar's Daughter*, for example, when Henny speaks in the courtroom in spite of the legal conventions that prohibit African American testimony, that we see most vividly how Hopkins exposes and critiques the mechanisms of a systemically racist legal system. This essay adds to our ability to understand Hopkins's generic manipulation and experimentation; it also brings to our attention how naturalized processes—or genres—such as those in the legal system can and should be denaturalized in order to understand the assumptions that ground their authority.

Part 2, "Intertexts," specifically grapples with Hopkins's extensive use of unattributed texts. Each of these essays makes vital contributions to how and perhaps why Hopkins wove the intertextualities in the manner she did. They probe Hopkins's use of sources, their effects, and their implications, raising new questions and providing new frameworks for addressing them. The essays examine the appropriations through a cultural lens that situates Hopkins as stenographer (Hooks); through a politicized lens that emphasizes a rebuke of colonialism (O'Brien); through Hopkins's genre experimentation (Novosat); through a critique of the historical amnesia of the post-Reconstruction era (Engwer); and through an explication of gender, power, and property as represented by Hopkins and by one of her source texts (Wallinger).

Hanna Wallinger leads this part with an essay, "Intertextual Transformations: Pauline E. Hopkins and Alice French [Octave Thanet]," that spans four novels and the Du Bois / Washington debate. She examines *Winona* and *Contending Forces* via one of *Winona*'s primary source authors, Octave Thanet, the pen name for Alice French, and two of her novels, *Expiation* (1890) and *By Inheritance* (1910). French was a contemporary of Hopkins who, at the peak of her career, was an extremely popular, wealthy, and politically conservative novelist and who was almost certainly a lesbian. Wallinger's essay examines the "negotiations of the power politics relevant to occupying, owning, and inheriting land," demonstrating that all four novels "feature gender constellations in which the brave and courageous women take care of, rescue, or motivate the masculinization of the male characters." The similarities between texts of writers holding radically different subject positions highlight the differentials in power and attitudes to property, especially in the context of post--Reconstruction debates about the role and capacities of Black citizens, as the authors "actively rearrange their era's discourses, overlapping and intersecting with each other." Wallinger, the author of *Pauline E. Hopkins: A Literary Biography* (2005), demonstrates the value of sustained investigations of Hopkins's source texts to illuminate Hopkins's work and the period's literary and political conversations.

In "Pauline Elizabeth Hopkins: Nineteenth-Century America's Cultural Stenographer," Karin L. Hooks follows a very different critical path in her examination of stenography as both a concept and a practice, including Hopkins's own experience with it, and its relation to her first novel, *Contending Forces*. Whereas Sappho Clark's profession is most frequently ignored by readers, Hooks's focus on it provides an apt tool for understanding Hopkins's appropriative methodology. Hooks reminds us that Hopkins's career as a stenographer, roughly 1890 to her death in 1930 with, perhaps, a hiatus while she was at the *Colored American Magazine*, occurred at a cultural moment when new technologies such as stenography, the phonograph, and the typewriter "induced anxieties about how different types of mechanized writing impacted authorial agency." Hooks views Hopkins as a "cultural stenographer who employed an emerging technology as a means of inserting the Black female voice into late nineteenth-century public discourse." Concentrating on Hopkins's "skillful editing" of Ralph Waldo Emerson's abolitionism, Hooks demonstrates how Hopkins recorded and updated midcentury Emersonian discourse to make it "effective in African Americans' turn-of-the-century demands for social equality and full citizenship."

Sabine Engwer's essay, "'It's This Cursed Slavery That's to Blame': Nineteenth-Century Discourse on Slavery and Pauline Hopkins's Historiographic Counternarratives," addresses the plantation tradition, as does Wallinger. However, Engwer's essay explicates Hopkins's representation of the continuity between the antebellum realities of slavery and the post-Reconstruction period's attempt to reinstate it. Engwer argues that Hopkins attempted to change the cultural conversation that rewrote enslavement as a time of harmony between the races by bringing texts that celebrate antebellum relations into dialogue with her own, in this case, William Grayson's proslavery poem "The Hireling and the Slave." This poem, included but unattributed in *Contending Forces*, is an intertextual source that heretofore has not been discussed by Hopkins scholarship and that Hopkins incorporated "in a narrative invested in exposing the evils of the institution it so fervently defends," thus making the poem "complicit in its own deconstruction."

Hopkins's last novel, *Of One Blood*, seems poised for a new generation of analysis. The emergence of contemporary Afrofuturism retroactively marks

Hopkins as one of its important progenitors. In "'Gazing Hopelessly into the Future': Utopia and the Racial Politics of Genre in *Of One Blood; or, The Hidden Self*," Courtney Novosat highlights the racial anxiety inherent in the utopian genre and, significantly, further explores intertextuality as conventional to it. She explicates *Of One Blood* in the context of Edward Bellamy's *Looking Backward* (1889) and in relation to *Iola Leroy; or, Shadows Uplifted* (1892), by Frances Harper, and *Imperium in Imperio* (1899), by Sutton Griggs. The essay concludes that these novels, as part of an underexplored tradition of early Black utopias, highlight a long-standing use of speculative fiction as a site for nonwhite writers to intervene in white supremacist discourse. Novosat continues this collection's emphasis on comparative analysis and Hopkins's generic experimentation and increases our awareness of the relationship between utopian genre conventions and practices most typically understood as plagiarism, cautioning against any one definition of the term or practice.

Colleen O'Brien, an early contributor to Hopkins's recovery, concludes this part with "Stolen Words: Literature as a Tool for Revolution," an analysis that revisits one of O'Brien's previous arguments in light of the textual appropriations in *Winona*. *The White Islander* (1893), by Mary Hartwell Catherwood, set in eighteenth-century Native American territory at the northern reaches of Lake Michigan, is a primary source text for *Winona*. O'Brien argues that Hopkins's use of *The White Islander* is an attempt to revise the terrain of both American literature and American history. Hopkins thereby aspired to "reclaim the territory, both literary and geographic, stolen in four hundred years of colonial conquest." O'Brien's essay emphasizes the fundamental problem of the epistemological appropriation and theft that accompanied the genocide and enslavement of African and Indigenous North American people. She thus reframes Hopkins's appropriations in order to understand their larger historical implications.

Part 3, "Textual Practices," brings Hopkins studies firmly into the present with two essays that demonstrate Hopkins's relevance to twenty-first-century culture and classrooms. Geoffrey Sanborn's essay, "'Coming Unalone': Reflections on Teaching Pauline Hopkins," describes "how a recognition of Hopkins's profoundly relational understanding of subjectivity can affect the way in which her works are experienced in the classroom." The essay begins with a meditation on the relationship between language, consciousness, and the subjectivity engendered by our culture of possessive individualism, in particular, our narrow understanding and adjudication of copyright and plagiarism. Sanborn sees Hopkins's compositional practices as an antidote to the limitations of this entrenched and alienating possessive individualism. His students found that the difficulty of knowing who is originating what became a jumping-off point for a discussion of the ways in which the phenomenon of literature exceeds "the boundaries that have been established by the culture of possessive individualism." In this process, Sanborn's class came to understand whiteness as the reification of atomistic individuality and how it works against a recognition of human relationality. Sanborn suggests that studying Hopkins's compositional practices can result in a "transformative opening-up of relational possibilities" where readers experience a "collective reaching-out" to meaning beyond narrow and limiting notions of any one individual's words.

In her essay, "The Serial Pleasures of Reading Pauline Elizabeth Hopkins," Cherene Sherrard-Johnson reminds us of the pleasures of fandom. She surveys Hopkins's literary genius and popular relevance with a delightfully wide scope that includes Meghan Markle's marriage into the British royal family, the blockbuster films *Black Panther* and *The Help*, Valerie Martin's novel *Property*, and nineteenth-century Black women writers such as Elizabeth Potter and Elizabeth Keckley, in addition to Hopkins's *Of One Blood* and *Hagar's Daughter*. The essay celebrates Hopkins's "fusion of political and aesthetic aims" in audience-pleasing plots and tropes that "unsettle and galvanize, as well as entertain." She writes that the intransigence of a class-based hierarchy within dominant culture and racialized groups operates in popular culture's continued fascination with mixed-race women and its seemingly oblivious traffic in domestic stereotypes of Black womanhood that refuse to allow them the full spectrum of human desire, complexity, and interiority. Sherrard-Johnson juxtaposes Hopkins and other women of her period to "the nostalgic traffic" in *The Help* to "explore the audacious desires of domestic workers whose negotiation of class boundaries and strategic maneuvers provide textured conversation about the intimacy of the upstairs/downstairs relationship."

Taken as a whole, the essays in this collection significantly broaden the critical conversation on Pauline Hopkins in an attempt to match the breadth and depth of her vision and work. In a discussion of *Of One Blood*, Ira Dworkin argues that Hopkins's appropriations are consistent with "her strenuous, broad-based critique of existing forms of knowledge" (26e). As the essays in this collection attest, Dworkin's insight is relevant to Hopkins's entire corpus, in which she continually adapted "existing forms"—fiction genres, journalism, and more—in order to critique their insufficiencies and simultaneously to fashion new forms and structures of knowledge. She engaged in literary civil disobedience, figuratively ignoring "no trespassing" signs put up by the white readers of *CAM*, by the Booker T. Washington machine, and by the many gatekeepers around her in pursuit of ends that she clearly considered urgent. With an uncompromising drive and willingness to experiment, she created works with "all the fire and romance" (Hopkins, *Contending Forces* 14) of African American culture and history and with a broad and complex vision adequate to the magnitude and difficulty of her aims.

NOTES

1. One example of the complexity of Hopkins's oeuvre and life for critical assessments is her musical and theatrical experience. Hopkins appears to have been the first Black playwright with her production of *Peculiar Sam; or, The Underground Railroad*. "Peculiar Sam is a dramatic ballad opera in four acts and was written as a benefit for the then famous minstrel Sam Lucas. The central character was created by Lucas, and Hopkins planned her text around 16 different vocal numbers using plantation songs, ballads, and spirituals as the basis for her score. The premiere of *Peculiar Sam* took place at the Boston Young Men's Christian Union on December 8, 1879. For a year, the show toured under the management of Z. W. Sprague, a white minstrel and impresario. The most successful production occurred in July 1880 at Boston's Oakland Gardens. Large crowds attended, and the play, revised into three acts and staged by Hopkins' group, the Hyers Sisters Combination, was a huge success. The plot of the drama is reminiscent of that of the ballad opera *Out of Bondage*, by Joseph Bradford, which may have inspired the story. It documents the lives of several escaped slaves; scenes take place at various stops along the underground railroad, and the final scenes show them as successful professionals in different walks of life" (Cristi). Subsequent productions were not staged again until 2018 and 2019. Further research on this dimension of Hopkins's talents is badly needed. These youthful achievements need to be better understood in terms of their historical moment, as well as for what they harbor about Hopkins's more mature cultural productions.

2. Brown's and Wallinger's biographies are essential. There is not much biographical criticism on Hopkins, yet Brown's biography in particular insists on a Pauline Hopkins who consciously crafted a respectable middle-class public persona as she negotiated the liabilities that accompanied a Black woman in theater at a time when being on the stage was often perceived as a sign of loose virtue. Black women suffered that kind of crass sexualization exponentially.

3. In 2010 Michelle Alexander's *The New Jim Crow: Mass Incarceration in the Age of Colorblindness* was published. Alexander's book and others that have followed occasioned a reckoning with the post-Reconstruction era that continues to reverberate in numerous fields. In literary cultural studies, the creation of C19: The Society of Nineteenth-Century Americanists and its journal, *J19*, has been a part of this important trend. Whereas much of this new work is academic, there have been documentaries on the period produced by, among others, Henry Louis Gates Jr.

4. There has been much scholarly engagement with Hopkins's representations of gender since 1988 and the republication of her four novels. John Cullen Gruesser's foreword outlines some of this critical history and offers an excellent starting point for interested readers.

5. Whereas Hopkins's intertextuality has been acknowledged for many years, recent publications by Geoffrey Sanborn, myself, and Lauren Dembowitz brought to critical attention the more extensive nature of it. While it is certain that we have not yet discovered all of Hopkins's sources, we do know that in addition to an obvious intertextuality with over fifty authors, Hopkins structured her plots, developed characters, described landscapes, and produced dialogue through the copious use of wildly different sources.

6. I wish to thank Dr. April Logan for sharing her concerns and helping me to better understand the stakes in this discussion. Racism in academia can be as subtle—or blatant—as the (ex)inclusion of particular authors on reading lists, for example, and it is never too late for a figure to return to the obscurity from which recent scholarly efforts have attempted to rescue them.

7. As I write this introduction in the summer of 2021, debates on race, tenure, and acceptability rage. The University of North Carolina's board of trustees intervened to deny Nikole Hannah-Jones tenure in light of *The 1619 Project*, which she and other writers created with the *New York Times* and the *New York Times Magazine*. Other faculty of color with less claim to fame struggle with marginalization or rejection, and states across the nation have acted to restrict the teaching of critical race theory specifically and race generally. The potential for further marginalization of Hopkins is real, and we must not be naive about it.

8. Notions of authorship, originality, and plagiarism had developed into the concepts used in most current college classrooms by the early twentieth century. It was an uneven development, however. For specifics about these changes in print culture between the antebellum period and the twentieth century, consult Lara Cohen's *Fabrication of American Culture: Fraudulence and Antebellum Print Culture*; Geoffrey Sanborn's *Plagiarama! William Wells Brown and the Aesthetics of Attraction*; Pavletich; and Yarborough et al.

9. Sanborn makes his argument in a recent essay in *American Literary History*, "The Pleasure of Its Company: *Of One Blood* and the Potential of Plagiarism." John Gruesser's thoughts are from a personal email, 28 Dec. 2018. Additionally, the Pauline Elizabeth Hopkins Society maintains a web page that lists the known sources in each of Hopkins's three serialized novels: http://www.paulinehopkinssociety.org/inspired-borrowings.

WORKS CITED

Barnes, Ashley C. "Variations on a Melodrama: Imagining the Author in *Pierre* and *Of One Blood*." *Arizona Quarterly: A Journal of American Literature, Culture, and Theory*, vol. 73, no. 3, 2017, pp. 23–47.

Brown, Lois. *Pauline Elizabeth Hopkins: Black Daughter of the Revolution*. University of North Carolina Press, 2008.

Cooper, Brittney C. *Beyond Respectability: The Intellectual Thought of Race Women*. University of Illinois Press, 2017. EBSCOhost, doi:10.5406/illinois/9780252040993 .001.0001.

Cristi, A. A. "On Her Shoulders Presents Pauline Hopkins, 3/15." *Broadway World*, 19

Feb. 2018. https://www.broadwayworld.com/article/On-Her-Shoulders-presents
-PAULINE-HOPKINS-315-20180219.

Dembowitz, Lauren. "Appropriating Tropes of Womanhood and Literary Passing in Pauline Hopkins's *Hagar's Daughter.*" "Rethinking Pauline Hopkins: Plagiarism, Appropriation, and African American Cultural Production," by Richard Yarborough, JoAnn Pavletich, Ira Dworkin, and Lauren Dembowitz. *American Literary History*, vol. 30, no. 4, Winter 2018, https://academic.oup.com/alh/article/30/4/e3/5099108 ?login=true.

Dworkin, Ira. "Black Livingstone: Pauline Hopkins, *Of One Blood*, and the Archives of Colonialism." "Rethinking Pauline Hopkins: Plagiarism, Appropriation, and African American Cultural Production," by Richard Yarborough, JoAnn Pavletich, Ira Dworkin, and Lauren Dembowitz. *American Literary History*, vol. 30, no. 4, Winter 2018, https://academic.oup.com/alh/article/30/4/e3/5099108?login=true.

Hack, Daniel. "Contending with Tennyson: Pauline Hopkins and the Victorian Presence in African American Literature." *American Literary History*, vol. 28, no. 3, 2016, pp. 484–511.

Hopkins, Pauline Elizabeth. *Contending Forces: A Romance Illustrative of Negro Life North and South.* Oxford University Press, 1988.

McKay, Nellie. Introduction. *The Unruly Voice: Rediscovering Pauline Elizabeth Hopkins,* ed. John Gruesser, University of Illinois Press, 1996. EBSCOhost, search--ebscohost-com.ezproxy.uhd.edu/login.aspx?direct=true&db=mzh&AN=1996020316 &site=ehost-live.

Paulin, Diana. "The Futurity of Miscegenation: James Weldon Johnson's *The Autobiography of an Ex-Colored Man* and Pauline Hopkins's *Of One Blood.*" *New Perspectives on James Weldon Johnson's "The Autobiography of an Ex-Colored Man,"* edited by Noelle Morrissette and Amritjit Singh, University of Georgia Press, 2017, pp. 87–111.

Pavletich, JoAnn. "'We Are Going to Take That Right': Power and Plagiarism in Pauline Hopkins's *Winona.*" *CLA Journal*, vol. 59, no. 2, Dec. 2015, pp. 115–30.

Randall, Kelli V. *American Realist Fictions of Marriage: From Kate Chopin, Edith Wharton to Frances Harper, Pauline Hopkins.* Peter Lang Publishing, 2017.

Randall, Marilyn. *Pragmatic Plagiarism: Authorship, Profit, and Power.* Editions Klincksieck, University of Toronto Press, 2001. EBSCOhost, search-ebscohost-com .ezproxy.uhd.edu/login.aspx?direct=true&db=mzh&AN=2001460026&site=ehost-live.

Sanborn, Geoffrey. "The Wind of Words: Plagiarism and Intertextuality in *Of One Blood.*" *J19: The Journal of Nineteenth-Century Americanists*, vol. 3, no. 1, Spring 2015, pp. 67–87.

Wallinger, Hanna. *Pauline E. Hopkins: A Literary Biography.* University of Georgia Press, 2005.

Wooley, Christine A. "Haunted Economies: Race, Retribution, and Money in Pauline Hopkins's *Of One Blood* and W. E. B. Du Bois's *The Quest of the Silver Fleece.*" *Haunting Realities: Naturalist Gothic and American Realism*, edited by Monika Elbert and Wendy Ryden, University of Alabama Press, 2017, pp. 132–44.

Wong, Edlie. "An Unexpected Direction: Pauline Hopkins, S. E. F. C. C. Hamedoe, and 'The Dark Races of the Twentieth Century.'" *American Literary History*, vol. 32, no. 4, 2020, pp. 723–54. EBSCOhost, search-ebscohost-com.ezproxy.uhd.edu/login .aspx?direct=true&db=mzh&AN=202120815620&site=ehost-live.

Yarborough, Richard. Introduction. *Contending Forces: A Romance Illustrative of Negro Life North and South,* by Pauline Hopkins, Oxford University Press, 1988, pp. xxvii–xlviii.

Yarborough, Richard, JoAnn Pavletich, Ira Dworkin, and Lauren Dembowitz. "Rethinking Pauline Hopkins: Plagiarism, Appropriation, and African American Cultural Production." *American Literary History*, vol. 30, no. 4, Winter 2018, https:// academic.oup.com/alh/article/30/4/e3/5099108?login=true.

PART I

Texts and Contexts

"Strun 'Em Up fer a Eggsample to the Res'"

LYNCH LAW'S RHETORIC OF EXEMPLARITY
AND PAULINE E. HOPKINS'S
CONTENDING FORCES

John Cyril Barton

In a historic vote on February 26, 2020, the U.S. House of Representatives passed the Emmitt Till Justice for Lynching Act, a bill that would enable the federal government to prosecute racially motivated acts of mob violence for the first time ever. On March 7, 2022, the bill was approved by the Senate and now waits to be signed into law by the president of the United States. Over fifteen years earlier, on June 13, 2005, Congress officially apologized for its failure to pass such legislation, even though over two hundred anti-lynching bills were presented before the Senate or House from the early 1890s through the 1920s (Curtius). Three of those bills had passed in the House, but none ever made it out of the Senate. The most famous of those proposals was the Dyer Bill, first introduced in 1918 and vigorously debated on several occasions in Congress until its ultimate defeat in the Senate by filibuster in 1922. One of the earliest of such anti-lynching proposals, however, was the 1894 Blair Bill, which requested $25,000 in federal funds and called upon the national government "to investigate, ascertain, and report" (*New York Times*, September 11, 1894) facts and circumstances concerning alleged acts of rape and racially motivated mob violence from the previous decade. Noted African American activists supported the Blair Bill, including T. Thomas Fortune, the influential journalist and editor of the *New York Age*, and Ida B. Wells, the tireless race crusader who championed the bill in the concluding chapter of her second anti-lynching pamphlet, *A Red Record: Tabulated Statistics and Alleged Causes of Lynching in the United States* (1894).

Around the turn of the twentieth century, when Congress was first seriously considering a federal solution to racial lynching, several prominent Black writers turned to fiction, particularly the novel, to attack the systemic problem of white mob violence.[1] W. E. B. Du Bois, for instance, concluded "Of the Coming of John"—the penultimate chapter of *The Souls of Black Folk* (1903) and the only work of fiction in the book—with an imminent lynching to express symbolically the problems of the color line in the starkest terms. Sutton E. Griggs, a prominent Baptist minister, activist, and compatriot of Du Bois in the Niagara Movement, penned four novels between 1899 and 1905 that significantly involved or revolved around acts of mob violence. Likewise, Paul Laurence Dunbar, unquestionably the period's most famous Black poet, turned from poetry to fiction to analyze the psychology of white mobs in "Tragedy at the Forks" (1898) and especially "The Lynching of Jube Benson" (1902). Charles W. Chesnutt, the most distinguished Black novelist of the day, left his successful legal stenography business and budding career in law to pursue literature full time, writing two novels in which lynchings or near lynchings figured prominently.

Elsewhere, I have explored at length Chesnutt's work in the context of anti-lynching legislation, giving special attention to *The Marrow of Tradition*, which, I argue, drew from Ohio's successful passage of a state anti-lynching bill to make a case for a federal law modeled after it. Building on what I call "lynch law's cultural rhetoric of legitimation, that is, the narratives, tropes, and arguments through which participants in and apologists for lynching justified the mob murder of African Americans and other minorities" (Barton 27), this essay examines Pauline E. Hopkins's *Contending Forces* (1900) in light of an important literary antecedent and in relation to anti-lynching activism, an important goal of which was the passage of a federal anti-lynching bill. Working both within and against this broader cultural rhetoric, the present essay focuses on *lynch law's rhetoric of exemplarity*, what I define here as dramatic representations of mob violence that not only self-consciously call upon the judgment of readers but overtly thematize the idea of "example" as pattern, punishment, or model. For the means and modes of persuasion in any discourse that condones or condemns lynching often hinge on references, descriptions, or citations of particular acts of mob violence presented with particular audiences in mind.

My formulation of this term owes much to the insightful theoretical work of Alexander Gelley and the contributors to his collection, *Unruly Examples: On the Rhetoric of Exemplarity*, especially what Gelley identifies as "the performative and ethical aspect of a rhetoric of exemplarity" (13). The "example," in Gelley's words, is "oriented" not only "toward a conclusion, a truth or principle that the speaker may have in view . . . but also . . . to an interlocutor, an addressee, for whom the example has, to a certain extent, been selected and fashioned" (4). This act of selection and refashioning, as we shall see, is crucial to lynching's rhetoric of exemplarity in African American literature because it forces judgment and solicits a response from readers, thus rendering the lynching scene much more of a performative act than a constative description or a so-called report. As Gelley goes on to theorize exemplarity by virtue of performativity, "The rhetorical force of example is to impose on the audience or interlocutor an obligation to judge. Whether it be in argument or narrative, the rhetoric of example stages an instance of judgment, and the reader . . . occupies, however provisionally, the seat of judgment" (14).

It is precisely this staging of judgment, this "obligation to judge," to which overt depictions of lynching rhetorically appeal in African American literature. Such scenes, I would argue, are always overdetermined sites, reverberating with residues of injustice and dramatizing the conflict between Black subjectivity and white (supremacist) authority in its starkest terms. Historically and symbolically laden with signification, the lynching scene presents writers with an ethical and aesthetic conundrum. After all, with the high stakes of representing white violence and the display of the murdered, often tortured, Black body before them, how are writers to represent the violence? Realistically, surrealistically, sentimentally, ironically, or sardonically, to name only a few narrative modes? And from whose perspective should the scene be seen: the narrator, the white press, a member of the mob, a Black witness, the victim's relative, and so on? Or is it best *not* to dramatize the violence in the first place, lest one gratifies the perverse desires of some readers? Whether taking place onstage or off, lynchings in African American literature constitute critical nodes in a literary work's dramatic form, often providing the structural center around which a narrative turns or the climax or dénouement toward which it builds. Whereas Chesnutt's *The Marrow of Tradition* (1901), Griggs's *The Hindered Hands* (1905), and Hopkins's *Contending Forces* exemplify the former, Du Bois's "Of the Coming of John" (1903), Dunbar's "The Lynching of Jube Benson" (1903), and James Weldon Johnson's *The Autobiography of an Ex-Colored Man* (1911) illustrate the latter. In each of these works, however, examples qua examples of mob violence play an essential role in criticizing lynching's cultural rhetoric of legitimation, given that lynch logic can *only* be fully expressed by way of the example, through a particular illustration or instance. For without the example—the exemplification or instantiation of lethal and extralegal racial violence—lynch law itself would be merely "rhetorical," a figure for an abstract principle rather than a historical practice whose examples are legion.

Concentrating on the two acts of lethal and extralegal violence that help to structure *Contending Forces*, in what follows I read Hopkins's first published novel in light of an important literary antecedent and alongside fiction by like-minded contemporaries who engaged with and criticized the concept of lynching's exemplarity. The first of these acts in *Contending Forces* constitutes what we might think of as the novel's primal scene of racial violence, which is expressed through mob murder and a sublimated rape scene in the Old South "Before the War," as Hopkins puts it in a chapter title. "The Montfort Tragedy," as the event is called, marks the climax of the novel's historical frame, which is set in North Carolina at the turn of the nineteenth century. The second act, which transpires a century later in Boston, unfolds at the structural core of the narrative proper and is communicated through a turn-of-the-twentieth-century syndicated lynching report from the white southern press. Culminating in a comparative analysis of these two disparate, albeit historically and symbolically entwined events in *Contending Forces*, I begin with a close examination of lynch law's rhetoric of exemplarity in William Wells Brown's *Clotel; or, The President's Daughter* (1853) for two reasons. First, I suggest that Brown's lynching scene provided a model, an example, for later African American writers, particularly Hopkins, a great admirer of Brown.[2] Second, I show that racialized mob violence against African Americans has a history and presence well before the Civil War, the traditional starting point for the vast majority of historians and literary critics who study anti-Black lynching, with most scholars concentrating on the period between 1880 and 1940, during which at least thirty-two hundred African Americans were put to death by white mobs.[3]

In fact, such scholarship from across disciplines has almost exclusively examined the topic as a postbellum phenomenon for obvious and important reasons. Enslaved people, after all, were valuable property and sources of profit for their owners, who had a vested interest in protecting them from *lethal* violence (while, of course, subjecting them to all sorts of *nonlethal* violence). Moreover, enslaved persons who committed capital crimes could be lawfully executed by the state, which would often compensate slaveholders for their loss of property. Even so, at least "fifty-six mob executions of blacks in the South [occurred] in the years 1824–1862" (34), as historian Michael Pfeifer documents in *The Roots of Rough Justice*, the only book-length study to date with an emphasis on racial lynching before Emancipation.[4] Hopkins's beloved Brown wrote about two of those lynchings. One was the infamous 1835 public burning of Francis McIntoch in St. Louis, an event Brown directly referenced in his 1846 *Narrative of William W. Brown, a Fugitive Slave* and about which he provided supplementary press clippings in the appendix to the revised 1848 edition of his *Narrative*.

The second was a gruesome 1842 lynching report published in the southern white press that Brown included in his revised *Narrative*'s appendix and from which he extensively quoted in the narrative of *Clotel*, reframing it for rhetorical purposes. Brown's repurposing of this report provides my starting point because of how it influenced and helped to shape, as I shall argue, subsequent representations of lynchings by later Black writers—again, Hopkins in particular. Writing in the antebellum period, Brown of course could not have anticipated the horrors of so-called lynch law during the (post-)Reconstruction period; nonetheless, his early reckoning with lethal and extralegal mob violence helps to establish a historical link between racialized lynching before and after the Civil War—a connection Hopkins strove to reinforce by interlinking the two lynching scenes, one in the 1790s and the other in the 1890s, that serve as structural poles or organizing principles in *Contending Forces*.

"He Must Be Made an Example"

Depictions of white mob violence against Blacks abound in African American literature, as any reader familiar with the tradition can readily attest. One of the earliest references to anti-Black "Lynch law," however, occurs in Frederick Douglass's 1845 *Narrative*, when Douglass describes a mob beating to which he was subjected in a shipyard that could have easily turned fatal had he not fled. Jeered and attacked by a group of white men while working in the Baltimore shipyard, Douglass fights back, but "to strike a white man is death by Lynch law," Douglass informs readers about his decision to run away, "and that was the law in Mr. Gardner's ship-yard; nor is there much of any other out of Mr. Gardner's ship-yard" (*Narrative* 102).

If Douglass provided an early reference to "Lynch law," the first out-and-out depiction of what today we would define as *lynching*—summary punishment (usually execution) by a mob—in African American literature appears in Brown's *Clotel*, itself the first published novel by a Black writer.[5] The scene in question accounts for the climax of chapter 3 of *Clotel*, "The Negro Chase." This early and horrific scene, perhaps more than any other in the novel, epitomizes the terrors and savagery of slavery. It also provides a model or pattern, an example for later Black writers, offering an archetype of sorts for representing racialized lynch law, thus establishing some of the conventions and rhetorical strategies one finds at play in lynching or near lynching scenes dramatically rendered in later works by Wells, Hopkins, Chesnutt, Dunbar, and Griggs. We can see how those conventions were established by looking closely at *Clotel*'s lynching scene in the context of such later depictions; doing so will also enable me later to show how Hopkins in particular drew from Brown in subtle yet significant ways in fashioning the central lynching scene toward which the drama of *Contending Forces* builds.

The lynching graphically depicted in "The Negro Chase" from *Clotel* is indeed exemplary in how Brown selected and fashioned a particular historical incident—well documented in the antebellum press—to represent, exhibit, and stand in for the generalizable practice or principle of racialized lynch law. To begin with, Brown's description sets the stage for scenes to come by emphasizing the obvious "inhumanity and barbarity" that transpire when two enslaved men "run off owing to severe punishment" (96). Throughout the chase, Brown emphasizes how the two runaways are dehumanized, treated like "prey" (99) and pursued by so-called negro dogs, bloodhounds trained to "attack a negro at their master's bidding and cling to him as the bull-dog will cling to a beast" (96). At the same time, however, Brown humanizes and sympathizes with the enslaved men as victims of unchecked tyranny. Later, Brown lets the horror of mob violence speak for itself, narrating the capture and subsequent lynching of one of the runways from a detached, matter-of-fact perspective and then quoting extensively from an 1842 Natchez paper reporting an actual lynching.

One finds all of these strategies—citation from the white press, sympathy with a dehumanized victim, and use of a detached narrative voice—not only in *Contending Forces*, as we shall see in detail, but also in works by Dunbar, Chesnutt, Wells, and Griggs. In "The Lynching of Jube Benson," for instance, Dunbar dramatized a chase in which the story's titular Black victim is depicted as a "human tiger" and hunted as "quarry" by a white mob itself likened to a pack of "hungry tigers" (234–35), whereas use of the white press and a detached, ironic perspective constitute hallmark strategies of Wells's influential anti-lynching campaign. Other Black writers similarly drew from Brown's playbook. Griggs, for instance, closely based the primary lynching scene in *The Hindered Hand* on an actual double lynching in 1904 reported in a Nashville paper; moreover, he sardonically framed the scene by introducing it from the perspective of a young white boy eager to witness the violence. Chesnutt likewise sustained a detached, ironic point of view to register the horrors and hypocrisies of lynch law in *The Marrow of Tradition*. In fact, this tone and perspective dominate two chapters at the center of the novel that satirize lynching's exemplarity. Whereas the first, "The Necessity of an Example," offers a sardonic critique of an ideology of white supremacy that legitimates lynching as a necessary example, the second, "How Not to Prevent a Lynching," provides a negative example à la the Dickensian parody of "how *not* to do it" (in *Little*

Dorrit), thus mocking the legal, political, and social institutions that foster mob violence.

Yet to uncover the ideology undergirding lynch law's rhetoric of exemplarity and the critique inaugurated in *Clotel*, we have to consider more closely what is at stake in Brown's thematicization of lynching as example, pattern, warning—a concept or idea invoked on three separate occurrences in "The Negro Chase." The first occurs through free-indirect discourse as Brown, impersonating the voice of white authority, narrates the capture of the fugitive and his fatal act of insubordination: "While being tied," Brown writes of the runaway, "he committed an unpardonable offence: he resisted, and for that he must be made an example on their arrival home. A mob was collected together, and a Lynch court was held, to determine what was best to be done with the negro who had had the impudence to raise his hand against a white man. The Lynch court decided that the negro should be burnt at the stake" (98–99). Ironically accepting the necessity-of-an-example argument that Chesnutt later savages, this scene explicitly articulates lynch law's exemplarity, for the captured enslaved man "must be made an example." Simple and direct, the statement merits little attention on the surface, but its underlying logic calls for scrutiny. Ostensibly holding up a case for consideration, this straightforward declarative and description of the "Lynch court" that follows foreclose any meaningful judgment. The reasoning here suggests both prejudice and prejudgment—an evaluation that announces its verdict in advance, like a foregone conclusion or a rhetorical question that posits its own answer. There is, in other words, no thoughtful decision but rather a preprogrammed, programmatic response that goes without saying and ought *not* to be questioned. Clearly, Brown's point in narrating the scene through *this* voice is to show that so-called lynch law is really no law at all. Rather, it is a racialized—we could just say racist—practice or custom (without due process) stemming from what Chesnutt calls "the marrow of tradition" in his later novel by that name and what Dunbar simply dubs "Tradition" from the perspective of a remorseful member of a white lynch mob in "The Lynching of Jube Benson" (236). Likewise, the "Lynch court" in Brown's account is no court but instead a mob appropriating legal forms of authority, such as holding court or trial in the first place, presenting evidence, calling for testimony, and—of course—rendering a verdict.

The verdict to lynch in "The Negro Chase" is immediately followed by the horrific and grisly account taken from the southern press. Brown's selection and extensive quotation from this report are crucial for our understanding not only of Brown's critique of lynch law's rhetoric of exemplarity in *Clotel* but also of the similar critique Hopkins levies in *Contending Forces*. Hopkins, as we shall see, not only followed Brown by staging and quoting from the white press but literally drew from his example, with textual echoes and resonances suggesting that she used the scene as a model. The example from *Clotel* appears as follows:

> A Natchez newspaper, the *Free Trader*, giving an account of it says,
>
>> "The body was taken and chained to a tree immediately on the banks of the Mississippi, on what is called Union Point. Faggots were then collected and piled around him, to which he appeared quite indifferent. When the work was completed, he was asked what he had to say. He then warned all to take example by him, and asked the prayers of all around; he then called for a drink of water, which was handed to him; he drank it, and said, 'Now set fire—I am ready to go in peace!' The torches were lighted, and placed in the pile, which soon ignited. He watched unmoved the curling flame that grew, until it began to entwine itself around and feed upon his body; then he sent forth cries of agony painful to the ear, begging some one to blow his brains out; at the same time surging with almost superhuman strength, until the staple with which the chain was fastened to the tree (not being well secured) drew out, and he leaped from the burning pile. At that moment the sharp ringing of several rifles was heard: the body of the negro fell a corpse on the ground. He was picked up by some two or three, and again thrown into the fire, and consumed, not a vestige remaining to show that such a being ever existed." (W. Brown 98–99)

It is important for us to confront this brutal and sickening example of slavery's terrors for precisely the reason Saidiya V. Hartman refrains from reproducing such "terrible spectacle[s]" in her seminal study, *Scenes of Seduction: Terror, Slavery, and Self-Making in Nineteenth-Century America*. Doing so, according to Hartman, "call[s] attention to the ease with which such scenes are usually reiterated, the casualness with which they are circulated, and the consequences of this routine display of the slave's ravaged body" (3). First published in Mississippi's *Natchez Free Trader*, this report was reprinted in over twenty northern antebellum papers, including William Lloyd Garrison's *The Liberator*, from which Brown likely transcribed it into his novel, thus making it an exemplary display of racial violence in the popular press by the time Brown repurposed it for his novel. Brown, contra Hartman, cited the report precisely to illustrate the casual reiteration and circulation of such violence as a form of cultural critique. He thus reproduced and reiterated the violence to show how casual and routine such racial violence had become. The enslaved man in Brown's cited account is more "body" than person, more object than subject. Yet his suffering rings out plangently, with the reporter expressing a mixture of pathos and terror, noting the condemned's "cries of agony" and plea for "someone to blow his brains out" while marveling at the "superhuman strength" with which he bursts momentarily from the fire before "several rifles," a synecdoche for the mob, collectively fire into "the body," thereby providing a ritualized scene of overkill so familiar in anti-Black lynching reports that glutted the postbellum press.

It is within this quoted report that the second instance of exemplarity occurs, specifically when the report's author states: "He then warned all to take example of him, and asked the prayers of all around." This appeal, attributed to the condemned, comes of course neither from Brown's narrator nor from the enslaved man himself but instead from the white press. In other words, the "he" in the *Free Trader* who "warn[s] all to take example of him" is not the enslaved man himself, speaking in his own voice, but rather the white press speaking through or for him. In this way, we could say that the *Natchez Free Trader* made the subaltern speak, to borrow from Gayatri Chakravorty Spivak's famous formulation of postcolonial subjectivity—or the lack thereof. And the white press does so by having the captured enslaved man endorse his own extralegal execution, just as condemned felons in early American gallows literature were so often represented by ministers or in the popular press as holding themselves up as examples and justifying the lawful processes through which they were publicly put to death.[6]

The third instance of lynching's exemplarity transpires when Brown resumes his narration following the *Free Trader* citation. "Nearly 4,000 slaves were collected from the plantations in the neighborhood to witness this scene," Brown writes of the immense spectacle. "Numerous speeches were made by the magistrates and ministers of religion to the large concourse of slaves, warning them, and telling them that the same fate awaited them, if they should prove rebellious to their owners" (99). In concluding his account, as in introducing it, Brown employed a series of passive constructions to suggest both the enslaved man's lack of agency and the so-called official voice and action of the state, represented here by "magistrates and ministers" who echo and reinforce the condemned's appeal to his own exemplarity. They, too, use him as a "warning" and telling example to this "large concourse of slaves" of a fate that "awaited them" should they "prove rebellious to their owners."

It is precisely through these different voicings of lynching's exemplarity that Brown engaged a subtle critique of what Jacqueline Goldsby, writing about anti-Black mob violence at the turn of the twentieth century, calls lynching's "cultural logic." In identifying "several interpretive facets" that make up this logic, Goldsby broadly defines the term to promote an understanding of "antiblack mob murders as a networked, systematic phenomenon indicative of trends in national culture" rather than acts of regional violence perpetrated in the backwoods of the South and motivated by "scapegoating, purity taboos, or identity politics" (5). With the example of Brown's *Clotel* before us, we can identify another facet of this deep-seated cultural logic—one that works through an assumed or presumed reasoning that goes without saying and that operates according to a rhetoric of sheer self-assertion. Again, as Brown laconically (and ironically) puts it: "He resisted, and for that he must be made an example." Brown's example of the enslaved man out of whom "an example" is made also shows how a cultural practice legitimating lynching through dehumanization, overkill, and discretion of the Black body, along with appeals to exemplarity, existed well before the Civil War. Of course, that practice was much more prevalent and pronounced during the postbellum period, reaching its sickening fruition in the 1890s, when first Wells and then Hopkins and her contemporaries were writing. Nonetheless, as Brown illustrated and as Hopkins strove to show, racialized lynching had not only a cultural logic but also an accompanying rhetoric of legitimation with roots that reached deep into America's past.

"Ter Be Made a Eggsample Of"

Published almost a half century after *Clotel*, Hopkins's *Contending Forces* offers a direct yet nuanced response to the crime of lynching and a plea for anti-lynching activism, as several critics have argued.[7] Moreover, Hopkins's indebtedness to Brown and the influence of *Clotel* upon her work, as noted earlier, have been well documented by scholars. No one, however, has examined Hopkins's novel in relation to *Clotel*'s lynching scene or either works in terms of what I've been calling lynch law's rhetoric of exemplarity.

The influence of *Clotel*'s scene of racial mob violence on the composition of *Contending Forces* can be seen in how Hopkins introduces lynching as a topic and trope in the narrative's historical frame. Like Brown near the beginning of his novel, at the outset of hers Hopkins invokes lynch law and builds up to an enactment of it to expose readers to the horrors and hypocrisies of slavery in the United States, a country ironically esteemed by Charles Montfort, the protagonist of the novel's historical frame, for its democratic practices and republican institutions (*Contending* 28–29). Yet while Brown pulls his account of racial mob violence from the contemporary antebellum press, Hopkins unearths the source for hers, as she notes in the novel's preface, from "the archives of the courthouse at Newborne, N.C., and at the national seat of government, Washington, D.C." (*Contending* 14). In addition, whereas Brown's criticism of lynch law's rhetoric of exemplarity is bound up with the spectacle of its violence, Hopkins initially uncouples the rhetoric from the example in order to give fuller attention to each. Doing so enables her not only to fill in the ideological gaps of what goes without saying in Brown's critique but also to situate historically the origins of lynching's legitimation rhetoric long before the Civil War.

In a chapter significantly titled "The Days Before the War," Hopkins first broaches the subject of lynching indirectly through a callous and all-too-casual conversation between two repugnant white characters, Bill Sampson and Hank Davis, on the docks of a North Carolina port in the late eighteenth century. Uncouth, "burly," tobacco-spitting "idlers" and overseers (Hopkins, *Contending* 35), Bill and Hank muse over the authority and perverse pleasures lynch law bestows upon them (as white men) as they watch an incoming ship bearing from Bermuda (a British colony that had just abolished slavery) Charles Montfort and his family, the source of the narrative's future progeny. When Hank, speaking of the ship, asks, "Whar's she from?" the following exchange ensues:

> "Hain't been in town lately, I reckon, or you'd know all about the 'Island Queen' from Bermudy. Planter named Montfort on her. He's movin' his niggers here to Caroliny; gittin' too hot fer him back thar," replied Bill, with a backward jerk of his thumb in the supposed direction of Bermuda. "How's things up yer way?"
>
> "Fair, fair to middlin', Bill; thar's been some talk 'bout a risin' among the niggers, and so we jes tuk a few o' them an' strun 'em up fer a eggsample to the res'. I tell you, Bill, we jes don't spec' to hav' no foolin' 'bout this yer question of who's on top as regards a gentleman's owning his niggers, an' whomsoeveder goes ter foolin' with that ar pertickler pint o' discusshun is gwine ter be made a eggsample of, even ef it's a white man. Didn' hyar nuthin' 'bout a circus up our way, did yer?" (Hopkins, *Contending* 35–36)

Through this dialogue, Hopkins introduces lynch law by belittling and debasing its logic, particularly in terms of a rhetoric of exemplarity that we have seen at work in *Clotel*. The laconic and understated "he must be made an example" of Brown's "Lynch court" is echoed and lampooned through Hank's argument for a few enslaved Blacks "ter be made an eggsample of." Yet in Hopkins's account, there is no dignified and self-righteous voice from the white press or solemn warnings issued by distinguished magistrates and ministers in *Clotel*. Instead, Hopkins mounts her critique through these two clownish "crackers," who make poor spokespersons for the virtues of lynching. The term "crackers" (*Contending* 90) is later used by Hopkins herself to describe the class to which Bill and Hank belong in old Carolina; I have added *clownish* here to get at the sense of entertainment and brutality with which Hopkins associates lynching and the circus in its pre-antebellum state, long before the circus-like environment that would come to characterize spectacle lynchings of Hopkins's own day.

Thus, Hopkins not only ridicules the ridiculous logic of Hank's appeal through dialect—his comical yet self-righteous appeal to "as an eggsample to the res'"—but also exposes the irrational motives behind the practice, showing it to be a barefaced form of racial terrorism, what sociologists Stewart E. Tolnay and E. M. Beck identify as a predominant argument in lynching practices.[8] In this respect, Hopkins's criticism differs from Brown's more subdued use of irony. Nonetheless, it shares with Brown's the same logic of self-evidence, one that goes without saying among southern whites and that ought *not* to be questioned, thereby conveying a similar sense of prejudice and entitlement on the part of those who participate in or apologize for mob violence. Hank makes this point when, stating the obvious for whites like himself, he insists: "I tell you, Bill, we jes don't spec' to hav' no foolin' 'bout this yer question of who's on top as regards a gentleman's owning his niggers." In fact, Hank, pontificating on this principle, takes the argument a step further when he concludes: "An' whomsoeveder goes ter foolin' with that ar pertickler pint o' discusshun is gwine ter be made a eggsample of, even ef it's a white man."

Hank's "pertickler pint" here refers not just to a general political principle —that is, using lynching as racial terrorism—but also to a particular example, for his justification of lynching "even . . . a white man" foreshadows the fate of Charles Montfort, the naive patriarch of the novel's historical frame who indeed is made "a eggsample of" for his liberal beliefs and practices as a slave owner. Hopkins later makes this link explicit when a rhetoric of "eggsamplarity" again crops up in an exchange between these two lowly idlers. This time, however, it is Bill speaking to Hank about Montfort's "troubl[ing] . . . eggsample," especially the "bad eggsample" he has "set befo' the niggers roun' this town" (Hopkins, *Contending* 62). Citing an unstated and obviously trumped-up "law of the United States that ef eny man is caught creatin' dissatisfacshun among the slaves he desarves death, and death he gits" (62), Bill helps set in motion a plot to kill Montfort and take possession of his extensive assets. In addition to Bill and Hank, that plot involves the covetous Anson Pollock, an influential and well-respected member of the white community who conspires with them and assumes a leadership role in the conspiracy. Besides promulgating news of

Montfort's private plans to manumit his enslaved subjects within ten years and intimating that insurrections on other plantations would certainly follow, the lynching plot gains momentum through rumors that Bill and Hank circulate about the African ancestry of Montfort's wife, Grace. As Pollock's henchmen, Bill and Hank serve an important role in that they show the extent to which the interpolation of lynch logic permeates southern culture, bringing into material form the abstract, detached voice of "official" white culture we saw in Brown's critique. For unlike Pollock, these crackers stand to gain little themselves through mobbing the Montforts but are part of a power apparatus that naturalizes assumptions about race and condones anti-Black violence.

Scholarship on Hopkins, beginning with Hazel Carby's seminal work, has productively read the subsequent beating of Grace as a metaphorical rape, with the "snaky, leather thong" ("'On the Threshold'" 269) of each man's whip standing in for phalluses.[9] If it is important to understand the assault upon Grace (who personifies womanly "grace," as her name suggests) in these terms, then it is equally important to see Montfort's murder as a symbolic lynching. Even though the rope, the fire, and the fagot—conspicuous trappings of later lynching scenes—are absent from Montfort's execution, the scene nonetheless features telltale signs of racial mob violence. For starters, not only is the conspiracy motivated by issues of race, but the vigilante group that plans the murder does so under the guise of a "committee on public safety," a common cover for lynch mobs, with an important historical example found in the "Committee of Safety" (qtd. in Waldrep 66–67) that lynched at least twelve enslaved men in what historians have called the Madison Insurrection Scare of 1835.[10] Moreover, the murder of Montfort itself, which involves a KKK-style surprise attack at the victim's home, is carried out by a "crowd of angry men" (Hopkins, *Contending* 67). Hopkins also imbues the scene with elements of anonymity and secrecy that evoke more associations with organizations such as the Ku Klux Klan, which formed in the aftermath of the Civil War but had clear roots in the kind of antebellum "Lynch court" Brown describes and the postrevolutionary "committee" about which Hopkins writes in her novel's historical frame. For instance, the so-called committee that mobilizes (we could say *mob*-ilizes) the "angry men" is comprised of secret members and has an invisible power structure. The organization, Hopkins's narrator tells us, "had a chairman, but no one knew of his identity save a chosen few of the committee," and "very little was known positively as to the identity of any members" (*Contending* 53). Similarly, when the murder itself takes place, we are told that the bullet killing Montfort was "sped by an unseen hand" (67). This detail, coupled with the collective guilt associated with the crowd of unidentified men, a Klan of sorts, calls to mind the self-righteous, indignant members of lynch mobs from the (post-)Reconstruction period, the great majority of whom escaped responsibility for crimes the courts ultimately determined to be perpetrated "at the hands of persons unknown."[11]

Taken together, the symbolic rape and lynching of the Montforts account for what we can think of as the novel's "primal scene" of racial violence, a term I'm generally borrowing from the psychoanalytic tradition but with specific reference to Hartman's use of it to characterize the "terrible spectacle" of sex and violence with which Douglass's 1845 *Narrative* begins (3). The Montfort tragedy is indeed "primal" not only because it involves mob violence and rape but also because it constitutes an origins tale of sorts, providing both a genealogy for the central characters of the narrative proper and a historical backdrop against which readers are eventually encouraged to compare current race relations of Hopkins's day to the conditions of slavery a century before. Equally important, this scene is primal (we could also say *primary*) given its relation to the novel's *central* lynching scene: a syndicated news report from the South that Hopkins situates at the center of the narrative proper. This central scene bears no direct causal relation to the primal one a century earlier; nonetheless, it resonates with the horrors and hypocrisies of the earlier scene, thereby revealing a deeper logic uniting them based in part, as we shall see, on a rhetoric of exemplarity.

"A Salutary Spectacle"

While the historical frame of *Contending Forces* focuses on the Montfort family and the tragedy that befalls them in North Carolina in the 1790s, the narrative proper takes place in Boston in the 1890s and principally concerns Will and Dora Smith, siblings and descendants of the Montforts, and their respective love interests: Dora's suitors, John P. Langley and Dr. Arthur Lewis, and the beautiful, mysterious Sappho Clark, a boarder from the South at Ma Smith's lodging house who becomes Dora's good friend and later Will's beloved. The overt racial tension that pervades the novel's historical frame is relatively absent from the first half of the narrative proper. In fact, up to the point where the lynching report appears, the narrative proper has taken shape as a polite domestic romance about racial uplift and the construction of a Black middle class. Early chapters chronicle the vibrant lives of African Americans in Ma Smith's boardinghouse and its surrounding environs, particularly the friendship that develops between Dora and Sappho. Chapters leading up to the lynching report take readers first inside a "sewing circle" sponsored by a women's club, where important issues about race and gender are discussed, and then into a planning committee meeting for a church fundraiser where a petty (yet humorous) conflict develops over a fair raffle contest for which first prize is a grand piano—the very symbol of upper-class establishment and bourgeois domesticity. In these ways, *Contending Forces* constitutes a representative post-Reconstruction domestic romance, a popular literary form of the late nineteenth century whose conventions, as Claudia Tate insightfully demonstrates, Hopkins (along with other Black women writers) manipulated to create allegories of political desire for her contemporary readers. It is into the apparently peaceful quotidian world of such a novel that Hopkins drops a jarring and graphic lynching report, which disrupts and discombobulates the novel's structure like the proverbial monkey wrench thrown into a machine.

That Hopkins strives for such an effect is evident in how she introduces the novel's central lynching report, which, to switch to Hopkins's metaphor, comes out of the clear blue sky like a storm without warning:

> Up from the South there came one morning early in March the report of another lynching. The skies were heavy with gray, storm-laden clouds, not darker nor more threatening than the dire and bloody news the daylight ushered in. For a month or two peace had seemingly reigned in southern latitudes, but it was the slumbering of passion, not its subsidence. At table, in the cars, at the office, in the workshop, men read with sick hearts the description of another illegal act of distorted justice, wherein the sufferings of the poor wretches were depicted only too truthfully for the peace of the community:
>
>> Jim Jones, a burly black Negro accused of the crime of rape against the person of a beautiful white woman, was taken from his home by a number of our leading citizens, and after being identified by his victim, was carried into the woods, where, before an immense concourse of people, he was bound to a tree, pieces of his flesh were stripped from his body, his eyes were gouged out, his ears cut off, his nose split open, and his legs broken at the knees. After this the young woman stepped forward and poured oil upon the wretch, and the wood being piled about him, she applied the torch to light the fire which was to consume the black monster. Leaving some of the party to watch the funereal pile, a posse went into the city and brought to the scene of vengeance Sam Smith, Bill Sykes and Manuel Jackson, who were accused of hiding the guilty wretch from the justice of the populace. These

three men were hanged to the nearest trees in full sight of the burning wretch, who made the day hideous with his cries of agony. We
think the Negroes of this section have been taught a salutary lesson.
—*Torchlight* (*Contending* 223–24)

I quote Hopkins's narrator citing a southern lynching report not only to invite
comparisons with the report in Brown's *Clotel* and its introductory frame but
also to signal its centrality to the novel's anti-lynching politics *through* its exemplarity, Hopkins's selection and fashioning of the example to force judgment
and elicit a response from readers. We can see how by looking more closely first
at the framing paragraph introducing the report and then at the report itself.

While Hopkins, on the one hand, uses the metaphor of a sudden storm to
register the unexpected violence of lynch law in general, on the other, she sets
up the citation to follow by emphasizing the routine, unsurprising occurrence
of particular acts of mob violence, noting this one as "the report of another
lynching," "the description of another illegal act of distorted justice." The repeated use of "another" here underscores just how commonplace lynchings
have become in the United States, a country that prides itself on being an example to the world of republican virtues and democratic institutions. Introducing the report in these terms frames it as, paradoxically, both shocking and extraordinary, banal and ordinary. In doing so, Hopkins points to an important
tension between lynching as an unlawful, barbaric practice and the political
ideals of due process and equal protection, thus exposing a hypocrisy in American democracy similarly found in the Montfort tragedy. In analyzing this introductory paragraph, it is also important to note that, of all the places where
the report is being read "with sick hearts"—around dinner tables, in street-
cars, and at places of employment, we are told—readers learn of it from behind the closed office doors of "A Colored Politician," as the chapter in which
it appears is titled. Informing us of the lynching here, wherein two politicians
(one white and one Black) negotiate how it is to be interpreted and publicly
handled, suggests how such reports are always already politicized events by the
time they reach a print audience. In this way, Hopkins signals the lynching report to come as an overdetermined site, one composed of different voices and
in different registers to demand judgment from readers.

Nothing in this prefatory paragraph, however, properly prepares us for
the report itself—which is part of the point. Its graphic depiction of violence
and racist overtones, written from the perspective of white supremacy and attributed to the *Torchlight*, a representative southern paper, stand in sharp contrast to the measured tone of Hopkins's narrator, who sustains a compassionate

and progressive perspective throughout the novel, even if at times that viewpoint is more tolerant of racial prejudice or shaped by an ideology of white supremacy than modern readers would allow.[12] In letting the voice of the white press speak for and against itself, Hopkins not only follows Brown's early example in *Clotel* but also borrows from a hallmark strategy of her contemporary, Ida B. Wells, from whose anti-lynching pamphlets Hopkins later drew in both Luke Sawyer's testimony and Will Smith's speech before the Boston American Colored League, whose meeting is prompted by the *Torchlight* report.[13]

If Brown was the first literary figure to cite a lynching report to *incite* a negative reaction to it, that technique was used at length and perfected by Wells, who extensively quoted from actual lynching reports in her anti-lynching pamphlets, recontextualizing them in light of suppressed, doctored, or mistaken facts to expose racist assumptions and to highlight the familiar tropes, arguments, and narratives according to which lynch law operates. Through a process of first appropriating and then displacing white authority in her pamphlets, Wells drew from a recent archive of lynching reports and editorials to write a new historiography in their place and through their own language—an approach dramatically enhanced through her masterful use of irony and understatement. Wells herself characterized this technique in the opening chapter of her second anti-lynching pamphlet, *A Red Record*: "The purpose of the pages which follow shall be to give the record which has been made, not by colored men, but that which is the result of compilations made by white men, of reports sent over the civilized world by white men in the South. Out of their own mouths shall the murderers be condemned" (82). By calling attention to the production and distribution of these lynching reports, Wells described her approach as one of reading against the grain in order to condemn the *abuse* of white authority (vigilante acts of mob justice) through the *use* of white authority (reports in the white southern press). She thus produced a double-voiced discourse that served to displace the official record with what her title figures as "a red record," a record of barbarism, cruelty, and profound injustice that bleeds through an official record created and "sent over the civilized world by white men in the South" (Wells 82).

It is precisely such an approach that Hopkins adopted in crafting an exemplary lynching report attributed to the *Torchlight*, the name of an actual southern paper from North Carolina (the site of the novel's historical frame and the Montfort tragedy) that published such reports in the late nineteenth century, although the one Hopkins "cites" is almost certainly her own invention.[14] Like Wells, she thus dialogizes the monologic voice of white authority, highlighting lynch law's racist assumptions and calling into question its stereotyped tropes, threadbare arguments, and predictable narratives. To this end, Hopkins's *Torchlight* report begins with the familiar and often fallacious charge of rape, racializing the subject positions of victim and perpetrator through an oft-cited Black-and-white binary: the "beautiful white woman," on the one hand, and the equally alliterative "burly black Negro," on the other. An additional subject position is occupied by presumed white readers in the ever-present "leading citizens," who lend authority and ethos in their support of or participation in racial mob violence.

Hopkins's appropriation of these conventions not only talks back to lynch logic but also dialogues with other Black authors who contested white authority. For instance, claims that the "best" or "leading citizens" supported or participated in lynchings were consistently mocked by Wells, who even interpolated ironic question marks ("[?]") after quoting the phrase (102). Likewise, Wells and others scoffed at the ubiquitous trope of the "burly black Negro." Whereas Wells repeatedly cited the stereotype to expose it as fiction—a construction of the southern press—journalist and newspaper editor Alexander Manly made special reference to it in an 1898 editorial published in the *Wilmington Daily Record* shortly before Hopkins wrote *Contending Forces* and in response to an 1897 defense of anti-Black mob violence in the popular press by Rebecca W. Felton, a famous feminist, suffragist, and Georgia white supremacist. In reply to Felton's declaration, "If it needs lynching to protect woman's dearest possession from the ravenous human beasts, then I say lynch a thousand times a week if necessary" (qtd. in Waldrep 144), Manly challenged Felton's characterization of white women as helpless, innocent victims of "ravenous human beasts" and retorted: "Every negro lynched is called 'a big, burly, black brute,' when in fact many of those who have thus been dealt with had white men for their fathers, and were not only not 'black' and 'burly' but were sufficiently attractive for white girls of culture and refinement to fall in love with them, as is well known to all" (qtd. in Waldrep 144, 147). Channeling the fearless tone with which Wells debunked popular myths and blatant lies about sexual relations between Black men and white women in the early 1890s, and anticipating Will Smith's argument to this effect before the American Colored League in *Contending Forces*, Manly points here to the attraction white women have for Black men, as well as historical evidence (evinced in the so-called mulatto race) that white men have sexually exploited Black women since the earliest days of slavery—a point Hopkins emphasized symbolically through the rape of Grace Montfort, which is later echoed through the revealed rape of Sappho Clark in the story Luke Sawyer tells of Mabelle Beaubean.

Charles Chesnutt, who used Manly's editorial as a source for his novel based on the Wilmington Race Riots, similarly ridiculed the stereotype. Noting in *The Marrow of Tradition* the damage done to the national reputation of Black men, despite the thwarted lynching and proven innocence of Sandy Campbell, an African American character accused of rape, robbery, and murder, Chesnutt's narrator comments: "All over the United States the Associated Press had flashed the report of another dastardly outrage by a burly black brute,—all black brutes it seems are burly,—and of the impending lynching with its prospective horrors" (187). Hopkins's use of "burly black Negro" in her fictive report, syndicated through the Associated Press like the one Chesnutt references, carries with it the same criticism of the racist stereotype, yet she lets the racism speak for itself. There is, then, a sort of double irony at play in Hopkins's appropriation that distinguishes her work from that of Chesnutt and Manly. She turns the tables on a white supremacist ideology that assumes Black inferiority as a naturalized fact and lynch logic as self-evident that needs no explanation. Hopkins, in other words, does not spell out her point, as Manly and Chesnutt do. Rather, she lets readers see the stereotype as such for themselves, given that no Black characters within the novel are remotely like the constructed rapist, Jim Jones, in Hopkins's report. Even John P. Langley, a mixed-race descendant of Anson Pollock who emerges as the main narrative's conniving villain, is anything but a "burly black Negro." Yet Jones is not only stereotyped in the report but also demonized as a "black monster," another common trope in lynching's legitimation rhetoric. Such a characterization renders Jones at once utterly unrelatable (again, he is like no Black character but in fact is closer to the brutish white rapists and murderers, Bill and Hank) *and* entirely relatable—though only through the racial stereotype. It is precisely this logic of supposed self-evidence that Hopkins undermines by appropriating a rhetoric that goes without saying in her own criticism of lynch law.

If Hopkins draws from and criticizes the general conventions for representing lynching in her exemplary report, she also alludes in it to some specific enactments of white mob violence. Doing so enables her at once to link her literary lynching to the historical record and to use her fiction as a form of political intervention. As Thomas Cassidy and Lois Brown point out, one such historical event was the infamous and horrific spectacle lynching of Sam Hose in Newnan, Georgia, in 1899, the year Hopkins wrote *Contending Forces* and two years after Felton delivered her infamous speech in the state. Reports from the southern press of this lynching garnered attention in Boston papers and in the city's African American community (L. Brown 188), just as the *Torchlight* report does in Hopkins's novel, set in contemporary Boston. Not only did the Hose lynching involve a burning and attract a crowd of nearly two thousand (like the "immense concourse" of Hopkins's scene), but certain details from it found their way into Hopkins's depiction of Jones's gruesome torture, including Hose's stripped flesh and cut-off ears. Another probable source was a notorious lynching that took place in Arkansas in 1892. Reports of that lynching included a striking detail found in Hopkins's *Torchlight* report but not in the report of the Hose lynching: the burning initiated by a white woman, presumably the alleged victim. Douglass, about whom Hopkins would write for her Famous Men of the Negro Race series in the *Colored American Magazine*, emphasized this detail in his "Lynch Law in the South" (1892), an article featured in the *North American Review* the same year. "Think of an American woman," Douglass sardonically muses near the beginning of the essay, "mingling with a howling mob, and with her own hand applying the torch to the fagots around the body of a negro, condemned to death without a trial, and without a judge or jury, as was done only a few weeks ago in the so-called civilized State of Arkansas" ("Lynch" 17). Hopkins indeed may have been thinking of Douglass's example when she imagined a white woman performing such a role in her report. Further evidence to support this claim can be found in Hopkins's attention to Jones's grim execution as "an illegal act," an instance of "distorted justice" (descriptors that resonate with Douglass's attention above to the illegality of the Arkansas lynching), as well as the fact that she referenced two of Douglass's other *North American Review* articles from 1891 in her own article on the pre-eminent orator and abolitionist published in the *Colored American Magazine*.[15]

The work of another illustrious author about whom Hopkins wrote in her Famous Men of the Negro Race series also found its way in Hopkins's *Torchlight* report. That work is one we have already carefully considered and to which I return here to conclude this essay and to bring us back to lynching's exemplarity. That source, of course, is Brown's *Clotel*. The lynching scene from Brown's novel, like Hopkins's, not only is ripped from the headlines (literally, in Brown's case) but also involves a public burning witnessed by a "large concourse" (Hopkins uses the term "immense concourse," a close echo of Brown's description). It also describes the victim's suffering in similar language and perhaps provided the inspiration for the title Hopkins gave to her (fictive) southern paper. For just as the victim in Brown's cited report sends "forth cries of agony painful to the ear" when consumed by the flames, the victim in Hopkins's report makes "the day hideous with his cries of agony" when the fire engulfs him. Additionally, there are similar resonances in both accounts about the use of torches, with Brown's description of how "the torches were lighted" echoed in Hopkins's title, *Torchlight*, and repeated in the report itself ("the torches to light") at the same critical juncture.

Yet there is a more substantial way in which Hopkins builds upon Brown's example as a form of political intervention. Whereas Brown provides an example that is desultory and extraneous to *Clotel*'s central plot, Hopkins artfully organizes her novel around lynching's spectacle and rhetoric of legitimation. Her report, moreover, goes beyond Brown's in thematizing lynch law's rhetoric of exemplarity (as warning, model, and pattern) by demanding judgment and eliciting a response from characters and readers alike. The brutal lynching of Jim Jones not only serves as an *example* and *warning* but also fits within a *pattern* and produces one itself, as three other men are lynched, modeled after the first, as additional examples and warnings to the Black community. As the voice of white supremacy proudly concludes the *Torchlight* report, "We think the Negroes of this section have been taught a salutary lesson" (Hopkins, *Contending* 224). Through this flagrant endorsement of racial terrorism—lynching as exemplum, "a salutary lesson"—Hopkins chimes a keynote first sounded in the novel's historical frame, namely, Hank's argument for stringing up a handful of enslaved people to make "an eggsample to the res'." No doubt the white authority behind the *Torchlight* report, spoken in the collective first person (the royal "we"), couches the argument in more genteel (and thus more insidious) terms. Even so, the underlying principle of exemplarity is at work here, too, as Jim Jones and the other three men—Sam Smith, Bill Sykes, and Manuel Jackson—are "ter be made a eggsample of," to return us to the more explicitly racist language of Bill and Hank, which closely echoes and caricatures Brown's "to be made an example" underlying the scene in *Clotel*. Hopkins, however, pushes the critique much further by making lynching the example par excellence of an ideology of white supremacy rather than one example among others expressing that ideology.

Every act of lynching constitutes a unique act, an *event* if there ever was one. But the representation of such acts also fits into a pattern from which we can derive a formula, as Hopkins has done by crafting a lynching scenario that features many conventions and common arguments from white reports and dialogues with other Black writers on the subject. Those conventions, as we have seen, include the frequent and often fallacious charge of rape, the dehumanization and demonizing of the Black suspect, and the presence of a so-called dignified white vigilante group comprised of a community's "leading citizens." Each of these conventions, to differing degrees, is present in the novel's primal scene of racial violence. For instance, the group of "leading citizens" in the *Torchlight* report is analogous to the "committee for public safety" that plots the Montfort tragedy. In this way, the contemporary lynching report that Hopkins drops into the center of the narrative proper calls to mind or triggers—like a repressed memory—the primal violence used to frame the work as a whole. As such, the Montfort tragedy functions as a deep-seated, symbolic, and latent source for the manifestations of racial violence that erupted in Hopkins's contemporary reality with alarming frequency. What is more, connecting the novel's two disparate lynching scenes, as I've argued here, suggests that racial mob violence in America has a history dating back much further than the Civil War, a standard starting point for studies of lynch law as a racialized form of mob violence. That violence, we might say (and Hopkins suggests), is rooted in postrevolutionary America and coextensive with the founding of the United States, thus making lynch logic one of the foundational hypocrisies of American democracy.

Literally central to the narrative proper, the *Torchlight* report is also central to the novel's thematic focus, as it *re*centers the work around anti-lynching activism, with four subsequent chapters devoted to public debate and testimony or private conservations about "the philosophy of lynching" (*Contending* 287), as Hopkins's narrator puts it in the last of these chapters. Much of the scholarship that treats lynching in *Contending Forces* has, for good reason, focused on these chapters.[16] In this essay, I have given considerable attention instead to the novel's central lynching scene not merely because it has received scant attention in Hopkins criticism but also because of the performative role it plays in the novel's anti-lynching politics. The spectacle not only places readers in the seat of judgment but also serves as a call to action. Through the example of lynch law's gruesome and reprehensible violence, Hopkins intended her novel to have a galvanizing effect upon her readership, just as that spectacle does within the novel itself, thus bringing together "contending forces" within the Black community to counter and countermand an ideology of white supremacy and lynching's cultural rhetoric of legitimation. Indeed, it is through the meeting sponsored by the Colored American League that Hopkins crafts her response to lynch law's rhetoric of exemplarity, first through Luke Sawyer's testimony of its horrors and then through Will Smith's arguments against its practice. But again, it is the example of lynching—intimated in the Montfort tragedy and epitomized in Jim Jones's horrific torture and burning, culled from representative reports—that brings about the book's agitation and anti-lynching activism.

NOTES

1. One important federal anti-lynching bill was House Resolution 6963, proposed by Representative George H. White of North Carolina, the last African American to serve a southern state in the House for seventy years. Among other things, White's 1900 bill proposed to "make the act of lynching a crime against the United States . . . and to empower the President . . . to make it his duty to intervene whenever and wherever necessary with the armed force of the nation to prevent the commission of this atrocious crime, and to rescue any person or persons from the hands of any mob in any state of the Union" (United States Congress, House, HR 6963, 56th Cong., 1st sess. [1900]). For scholarship on early federal efforts for anti-lynching legislation, see Zangrando; Burns; and Ferrell.

2. Even a casual reading of Hopkins evinces Brown's influence. For instance, Hopkins borrowed several scenes from Brown's *Clotel*, such as Pompey primping enslaved persons for auction at the New Orleans market and the tale of an enslaved boy serving as a wager for a southern gentleman's bet at the beginning of *Hagar's Daughter*, Hopkins's second published novel but the first she began writing. For a discussion of Hopkins's intimate knowledge of *Clotel*, see L. Brown (346–50). At the very beginning of her career, a young Hopkins won an essay contest sponsored by Brown himself, and some thirty years later Hopkins wrote about Brown for her Famous Men of the Negro Race series for the *Colored American Magazine*. Moreover, she drew upon Brown in writing *A Primer of Facts Pertaining to the Earlier Greatness of the African Race* (1905) and other works. As Ira Dworkin notes in his introduction to *Daughter of the Revolution*, Brown "remained a major influence throughout [Hopkins's] career" (xxii). Along with Parker Pillsbury and Wendell Phillips, Brown is the author Hopkins cites most frequently in her essays and journalism (xxxvi).

3. The figure of thirty-two hundred is taken from Wood 3. Scholarship on lynching, from different perspectives and in multiple disciplines, has flourished over the past three decades. Historian Jacquelyn Dowd Hall and literary critic Trudier Harris pioneered new investigations into the subject, to which numerous scholars contributed in the 1990s and early 2000s, including Ayers; Gunning; Hale; Apel; Pfeifer; Dray; and Waldrep. In addition to these scholars, sociologists Stewart Tolnay and E. M. Beck and historian W. Fitzhugh Brundage engaged quantitative analysis and compiled statistical data that generated new models and created a wealth of source material for studying lynching in the South generally or in specific southern states. More recently, major cross-disciplinary studies by Jacqueline Goldsby and Amy Wood have moved beyond the South as region to link lynching not only to national trends and cultural practices but also to technical forces associated with modernism. This rich and diverse body of research is representative of a larger body of scholarship that focuses on racial lynching since Emancipation that is too copious to cite in a brief note here.

4. In addition to Pfeifer, see Dyer; Jones; and Campney for book chapters that examine the lynching of enslaved Blacks before the Civil War. Waldrep provides an invaluable collection of edited primary sources related to antebellum (and earlier) lynchings in America.

5. In her pioneering work, Harris was the first scholar to identify this scene in *Clotel* as the first representation of lynching in African American literature. See also Blight 109 and Karcher 196 for discussions of this scene as the first lynching dramatized by a Black writer.

6. For a discussion of the lawfully condemned's role in legitimating capital punishment in the Puritan execution sermon, see Cohen; Halttunen. DeLombard concentrates on the African presence in early American gallows literature, arguing that criminality played a constitutive role in the formation of Black subjectivity in early white print culture in America and demonstrating that "the criminal confession" was the "most widely circulated, influential form of early black personal narrative" (13).

7. Hazel Carby first broke ground on the subject in *Reconstructing Womanhood* and her oft-reprinted essay, "'On the Threshold of the Woman's Era.'" Claudia Tate, following Carby, touches on the topic, while Sandra Gunning and Thomas Cassidy make it a central focus in their scholarship. William Moddelmog offers the most sustained and sophisticated formal analysis of *Contending Forces* in relation to law and anti-lynching activism, whereas Lois Brown provides a rich and invaluable context for understanding *Contending Forces* as the product of local and national anti-lynching campaigns in her critical biography of Hopkins, although she gives relatively little attention to the text itself in terms of lynching. As Brown puts it, "*Contending Forces* was a direct outgrowth of Hopkins's exposure to the Colored National League debates in Boston about African American civil rights in local anti-lynching campaigns" (190). For an essay that reads *Contending Forces* in relation to lynching and Hopkins as a forerunner of critical race theory, see Watkins.

8. This argument falls under Tolnay and Beck's "social threat" model for understanding white motivations for lynching. They also theorize models based on popular justice and both social and economic competition for explaining white mob violence against Blacks. See in particular chapter 3, "Social Threat, Competition, and Mob Violence," in their study, *A Festival of Violence*.

9. See Carby, *Reconstructing Womanhood* 131–32; and Carby, "'On the Threshold'" for her influential discussion of Grace's beating as a symbolic rape scene. Numerous critics have noted Carby's interpretation of this scene in their work. For the most sustained engagement with this scene and the symbolic raping, see McCoy.

10. Thomas Shackleford, one of the lynchers involved in the insurrection scare, euphonized the lynch mob as a "Committee of Safety" in *Proceedings of the Citizens of Madison County, Mississippi, in July 1835, in Relation to the Trial and Punishment of Several Individuals Implicated in a Contemplated Insurrection in This State*, a quasi-official extralegal pamphlet justifying the lynchings. See McKibben; Miles; and Morris for accounts of the 1835 Madison Insurrection Scare.

11. For use of this trope, see Dray.

12. I am referring here to Gwendolyn Brooks's assessment that in *Contending Forces*, Hopkins belies the mentality of a slave through her narrator's not infrequent remarks about the so-called superiority of whites in drawing racial comparisons. See Richard Yarborough's introduction to the Schomburg edition of the novel for a discussion of Brooks's reading. For an opposing perspective on Hopkins's use of free-indirect discourse

and an "unreliable" narrator informed through a Bakhtinian understanding of dialogism, see Cassidy.

13. On this point, see especially Cassidy; Moddelmog.

14. In my own research, I have located several lynching reports in North Carolina's *Torchlight* during the 1890s, but nothing involving a victim named Jim Jones or the specific circumstances described in Hopkins's novel.

15. Dworkin, in a note to Hopkins's reference to the *North American Review* in "Hon Frederick Douglass" for her Famous Men of the Negro Race series, published in the *Colored American Magazine*, identifies these works: "Frederick Douglass, 'Haiti and the United States: Inside History and the Negotiations for the Mole St. Nicolas,' Pts. 1 and 2, *North American Review* 153 (Sept 1891): 337–345; 153 (Oct 1891): 450–459."

16. See Gunning; Moddelmog; L. Brown; Carby, *Reconstructing Womanhood*; Carby, "'On the Threshold'"; Cassidy; and Watkins.

WORKS CITED

Apel, Dora. "On Looking: Lynching Photographs and Legacies of Lynching after 9/11." *American Quarterly*, vol. 55, no. 3, 2003, pp. 457–78.

Ayers, Edward L. *The Promise of the New South: Life after Reconstruction*. 1992; Oxford University Press, 2007.

Barton, John Cyril. "'The Necessity of an Example': Chesnutt's *The Marrow of Tradition* & the Ohio Anti-lynching Campaign." *Arizona Quarterly*, vol. 67, no. 4, 2011, pp. 27–58.

Blight, David W. *Race and Reunion: The Civil War in American Memory*. Harvard University Press, 2002.

Brown, Lois. *Pauline Elizabeth Hopkins: Black Daughter of the Revolution*. University of North Carolina Press, 2008.

Brown, William Wells. *Clotel; or, The President's Daughter*, edited by Robert S. Levine, Bedford, 2000.

Brundage, W. Fitzhugh. *Lynching in the New South: Georgia and Virginia, 1880–1930*. University of Illinois Press, 1993.

Burns, Adam. "Without Due Process: Albert E. Pillsbury and the Hoar Anti-lynching Bill." *American Nineteenth-Century History*, vol. 11, no. 2, June 2010, pp. 233–52.

Campney, Brent. *Hostile Heartland: Racism, Repression, and Resistance in the Midwest*. University of Illinois Press, 2019.

Carby, Hazel V. "'On the Threshold of the Woman's Era': Lynching, Empire, and Sexuality in Black Feminist Theory." *Critical Inquiry*, vol. 12, no. 1, 1985, pp. 262–77.

———. *Reconstructing Womanhood: The Emergence of the Afro-American Woman Novelist*. Oxford University Press, 1989.

Cassidy, Thomas. "Contending Contexts: Pauline Hopkins's *Contending Forces*." *African American Review*, vol. 32, no. 4, 1998, pp. 661–72.

Chesnutt, Charles. *The Marrow of Tradition*, edited by Eric J. Sundquist, Penguin, 1999.

Cohen, Daniel A. *Pillars of Salt, Monuments of Grace: New England Crime Literature and the Origins of American Popular Culture, 1674–1860*. Oxford University Press, 1993.

Curtius, Mary. "Senate Issues an Apology for Inaction on Lynchings." *Los Angeles Times*, 14 June 2005.

DeLombard, Jeannine. *In the Shadows of the Gallows: Race, Crime, and American Civic Identity*. University of Pennsylvania Press, 2012.

Douglass, Frederick. "Lynch Law in the South." *North American Review*, vol. 55, no. 428, July 1892, pp. 17–24.

———. *Narrative of the Life of Frederick Douglass* (1845), edited by David W. Blight, 2nd ed., Bedford / St. Martin's, 2003.

Dray, Philip. *At the Hands of Persons Unknown: The Lynching of Black America*. Modern Library, 2002.

Dunbar, Paul Laurence. "The Lynching of Jube Benson." *The Heart of Happy Hollow*. Mnemosyne Publishing, 1969, pp. 220–40.

Dworkin, Ira, editor. *Daughter of the Revolution*. Piscataway, 2007.

Dyer, Thomas G. "A Most Unexampled Exhibition of Madness and Brutality: Judge Lynch in Saline County, Missouri." *Under Sentence of Death*, edited by W. Fitzhugh Brundage, University of North Carolina Press, 1997, pp. 269–89.

Ferrell, Claudine. *Nightmare and Dream: Antilynching in Congress, 1917–1921*. Garland Publishing, 1986.

Gates, Henry Louis Gates, Jr. *Figures in Black*. Oxford University Press, 1987.

———. *The Signifying Monkey: A Theory of African-American Literary Criticism*. Oxford University Press, 1988.

Gelley, Alexander. Introduction. *Unruly Examples: On the Rhetoric of Exemplarity*, edited by Alexander Gelley, Stanford University Press, 1995, pp. 1–24.

Goldsby, Jacqueline. *A Spectacular Secret*: Lynching in American Life and Literature. University of Chicago Press, 2006.

Griggs, Sutton E. *The Hindered Hand*, edited by John Cullen Gruesser and Hanna Wallinger, West Virginia University Press, 2017.

Gunning, Sandra. *Race, Rape, and Lynching: The Red Record of American Literature, 1890–1912*. Oxford University Press, 1996.

Hale, Grace Elizabeth. *Making Whiteness: The Culture of Segregation in the South, 1890–1940*. Random House, 1998.

Hall, Jacquelyn Down. *Revolt against Chivalry: Jessie Daniel Ames and the Women's Campaign against Lynching*. 1979; Columbia University Press, 1993.

Halttunen, Karen. *Murder Most Foul: The Killer and the American Gothic Imagination*. Harvard University Press, 1998.

Harris, Trudier. *Exorcising Blackness: Historical and Literary Lynching and Burning Rituals*. Indiana University Press, 1984.

Hartman, Saidiya. *Scenes of Subjection: Terror, Slavery, and Self-Making in Nineteenth-Century America*. Oxford University Press, 1997.

Hopkins, Pauline E. *Contending Forces*. Oxford University Press, 1988.

———. "Men of Vision." *New Era Magazine*, Feb.–Mar. 1916.

————. *Winona*. Reprinted in *The Magazine Novels of Pauline Hopkins*, edited by Henry Louis Gates Jr., Oxford University Press, 1988, pp. 285–437.

Jones, Kelley Houston. "'Doubtless Guilty': Lynching and Slaves in Antebellum Arkansas." *Bullets and Fire*, edited by Guy Lancaster. Fayetteville: University of Arkansas Press, 2018, pp. 17–34.

Karcher, L. Carolyn. *A Refuge from His Race: Albion W. Tourgée and His Fight against White Supremacy*. University of North Carolina Press, 2016.

Korobkin, Laura H. "Imagining State and Federal Law in Pauline E. Hopkins's *Contending Forces*." *Legacy: A Journal of American Women Writers*, vol. 28, no. 1, 2011, pp. 1–23.

McCann, Sean. "'Bonds of Brotherhood': Pauline Hopkins and the Work of Melodrama." *ELH*, vol. 64, no. 3, 1997, pp. 789–822.

McCoy, Beth. "Rumors of Disgrace: White Masculinity in Pauline Hopkins's *Contending Forces*." *African American Review*, vol. 37, no. 4, Winter 2003, pp. 569–81.

McKibben, Davidson Burns. "Negro Slave Insurrections in Mississippi, 1800–1865." *Journal of Negro History*, vol. 34, no. 1, 1949, pp. 73–90.

Miles, Edwin A. "The Mississippi Slavery Insurrection of 1835." *Journal of Negro History*, vol. 42, no. 1, 1957, pp. 48–60.

Moddelmog, William. *Reconstituting Authority: American Fiction in the Province of the Law, 1880–1920*. University of Iowa Press, 2001.

Morris, Christopher. "An Event in Community Organization: The Mississippi Slave Insurrection Scare of 1835." *Journal of Social History*, vol. 22, no. 1, 1988, pp. 93–111.

Pfeifer, Michael. *The Roots of Rough Justice*. University of Illinois Press, 2014.

Spivak, Gayatri Chakravorty. "Can the Subaltern Speak?" *Marxism and the Interpretation of Culture*, edited by Cary Nelson and Lawrence Grossberg. Macmillan, 1988, pp. 271–313.

Tate, Claudia. *Domestic Allegories of Political Desire: The Black Heroine's Text at the Turn of the Century*. Oxford University Press, 1992.

Tolnay, Stewart E., and E. M. Beck. *A Festival of Violence: An Analysis of Southern Lynchings, 1882–1930*. University of Illinois Press, 1992.

Waldrep, Christopher, editor. *A History in Documents: Lynching in America*. New York University Press, 2006.

Watkins, Patricia D. "Rape, Lynching, Law and *Contending Forces*: Pauline Hopkins—Forerunner of Critical Race Theorists." *CLA Journal*, vol. 46, no. 4, June 2003, pp. 521–42.

Wells, Ida B. *The Anti-lynching Campaign of Ida B. Wells, 1892–1990*, edited by Jacqueline Jones Royster, Bedford, 1997.

————. *A Red Record: Tabulated Statistics and Alleged Causes of Lynching in the United States*. 1894; Bedford, 1997.

Williams, Andrea N. *Dividing Lines: Class Anxiety and Postbellum Black Fiction*. University of Michigan Press, 2013.

Wood, Amy Louise. *Lynching and Spectacle: Witnessing Racial Violence in America, 1890–1940*. University of North Carolina Press, 2011.

Yarborough, Richard. Introduction. *Contending Forces*, by Pauline E. Hopkins, Oxford University Press, 1988, pp. xxvii–xlviii.

Zangrando, Robert. *The NAACP Crusade against Lynching, 1909–1950*. Temple University Press, 1980.

Pauline E. Hopkins's Editorial Rise and Radical Racial Uplift in Fiction Publishing at the *Colored American Magazine*

Elizabeth J. Cali

In May 1900 Pauline Hopkins began her literary and editorial journey with the *Colored American Magazine* (*CAM*), a periodical that intended to "develop and intensify the bonds of that racial brotherhood, which alone can enable a people, to assert their racial rights as men, and demand their privileges as citizens" ("Editorial" 60). By that time, Hopkins's literary career and work as a race woman were well under way with her 1879 publication of the musical play *Peculiar Sam* and the 1900 publication of her first novel, *Contending Forces*. But as Alisha R. Knight observes, Hopkins's role as prolific contributor and rising editor at *CAM* played "no small part in earning her this distinction" as one of the most prominent and productive African American women writers at the turn of the century (27). Further, Hazel Carby's insight in *Reconstructing Womanhood* that "any attempt to gain a comprehensive understanding of her [Hopkins's] fiction must begin with an analysis of all her work for the *Colored American Magazine*" inspired a watershed of scholarship that collects and analyzes volumes of Hopkins's fiction and nonfiction works originally published in *CAM* (122).[1] While research examining Hopkins's written works for *CAM* has expanded, her editorial and publishing practices at the magazine have not seen the same volume of attention.

The primary attention to Hopkins's editorship—from Hopkins's own contemporaries and from current scholarship—understandably fixates on unraveling the reasons for her rapid departure from the publication in March 1904. Scholars often focus on Hopkins's exit to determine a causal relationship between Hopkins's actions while editor of the magazine and her resulting exit. As early as 1912, W. E. B. Du Bois suggested that Hopkins's editorship ended because her "attitude was not conciliatory" enough (33).[2] Alisha Knight's work in particular offers a key overview of the speculation, tracking arguments by Jill Bergman that Hopkins's departure was a direct result of gender bias and by Hanna Wallinger that Hopkins's experience of Bookerite vengefulness led to her exit. Knight's own study suggests that Hopkins lost her editorial position and control at *CAM* because she used her nonfiction articles to position herself as a bold and unflappable critic of both Booker T. Washington's brand of racial uplift and broader U.S. policies that aligned African American success with achievement of the American Dream. While this essay is less interested in determining a definitive reason why Hopkins left *CAM*, these arguments cue a keener attention to the intersecting power dynamics that inform how Hopkins carried out her vision of the magazine's mission as a race publication.

The scholarship unraveling Hopkins's departure from the magazine also presents a foundation for unpacking the politicization of Hopkins's term at the magazine. Thorough archival research in Hopkins's correspondence both grounds the debate on Hopkins's departure and underscores the ways that opposition to Hopkins's role as civil rights agitator intersected with the gendered bias she faced as the only woman editor at *CAM*, leading to the "double jeopardy" that she experienced at the magazine (see Beal). Hence, taken together, Knight, Bergman, Wallinger, and others delineate the "manifold and simultaneous oppressions" that Hopkins faced and through which I argue she built her editorial resistance (Combahee River Collective 13).[3] Situated in this way, Hopkins's editorial practices illuminate a radical ideology of racial uplift that directly targets the intersection of racial and gendered injustice as the nexus for uplift agitation.

The intersecting oppressions that impelled Hopkins's exit most certainly did not emerge from the ether. Rather, pressure to assimilate to white American cultural norms, budding tensions between supporters of Bookerite uplift politics and civil rights agitators, and the exclusionary biases of patriarchal men and racist white women all contextualize Hopkins's work as *CAM* editor. The choices she made in her editorship convey an unflinching multipoint corrective to racist white women's movements, male-centered approaches to civil rights, and accommodationist uplift policies that undermined the need for urgent responses to white supremacist violence.

This study of Hopkins's editorial practices with fiction selections in particular—the author demographics, inclusion, and proliferation of fiction entries in *CAM*—argues that explicating Hopkins's decisions with fiction demonstrates that the raced and gendered politics contextualizing her editorship at *CAM* and her subjectivity as a Black woman were in fact critical to her brand of racial uplift.[4] Analysis of Hopkins's fiction selections reveals that for thirty--

three months *CAM* featured nearly all Black-authored imaginative works and among these works foregrounded African American women writers. While racial uplift proponents within and beyond *CAM* often encouraged demonstrations of Black people's ability and preparedness to assimilate into white American social conventions and cultural norms, Hopkins's fiction selections turned away from cultural assimilation and instead cultivated Black cultural expression. I argue that Hopkins's editorial choices allowed her to alternately reject accommodationist visions of racial uplift and pressures to assimilate African American literature into a white Western writerly tradition, to rebuke patriarchal gender biases that sidelined Black women race thinkers, and to check white women's divisive efforts to separate Black women's gendered experiences from their racial identities. As such, Hopkins's fiction selections speak to and through the nexus of racial and gendered antagonisms that concerned her, carving out a radical practice of racial uplift in a sociopolitical environment that rarely made space for a joint raced and gendered critique.

The Timeline of Hopkins and *CAM*

This essay follows Hopkins's chronological editorship with *CAM* alongside a timeline of key changes in management and sociopolitical influence during Hopkins's involvement with *CAM* and her rise to editor.[5] Hopkins's tenure and involvement with *CAM* can be categorized in three key overlapping periods: her rise to editorial power (May 1900–July 1901); her key period of editorial influence (March 1901–November 1903); and her exit as editor of *CAM* (December 1903–September 1904). The first two sections of the essay discuss Hopkins's rise to editorial power. Section 1 concerns *CAM* from May 1900 through July 1901 and situates Hopkins's entry into her editorial position at *CAM* within a network of intersecting and shifting business interests and raced and gendered politics. The shifts in *CAM*'s sociopolitical environment and leadership anchor this section's theorization that a small subset of fiction publications in the magazine became a critical edge from which Hopkins navigated the institutional, gendered, and raced sanctions she faced as a single Black woman on the *CAM* staff. Section 2 also concentrates on Hopkins's rise to editorial influence to chart the remarkable and drastic shifts in the race and gender demographics of fiction selections across the months immediately before and after Hopkins took control over literary publications for the magazine. Publication of all Black fiction authors and, of these, primarily Black women in the early months of her editorship foreshadows Hopkins's expanding construction of a racial uplift ideology that prioritized the intersection of racial and gendered injustices.

The third section of the essay focuses on the key period of Hopkins's editorial prominence from March 1901 to November 1903. During this time, Hopkins shouldered primary editorial responsibilities at *CAM*. Charting the race and gender demographics of Hopkins's fiction selections as she gained additional editorial influence illustrates key developments in Hopkins's racial uplift politics, including an alignment with civil rights agitation against the will of Bookerites and simultaneously daring to offer a corrective to patriarchal exclusions of Black women writers as intellectuals. Further, this section compares charts of the racial demographics across fiction and nonfiction publications, interpreting Hopkins's inclusion of nearly all Black authors during this time as a contribution to building a Black literary tradition rather than attempting to assimilate into a Western literary canon, thus fusing and infusing imaginative literature with her own embrace of a Black vision for racial uplift that was centered on both culture and women. Here we can see in full view Hopkins's utilization of the fiction section of *CAM* to address resistance she faced in articulating both race and gender fealty.

In November 1903 *CAM* president and then owner William Dupree solicited white newspaperman and Bookerite John C. Freund for financial and production assistance and thus initiated the final period of Hopkins's tenure as editor of *CAM* from December 1903 to September 1904, which compels the focus of the final section of the essay (Hopkins to W[illiam] M[onroe] Trotter, 16 Apr. 1905). The final section of the essay analyzes charts focused on fiction publications and their race and gender demographics in the months leading up to and immediately following Hopkins's departure from *CAM*, a period that was increasingly fraught with racial and gendered tension for Hopkins in particular. In May 1904 the publication officially changed hands when Fred R. Moore purchased *CAM*, purportedly at the behest of Booker T. Washington.[6] Contextualized by these rapid changes in magazine leadership and a significant volume of correspondence between Hopkins, Freund, and Dupree, this analysis shows the staggering tension that Freund's arrival created around the role of fiction at *CAM*. Though Hopkins did not officially exit *CAM* until September 1904, given Hopkins's April 1905 account of "unbearable" working conditions at the *CAM* office, which necessitated her absence for a "number of days," I consider May 1900–March 1904 to be a more accurate timeline of her tenure at the publication (Hopkins to Trotter). Following the timeline of Hopkins's rise to editorial prominence and eventual exit from *CAM* while tracking the demographic shifts in the body of fiction published in the magazine underscores the profound influence Hopkins exerted over fiction publishing and specifically the foregrounding of Black women's fiction in the magazine.

May 1900–March 1901:
Hopkins's Editorial Beginnings

William Stanley Braithwaite's 1947 commentary on the internal business practices, politics, and disputes at *CAM* assists in clarifying the politicization of
Hopkins's point of entry into editorial control over literary publications in the
magazine. Braithwaite was a key contributor to *CAM* and a close associate of
the founding members. His commentary details Hopkins's increased influence
over *CAM*'s literary publications as it arose from four key intersecting factors.[7]
First, *CAM* managing editor Walter Wallace engaged an experienced white
newspaperman, R. S. Elliott, to handle the mechanical details of publishing the
magazine.[8] As Braithwaite puts it, Elliott was far from a benign presence at
CAM. Early on he "sensed an opportunity that might be profitable for himself"
and "soon began to exert a dominant influence in the affairs of the magazine,"
an influence that Hopkins "resented bitterly" (117, 120). Elliott's business interests in a potentially profitable race publication coalesced with the Bookerites'
lack of interest in literary matters, and he focused his attention on the nonfiction content of *CAM*.[9] Second, Elliott's disregard for literary content also coalesced with Dupree's general uninterest in literary matters, which Braithwaite
describes as "beyond the scope of his personal interest" (119–20). These two
points reveal the tension between Hopkins's investment in fiction and Elliott's
and Dupree's nonliterary interests. Both men were powerful influences at the
magazine.[10] While their uninterest in fiction likely presented Hopkins with less
opposition to claim it as her purview, that uninterest likewise ensured that a
key interest for Hopkins—imaginative genres—did not appear in significant
quantities in the magazine.

Third, as Braithwaite explains it, while Wallace demonstrated enthusiasm
for literary publications, he had little knowledge or expertise in the area. Early
on, then, Wallace focused on soliciting the magazine's nonfiction and visual
contents and deferred to Hopkins's literary regard for herself as an author "in
the company of Charles W. Chesnutt and Paul Laurence Dunbar" for the cura-
tion of literary content in *CAM* (Braithwaite 120).[11] From this angle, it is feasi-
ble that Hopkins's control over fiction in *CAM* was due not only to her express
interest in the subject but also to the disregard and lack of knowledge in areas of
imaginative literature that leading men at the magazine demonstrated. Fourth,
Braithwaite's account reveals a gendered dismissal of Hopkins's presence and
significance to the literary value of the publication.[12] Braithwaite describes
Hopkins as "temperamental," requiring behind-the-scenes maneuvering from
the male editorial staff. Further, as Carby observes, Braithwaite makes it clear

FIGURE 1.01. Total Fiction Entries per Issue Compared to Total Table of Contents Entries per Issue

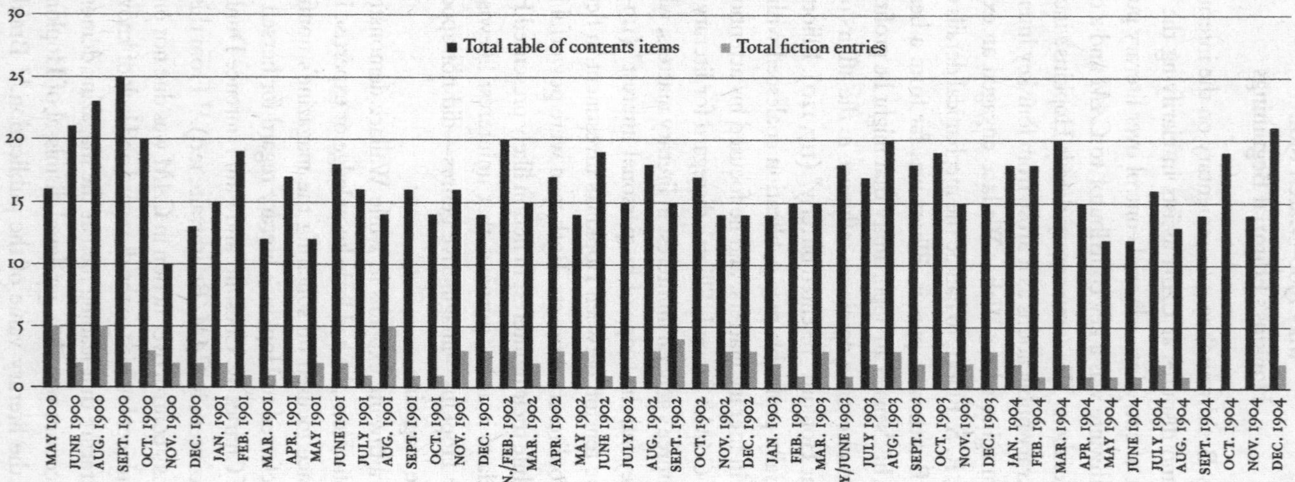

■ Total table of contents items   ■ Total fiction entries

■ Total fiction entries

MAY 1900, JUNE 1900, AUG. 1900, SEPT. 1900, OCT. 1900, NOV. 1900, DEC. 1900, JAN. 1901, FEB. 1901, MAR. 1901, APR. 1901, MAY 1901, JUNE 1901, JULY 1901, AUG. 1901, SEPT. 1901, OCT. 1901, NOV. 1901, DEC. 1901, JAN./FEB. 1902, MAR. 1902, APR. 1902, MAY 1902, JUNE 1902, JULY 1902, AUG. 1902, SEPT. 1902, OCT. 1902, NOV. 1902, DEC. 1902, JAN. 1903, FEB. 1903, MAR. 1903, MAY/JUNE 1903, JULY 1903, AUG. 1903, SEPT. 1903, OCT. 1903, NOV. 1903, DEC. 1903, JAN. 1904, FEB. 1904, MAR. 1904, APR. 1904, MAY 1904, JUNE 1904, JULY 1904, AUG. 1904, SEPT. 1904, OCT. 1904, NOV. 1904, DEC. 1904

0, 5, 10, 15, 20, 25, 30

he and the staff frequently resented and worked around Hopkins at *CAM*. We might read this "behind-the-scenes maneuvering" and "working around" Hopkins as nudging or edging her to the side, a paternalistic permissiveness that released to Hopkins the subject matter that men at the publication did not see as particularly useful for financial gain or for racial uplift. Even Braithwaite, the lone literary artist of involved men at the publication, signals a resigned frustration with Hopkins's claim over the literary segment of the magazine, both allowing her to "have" it while dismissing her attempts at influencing the publication as petulant or "temperamental." Further, *CAM* editors quickly assigned Hopkins purview over the Women's Department as a marginalized segment of the magazine, further underscoring where the editorial board placed Hopkins in their hierarchy. Taken together, the evidence suggests that Hopkins's rise to crucial control of *CAM*'s fiction selections resulted from a combination of gendered dismissals and political ambivalence toward Hopkins and toward fiction's place in the larger racial uplift movement. In short, Hopkins saw opportunity in what dominant white and Black male figures at the magazine deemed marginal to the magazine's success. She leveraged these factors into largely unmitigated editorial control over fiction publications at the magazine.

As figure 1.01 demonstrates, fiction entries comprise a relatively small proportion of each issue's contents. Issues of *CAM* from May 1900 to September 1904 averaged sixteen total entries per issue, with fiction representing two of these entries per issue. The editorial board's politics delimited where Hopkins had the most opportunity to impact the magazine, positioning the fiction section—largely dismissed by those in power at *CAM*—as an ideal location for Hopkins to advance an uplift ideology that foregrounded Black women writers. Borrowing from bell hooks, I suggest that Hopkins chose the margin and, as Brittney Cooper observes about Black women's intellectual traditions, "did [her] theorizing in unexpected locations," converting the very space of her marginalization into a site of resistance and empowerment (12).

In addition to the inner workings of *CAM*'s editorial offices, Hopkins's subjectivity as an educated Black woman facing the prejudices of a racist and sexist society almost certainly pushed her to advance some of her boldest visions for racial progress from this strategic and marginalized location of fiction publishing within *CAM*.[13] As a child in a family with a tenuous position as middle class, Hopkins had access to education while remaining vulnerable to the financial pitfalls undercutting Black people's progress and security. More, Hopkins's stepfather, William Hopkins, was an "active race man" with abolitionist ancestors (see Brown 46–56) and brought his experience and history to bear on Hopkins's views on dismantling racial hierarchies, certainly a strength that drove Hopkins's magazine work and literary career. Further, her status as an unmarried Black woman required her to find work in the public sphere, sacrificing access to the "true womanhood" available to white women with the means to tend their domestic lives (see Welter 151–74). The burgeoning era of the New Woman fostered Hopkins's participation in Black women's clubs, yet she did so while facing the persistent racism and rejection of white women's movements. This matrix created intersecting constraints and liberties for Hopkins that channeled some of her most radical resistance into a small subset of the magazine's publications: fiction selections. In choosing the margin of fiction publications to assert key components of her racial uplift politics, Hopkins departed radically from male-centered civil rights politics, conciliatory accommodationist politics, and exclusionary white women's rights programs through the contours of a genre that those she critiqued had largely dismissed.

May 1900–November 1901:
Hopkins's Initial Impacts

While revealing the relatively small numbers of fiction entries per issue, figure 1.01 also demonstrates consistency in fiction entries published from month to month in *CAM*. From May 1900 to March 1904, with few exceptions (e.g., August 1901), the number of fiction publications per issue hovered between one and three entries. Hopkins's editorial rise at the magazine in early 1901 prompted no measurable change in the volume of fiction entries published per issue, though it is notable that under Hopkins's watch, the magazine always published at least one fiction entry. Hence, Hopkins's editorial practices with fiction are better evaluated according to the demographics of whose writing she included and the persistence with which she included that writing. Figure 2.01 offers data representing the demographic changes in fiction selections concurrent with Hopkins's growing editorial influence in 1901, and figure 2.02 reviews the racial demographics of nonfiction selections during the same time frame. A comparison of the two figures indicates that the move toward nearly all Black fiction writers while maintaining a fairly consistent set of white contributors of nonfiction entries in *CAM* signals two critical points. First, the drastic move away from white fiction authors to all Black fiction authors asserts Hopkins's commitment to representing Black imaginative works. Second, Hopkins's publication of nearly all Black fiction writers while continuing more voluminous publication of white nonfiction authors reinforces her positioning of fiction publication as the locus for racial uplift politics.

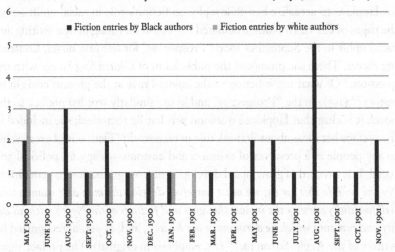

FIGURE 2.01. Fiction Entries by Black and White Authors (May 1900–Nov. 1901)

The *CAM* did not put out a July 1900 issue.

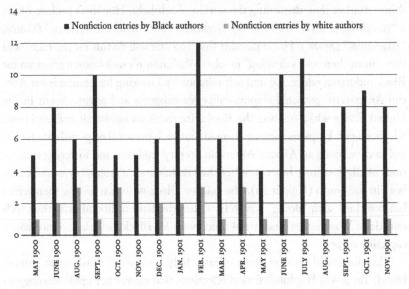

FIGURE 2.02. Nonfiction Entries by Black and White Authors (May 1900–Nov. 1901)

Editorial control over the fiction section in *CAM* created new opportunities for Hopkins to actualize her philosophy on fiction's role in racial uplift across the pages of *CAM*. Hopkins articulated her vision for fusing fiction writing and racial uplift in the September 1900 "Prospectus" for her first novel, *Contending Forces*. There she promoted the publication of *Contending Forces* with the question: "Of what use is fiction to the colored race at the present crisis in its history?" (195). In the "Prospectus" and in her similarly worded preface to the novel, it is clear that Hopkins's question was hardly rhetorical; she included in the preface her ideas about fiction's role in race work: "Fiction is of great value to any people as a preserver of manners and customs—religious, political and social. It is a record of growth and development from generation to generation. *No one will do this for us; we must ourselves develop the men and women who will faithfully portray the inmost thoughts and feelings of the Negro with all the fire and romance which lie dormant in our history*, and, as yet, unrecognized by writers of the Anglo-Saxon race" (14, emphasis in original). The preface signifies on Booker T. Washington's self-help brand of racial uplift in this early articulation of her desire to build a cohort of Black fiction writers for *CAM*. Here I suggest that Hopkins's installment of a Black fiction-writing tradition within *CAM* serves as another method for rejecting Bookerite uplift in addition to the tropological critiques of Washington's politics revealed in Knight's scholarship.[14] Rather than discarding the notion of self-help, Hopkins's preface offers a "rewriting of a received literary tradition," but "with a difference" (Gates, "Blackness" 285–86). Her statement that "no one will do this for the race" and they "must themselves develop" invokes Washington's well-known program for Black industrial education and self-reliance by invoking his emphasis on African Americans' personal responsibility for progress and advancement in the United States while revising the Bookerite focus on industrial and economic advancement. Hopkins suggests instead that such personal responsibility is critical in developing an African American literary tradition and fostering generations of Black culture bearers rather than reclaiming "a monopoly of skilled labor" in the South (Knight 29). She calls on Black writers to do for themselves but positions such "doing" squarely within the field of liberal arts, thus well outside of Washington's industrial framework for Black assimilation into white capitalist success.

This discursive revision alone offers a bold critique of Washington's uplift brand. Yet it was Hopkins's fiction selections that moved her uplift ideology to action, signifying on Washington's uplift program in both word and deed. In the nine months prior to March 1901 (from May 1900 to February 1901), eleven of the fiction entries in *CAM* were authored by African American authors and ten by white authors. As Figure 2.01 shows, March 1901 and the eight months following mark a turning point at *CAM* during which Hopkins published sixteen items of fiction, all by Black authors. Hopkins's fiction selections as she came to editorial power early in 1900 transformed her September 1900 ideations of fiction's role in creating a long-standing literary tradition of uplift into an editorial practice.

Hopkins's early editorial decisions moved beyond critique of Bookerite politics, also signaling her stance against patriarchal uplift ideals that foregrounded Black male intellectual leadership and white women's exclusionary progressivism. As figure 2.03 shows, Hopkins's elimination of white fiction writers from *CAM* parallels a concurrent reduction in (though not an elimination of) male-authored fiction and a growing prominence of Black women fiction authors in *CAM*. All of the women fiction writers represented in figure 2.03 are Black women authors, whereas figure 2.04 demonstrates that white women authors were regularly featured in the nonfiction publications. Simply put, Hopkins's fiction selections foregrounded Black women writers in a way that the nonfiction selections did not, curating the fiction section of *CAM* as a space for Black women writers' prominence. Concurrent with Hopkins's increasing control over fiction selections for *CAM*, her project articulated an intersecting raced and gendered approach to racial uplift, one that was simultaneously interested in securing Black women's authorial prominence and in solidifying the importance of Black-authored fiction throughout *CAM*.

FIGURE 2.03. Fiction Entries by Men and Women Authors (May 1900–Nov. 1901)

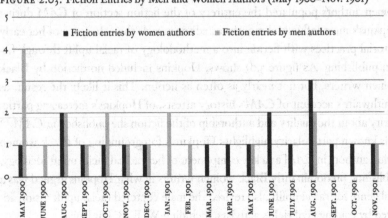

FIGURE 2.04. Nonfiction Entries by Men and Women Authors

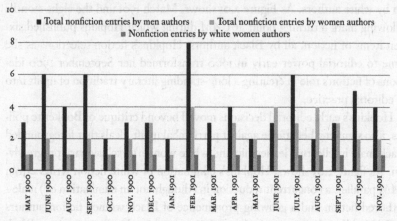

March 1901–November 1903: Hopkins's Key Period of Influence

While Hopkins's initial influence on fiction publications in *CAM* was striking, examining the development and consistency of that impact over her thirty-three most influential months (March 1901–November 1903) as editor confirms Hopkins's Black woman–centered selections as a gendered vision for racial uplift. Figures 3.01 and 3.02 demonstrate that Hopkins's early impact on fiction publications (figure 2.01), which focused on publishing Black authors and almost exclusively Black women authors, proved to be the rule for Hopkins's editorship. The consistency with which Black authors and specifically Black women authors populated the entirety of the fiction section of *CAM* during Hopkins's most influential months as editor reveals the coherence of her early editorial practices with fiction into a methodology of racial uplift through fiction publishing. As figure 3.03 shows, Hopkins included nonfiction by Black women writers, but not nearly as often as fiction. This is likely the result, as Braithwaite's account of *CAM*'s history attests, of Hopkins's increasing particularity about the quality and authorship of the fiction she published in *CAM*.[15] This known particularity highlights Hopkins's foregrounding of Black women fiction authors in *CAM* as a key component of her radical racial uplift ideology. Publishing predominantly Black women writers in what Hopkins argued was a vital genre for racial uplift also revised the male-centered racial uplift vision adopted by leading civil rights activists, including W. E. B. Du Bois.

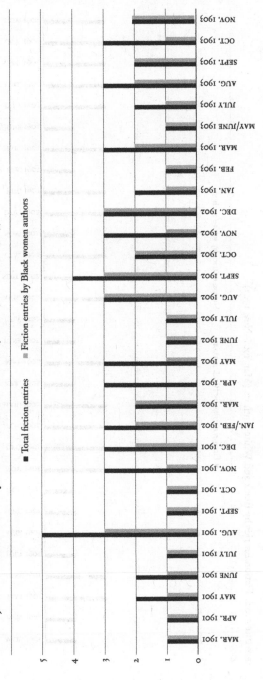

FIGURE 3.01. Fiction Entries by Black Women Authors (Mar. 1901–Nov. 1903)

■ Total fiction entries   ■ Fiction entries by Black women authors

FIGURE 3.02. Fiction Entries by Black and White Authors (Mar. 1901–Nov. 1903)

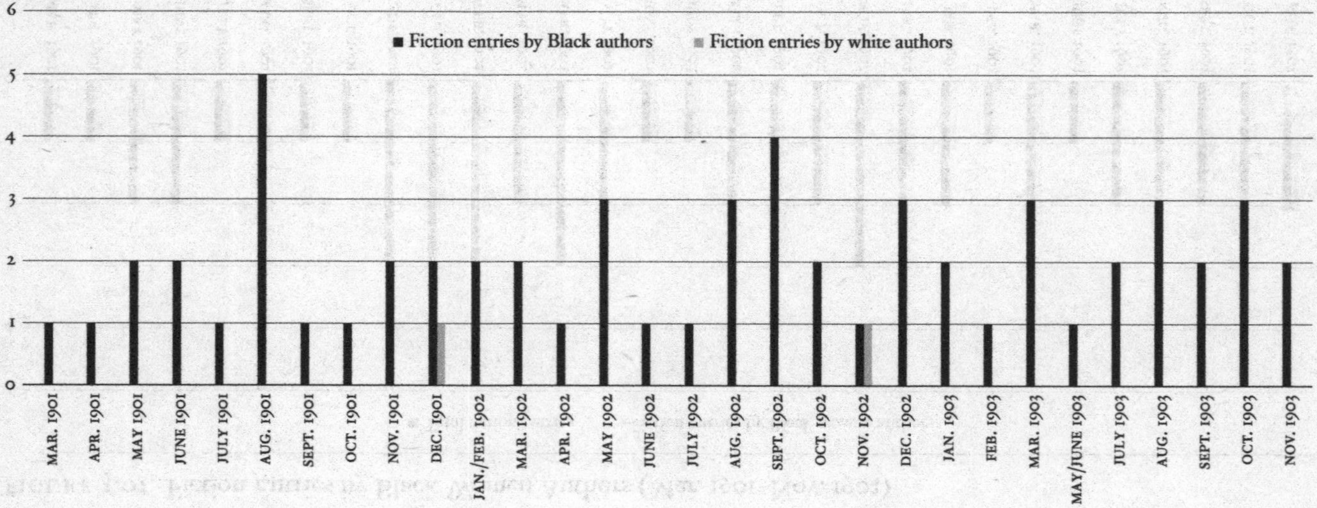

FIGURE 3.03. Nonfiction Entries by Black Women Authors (Mar. 1901–Nov. 1903)

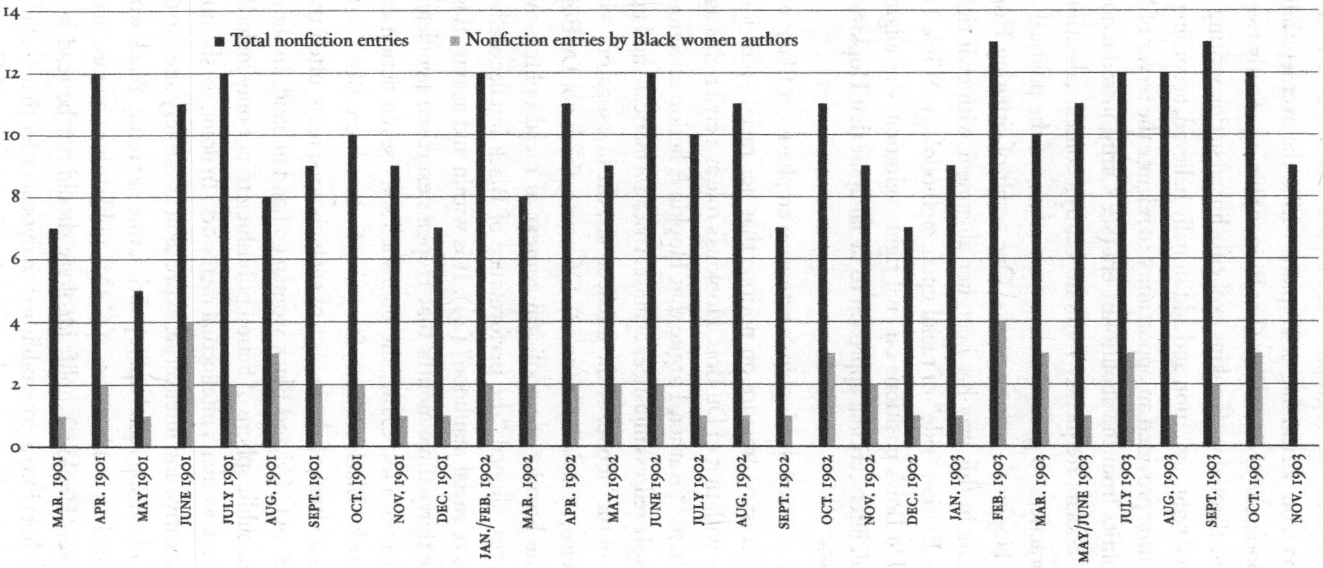

■ Total nonfiction entries ■ Nonfiction entries by Black women authors

MAR. 1901
APR. 1901
MAY 1901
JUNE 1901
JULY 1901
AUG. 1901
SEPT. 1901
OCT. 1901
NOV. 1901
DEC. 1901
JAN./FEB. 1902
MAR. 1902
APR. 1902
MAY 1902
JUNE 1902
JULY 1902
AUG. 1902
SEPT. 1902
OCT. 1902
NOV. 1902
DEC. 1902
JAN. 1903
FEB. 1903
MAR. 1903
MAY/JUNE 1903
JULY 1903
AUG. 1903
SEPT. 1903
OCT. 1903
NOV. 1903

0 2 4 6 8 10 12 14

Analysis of the demographics of Hopkins's fiction selections for *CAM* disturbs a common positioning of Hopkins within the overdetermined accommodation (Bookerite) / civil rights (Du Boisian) binary of early twentieth-century racial uplift theorizing. Hopkins explicitly linked fiction writing with racial uplift and civil rights agitation and additionally believed, according to Carby, that fiction writing provided an opportunity to reignite the fervor of New England's radical politics from the abolitionist era (see Carby, introduction xxxii–xxxv). Hopkins scholars frequently reiterate Carby's contextualization of Hopkins's written practices to ground their own analyses of the political and politicized tenors of Hopkins's written works. One result of situating Hopkins's politics and activism in this way has been her alignment with civil rights strategists, or the Du Boisian "side" of racial uplift methodology. While Hopkins shared many of Du Bois's positions on civil rights agitation, this alignment occludes the radical, intersectional approach to racial uplift that Hopkins's fiction selections evince.

Figure 3.01 reveals Hopkins's extensive emphasis on Black women writers, placing necessary pressure on notions that her racial uplift ideology aligned seamlessly with that of Du Bois. Hopkins's role as a civil rights agitator is not in question here.[16] Rather, I argue that Hopkins's fiction selections for *CAM* simultaneously redress injustices against African Americans and upend Du Bois's depiction of the "model of the intellectuals, the investigators who analyze Negro problems, as male" (Griffin 28). Of course, this is not Du Bois's view alone. Rather, the broader sociopolitical context of racial uplift movements, Cooper observes, aligned "the performance of Black intellectualism" with "performances of racial manhood" (49). It is within and against this context that, during the thirty-three months that Hopkins exercised significant control over fiction selections for *CAM*, she published sixty-seven fiction entries, sixty of which were by Black authors, forty-six of whom were Black women.[17] Figure 3.01 offers a visual of the impact of such choices; more often than not, fiction publication in *CAM* and Black women go hand in hand. In short, Hopkins reshaped the public sphere of fiction publishing to not only include but also foreground Black women's intellectual race work. In doing so, she positioned Black women's creative and intellectual expression at the very site she theorized as integral for advancing racial uplift politics, thus centering Black women's intellectual perspectives in a key area of *CAM*'s publications on race matters.

Moreover, Hopkins's uplift ideology should not be read as placing Black women authors into a preestablished analytical order that occludes their particular modes of analyzing racial and gendered oppression.[18] Hopkins did not simply publish Black women intellectuals who agreed with her agitation for civil rights. Rather, the Black women writers she published, herself included, offered a range of intellectual perspectives within the fiction pages of *CAM*. She included writings by authors Ruth Todd, M. Louise Burgess-Ware, and Gertrude Dorsey Browne, prominent Black intellectuals and clubwomen Gertrude Mossell and Fannie Barrier Williams, and authors and civil rights activists Anne Bethel Scales and Angelina Weld Grimké. Each of these women's writings addressed the specific and intersecting race and gender concerns of Black women, even as their uplift ideologies differed from one another and at times profoundly from Hopkins—Fannie Barrier Williams was a noted Bookerite, for example. As a whole, the cohort of Black women Hopkins published were intellectuals, artists, activists, and race workers whose thinking and writing about their experiences of racial and gendered discrimination already rejected these identities as discrete from one another, even as they promoted multivalent visions of racial progress. This publishing practice comprised a critical component of Hopkins's uplift ideology and in fact her commitment to civil rights agitation: she refused to sacrifice the publication and foregrounding of the fullness of Black women's intellectual perspectives on racial uplift in the interest of promoting a narrow path forward for racial progress. Instead, these publication choices suggest that a key component of Hopkins's uplift vision included a refusal to restrict Black women's intellectual expression.

Alternately, Hopkins's fiction-publishing practices ensured that her perspectives on agitation for civil rights would outweigh more conciliatory attitudes toward hostile white northerners and southerners even as she rejected the exclusion of Black women's intellectual work from racial uplift theorizing. The significant volume of Black women's fiction writing in *CAM* was due in no small part to Hopkins's publication of her own works. She authored thirty-four of the forty-six fiction entries by African American women. Hopkins's thirty-four fiction entries include her publication under two pseudonyms, Sarah A. Allen and J. Shirley Shadrach.[19] Likely, such voluminous self-publishing was the result of several factors, including Hopkins's vision of herself as a major fiction writer of the time and her struggle to secure quality submissions for publication in *CAM*. However, Hopkins's publication of her work under the names Sarah A. Allen and J. Shirley Shadrach would give *CAM*'s audience the impression that the publication offered a larger number of unique African American women's authorial voices. The subject matter of Hopkins's fiction also critiqued Booker T. Washington's uplift ideology and interrogated the antiblackness inherent in measuring racial progress according to Black assimilation into white American cultural practices.[20] Thus, Hopkins's publication of such a large volume of her own fiction allowed her to foreground both her support of cultivating distinct forms of Black cultural expression and her opposition to accommo-dationist and assimilationist uplift attitudes without sacrificing the importance of presenting a range of Black women's intellectual perspectives.

Hopkins's editorial selections of forty-six fiction entries authored by Afri-can American women not only launched a refutation of biased exclusions of Black women in racial uplift politics but also rebuked white women's attempts to excise issues of racial injustice from their progressive agendas for gender eq-uity. Jill Bergman documents Hopkins's wariness of offering unmitigated sup-port to white women's suffragist movements in her essay "'A New Race of Col-ored Women.'" As Bergman observes, Hopkins's concerns were "confirmed in May 1902, when the General Federation of Women's Clubs voted to ex-clude 'colored' clubs" (94). Hopkins spoke out against these racist institutions of New Womanhood in her nonfiction series titled Famous Women of the Ne-gro Race in multiple issues of CAM, and Bergman argues that the "racism of white women showed Hopkins that gender solidarity must come second to race solidarity" (94). This analysis of Hopkins's critiques of white women's racism is hindered, however, by the assumption that gender solidarity for Hopkins was limited to association with white women. Hopkins's fiction selections signal that Hopkins did not sublimate issues of gender in the interest of race matters. Rather, in a bold rejection of white women's racism and an ideological invest-ment in securing Black women's gendered concerns as deeply rooted in their concerns for racial justice, she published issue after issue of CAM foreground-ing Black women's fiction writings, the space Hopkins herself theorized as an epicenter of racial uplift.

Under Hopkins's watch, in a publication that she herself noted struggled to secure quality literary work and at times to scrape together enough submis-sions for a full issue (see Braithwaite), Black-authored imaginative works flour-ished. Undoubtedly, her tenacious emphasis on Black literary arts represents Hopkins's continued mobilization of her anti-Bookerite vision for racial uplift. But more, looking at Hopkins's fiction-publishing legacy from March 1901 to November 1903 reveals that Hopkins's uplift strategy was not myopically con-sumed with rejecting accommodationist ideals, nor was she singularly commit-ted to addressing women's rights. Her vision for racial uplift also rejected white supremacist ideals that would measure racial progress by Black literary assim-ilation into a white Western canon of literature. Unlike Hopkins's editorial practices with the nonfiction selections in CAM (see figure 3.04), Hopkins's fiction selections focused singularly on Black imaginative writings, demonstrat-ing a deep pride and investment in Black artistic culture and tradition.[21] The tropes, vernacular, and prevailing conventions included in Hopkins's tradition

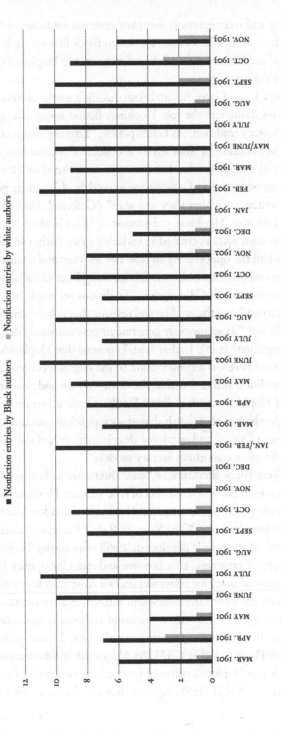

FIGURE 3.04. Comparison of Nonfiction Entries by Black Authors to Nonfiction Entries by White Authors during a Key Period (Early 1901–Nov. 1903)

■ Nonfiction entries by Black authors ■ Nonfiction entries by white authors

building will most certainly form key material for future scholarship. The emphasis here on Hopkins's contribution to Black literary traditions offers a philosophical and literary methodology for theorizing Hopkins's demographic selections of fiction writers.

Henry Louis Gates Jr.'s and Ann duCille's works on the making of literary traditions illuminate the role Hopkins's fiction selections played in building a Black literary tradition. As Gates puts it, "Literary works configure into a tradition not because of some mystical collective unconscious determined by the biology of race or gender, but because writers read other writers and *ground* their representations of experience in models of language provided largely by other writers to whom they feel akin" (*Collected Black Women's Narratives* xviii). Likewise, Hopkins's publication of Black authors and foregrounding of Black women authors created an enduring space within and across which Black writers had the opportunity to read one another and situate their literary representations and expressive modalities along lines of racial and gendered affinity. Moreover, as duCille argues, "Traditions are made not born, constructed not spawned," and the reading and revising that cohere among and between authors do not "spontaneously generate or autonomously define a particular literary tradition" (147). In that vein, I contend that Hopkins's fiction-publishing practices cohered as a contribution to the ongoing construction of a Black literary tradition situated within the nexus of race and gender concerns that informed Hopkins's uplift politics. Hopkins built a literary environment in and through which authors with shared sociopolitical concerns and connected experiences of racial and gendered discrimination had the opportunity to read and build on one another's literary models.

Linking Black literature or "race" literature as key to racial uplift was not uncommon in the written works of race women. Hopkins's contemporary Victoria Earle Matthews anticipated Hopkins's vision for African American literature in her 1895 essay, "The Value of Race Literature," stating that "when the literature of our race is developed, it will of necessity be different in all essential points of greatness, true heroism and real Christianity from what we may at the present time, for convenience, call American literature." Like Hopkins, Matthews construed the building of a Black literary tradition as discrete from the current body of American literature and encouraged a proliferation of race writings. But Matthews, persuasive as she was, did not have the editorial position that Hopkins did at *CAM*. As Abby Arthur Johnson and Ronald Johnson argue, it was Hopkins's editorial work that encouraged "a renaissance of black literature" in *CAM* (326). Right as they are, Johnson and Johnson are conservative in their use of the word "encouraged." The data in figures 3.01 and 3.02 suggest that Hopkins did much more than encourage this renaissance, she ensured *CAM*'s central role in its construction.

Hopkins's fiction selections as a whole—sixty of sixty-seven entries by Black authors, forty-six of these sixty by Black women authors—and her persistent publishing of this fiction in every issue of *CAM* actualized her cultivation of a distinct Black literary tradition as part of the race work of *CAM*. Matthews's lecture looked forward to "when the literature of our race is developed," while Hopkins employed her editorial role at *CAM* to materialize Matthews's stunning vision for Black literary expression. More, as Hopkins stated in May 1902, "Our short stories, by our Race writers, are becoming more and more literary in style, and we shall soon see an era of strong competition in the field of letters." Hopkins wanted Black-authored fiction to compete rather than assimilate or wear the mask of white literary expression. This does not disregard the significant scholarship examining the ways that Black authors, Hopkins included, engaged and fused Western literary conventions with Black forms of cultural expression to create new meaning, creating what Bernard Bell and others refer to as the "dual tradition" of African American literature (451). Rather, Hopkins cultivated a community of Black writers doing the work of this dual tradition, fiercely positioning Black cultural expression in competition with a white Western literary canon as a central component of her editorial approach to racial uplift. Hopkins's editorial practices with fiction during this key period of her editorship activated, dually, an antiassimilationist and Black woman–centered vision for racial uplift, curating a space to bring together Black intellectual expression across gender identities in order to create and imagine their individual and collective place and experience in the world.

December 1903–November 1904:
John C. Freund's Arrival and Hopkins's Exit from *CAM*

The arrival of white Bookerite representative and newspaperman John C. Freund created a staggering tension around the role of fiction at *CAM*. Freund's commentary disparaging the value of Black literary works only serves to further underscore Hopkins's fiction selections as a radical political component of her vision for racial uplift in opposition to prevailing racist attitudes toward Black people. Here, correspondence between Freund, Hopkins, and *CAM* president William Dupree assists in contextualizing and theorizing the inverse relationship between Freund's increasing influence at *CAM* and the precipitous

FIGURE 4.01. Trends in Fiction and Black Men's Fiction
(Dec. 1903–Nov. 1904)

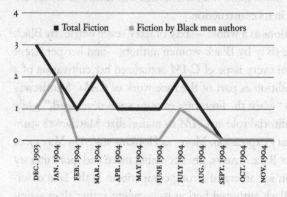

FIGURE 4.02. Trends in Fiction and Black Women's
Fiction (Dec. 1903–Nov. 1904)

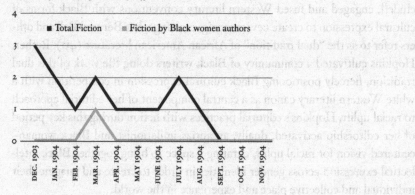

decline in Black-authored fiction publications and eventually all fiction publications in the magazine from December 1903 to November 1904 (see figures 4.01 and 4.02).

In a letter dated 19 November 1903 Dupree solicited Freund's assistance with the magazine. By January 1904, Freund's correspondence indicates that he had become deeply involved in the financial and day-to-day workings of *CAM* in this short time. From January 1904 to April 1904, Freund wove mention of his financial commitments to *CAM* with his editorial suggestions regarding magazine content and production, thus flexing his newfound influence over the publication. As Freund's correspondence with Hopkins and Dupree became routine, so too did his effort to alter the ideological focus and content of *CAM*, where his most repeated directives paired warnings to avoid offending or turn-ing off white readers with suggestions that Hopkins limit the volume of literary works included in the magazine. I quote Freund's correspondence with Hop-kins and Dupree at length to demonstrate the strain Freund placed on Hop-kins's ability to sustain her editorial practices with fiction and to highlight the inverse relationship between Freund's demands to alter the principles of *CAM* and the racial uplift principles Hopkins advanced through her fiction selections for the publication.

Repeatedly, Freund pushed for the removal of a literary emphasis in *CAM*, and repeatedly he linked that removal with the imperative to appeal to and avoid offending white readers. As the correspondence discussed here demon-strates, Freund's demands for fewer literary items and silenced civil rights agita-tion increased along with his involvement in *CAM*. The starkest indication of Freund's insinuation of Bookerite politics at *CAM* is the disappearance of fic-tion from the magazine altogether from September 1904 to November 1904, the same months that correspond with Hopkins's departure.[22] However, I contend that, given what we now know about Hopkins's fiction publication practices from early 1901 to November 1903, the demographics of the fiction publications in early 1904 alongside the additional evidence from Freund's correspondence offer an ominous indication of Hopkins's diminished editorial and ideological control at *CAM*.

In Freund's first extant correspondence with Hopkins, dated 27 January 1904, he demonstrated already his ease in giving instruction on editorial mat-ters at *CAM* while advocating an accommodationist vision for the publication: "Let me urge upon you the importance of keeping up a conservative tone in the magazine itself. . . . There must not be one word of reproach in the maga-zine. . . . Your people must look forward and not backward. You must not, as one of your number said, dwell on your wrongs. The higher the plane you are on, the more you will appeal to the people who mean to help you." In the same letter, Freund linked his caution against agitating white readers with transition-ing the magazine content away from imaginative genres, including fiction:

> Further, let me suggest that you, as far as possible, confine the *entire con-tents of your magazine* [emphasis mine] to reporting the work which is be-ing done by colored men and women, by their associations, their universities, their organizations and their clubs. This will serve two puporses [*sic*]. In the first place you will give the white people an adequate idea of the work you are doing; which they now have not, and acquaint them with what the better element in the colored race is doing. And, secondly, you will put heart and

life into the colored people themselves; thus, they will have a record of their work, which up to this time they have never had.

The extent to which Freund attempted to influence Hopkins in this manner may be best demonstrated through the series of demands he made in this regard for the duration of Hopkins's editorial influence at the magazine. In a letter dated 28 January 1904 to Dupree, Freund reemphasized his point: "There is one point ahich [*sic*] I want to impress upon you, as I have endeavored to do upon Miss Hopkins. You must not endeavor for a moment to publish a general literary magazine. . . . I would try and make *news* the leading feature of the magazine rather than criticisms, essays, and literary matter generally." And again in a letter dated 18 February 1904 Freund pressed Hopkins to make a content change, positioning Hopkins's investment in a Black literary publication as simultaneously oppositional to a white audience's interests and trivial to Black interests in racial uplift: "I send you herewith the editorial page of 'The Post', of last night, which will give you . . . some idea of what is being said on the other side with regard to the colored race problem. This editorial I want you to read most carefully for it is right in the line with what I have been endeavoring to say to you with regard to the conduct of the magazine. To supply the colored people with literary matter is, in the best event, a thankless task." In a letter dated 31 March 1904, Freund reiterated that he "would not cross the street to buy what is called a 'literary monthly.'" And in a letter dated 7 April 1904 to Hopkins, Freund referred to his own belaboring of these points while equally demonstrating his awareness that Hopkins's views on the matter did not align with his own: "That your taste shoule [*sic*] run to a literary monthly, and that you have dreamed for a long time of a great magazine which should present your race in hits noblest form . . . is grand. . . . The general literary weekly, however, noble though its scope, is dead. . . . We must deal with live issues, and above all, we must specialize. As I have again and again written you, everything that may offend must come out of the magazine."

Freund's impact on Hopkins's editorial practices is evident in the data representing fiction selections during this time. Concurrent with Freund's increased influence, the hallmarks of Hopkins's fiction-publishing practices receded. As figure 4.02 shows, after thirty-three months of publishing fiction almost entirely authored by African Americans, predominantly Black women, Black women fiction writers disappeared entirely from *CAM* for three months. Black men's fiction hardly fared better (figure 4.01), seeing a brief presence in December 1903 and January 1904 before also disappearing from February 1904 through June 1904. Conversely, fiction did not disappear immediately, as figures 4.01 and 4.02 show. *CAM* published white woman author Harriet Martineau's serialized fiction "The Hour and the Man" during this time. Thus, concurrent with Freund's involvement, white-authored fiction headlined the fiction section of *CAM* for the first time since Hopkins gained editorial control in early 1901.

There is indeed no question that the key demographic characteristics of Hopkins's editorial practices with fiction disappeared, and by the time of her official exit from the publication in September 1904, Hopkins's long-held commitment to publishing fiction as a critical component of racial uplift ceased to appear in the current pages of the publication. First, Hopkins's emphasis on Black fiction authorship receded, nearly concurrent with the diminished presence of Black women fiction writers. Then, as Hopkins's official exit in 1904 became imminent, the magazine published zero fiction entries for the first time since Hopkins took editorial control. This inverse relationship highlights the extent to which Hopkins's particular vision for racial uplift, her antiaccommodationism, her foregrounding of Black women's intellectual work as central to racial uplift, and her investment in celebrating and cultivating Black literary expression cohered in and through her fiction selections. Perhaps, like many histories of loss, we are made most keenly aware of Hopkins's radical uplift influences where and when her interventions disappeared from *CAM*.

Conclusion

Through her editorial practices with fiction, Pauline Hopkins articulated a radical politics of racial uplift. The intersecting structures of power that likely combined to precipitate Hopkins's exit from *CAM* also represented the ideological perspectives that Hopkins's vision for racial uplift contested. Hopkins faced the difficult task of writing for and editing a journal that "mediated between its identity as a 'race magazine' and a pragmatic editorial policy of appealing to white, middle-class audiences for economic, social, and political support" (Cordell 53). She encountered racist white women's rejections of her vision of a Black New Womanhood even as she encountered gendered biases that interpreted her editorial opinions as temperamental and sought to sideline Black women's intellectual work. Hopkins confronted these intersecting oppressions at a time when twentieth-century public race and gender conversations separated the fight for racial uplift from women's rights struggles. This left scant room for her to assert a vision for racial uplift that incorporated the various values that informed her ideas for racial progress, values that included her critiques of Bookerite politics, male-centered civil rights strategies, *and* the exclusionary practices of white women. Hopkins's editorial control over fiction served as a critical edge from which she deployed her own Black woman–centered program of racial uplift, one that addressed racial injustice at the intersection of racial and gendered concerns while investing deeply in advancing Black literary culture. Hopkins converted the very conditions that contributed to her marginalization as an editor at *CAM* and as a race woman in Boston into an opportunity to utilize the fiction section of *CAM* as a mechanism for voicing her vision for racial progress.

The preoccupation with Hopkins's exit from *CAM* often turns toward what she could have accomplished had she remained at the publication with some editorial power. As Nellie McKay puts it, Hopkins and other Black women editors "saw in periodical editorship a promise of access to a multidimensional public voice in the interests of the groups to which they were committed," but "their intentions were given less credit and often used against them. The world is poorer for what they were not permitted to do" (11–12). In response to McKay's concern, this focus on Hopkins's editorial choices at *CAM* assists in identifying more of the work Hopkins was able to do, work that was accomplished in the face of significant deterrence and opposition. This approach to analyzing Hopkins's editorial decisions carves a path toward delineating how she participated in the larger trajectories of Black women's intellectual and literary activism, early Black feminisms, Black community and nation building, and more.

NOTES

1. See Gruesser; Dahn and Sweeney; Schomburg Library; and Dworkin.

2. See Knight 46 for the political environment motivating Du Bois's discussion of Hopkins.

3. See Crenshaw's definition of "intersectionality" in "Demarginalizing" and "Mapping."

4. I built and interpreted the dataset with a multipoint approach to verifying, interpreting, and contextualizing the digitized information. The dataset is a product of extensive cross-checking across Google Books' digitization of *CAM* and digitized issues and accompanying scholarly commentaries from Dahn and Sweeney. Where an author's identity could not be confirmed through historical research, the data are marked as unknown. Anonymous designations are reserved for texts with unattributed authorship and texts signed "Anonymous."

5. Timeline constructed from Hopkins's 16 April 1905 letter to William Monroe Trotter. All letters cited throughout the text are found in folder 9, box 1, Pauline Hop-

kins Collection, 1879–99, John Hope and Aurelia E. Franklin Library Special Collections, Fisk University, Nashville, Tenn. Additional research for the timeline derives from Knight.

6. See Knight 46 for a detailed account of behind-the-scenes developments in the ownership of *CAM*.

7. See McKay 4–5; Carby, introduction xxxii; and Knight 45 for evidence of Hopkins's control over fiction publications in *CAM*.

8. Walter Wallace founded the Colored Co-Operative Publishing Company in May 1900. For background on Hopkins's role as board member of the Colored Co-Operative, see Wallinger 50.

9. *CAM* editorial staff navigated between showing respect for Booker T. Washington's uplift program and publishing the magazine's interests in civil rights injustices. See the May 1900 issue of *CAM*, in which the editors published an article dismantling the separate but equal logic of the "separate car law," while the Editorial and Publishers' Announcements section cautions readers against critiquing Booker T. Washington's views.

10. Braithwaite confirms Hopkins's increased editorial influence leading up to William Dupree's appointment as *CAM* president in July 1901.

11. Braithwaite credits Wallace with securing artwork, articles, and essays for publication in the magazine.

12. Yarborough offers a thorough analysis of early gendered dismissal of Hopkins's literary works in his 1988 introduction to *Contending Forces* (xxviii).

13. See Tate, *Domestic* 9 for a thorough discussion of the intersecting social, political, and economic sanctions shaping Black women's navigation of public spheres at the turn of the century.

14. This analysis builds from Knight's analysis of Hopkins's revisions of the archetype of the self-made man.

15. See Braithwaite 119 for insight into Hopkins's control over fiction publications.

16. Knight demonstrates that Hopkins was early on "labeled an agitator" (30).

17. Of the seven fiction entries during this time that are not authored by Black authors, two of the entries are by Charles Winslow Hall, and the remaining five entries are authored by either anonymous authors or named authors whose identities cannot be verified.

18. See Crenshaw, "Demarginalizing" 140 for a thorough discussion of the compounded impacts of racial and gendered oppression for Black women.

19. See Knight; Wallinger; and Brown for full discussion of Hopkins's use of pseudonyms Sarah A. Allen and J. Shirley Shadrach.

20. See Knight for a thorough examination of Hopkins's multivalent critiques of Bookerite accommodationism.

21. Use of "imaginative writings" derives from Bell.

22. In the Editorial and Publishers' Announcements of the November 1904 issue of *CAM*, editors announced that Hopkins had left the publication due to ill health (vol. 7, no. 2, p. 700). Hopkins corrected this in her 16 April 1905 correspondence with Trotter, stating that she was "frozen out" and "forced to resign" in September 1904.

WORKS CITED

Ammons, Elizabeth. "Afterword: *Winona*, Bakhtin, and Hopkins in the Twenty-First Century." *The Unruly Voice: Rediscovering Pauline Elizabeth Hopkins*, edited by John Cullen Gruesser, University of Illinois Press, 1996, pp. 211–19.

Beal, Frances M. "Double Jeopardy: To Be Black and Female." 1970. *The Black Woman: An Anthology*, edited by Toni Cade Bambara, Washington Square Press, 2005, pp. 109–22.

Bell, Bernard. "Dual Tradition of African American Fiction: An Interpretation." *The Encyclopedia of African American Experience*, edited by Kwame Anthony Appiah and Henry Louis Gates Jr., 2nd ed., 2005, pp. 450–57.

Bergman, Jill. "'A New Race of Colored Women': Pauline Hopkins at the *Colored American Magazine*." *Feminist Forerunners: New Womanism and Feminism in the Early Twentieth Century*, edited by Ann Heilmann, Pandora, 2003, pp. 87–100.

Braithwaite, William Stanley. "Negro America's First Magazine." 1947. *The William Stanley Braithwaite Reader*, edited by Philip Butcher, University of Michigan Press, 1972, pp. 114–22.

Brown, Lois. *Pauline Elizabeth Hopkins: Black Daughter of the Revolution*. University of North Carolina Press, 2008.

Carby, Hazel V. Introduction. *The Magazine Novels of Pauline Hopkins*, Schomburg Library of Nineteenth Century Black Women Writers, Oxford University Press, 1988, pp. xxix–l.

———. *Reconstructing Womanhood: The Emergence of the Afro-American Woman Novelist*. Oxford University Press, 1987.

Colored American Magazine, vols. 1–2, 1900–01; vols. 3–4, 1900–01; vol. 5, 1902; vol. 6, 1903; and vol. 7, 1904, all in The Black Experience in America: Negro Periodicals in the United States, 1840–1960, series, Negro Universities Press, 1969.

Colored American Magazine, vol. 1, no. 3, Colored Co-Operative Publishing Company, Aug. 1900, *The Digital Colored American Magazine*, directed by Eurie Dahn and Brian Sweeney, http://coloredamerican.org/wp-content/uploads/2017/02/CAM _1.3_1900.08.NS_.pdf, accessed 10 May 2018; vol. 1, no. 5, Colored Co-Operative Publishing Company, Oct. 1900, *The Digital Colored American Magazine*, directed by Eurie Dahn and Brian Sweeney, http://coloredamerican.org/wp-content/uploads /2016/08/CAM_1.5_1900.10.pdf, accessed 10 May 2018; vol. 4, no. 3, Colored Co--Operative Publishing Company, Jan./Feb. 1902, *The Digital Colored American Magazine*, directed by Eurie Dahn and Brian Sweeney, http://coloredamerican.org /wp-content/uploads/2017/07/CAM_4.3_1902.0102.pdf, accessed 10 May 2018; vol. 4, no. 4, Colored Co-Operative Publishing Company, Mar. 1902, *The Digital Colored American Magazine*, directed by Eurie Dahn and Brian Sweeney, http://colored american.org/wp-content/uploads/2017/03/CAM_4.4_1902.03.NS_.pdf, accessed 10 May 2018.

Combahee River Collective. "A Black Feminist Statement." 1977. *All the Women Are White, All the Blacks Are Men, but Some of Us Are Brave*, edited by Gloria T. Hull, Patricia Bell Scott, and Barbara Smith, Feminist Press, 1982, pp. 13–22.

Cooper, Brittney C. *Beyond Respectability: The Intellectual Thought of Race Women.* University of Illinois Press, 2017.

Cordell, Sigrid Anderson. "'The Case Was Very Black Against' Her: Pauline Hopkins and the Politics of Racial Ambiguity at the *Colored American Magazine*." *American Periodicals*, vol. 16, no. 1, 2006, pp. 52–73. *Project Muse*, DOI: 10.1353/amp.2006.0003.

Crenshaw, Kimberlé. "Demarginalizing the Intersection of Race and Sex: A Black Feminist Critique of Antidiscrimination Doctrine, Feminist Theory and Antiracist Politics." *University of Chicago Legal Forum*, vol. 1989, no. 1, pp. 139–67. *Nexis*, http://chicagounbound.uchicago.edu/uclf/vol1989/iss1/8.

———. "Mapping the Margins: Intersectionality, Identity Politics, and Violence against Women of Color." *Stanford Law Review*, vol. 43, no. 6, 1991, pp. 1241–99. *ResearchGate*, DOI: 10.2307/1229039.

Dahn, Eurie, and Brian Sweeney, project directors. *The Digital Colored American Magazine.* http://coloredamerican.org/. Accessed 10 May 2018.

Doreski, C. K. "Inherited Rhetoric and Authentic History: Pauline Hopkins at the *Colored American Magazine*." *The Unruly Voice: Rediscovering Pauline Elizabeth Hopkins,* edited by John Cullen Gruesser, University of Illinois Press, 1996, pp. 71–97.

Du Bois, W. E. B. "The Colored Magazine in America." *The Crisis,* vol. 5, no. 1, 1912, p. 33.

duCille, Ann. *The Coupling Convention: Sex, Text, and Tradition in Black Women's Fiction.* Oxford University Press, 1993.

Dworkin, Ira, editor. *Daughter of the Revolution: The Major Nonfiction Works of Pauline E. Hopkins.* Rutgers University Press, 2007.

Editorial and Publishers' Announcements. *Colored American Magazine,* vol. 1, no. 1, May 1900, p. 60, and vol. 7, no. 2, Nov. 1904, p. 700.

Gates, Henry Louis, Jr. "The Blackness of Blackness: A Critique of the Sign and the Signifying Monkey." *Black Literature and Literary Theory,* edited by Henry Louis Gates Jr., Routledge, 1990, pp. 285–321.

———, editor. *Collected Black Women's Narratives.* Schomburg Library of Nineteenth-Century Black Women Writers. Oxford University Press, 1988.

———. *The Signifying Monkey: A Theory of African American Literary Criticism.* Oxford University Press, 2014.

Griffin, Farah Jasmine. "Black Feminists and Du Bois: Respectability, Protection, and Beyond." *Annals of the American Academy of Political and Social Science,* vol. 568, 2000, pp. 28–40. *JSTOR*, www.jstor.org/stable/1049470.

hooks, bell. "Choosing the Margin as a Space of Radical Openness." *Framework: The Journal of Cinema and Media,* no. 26, 1989, pp. 15–23. *JSTOR*, www.jstor.org/stable/44111660.

Hopkins, Pauline E. Famous Women of the Negro Race. *Colored American Magazine,* vol. 5, no. 3, July 1902, pp. 210–11; vol. 5, no. 4, Aug. 1902, pp. 273–77; and vol. 5, no. 6, Oct. 1902, pp. 445–50, all in The Black Experience in America: Negro Periodicals in the United States, 1840–1960, series, Negro Universities Press, 1969.

———. Letter to the Editor. *Colored American Magazine,* vol. 6, no. 5, Mar. 1903, p.

399, The Black Experience in America: Negro Periodicals in the United States, 1840–1960, series, Negro Universities Press, 1969.

———. Preface. *Contending Forces: A Romance Illustrative of Negro Life North and South*. 1900. Oxford University Press, 1988, pp. 13–16.

———. "Prospectus." *Colored American Magazine*, vol. 1, no. 4, Sept. 1900, p. 195, The Black Experience in America: Negro Periodicals in the United States, 1840–1960, series, Negro Universities Press, 1969.

Johnson, Abby Arthur, and Ronald M. Johnson. "Away from Accommodation: Radical Editors and Protest Journalism, 1900–1910." *Journal of Negro History*, vol. 62, no. 4, 1977, pp. 325–38. *JSTOR*, www.jstor.org/stable/2717109.

Knight, Alisha R. *Pauline Hopkins and the American Dream: An African American Writer's (Re)visionary Gospel of Success*. University of Tennessee Press, 2012.

Masthead. *Colored American Magazine*, vol. 1, no. 1, May 1900, The Black Experience in America: Negro Periodicals in the United States, 1840–1960, series, Negro Universities Press, 1969.

Matthews, Victoria Earle. "The Value of Race Literature: An Address Delivered at the First Congress of Colored Women of the United States," Boston, Mass., 30 July 1895. Beinecke Rare Book and Manuscript Library, Yale University, New Haven, Conn.

McKay, Nellie Y. Introduction. *The Unruly Voice: Rediscovering Pauline Elizabeth Hopkins*, edited by John Cullen Gruesser, University of Illinois Press, 1996, pp. 1–20.

Pavletich, JoAnn. "'Inspired Borrowings': Pauline Hopkins's Literary Appropriations." The Pauline Hopkins Society, www.paulinehopkinssociety.org/inspired-borrowings/, accessed 8 March 2018.

———. "Pauline Hopkins and the Death of the Tragic Mulatta." *Callaloo*, vol. 38, no. 3, 2015, pp. 647–63. *Project Muse*, DOI: 10.1353/cal.2015.0103.

Schomburg Library of Nineteenth Century Black Women Writers. *The Magazine Novels of Pauline Hopkins*. Oxford University Press, 1988.

Shockley, Ann Allen. "Pauline Elizabeth Hopkins: A Biographical Excursion into Obscurity." *Phylon*, vol. 33, no. 1, 1972, pp. 22–26. *JSTOR*, www.jstor.org/stable/273429.

Tate, Claudia. *Domestic Allegories of Political Desire: The Black Heroine's Text at the Turn of the Century*. Oxford University Press, 1992.

———. "Pauline Hopkins: Our Literary Foremother." *Conjuring Black Women, Fiction, and Literary Tradition*, edited by Marjorie Pryse and Hortense Spillers, Indiana University Press, 1985, pp. 53–66.

Wallinger, Hanna. *Pauline E. Hopkins: A Literary Biography*. University of Georgia Press, 2005.

Welter, Barbara. "The Cult of True Womanhood: 1820–1860." *American Quarterly*, vol. 18, no. 2, 1966, pp. 151–73. *JSTOR*, www.jstor.org/stable/2711179.

Yarborough, Richard. Introduction. *Contending Forces: A Romance Illustrative of Negro Life North and South*, by Pauline E. Hopkins, 1900. Oxford University Press, 1988, pp. xxvii–xlviii.

Literary and Legal Genres in Pauline Hopkins's *Hagar's Daughter*

BLACK TESTIMONY, THE PRODUCTION OF TRUTH, AND THE REGULATION OF PROPERTY

Valerie Sirenko

When examining nineteenth-century African American novels, it is striking how frequently their plots revolve around stolen inheritance, including not only slavery's hereditary theft of personhood but also the theft of literal fortunes. For example, in Frank Webb's *The Garies and Their Friends* (1857), a white lawyer steals the inheritance of his cousin's Black children. In Hannah Crafts's *The Bondwoman's Narrative*, the narrator's mistress loses her inheritance to a blackmailing lawyer who discovers her hidden Black ancestry while executing her father's estate. In Frances Harper's *Iola Leroy* (1892), Iola and her mother are disinherited and sold into slavery after her white father dies. In Charles Chesnutt's *The Marrow of Tradition* (1901), a white woman steals her brother-in-law's will and marriage license to prevent his Black wife and daughter from claiming the property. These stolen inheritances often signal the broken promises of contract ideology in a legal era in which restrictions against Black testimony prevented African Americans from defending themselves and their property in court.[1] In each of these novels, Black heirs lose their rightful inheritances when legal documents fail to secure the property rights that a contract ostensibly confers. In *Hagar's Daughter* (1901), Pauline Hopkins employs a stolen inheritance plot but with a significant difference in that the inheritance is saved: a forged will threatens to disinherit two biracial Black women, but a detective uncovers the forger's involvement in a separate but related crime. Although the forgery of the will is never proven, discrediting the man behind the scheme saves Hagar/Estelle and her daughter, Jewel, from being disinherited and allows the true will to follow through on the contract's promise. In this way, Hopkins suggests that exposing the way legal authority is embodied in white persons can combat the pattern of Black disinheritance foregrounded by her literary predecessors.

Representing law as the result of embodied, racialized authority also highlights the function of the legal contract as a genre that in theory designates predetermined actions but that in practice can be manipulated by legal authorities to dispossess racialized others. Significantly, the contract's failure to protect Black property occurs at the point of a text's enactment, when embodied persons—white lawyers, executors, and judges—refuse to enact the document's stipulations in direct contradiction to contract law's promise that a written document will convey the writer's legal agency. When African American authors highlight the moment when legal texts fail to transform into action, they encourage us to think about law's operation as a genre with conventions, expected forms, and predictable outcomes that become visible at moments of deviation. When Hopkins shows the contract failing to produce its expected outcome, she correlates the shared function of literary and legal genres: both are designed to produce an expected outcome, but when this expectation is unfulfilled, they can produce powerful critiques of the normative operations of the genre.

In Hopkins's novel, it is the operation of a popular literary genre, detective fiction, that achieves this crucial representation of law as the outcome of racially embodied actors. While critics have at times dismissed or ignored Hopkins's work because it appears to follow the patterns of popular genre fiction, I argue that it is precisely through her disruption and reinterpretation of detective fiction that Hopkins produces an incisive critique of the way racialized law dispossesses Black subjects.[2] In *Hagar's Daughter*, the white detective, Chief Henson, testifies at the novel's climactic trial to verify the statements made by the crime's only witness, Henny, whose testimony is questioned because she is Black. Henny's testimony exposes two white men as criminals and saves Hagar/Estelle and Jewel's endangered inheritance because Henson and Henny successfully manipulate the courtroom audience's generic expectations. Hopkins pushes back against her era's legal restrictions on Black testimony by representing the courtroom as a public sphere in which Black voices can indict white crimes even when those voices are rejected as impermissible evidence. Hopkins suggests that the combined power of embodied Black testimony, which she represents as the only source of unmediated truth, and white authority, which she represents as the only way to produce legally permissible evidence, can protect African American inheritances.

In this way, Hopkins used the popular literary genre of detective fiction, defined by a narrative structure built around methods of producing and evaluating evidence, to draw attention to the racialized operating assumptions behind legal genres such as contracts, testimony, and evidence law that white legal authorities used to invalidate Black voices in the courtroom. Hopkins called attention to the potential of genre, when applied to an understanding of law as a collection of legal genres, to disrupt the normative operations of a legal system designed to deny the agency of racialized persons. The legal genres Hopkins examined include testimony, which functions as embodied authority so that racialized voices do not qualify; forensics, in which physical objects are represented as providing unmediated access to a crime's events but in fact hide the role of white interpreters; and legal contracts such as the last will and testament, which seem to give one the power to control property after death but in fact permit intervention by legal authorities who invalidated wills that transgressed racial boundaries.[3] By exposing how each legal genre produces white authority, Hopkins also demonstrated how these genres can be repurposed to produce Black authority, such as when Chief Henson confirms Henny's rejected testimony.

While scholars have examined how Hopkins indicted racialized legal discrimination and how she employed certain genres such as detective fiction, none have examined how Hopkins used popular literary genres to unpack the function of legal genres in producing racialized law.[4] My approach reads the novel's restricted testimony, forensic discourse, and contested wills as legal genres that reveal how a racialized legal system controls who has the right to speak in court, whose voice carries legal weight, and what counts as legal truth. Understanding genre as a form of knowledge production that encodes structures of power reveals white authorities' mechanisms for controlling the production of legal truth and suggests that genre provides an opportunity for Black voices to intervene in this process. Law and literature scholars invested in critical race studies have recently emphasized how racial restrictions on testimony regulate what types of knowledge and evidence become legally persuasive in court (see Wong; Hsu). Drawing on this scholarship's method of examining "law's narrative structures—its perspectives, tropes, and plots—to better understand the mechanisms of power at the site of the law," I argue that the legal genres explored in *Hagar's Daughter* reveal that exercising legal agency is a matter of navigating the proper genres (Wong 9).

I will begin by examining how Hopkins depicts white authorities' use of forensics to deny legal recognition to Hagar's voice, a loss of agency that Hopkins contrasts against Henny's ability to subvert restrictions against Black testimony by speaking in the courtroom's public sphere. Next, by considering how Chief Henson's authority emerges from his partnership with a working-class Black woman, Venus Johnson, who solves the case by scrutinizing how her father acquired the money to pay her family's mortgage, I suggest that Hopkins repurposes the conventions of the detective genre to position vulnerable Black property as the essential clue that exposes white crimes. In contrast to the way white legal authorities manipulate the production of truth, Hopkins repositions two Black women, Henny and Venus, as more reliable sources of truth. I conclude that the absence of an heir to the fortune at the novel's conclusion, which further complicates the stolen inheritance plot, provides Hopkins with the opportunity to reposition Henny, her daughter, Marthy, and Marthy's children as Black heirs to a form of American property that, like a mortgage, they seem to possess without ever truly owning.

Speaking Objects and Black Testimony

In *Hagar's Daughter*, white legal authorities use the discourse of forensics to silence Black voices by personifying objects with a figurative voice that the authorities can interpret according to their own narratives. Within the genre of evidence law, which is codified with complex rules in the U.S. legal system, different forms of testimony and evidence are accorded differing levels of credibility depending on how closely they are perceived as representing the truth (Gallanis). Over the course of the nineteenth century, the status of eyewitness testimony within U.S. evidence law declined as other forms of evidence, especially physical and circumstantial evidence, came to be seen as more reliable than human beings (Chinn 7–15). As this conception of evidence came to the foreground, it provided legal authorities with a language and a set of logical assumptions that worked in tandem with exclusionary laws against Black testimony.[5] Hopkins juxtaposes the authority produced by physical objects and by Black testimony to reveal the way evidence law's use of forensics prevents Black speech from becoming legally valid. The discourse of forensics privileges physical evidence as revealing the unmediated truth of a crime, while in contrast, Henny's testimony against a white man is dismissed as incredible because whiteness is presumed to embody authority, and human speech, especially Black speech, is presumed to be unreliable.

In this way, Hopkins demonstrated how law's production of truth depends on the forensics genre's ability to produce the impression of objectivity by presenting the meaning of physical evidence as self-evident. Within the forensics genre, it is commonplace to present physical evidence as needing no interpretation, a rhetorical gesture that correlates objects with the objectivity so highly valorized in the modern era.[6] Of course, legal authorities' interpretations of the meaning behind physical evidence remain dependent on subjective human constructions despite the forensics genre's rhetorical gestures to self-evident truth. Hopkins used the detective genre to unpack the assumptions hidden within forensic discourse. Like forensic discourse, the detective genre valorizes a method of truth production in which physical evidence is interpreted as telling the story of past events to reveal the events of a crime. By comparing the literary genre of detective fiction, which celebrates the detective's deductive powers, against the legal genre of forensics, in which the law's interpretive function is deliberately downplayed, Hopkins demonstrated that white legal authorities employed the forensics genre in order to produce the effect of an objective truth while retaining control over the narratives they allow objects to tell. In this way, Hopkins exposed forensic discourse's operation as a legal genre that uses particular rhetorical conventions to produce a narrative in service of white structures of power.

In Ronald Thomas's characterization of the detective genre, detectives prove their truth-finding power through methods of reading physical signs on bodies, which "enable[s] the body to function both as a text and as politics in these narratives" (3). In the same way, in the first section of *Hagar's Daughter*, a white coroner's jury reads the objects found on Hagar's husband's body to reconstruct a presumed narrative of how he died. Hagar has grown up believing she is the white heiress to a Maryland plantation, but the revelation of her Black ancestry invalidates her marriage to Ellis Enson, a white man, and remits her to slavery. Transformed into a Black slave, Hagar loses the embodied authority of whiteness yet continues to voice resistance to white legal narratives and their interpretations of evidence. Shortly after Hagar's race is revealed, a body presumed to be that of her husband is found dead in the woods. Ellis's conniving brother, St. Clair, convinces the coroner's jury that Ellis must have committed suicide when he learned of his wife's race. The body, when examined and interpreted by white legal authorities, becomes a political narrative in which a white man, upon discovering his wife's African ancestry, self-destructs rather than come to terms with the idea of miscegenation. The objects found nearby allow St. Clair to interpret the death as a suicide: "An empty pistol by the side of the body tells its own pitiful tale" (Hopkins 67). The white coroner's jury agrees with the inference that because a "large sum of money is on the body; papers and his watch," Ellis has not been murdered (67). When the coroner's jury imagines these objects as "tell[ing]" the "tale" of Ellis's suicide, this rhetorical move personifies the objects as giving an unmediated account (67). In the classic detective narrative, the expert sleuth demonstrates his or her deductive skills by reading signs in common objects that others fail to notice and by drawing inferences from them that allow him or her to reconstruct the crime. When this role is performed by St. Clair, an obvious villain who seeks to disinherit Hagar and her infant daughter so that he can claim the estate for himself, Hopkins signals the potentially nefarious purposes behind forensics as a discourse that transforms objects into narratives that take on the capacity to become legal fact.

At the inquest, the reconstructed narrative, presented in the form of white testimony, assumes a central role in legally defining Ellis's death as suicide, not murder: "Walker, the speculator, corroborated the evidence of St. Clair Enson—that the deceased was laboring under great depression at the time of his leaving home, and of his avowed purpose to shoot himself as the shortest way out of his family difficulties. This testimony so clearly given produced a profound impression upon the listeners" (Hopkins 68). In this way, Hopkins shows how the interpreted objects have given way to the white narrative that has been constructed out of them. The manner in which Walker's story is told—"so clearly given"—achieves acceptance as the official narrative by the jury because of its "impression" on the audience. With the word "impression," Hopkins alludes to the epistemological function of genre to produce rhetorically what counts as knowledge in the legal sphere. Walker knows how to employ the correct generic form to produce an authoritative legal truth. Walker's testimony, which convinces the courtroom audience that the physical evidence corresponds to the narrative they most expect, functions as the genre was designed: to turn white narratives into legal facts.

By first highlighting how the genre of testimony functions to produce white authority, Hopkins then points to an opportunity for Black voices to intervene using this same genre. When Hagar rejects the story told by the objects, she rejects white legal authority's interpretation of them. Hagar challenges the legal verdict that has been derived from the objects by dismissing the forensic language of "proof." As she says, "What did the pistol prove? Nothing. His pockets had not been rifled. That proves nothing. Neither his great trouble brought to him by his marriage with me—a Negro—would have driven him to self-destruction. He was murdered!" (Hopkins 70). In this way, Hopkins demonstrates that when evidence appears to "speak," this speech serves the purposes of the legal authorities who determine how the evidence is interpreted. The local community retains respect for Hagar's voice, despite her revealed racial origins: "It was hoped by many that Hagar would testify, but they were doomed to disappointment" (68). The community desires to hear this Black woman's excluded testimony, which positions the public sphere as a potential space for Black redress in opposition to the legal sphere. When Hopkins depicts the community's desire to hear Hagar's voice, she suggests that the public sphere is an alternative rhetorical space where Black voices may speak and be heard despite exclusionary evidence laws.

Even if Hagar's testimony would have been invalidated in court due to her race, Hopkins implies that the attending public audience would have listened to it anyway. The historical record reveals that in some cases Black testimony was permitted despite objections; these apparent anomalies evince the courtroom as a contested site in which the uneven application of laws and customs sometimes allowed racialized voices to speak and be heard.[7] The laws and practices excluding Black testimony in the nineteenth century varied from state to state and changed over time.[8] This inconsistent application suggests that legal authorities employed restrictions against Black testimony as a flexible genre, one that held the potential to protect whites against damning testimony when necessary yet could also be ignored when it served their purposes. In the genre's malleability, Hopkins locates the potential for intervention and reappropriation.

Hopkins depicts an alternative space in which Hagar's voice finds purchase by repurposing the forensics genre. Unable to speak in court, Hagar voices her resistance directly against St. Clair and rejects the legally sanctioned story determined by the jury. Ultimately, "the jury rendered a verdict of suicide. Plainly, Ellis Enson had died by his own hand" (Hopkins 69). In defiance, Hagar accuses St. Clair of the murder, declaring, "You are his slayer, and his blood is crying from the ground against you this very hour" (71). Just as the forensics genre personifies physical evidence as telling the story of a crime, Hagar personifies Ellis's blood with the power of speech. Hagar imagines Ellis's blood speaking or "crying [out]" for justice against his killer. In this way, Hagar personifies the bloodstains as speaking with Ellis's voice, the voice of a white man, thus marshaling the embodied authority of Ellis's whiteness to support her story, just as Henny later draws on Henson's white authority at the murder trial.

In the novel's second climactic legal event, the murder trial of Elise Bradford, who was murdered by General Benson (St. Clair Enson) after she threatened to reveal their affair, Hopkins correlates the forensics genre's reliance on the personified authority of physical evidence with the function of exclusionary laws that invalidated Black testimony. By locating authority in objects, forensics minimizes the power of human testimony to challenge the narratives white legal authorities have constructed. Analogously, when a case depends on human testimony, exclusionary testimony laws define authority in court as white. Henny, a formerly enslaved Black woman, is the only person who witnesses the white General Benson murder his secretary, Elise Bradford. At the trial, Henny exposes General Benson's crimes, but the prosecutor moves to dismiss her testimony: "On what would you base such an unheard of precedent? on the evidence of a Negress?" (Hopkins 257). Hopkins couples the prosecutor's appeal to precedent and evidence law with the reactions of the courtroom to demonstrate the powerful influence of public opinion on criminal procedure: "Instantly a chorus of voices took up the refrain—'That's the talk! No nigger's word against a white man!'" (257). This "chorus of voices" and their repeated "refrain" stage the racialized struggle of the post-Reconstruction era to silence Black voices at law. Significantly, just a few years after the Supreme Court legalized "separate but equal" racial segregation in *Plessy v. Ferguson* (1896) using the argument that the issue should be determined by the "usages, customs, and traditions of the people," Hopkins showed restrictions against Black testimony coming from the white masses.[9] The outcries of the white populace attempt to regulate whose evidence counts as legally permissible and whose story can become legal truth. The elements of "chorus" and "refrain" in these objections, however, suggest that the white audience is following the patterns of a genre that dictates the form of their response. Therefore, by changing the tune, Chief Henson is able to elicit a different response when he testifies, one that is nonetheless predicated on the expected generic response to his embodied white authority.

The genre of testimony, built around expectations concerning where authority is located and the exclusionary logic that whiteness equates authority, relies on the embodiment of the speaker. When the speaker is embodied by a supposedly respectable white man such as General Benson, the genre functions according to its expected conventions. When the speaker is revealed to be a criminal, as Hopkins shows, the genre breaks down and cannot function to produce white authority. The prosecuting attorney evokes General Benson's reputation and standing as a white gentleman to counter Henny's story: "Such a man as General Benson cannot be condemned and suspicioned by the idiotic ramblings of an ignorant *nigger* brought here by the defense to divert attention from the real criminal, who attempts to shield himself under the influence of the Bowen millions" (Hopkins 257, emphasis original). Feeling the backing of the assembled courtroom public, the prosecutor raises the possibility of mob violence as an extralegal means of community enforcement: "I would feel myself justified in sounding the slogan of the South—lynch-law! if I thought this honorable body could be influenced to so unjust a course as is suggested" (257). Figuring the white audience as a single "body" that can take the law into its own hands, the prosecutor's evocation of the specter of lynching, by which the post-Reconstruction white public can reinforce legal exclusion with extralegal violence, reminds Hopkins's readers that law and public opinion often work in complementary ways to enforce racial boundaries.

The assembled public, however, also provides Hopkins with the means to transform the courtroom into an arena for revealing the repressed crimes of slavery. Hopkins rewrites the expected outcome of the trial when Henny's testimony is ultimately confirmed. As a result, Hagar and Ellis (who is not dead and is, in fact, Chief Henson in disguise) are reunited despite their new status as an interracial couple. Although Henny's testimony is officially struck from the record, her story has been heard by the courtroom audience, and all it takes to transform it into fact is for Chief Henson to lend his white authority to confirm Henny's testimony "[i]n a brief, incisive way, which carried weight to many doubting minds" (Hopkins 259). Chief Henson declares, "It now becomes my duty to make a statement in regard to the testimony of the last witness. . . . What she has said concerning Gen. Benson is absolutely true" (260). In Henson's "statement," a white authority figure gives the final word concerning what is "absolutely true" (260). Just as white legal authorities create a narrative through their interpretation of objects, Henson's testimony manipulates the expectations of the genre—that white speech carries authority—to disrupt the genre's normal function. Henson uses white authority to produce an unexpected outcome: Black production of truth, embodied by Henny. Henny's testimony also facilitates the recovery of Black property; Hagar/Estelle is able to reclaim the fortune St. Clair stole from her after St. Clair (disguised as General Benson) is proven to be a murderer.

The conventional assumptions behind legal testimony as a genre, in which whiteness equals authority, can be seen in the legal discourse of the late nineteenth century. As legal historian Pamela Brandwein explains, Reconstruction era justices understood that "to bar blacks from testifying in court was to administer justice in a hostile spirit, for such bars permitted whites to commit crimes against blacks free from punishment or penalty" (47). In *United States v. Rhodes* (1867), the Supreme Court considered whether the Civil Rights Act of 1866 allowed the federal government to prosecute white individuals who had stolen from a Black citizen despite a Kentucky state law that barred Blacks from testifying (47). Supreme Court justice Noah Swayne argued that the Kentucky law excluding Black testimony violated the rights secured in the Civil Rights Act, which corrected the injustice of crimes "committed by white men with impunity" "by giving to the colored man everywhere the same right to testify 'as is enjoyed by white citizens,' . . . wherever the right

to testify as if he were white is denied to him or cannot be enforced in the local tribunals of the state" (qtd. in Brandwein 47). The statement "as if he were
white" demonstrates how testimony operates based on the assumption that authority can only be found in embodied whiteness. Justice Swayne does not say
that Black testimony is valid; instead, he redefines Black testimony "as if" it is
white in order to prove its validity. The production of legally valid speech is still
reserved for whiteness and simply extended to include Blacks when dictated by
positive law. Even when Justice Swayne draws attention to the "denial of justice" caused by excluding Black testimony, he argues for Black citizens' right
to testify "everywhere" based on the assumption that only by equating Black
voices with white authority can their speech become legally recognized. In the
same way, Hopkins shows that Henny's Black testimony achieves its persuasive
power in the courtroom by harnessing the embodied white authority of Chief
Henson.

Hopkins uses the courtroom audience's reactions to draw attention to the
methods through which white testimony's persuasive effect on public opinion
produces legal truth. Rhetorically, it is Henson who produces the narrative that
becomes accepted as legal truth. After Henson tells a story that "held the vast
crowd spellbound," no one questions Cuthbert's innocence or General Benson's guilt (Hopkins 260). The prosecutor gives closing remarks only as a matter of formality because "he knew the verdict was a foregone one, that his own
remarks were but a form, that the weight of evidence in 'this most extraordinary case' left him but one course" (263). Although he formulaically references the legal procedure by which the jury decides "in accordance with the
evidence," the evidence seems to need no interpretation: the jury only con-
sults "for the sake of appearances" (264). Once a definitive narrative has been
reached, those involved follow through on a legal formalism evacuated of independent agency. The "evidence" that supposedly determines the jury's verdict
consists of one white man's authoritative speech, given validity by the legal system and confirmed by the public audience. The courtroom receives Chief Henson's testimony as carrying "the weight of evidence" that makes the verdict a
"foregone" conclusion, but in fact, he has no evidence at all—just his story
(263).

The necessity of using white testimony to validate Black testimony depicted
in *Hagar's Daughter* resembles historical cases in which African Americans had
to enlist the aid of white witnesses to swear to the truth of their statements and
evokes the literary convention in which slave narratives required an authenti-
cating preface written by a prominent white figure.[10] When a legal narrative,
given authority because it is spoken by a white man, emerges as definitive ev-

idence, Hopkins reveals the way testimony functions as a genre in which appealing to the right forms produces the desired result. When the desired result is a deviation from expected structures of power, such as the confirmation of a Black woman's testimony, Hopkins shows that the genre can be repurposed if one knows how to manipulate its form.

Black Labor and Homeownership

Vulnerable Black property provides the crucial link among the novel's multifarious crimes. A number of critics, situating *Hagar's Daughter* within the genre of detective fiction, have noted how Hopkins rewrote the role of the renowned detective when Chief Henson depends upon Venus Johnson, a young working-class Black woman, to make his discoveries.[11] Venus is one of the earliest (if not the first) African American detective figures in American literature. However, critics have overlooked the significance of the fact that Venus solves the case by scrutinizing how her father has mysteriously come up with the money to pay her family's mortgage. The post-Reconstruction Black family's struggle for homeownership provides the essential clue that solves the murder, suggesting that the deeper roots of the crime lie in a property dispute. In Hopkins's fiction, crimes are typically traced back to property. The detective genre's imperative to uncover the crime allows Hopkins to demonstrate the stakes of white legal authorities' manipulation of legal genres and legal truth: property. When Hopkins's Black detective, Venus, becomes the novel's expert sleuth, Hopkins demonstrates how the detective genre's key elements—such as connecting a chain of evidence—can be repossessed by Black women to override the language of forensics, which is so often manipulated by white interpretations.

The Johnson family's working-class employment history provides the link in the chain of evidence that allows Venus and Henson to solve the case. As Venus resolves to unravel the conspiracy, Hopkins juxtaposes Venus's race and gender against the detective genre's expectations: "I'll see if this one little black girl can't get the best of as mean a set of villains as ever was born" (221). In language that positions Venus as the detective hero, she muses to herself, "I'll see him out on this case or my name ain't Venus Johnson" (221). Venus comes to Henson with the exact information he needs to crack open a case that has heretofore stumped his renowned deductive powers. Venus explains that her father Isaac's service for General Benson has clued her in to their scheme: "*I* believe the old rapscallion has got [Jewel] shut up somewhere down in Maryland, and dad's helping him. Oh, I didn't tell you, did I, that dad's his private waiter?" (226, emphasis original). Henson has long suspected that General Benson has kidnapped Jewel, but he cannot prove it or locate their hiding place until Venus comes to his aid.

Venus begins her detective work at home, inquiring "carelessly" but with pointed purpose, "Daddy been home lately?" (Hopkins 220). When her mother, Marthy, tells her, "He brought me the mor'gage money. . . . [Y]ou could have knocked me down with a feather, I was so outdone from 'stonishmen'," Venus adopts the modern detective's method of following the money (220). "Now, ma, where'd he get *all* that money I'd like to know?" Venus says. "He never got it honest, that's my belief" (220, emphasis original). When Marthy reveals that Isaac got the money from General Benson, Venus cross-examines her brother, Oliver, "question[ing] him closely," and "learn[s] many things concerning her father that her mother had failed to mention" (221). Venus concludes, "[I]t's as sure as preaching. . . . Dad's up to his capers. He can fool ma, but he can't pull the wool over my eyes; I'm his daughter" (221). Venus assertively resolves that she, as the only "somebody who knows something," must "take hold" of the case (221). By shifting authority from the classic detective figure to the working-class Black woman, Hopkins disrupts the detective genre to reposition the knowledge of working-class Black women as a crucial asset to the production of legal truth.

While critics have focused on the injustices done to the light-skinned heroines Hagar/Estelle and her daughter, Jewel, who are dispossessed when their invisible racial ancestry is revealed, I argue that Henny, Marthy, and Venus, three generations of dark-skinned, formerly enslaved women who cannot pass for white, are also central characters through which Hopkins depicts Black struggles to acquire and keep property.[12] These working-class women's struggle to own their home in a post-Reconstruction legal system of mortgages, wages, debt, and credit shows both the persistence of a legal system designed to dispossess them and these women's skillful ability to navigate these systems. The Bowen family and the Johnson family, whose fates are intertwined by the detective genre's structuring narrative of solving a crime, hold starkly contrasting economic statuses. While the extravagantly wealthy Hagar/Estelle (Mrs. Bowen) and Jewel are fighting to prove that Senator Bowen's will is a forgery in order to protect their million-dollar inheritance, the novel's Black women, far from inheriting anything, toil at low-wage service positions to support themselves and to avoid foreclosure on their home. In the figure of Venus, Hopkins unites Black female labor with the detective's prowess for solving crime and positions Venus's working-class background as foundational to the process of uncovering the truth.

Although critics of *Hagar's Daughter* tend to focus on the wealthy Bowen family's financial crisis, Venus solves the crime because she is prompted by the impending financial crisis facing her own family, who may lose their home to foreclosure. As critic Karla Holloway has noted, homeownership is particularly fraught for African Americans because, after generations of struggling to use property to establish themselves as full participants in American society and to achieve full legal personhood, debt has systematically denied them secure ownership of their homes (see also hooks). For Holloway, Black claims to property, particularly homeownership, require a struggle for legitimacy that signals the "changing same" of U.S. legal history's "persistent patterns of address and redress" that make Black people's legal identity a continually contested site (85). After learning that the family owes five hundred dollars on their mortgage, Henny (Venus's grandmother) offers to contribute one hundred dollars she has saved. As she says, "Cayn't rightly feel de place is ourn till we's paid up. When I sees you an' de chillun under your own roof, I gwine ter gib up de ghos' in peace" (Hopkins 175). Henny expresses the notion that owning one's home would signal peace and rest from a lifetime of toil. What Henny longs for is the *feeling* homeownership confers; she wants to "rightly feel" the place belongs to her family. When Marthy forces Isaac to "fotch out de res'" of the money to pay the mortgage, she inadvertently creates the financial trail of clues that allows Venus to solve the novel's central crime (175).

The centrality of Marthy's labor signals the "changing same" of post-Reconstruction Black dispossession, which takes on a new form as debt emerges as a key mechanism of Black financial vulnerability. Immediately after Cuthbert is arrested for the murder that General Benson has committed, the novel shifts perspective to Venus's mother, Marthy, whose appearance explicitly connects the first and second halves of the novel: "We last saw Marthy on the Enson plantation" (Hopkins 168). While most of the characters change names and identities in the twenty-year gap separating Hopkins's novel into pre- and postemancipation sections, the formerly enslaved Marthy, Henny, and Isaac have retained their identities, forming a crucial link between the novel's disjointed double narrative.[13] Kristina Brooks has dismissed these three formerly enslaved characters as "[s]tuck in a time warp and in plantation culture," arguing that they are the stereotypical "mammy, wench, and buck" and "are not subjects but objects for the reader's gaze" (133–34). Along these same lines, Holly Jackson reads "the odd reappearance of antebellum stock characters" as "textual atavism" (147).[14] Marthy's strong dialect, it seems, has marked her as less than a full character for today's scholars, just as it would have marked her as belonging to a racialized, gendered, and classed position if she were speaking in the post-Reconstruction legal sphere. However, as Marthy's struggle for homeownership proves, far from being stuck in the past, this working-class Black woman confronts and overcomes a new set of problems and a new form of dispossession facing post-Reconstruction Black families.

When Marthy reenters the narrative, she is no longer enslaved, but she continues to be defined by her labor: "Marthy Johnson knelt on the kitchen floor surrounded by heaps of fine white clothing sorting them into orderly piles" (Hopkins 168). Her labor, however, now goes toward paying for her son Oliver's education, a strategy of upward mobility that nonetheless divides the family down a gendered line of women working to support men: "Your pa's never 'roun' when he's wanted, an' your sister's slavin' herse'f like a nigger to help ejekate yer. My Lord, how worthless men folks is!" (169). Describing Venus as "slavin' herse'f," Marthy suggests that the women of the family continue to work in a state of enslavement (169). Making the gender difference explicit, Hopkins's representation of the Johnson family shows that twenty years after emancipation, instead of working for white men, Black women are working for Black men.

Marthy's expression of her work ethic not only emphasizes that Black women work ceaselessly throughout their lives but also points to the social structures that make this labor seem inevitable. As she explains, "Yer mammy 'spec' to wurk 'tell she draps inter the grave. Colored women wasn't made to take their comfit lak white ladies. They wasn't born fer nuthin' but ter wurk lak hosses or mules. Jes' seems lak we mus' wurk 'tell we draps into the grave" (171). In *Hagar's Daughter*, three generations of Black women work tirelessly to support the family and in the process develop collective strategies for pooling their resources. Referring to her mother's position as cleaning woman for the Treasury Department, Marthy describes the impact of her mother's monthly income: "Then I was able to sen' yer sister to school an' keep her nice in spite 'o [*sic*] yer daddy's racketty ways. Yer granny's holped me powful. Yer pa's money don' 'mount to a hill o' beans in my pocket" (173). Because Marthy's husband fails to contribute financially, the burden falls to the women. Although Isaac has been "working 'stiddy,'" Marthy has not yet "seen the color of his money" and remains "dependent" upon her washing work and "the substantial help given by her old mother's labor at the treasury" (175). Marthy's economically dependent position requires the family's Black women to collaborate, pool their resources, and work well into their old age.

As we have seen, Isaac's employment history turns out to be pivotal to the success of the novel's detectives. When Marthy "applie[s] to her husband for money," as if he is a bank, Isaac reveals that he has never received any wages from General Benson: "I ain't drawed a red cent o' my wages. . . . I jes' lef' it in his han's fer 'ves'men'. Major Madison an' Gin'ral's spec'latin' in mines" (Hopkins 176). Isaac believes he has been "investing" his money in safe "hands," but Marthy despairs of ever recouping the money: "The Lawd save us, Ike! Then we'll done lose this place. . . . The mor'gage money done come due in June, an' Mis' Jenkins been mighty kind, but he's boun' to fo'close" (177). Isaac tries to reassure her, but Marthy distrusts white financial institutions: "I don' trus' no' white man. 'Member all the money went up in the Freedman's bank, don' yer?" (177). Marthy's distrust is historically informed by Reconstruction's failure to protect and secure Black economic mobility. The Freedman's Savings Bank, established by Congress in 1865 to promote savings among recently emancipated Black people, went bankrupt in 1874, and most of the Black families who had invested their money lost everything.[15] Marthy resists investing in white speculative ventures because postemancipation history has proven that white "gentlemen" will not hesitate to cheat Black people out of their earnings (177).

However, even those Black families who owned their homes remained vulnerable to systems of credit and debt. Henny warns Marthy about the danger of losing the house to creditors even if the mortgage is paid: "Marthy, don't neber be a plum fool an let Ike wurrit you into raisin' money on de place, ef he gits inter scrapes let him git out as he gits in, widout any holp but de debbil" (Hopkins 176). If her husband gets into debt and borrows money, using the house as collateral, they could lose their home even though they have become the rightful owners. In this passage, Hopkins's gendered critique contrasts Isaac's way of living "widout any holp but de debbil" against female collaboration—"Yer granny's holped me powful" (176, 173). Henny imagines herself exerting posthumous revenge if Marthy allows Isaac to threaten the family's financial security: "Ef you eber let dat mon take de bread outer yer mouf dat way, an I'm daid, I gwine ter riz up outer de grave" (176). Henny, who understands how debt and credit work to deprive Black people of their property, gives Marthy economic advice informed by post-Reconstruction African American experience.

Venus's family's working-class history provides the link in the chain of evidence that allows Henson to solve the case. The narrative's structure, in which Hopkins presents Venus unraveling the plot and then immediately cuts to the defeated Chief Henson, contrasts Venus's acuity against the stumped and stymied white male detective whose famous powers have been foiled: "[Henson] had just returned from New York, where he had carefully examined the ground. . . . He was much depressed over his failure to obtain a clue. His vast experience did not aid him" (222). Venus then enters Henson's office with just the clue he needs. Isaac's new position as Benson's valet and his sudden ability to produce the four hundred dollars needed for the mortgage lead Venus to the old Enson plantation, where Jewel and Henny have been kidnapped, so she can rescue them in time for Henny to testify at the trial. Hopkins positions the Johnson family's struggle to pay their mortgage at the crux of the clues that unravel a larger plot to steal the Bowen fortune.

As the scene in Detective Henson's office reveals, the case of Senator Bowen's forged will has become conflated with Elise Bradford's murder trial, and in Hopkins's hybrid narrative, the sensational trial resolves not only the identity of the true murderer but also Major Madison and General Benson's scheme to steal Hagar/Estelle and Jewel's inheritance. The murder investigation prompts Chief Henson to examine a seemingly unrelated legal document: the last will and testament of the wealthy Senator Bowen, Hagar/Estelle's second husband. Although the murder has no direct relationship to the senator's will, Henson assumes "very naturally" that the murder can be solved by unraveling the mystery behind the will (Hopkins 259). As he expects, the forged will leads him to the true murderer. Just before Venus arrives with the crucial clue, Chief Henson has been "trying to find a flaw in the Bowen will, drawn and signed in that city, but not a particle of encouragement had rewarded his efforts" (222). The family lawyer, likewise stumped, has "just left him after acknowledging *his* inability to fix a point that would legally stay the enforcement of the will" (222, emphasis original). Henson is just as concerned with defeating the will, which he is "convinced was a clever forgery committed by two dangerous men," as he is with solving the murder (222). When the novel's detective plot transforms into a stolen Black inheritance plot, Hopkins revises this popular literary genre to show how restrictions on Black testimony and the regulation of Black property are intertwined structures of power.

Inheritance and the Last Will and Testament

As the combined detective powers of Venus and Henson uncover, General Benson has killed Elise Bradford so that he can marry the wealthy Jewel Bowen, and he has forged Jewel's father's will to appoint himself as her legal guardian and the executor of the estate. The murder trial, designed to frame Jewel's former fiancé, Cuthbert, holds implications for the inheritance of a vast fortune. Hopkins sets into motion the detective genre's convention of revealing secrets in order to return, somewhat circuitously, to the long durée of Black disinheritance. The stolen inheritance elevates the stakes of the detective genre's methods of producing legal truth to a critique of the racialized legal structures that dispossess Black families. However, Hopkins thwarts expectations once again with the untimely death of Jewel, the Black heiress to the novel's multiple fortunes. With Jewel's premature death, Hopkins condemns restrictions against Black testimony at law as implicated in the erasure of Black heirs from the narrative structures guiding the nation's distribution of property and inheritance. By highlighting the function of the last will and testament as a legal genre with forms, conventions, and expectations, Hopkins emphasizes that inheritance requires a legal process by which property becomes vulnerable to intervention. When the operations of the detective genre uncover Benson's plot to steal the inheritance of a wealthy family with hidden Black ancestry, Hopkins depicts how Blackness interrupts the expected operation of the legal genre of the contract. Although contract, as a genre, promises that the written document will represent the writer's legal agency, Hopkins shows how this genre permits white legal authorities to intervene and use the document's formal features to disenfranchise racialized persons.

There are two major fortunes at stake in the novel: the Enson estate, an inherited plantation built on slave labor, and the Bowen fortune, the self-made millions of a California miner.[16] Both fortunes depend on the ability of a will, as a legal contract, to express and enact the intentions of the deceased, and in both cases, the will's ability to convey posthumous legal agency fails. The will's ability to follow through on its expected generic function to represent the deceased's posthumous wishes and direct property into the right hands, Hopkins warns, is highly compromised. Hopkins uses the figure of Jewel, the biracial Black heir to multiple white family fortunes, to raise the question of the ability of Black families to secure property over multiple generations. In discussing Jewel, scholars typically consider her death a commentary on prejudices against interracial marriage.[17] However, I suggest that Hopkins uses the endangered Black inheritance plot to critique the post-Reconstruction era's perpetuation of racial dispossession by highlighting the vulnerability of property when it passes from one generation to the next. Jackson has argued that Hopkins's "preoccupation" with inheritance indicates her era's obsession with "genealogical paradigms" that construct families as white or Black (137). But Hopkins is also concerned with how Black families secure economic mobility. As Jeffory Clymer has shown, nineteenth-century literary depictions of marriage across the color line were crucial to imagining how property could move from white hands to Black family members. Hopkins evokes the recurrent nineteenth-century plot of hidden Black ancestry and stolen inheritances to demonstrate how one's legal agency translates into property rights depending on one's ability to secure the proper generic function of a contract. Hopkins's attention to the racial politics of the marriage contract and the uneven application of contract law allows her to highlight law's objectification and silencing of Black subjects beyond the courtroom.

Demonstrating the expected function of the will as a legal genre, Enson Sr., a white property owner, writes his will under the assumption that he can use the will to control events and property after his death:

> By the terms of the will St. Clair received a small annuity, to be enlarged at the discretion of his brother, and in event of the latter's death without issue, the estate was to revert to St. Clair's heirs "if any there be who are an honor to the name of Enson," was the wording of the will. In the event of St. Clair's continuing in disgrace and "having no honorable and lawful issue," the property was to revert to a distant branch of cousins, "for I have no mind that debauchery and crime shall find a home at Enson Hall." (21–22)

Enson Sr. believes he can use the dictates of his will to produce posthumous agency, as demonstrated by the conditional language of "in the event" that dominates the will's text. When he makes provisions in his will for multiple imagined possible futures, however, he does not settle the issue of the property's distribution as he intends but in fact leaves the property's future in flux and subject to the machinations of his disinherited son, St. Clair, who manipulates these conditional terms to try to secure the inheritance for himself. Enson Sr. believes in the power of the will to enact his agency after death, but Hopkins's novel exposes this belief to be a legal fiction. The will's terms in fact motivate St. Clair to hatch a plot to disinherit his brother's newborn baby.

Because the motivation behind St. Clair's revelation of Hagar's racial ancestry is property, Hopkins demonstrates how the loss of a legal voice denies Black heirs their inheritance. St. Clair orchestrates Hagar's reenslavement and Ellis's death in order to steal their fortune. The novel presents the "terms of the will" as the causal agent driving St. Clair's scheme (Hopkins 47). After Ellis's death, St. Clair inherits the Enson estate, including the enslaved people, among whom Hagar is now included, *and* the Sargeant family fortune, which was incorporated into the estate after Hagar's marriage. Hagar Sargeant, raised as the white heiress to the neighboring estate, inherits the Sargeant property (which includes the enslaved Henny) after her mother passes away, and her marriage to Ellis Enson legally transfers the property to him. After Hagar's remission to slavery and Ellis's death, Hagar's patrimony, which has been absorbed into the Enson estate, descends to St. Clair: "So no papers, bearing upon the case, being found, all the Sargeant fortune reverted by law to the master" (73). The causal agent behind this transfer, "reverted by law," depicts the transfer as happening without any individual person's active intervention, a rhetorical gesture that encapsulates the tendency of white legal authorities to use similar language to represent law as an abstract, disembodied process that happens automatically. When property moves from Black to white ownership "by law," this phrase allows white legal authorities to hide their crucial role in the process.

However, Hopkins emphasizes that inherited property transfers do not happen automatically and require a complicated legal process that involves the active intervention of persons who claim legal authority. For example, after Hagar's mother dies, Hagar marries Ellis almost immediately, never becoming a property owner in her own right, because otherwise the estate would have become vulnerable to the power of an executor, a legal guardian, and the judgments of the court: "Ellis put the case plainly before her, and she yielded to his persuasions to have the marriage solemnized at once, so that he might assume his place as her rightful protector" (Hopkins 39). Because Hagar's fortune is at stake, their marriage becomes a "case" described in legal terms. Ellis wants to avoid the legal process by which Hagar, now orphaned, would require a legal guardian and executor. Once Hagar is married, the property belongs to Ellis under the laws of coverture, and thus they avoid the stage in which Hagar's fortune would be controlled by someone else. The consolidation of property in the "union of the houses of Enson and Sargeant" allows St. Clair to acquire both fortunes at once (40). Given this context, it is notable that Hopkins's conclusion, in which the heiress Jewel prematurely dies, prevents the repetition of a similar consolidation of wealth into the hands of her white husband, Cuthbert.

The second crucial will in *Hagar's Daughter*, that of the millionaire Senator Bowen, appears suspiciously after his death and is believed to be a forgery, but its flawless replication of the proper legal forms defies the family lawyer's ability to disprove its validity. After Senator Bowen dies, Hopkins foregrounds the uncertainty of the legal device. The family lawyer informs Bowen's wife, Hagar/Estelle, and daughter, Jewel, that "this later document leaves the one in my possession null and void" (Hopkins 200). A last-minute will of questionable origins disrupts the expected function of the genre. The new will gives General Benson legal authority over both the property and Jewel, since as a minor she must be entrusted to a legal guardian. Jewel imagines the will's power in terms of her coerced engagement to General Benson: "She dreaded, too, the coming of the day set apart for the reading of the will, for General Benson could no longer be avoided" (199). Benson takes advantage of the legal procedure in which wills are read to corner Jewel and pressure her to accept his marriage claim.

On the other hand, Hopkins demonstrates that the will as a genre also contains cultural conventions that can combat its legal power. Jewel's father, Senator Bowen, leaves an alternative set of final words on his deathbed that constitute a powerful although nonlegal statement of his last wishes. Aware of General Benson's intention to pressure Jewel into marriage, Bowen uses his last moments to assert his parental authority in favor of his daughter's right to choose her husband. As his fevered mind recognizes Jewel's danger, he vows, "No you don't, General; my little girl shan't be forced. I, her father, say it. When, where and who she likes; that's my idea. I tell you, no!" (Hopkins 197). Following the conventions of the deathbed promise, Bowen uses the authority of last words to attempt to protect his family. Suspecting foul play concerning his will, Bowen attempts to repossess the genre by shifting from legal ground to cultural authority. Senator Bowen's nonlegal last "testament" in the form of his dying words returns later in the novel to reestablish severed kinship ties when it leads to the discovery that Jewel is Hagar/Estelle's long-lost daughter. After the criminal trial has resolved the problem of the will, Hagar/Estelle remembers Bowen's dying words: "Suddenly Senator Bowen's last words, 'The little hair trunk!' flashed across the lady's mind" (274). Inside the trunk, Hagar/Estelle finds physical evidence that proves Jewel is her lost biological daughter, who was found in the Potomac River and adopted by Senator Bowen and his first wife after Hagar/Estelle fled slavery. Thus, Hopkins represents multiple types of inheritance simultaneously competing for space in the narrative.

In both cases, *Hagar's Daughter* emphasizes the instability of property supposedly settled in a will. The vulnerability of the will to forgery allows it to represent the violence of nineteenth-century contestations over property. During the novel's climactic criminal trial, the inheritance plot is bound up with and finally resolved by the detective work necessary to solve the murder. The revelation of the forged will also casts doubt onto earlier parts of the novel, particularly Hagar's racial ancestry. Knowing now that the slave trader Walker (later Major Madison) is an expert forger, having successfully forged a will that the Bowen family's lawyer could not invalidate, it becomes possible if not probable that Walker forged the papers proving Hagar a slave. At the time, Ellis tests the document's authenticity by turning to legal authorities. His lawyer, "one of the ablest men of the Maryland Bar," "pronounced the bill of sale genuine, for it had been drawn up by a justice, and witnessed by men who sent their affadavits [*sic*] under oath" (Hopkins 55). After the lawyer declares the document valid, Enson submits to it as truth. Hopkins describes in detail the legal process that convinces him, in which the bill of sale's authenticity derives from a legal system based entirely on the personal authority of various white men and their testimony—the judge and witnesses whose oaths have been recorded. Hagar's remission into slavery is caused by Ellis's submission to the legal system's method of producing truth based on the testimony of white men. Ellis fails to consider the possibility of forgery, but once the reader learns of Walker/Madison's expert forgery skills, the veracity of his documents and the racial origins based upon them become as speculative and unreliable as Senator Bowen's forged will.[18]

Conclusion:
The Erasure and Recovery of Black Heirs

Discrediting the forged will does not completely solve the problem of the Bowen inheritance. During the courtroom scene, Senator Bowen's widow, Estelle, reveals herself to be Hagar, a former slave. The impediment of the scheming legal executor has been removed only to allow society's racial prejudice to take center stage. Although the legal details are never discussed explicitly, it is presumed that Black ancestry has disqualified Hagar/Estelle from inheriting her white husband's wealth. After Hagar/Estelle's racial ancestry is revealed, the debate over what to do with the Bowen fortune produces an indecision that is never resolved but rather is suspended by leaving the wealth under the care of the Johnson family: "Ellis wished to settle the whole of Senator Bowen's immense fortune upon Jewel, but the latter would not hear of so unjust a proceeding. So the mansion was to be left in the care of Marthy Johnson, Aunt Henny and Oliver, while Mr. and Mrs. Enson were abroad" (Hopkins 274). Jewel rejects sole ownership of her inheritance as "unjust," labeling it in legal terms as a "proceeding" that would deny her mother an equal share. This somewhat bizarre passage does not explain what happens to the fortune, and the question of who inherits the Bowen millions remains unanswered after Jewel's death leaves no heir to the Bowen fortune. Hopkins uses the uncertainty surrounding who will inherit the Bowen fortune to suggest a nonlegal form of inheritance that recovers a prominent position for the Johnson family to receive the novel's immense wealth.

The prominence of Marthy, Henny, and Oliver in this passage presents them, in a limited sense, as recipients, albeit not legal heirs, to the Bowen mansion in terms of possession if not in ownership. Marthy, Henny, and Oliver are named in this passage in a way that evokes, rhetorically, the naming of heirs in a will. The fortune is described as being "left" to these three Black characters using the same language a will would use to describe its distribution of property. In this way, Hopkins gives this working-class Black family a limited but significant place in the inheritance of American property. Hopkins imagines the Johnson family sharing in the Bowen fortune by inhabiting and caring for the mansion, despite not owning it legally, a role that resembles legal guardians or life estate beneficiaries. Although a racially discriminatory legal system has erased Hagar/Estelle as an heir to this property, Hopkins recovers other Black characters as heirs who receive possession but not ownership, a liminal status that mirrors the ownership granted by a mortgage: although Marthy owns her home, the mortgage leaves it in constant danger of being repossessed. As the novel's unstable wills and Marthy's mortgage struggles have shown, ownership is never secure, and possession hangs dangerously close to dispossession. Therefore, Hopkins's fiction imagines Henny, Marthy, and Oliver inheriting a prominent position in the Bowen mansion despite law's failure to acknowledge them.

In contrast, the expected heir to the fortune at law, Jewel, dies prior to inheriting her family's wealth, which aborts the expected "rightful" inheritance plot that the trial recovers from General Benson / St. Clair's scheme. Clymer has suggested that this conclusion, in which no Black characters inherit any property and no offspring of interracial marriage survive, shows Hopkins's failure to imagine wealth crossing the color line (145). Clymer's reading, which focuses on the mixed-race characters, does not take into account Marthy's children, Venus and Oliver, who at the novel's conclusion are well on their way to upward mobility. Clymer assumes that St. Clair's illegitimate white son will inherit both fortunes because he is the only biological relative remaining to the Enson family, but there is no reason to believe this child could make any claim to the Bowen fortune. Jackson has argued that the novel's "abortive teleology" is redemptive because it allows Hopkins to critique how the institution of the family perpetuates the color line, but the Johnson family's cooperative labor, resource pooling, and shared economic insight provide a model for Black economic advancement based on a family unit managed by multiple generations of Black women (142). Most importantly, Jewel's death in fact prevents the consolidation of wealth into white hands. Because Jewel has already legally married Cuthbert, should she inherit, all of the novel's wealth would be consolidated into the hands of one white man: her husband. Thus, Hopkins disrupts an inheritance plot that would further normalize the consolidation of white male wealth.

Hopkins's reinvention of the detective genre has some similarities with other fiction from the period, such as Mark Twain's *Pudd'nhead Wilson* (1894), suggesting that Hopkins participated in the invention of a new thread of American literary history. Like Twain, who follows a convention of detective fiction arising from trial reporting, Hopkins describes a courtroom scene that gauges the effect of testimony through references to the audience's reactions, a strategy that casts the assembled public as the ultimate arbiter of which stories become legally persuasive. Although Hopkins was subsequently marginalized by literary history, her use of popular literary genres such as detective fiction highlights the function of testimony, forensics, and contracts as legal genres and performs a critique of law as genre that resonates with the central concerns of critical race theory and law and literature scholarship today.

Hagar's Daughter, at the intersection of the detective genre and the stolen inheritance plot, exposes the way legally recognized speech determines one's ability to transfer property over generations. While Hopkins demonstrates how white authorities use legal genres to undermine Black legal agency, she also suggests that these genres could be repurposed to allow Black voices to speak authoritatively in the public sphere. Hopkins highlights how forensic discourse's interpretation of physical evidence as self-evident could be manipulated to silence Black voices, but she also reveals how Black voices can intervene into these constructed narratives. Hopkins first exposes the operating assumptions behind these legal genres to show how law regulates racialized persons' ability to speak authoritatively in court, exercise legal agency, and inherit property. She then shows how skillful navigation of these legal genres can undermine these restrictions. Hopkins's critique of law's exclusion of Black voices in the courtroom highlights the vulnerability of Black property owners when legal battles over the interpretation of contracts, wills, and other legal documents threaten to redirect their inheritances, yet her novel proffers the courtroom as a public sphere in which Black voices crying against white crimes can be heard.

Hopkins believed that her fiction could combat patterns of racial injustice.[19] Her reinterpretation of the detective genre in *Hagar's Daughter* exposes the operating logic behind law's structures of racial dispossession and demonstrates the importance of popular literary genres to Hopkins's political project. Hopkins goes beyond simply critiquing law as a set of embodied, racialized practices by demonstrating how legal genres can be repossessed to produce Black authority at law and to protect Black property if one knows how the genres work. As her characters learn how to navigate and repurpose both literary and legal genres, her fiction provides a model for how to rework a genre to serve one's purposes. In doing so, Hopkins demonstrates literature's power as a tool by which racialized subjects can produce new narratives with persuasive claims to authority. If legal authority, agency, and truth are produced by particular genres operating according to their expected conventions, the ability to reshape these genres becomes a powerful tool to redefine the outcomes they produce.

NOTES

1. Brook Thomas has also identified *Iola Leroy*, *The Marrow of Tradition*, *Contending Forces*, and *Hagar's Daughter* as being similarly engaged with Reconstruction's failure to give African Americans their fair share of the national inheritance (284–327).

2. Several scholars have located Hopkins's manipulation of popular literary genres as part of her racial critique. For example, Pavletich argues that Hopkins attempted to revise the tragic mulatta figure to reclaim Black female agency but ended up confined by the genre's adherence to the cult of true womanhood. Others such as Tate and McCullough have argued that Hopkins reinterpreted the sentimental genre to combat negative stereotypes against Black women's sexuality.

3. See Clymer and Davis for the many ways legal authorities can intervene to prevent Black relatives from inheriting wealth from white family members.

4. For scholarship on Hopkins's engagement with law, see English; Godfrey; and Moddelmog. Law and literature scholars who have examined race, law, and property in Hopkins's work have tended to examine how race itself or whiteness functions as a type of property; see Korobkin; Nerad; and Watkins.

5. For the history of legal restrictions on Black testimony, see Johnson; Harris; and Higginbotham.

6. As Latour explains, modern Western epistemology grants the highest authority to an empirical, scientific method that relies on the notion that observable, inanimate objects offer an unprejudiced source of information and reliability that humans cannot. These scientific facts, however, are created by human experts interpreting what they observe: "Who is speaking when [the facts] speak? The facts themselves . . . but also their authorized spokespersons" (Latour 28–29). This logic, when applied to evidence law, diminished the credibility of first-person testimony while elevating the credibility of forensic objects, despite the fact that these objects always required interpretation.

7. For example, Sterling cites a Georgia divorce case in which an enslaved woman, Louisa, was allowed to testify against her master, who had attempted to rape her, despite objections raised against her race. "LOUISA, (colored)," the record reads, was "sworn [in] over the defendant's objection" (Sterling 26).

8. For example, what Brackett describes as Maryland's "very simple" law of evidence, which excluded Black testimony "based strictly on the color line," was not applied consistently (190). In 1810 the court upheld a ruling that excluded a free Black woman's testimony even though her brother, also a free Black man, had once been allowed to testify, without objection, in a similar case (192–93). In 1856 and 1860 there were instances of admitting Black testimony against whites "in certain cases" (193). As Brackett explains, "The court held that the declarations of a negro, when part of the *res gestae* of a case, were admissible as evidence, that it would be a most unjust theory, that the exclamation of any man when assaulted must be debarred from notice. Nor was the question a new one, for it was stated that the court for Baltimore county had in two previous cases admitted statements of negroes when part of the *res gestae*" (193). For the various state laws on Black testimony, see Higginbotham 58, 119–20, 124, 133, 142, 146, 205–06, 258.

9. U.S. Supreme Court, Plessy v. Ferguson, 163 U.S. 537 (1896).

10. For example, a free Black carpenter in Maryland who had conducted repairs on his neighbor's farm was unable, after the neighbor died, to settle the account with the estate's executor until a white man testified to the validity of the carpenter's statements (Brackett 194). As the historical record proves, Black Americans stood to lose considerable property when their testimony was excluded from court. In one antebellum Maryland case, James L. Bowers of Maryland was accused of helping slaves escape but, ironically, he could not be convicted because the only evidence came from the confessions of the runaway slaves (Fields 63–64).

11. See Gruesser; Crafton; DeLamotte; Bailey; and Huh.

12. For example, Bussey argues that Hopkins's light-skinned Black characters such as Hagar and Jewel are able to seek self-determination in a class-based society, yet she dismisses Henny, Marthy, and Isaac as insignificant: "Hopkins relegates her dark-skinned characters to minor roles, then objectifies them in such stereotypes as the simple-minded old mammy and the rebellious young buck. These depictions are double-edged, and sometimes subversive and sometimes complicit, but the Black characters are nonetheless eclipsed by mixed-race protagonists" (300). As I will show, it is today's critics, not Hopkins, who have diminished the importance of the novel's darker-skinned characters.

13. Critics have often noted the significance of this split narrative structure. As Jackson argues, "Hopkins ultimately utilizes this duplication to foreground the failure of Reconstruction to facilitate a bridge into freedom for African Americans" (133). See also Tuhkanen.

14. Likewise, Smith-Spears argues that Marthy and Isaac are "obvious minstrel characters" who are "clearly a representation of the slave past" designed "for the exact purpose of creating a distance from these characters of the past and the race of the future" (23). Smith-Spears dismisses Marthy's ability to adapt to the new challenges of postemancipation life, suggesting that her "slave mentality makes [her] ill-equipped for survival in a newly-free society" because she lacks "thoughtfulness" and "a longing for independence or a desire for growth" (24).

15. See Baradaran: "The bank caused financial ruin for many blacks who had been diligently saving their money to purchase a home, and those that were not ruined internalized a warning about banking" and "lost faith in banks in general" (31).

16. There are actually four fortunes at stake in the novel, including the Sargeant fortune and Cuthbert's family fortune. I focus on the two inheritances that involve the intervening agency of a last will and testament.

17. Critics have focused on Hopkins's critique of social and legal prohibitions against interracial marriage. Jackson, for example, has examined the significance of inheritance in *Hagar's Daughter* in terms of how Black blood challenges constructions of the nation as a white family (132–52). For Rohrbach, the inheritance plot, in which "the process of handing down the family fortune uncovers some hidden aspect of a character's identity, forcing the character to be recast as someone else," exposes racial boundaries as shifting and undefinable (484). Focusing on the economic consequences of where the law draws the color line, Clymer argues that melodramatic plots of mistaken identity, missing wills,

and ambiguous racial ancestry allow authors such as Hopkins to "reimagine the relationship between wealth distribution" and "the social and legal infrastructure" that regulates it (15).

18. Brook Thomas has also suggested that there is no biological proof of Hagar's or Jewel's Black ancestry because Walker could have forged the bill of sale, which is the only evidence of their Black blood, just as he forged Senator Bowen's will. If so, Thomas concludes, then "the racial stigma attached to both women is the product of forged documents" (292).

19. As Carby argues, Hopkins advocated using fiction to promote greater social and political inclusion for African Americans by reaching a wider audience of readers. As seen in her other fiction and her work as literary editor of the *Colored American Magazine*, Hopkins designed her fiction to serve a political and pedagogical function (Carby 128).

WORKS CITED

Bailey, Frankie Y. *African American Mystery Writers: A Historical and Thematic Study*. McFarland, 2008.

Baradaran, Mehrsa. *The Color of Money: Black Banks and the Racial Wealth Gap*. Belknap, 2019.

Brackett, Jeffrey R. *The Negro in Maryland: A Study of the Institution of Slavery*. Johns Hopkins University, 1889.

Brandwein, Pamela. *Rethinking the Judicial Settlement of Reconstruction*. Cambridge University Press, 2011.

Brooks, Kristina. "Mammies, Bucks, and Wenches: Minstrelsy, Racial Pornography, and Racial Politics in Pauline Hopkins's *Hagar's Daughter*." *The Unruly Voice: Rediscovering Pauline Elizabeth Hopkins*, edited by John Cullen Gruesser, University of Illinois Press, 1996, pp. 119–57.

Bussey, Susan Hays. "Whose Will Be Done? Self-Determination in Pauline Hopkins's *Hagar's Daughter*." *African American Review*, vol. 39, no. 3, 2005, pp. 299–313.

Carby, Hazel V. *Reconstructing Womanhood: The Emergence of the Afro-American Woman Novelist*. Oxford University Press, 1987.

Chinn, Sarah E. *Technology and the Logic of American Racism: A Cultural History of the Body as Evidence*. Continuum, 2000.

Clymer, Jeffory. *Family Money: Property, Race, and Literature in the Nineteenth Century*. Oxford University Press, 2013.

Crafton, Robert E. *The African American Experience in Crime Fiction: A Critical Study*. McFarland, 2015.

Davis, Adrienne D. "The Private Law of Race and Sex: An Antebellum Perspective." *Stanford Law Review*, vol. 51, no. 2, 1999, pp. 221–88.

DeLamotte, Eugenia. "'Collusions of the Mystery': Ideology and the Gothic in *Hagar's Daughter*." *Gothic Studies*, vol. 6, no. 1, 2004, pp. 69–79.

English, Daylanne K. *Each Hour Redeem: Time and Justice in African American Literature*. University of Minnesota Press, 2013.

Fields, Barbara Jeanne. *Slavery and Freedom on the Middle Ground: Maryland during the Nineteenth Century*. Yale University Press, 1985.

Gallanis, T. P. "The Rise of Modern Evidence Law." *Iowa Law Review*, vol. 84, 1998, pp. 499–560.

Godfrey, Molly. "Of One Blood: Humanism, Race, and Gender in Post-Reconstruction Law and Literature." *CLA Journal*, vol. 59, no. 1, 2015, pp. 47–74.

Gruesser, John Cullen. *Race, Gender and Empire in American Detective Fiction*. McFarland, 2013.

Harris, Cheryl I. "Whiteness as Property." *Harvard Law Review*, vol. 106, no. 8, 1993, pp. 1707–91.

Higginbotham, A. Leon. *In the Matter of Color: Race and the American Legal Process: The Colonial Period*. Oxford University Press, 1978.

Holloway, Karla. *Legal Fictions: Constituting Race, Composing Literature*. Duke University Press, 2014.

hooks, bell. "House, 20 June 1994." *Assemblage*, vol. 24, 1994, pp. 22–29.

Hopkins, Pauline. *Hagar's Daughter. The Magazine Novels of Pauline Hopkins*, edited by Hazel Carby, Oxford University Press, 1988, pp. 1–284.

Hsu, Hsuan L. *Sitting in Darkness: Mark Twain's Asia and Comparative Racialization*. New York University Press, 2015.

Huh, Jinny. *The Arresting Eye: Race and the Anxiety of Detection*. University of Virginia Press, 2015.

Jackson, Holly. *American Blood: The Ends of the Family in American Literature, 1850–1900*. Oxford University Press, 2014.

Johnson, Sheri Lynn. "The Color of Truth: Race and the Assessment of Credibility." *Michigan Journal of Race and Law*, vol. 1, no. 2, 1996, pp. 261–346.

Korobkin, Laura. "Imagining State and Federal Law in Pauline E. Hopkins's *Contending Forces*." *Legacy*, vol. 28, no. 1, 2011, pp. 1–23.

Latour, Bruno. *We Have Never Been Modern*. Translated by Catherine Porter, Harvard University Press, 1993.

McCullough, Kate. "Slavery, Sexuality, and Genre: Pauline Hopkins and the Representation of Female Desire." *The Unruly Voice: Rediscovering Pauline Elizabeth Hopkins*, edited by John Cullen Gruesser, University of Illinois Press, 1996, pp. 21–49.

Moddelmog, William E. *Reconstituting Authority: American Fiction in the Province of the Law, 1880–1920*. University of Iowa Press, 2000.

Nerad, Julie Cary. "'So Strangely Interwoven': The Property of Inheritance, Race, and Sexual Morality in Pauline Hopkins's *Contending Forces*." *African American Review*, vol. 35, no. 3, 2001, pp. 357–73.

Pavletich, JoAnn. "Pauline Hopkins and the Death of the Tragic Mulatta." *Callaloo*, vol. 38, no. 3, 2015, pp. 647–63.

Rohrbach, Augusta. "To Be Continued: Double Identity, Multiplicity and Antigenealogy as Narrative Strategy in Pauline Hopkins' Magazine Fiction." *Callaloo*, vol. 22, no. 2, 1999, pp. 483–98.

Smith-Spears, RaShell R. "Uplift Ideology and the Fluidity of Racial Categories in Pauline Hopkins's *Hagar's Daughter*." *South Atlantic Review*, vol. 75, no. 4, 2010, pp. 21–36.

Sterling, Dorothy. *We Are Your Sisters: Black Women in the Nineteenth Century*. Norton, 1984.

Tate, Claudia. *Domestic Allegories of Political Desire: The Black Heroine's Text at the Turn of the Century*. Oxford University Press, 1992.

Thomas, Brook. *The Literature of Reconstruction: Not in Plain Black and White*. Johns Hopkins University Press, 2017.

Thomas, Ronald. *Detective Fiction and the Rise of Forensic Science*. Cambridge University Press, 1999.

Tuhkanen, Mikko. "'Out of Joint': Passing, Haunting, and the Time of Slavery in *Hagar's Daughter*." *American Literature*, vol. 79, no. 2, 2007, pp. 335–61.

Watkins, Patricia D. "Rape, Lynching, Law and Contending Forces: Pauline Hopkins—Forerunner of Critical Race Theorists." *CLA Journal*, vol. 46, no. 4, 2003, pp. 521–42.

Wong, Edlie. *Neither Fugitive nor Free: Atlantic Slavery, Freedom Suits, and the Legal Culture of Travel*. New York University Press, 2009.

PART 2

Intertexts

Intertextual Transformations

PAULINE E. HOPKINS AND ALICE FRENCH
[OCTAVE THANET]

Hanna Wallinger

One scene in Alice French / Octave Thanet's 1910 novel *By Inheritance* has the elderly, wealthy, white spinster Agatha Danforth, who is visiting her nephew on a plantation in Arkansas, open a book and say, "Speak for yourself . . . and I will listen" (288). The book is W. E. B. Du Bois's *The Souls of Black Folk*, and Agatha turns to it after she has overheard her protégé, Sidney Danton, a Harvard-educated, mixed-race young man who is hoping that she will endow a Black college in the South, refer to it in a conversation with her white maid and companion, Matilda. This moment is reminiscent of the often-quoted moment in the iconic early slave narrative by Olaudah Equiano in which the narrator tries to find answers from books he is unable to read. He puts his ear to the book, waits for an answer, and then finds out that the book remains silent (106–07, TEI pagination). The link between Agatha's reference to Du Bois and her indirect evocation of Equiano is intertextuality, which Gérard Genette defines as the "copresence between two texts or among several texts." It may take the form of quoting, plagiarism, or the practice of allusion (1–2). Genette uses "transformations" to denote a strategy in which Text B, called the hypertext, originates from Text A, the hypotext, which "it consequently evokes more or less perceptibly without necessarily speaking about it or citing it" (5). Alice French frequently refers to and quotes from Du Bois in a direct way, while further evocations of a text such as Equiano's are indirect. Like French, many authors of her period, white and Black, borrowed from, quoted, evoked, and adapted other texts. This essay pursues some of these intertextual transformations by pairing the popular and successful white writer Alice French with Pauline E. Hopkins, the eloquent advocate of Black women's rights.

This intertextual discussion offers a new approach mainly because Alice French is a writer with whom a critic of African American literature like myself comes into contact only because her 1890 novel, *Expiation*, served as one of the sources for Hopkins's 1902 serial novel, *Winona*, as JoAnn Pavletich has established ("'. . . We Are Going'"). This reversal of expected trajectories of intertextuality needs to be emphasized. There can be no doubt that French's *Expiation* was an important hypotext in the sense that Hopkins borrowed from it where necessary and digressed from it substantially when she found that it did not go far enough, misinterpreted some facts, and read history through the limited lens of her era's white supremacy. At the same time, Alice French, as a writer who otherwise might not be read in this context, becomes part of a project of revisionism and reevaluation. By teasing out and exploring in some detail the nuances and complexities of the appropriations and evocations running between these two female writers, taking into account their different positions on race, class, and current political issues, I hope to develop new methods and narratives that soften the canon and provide fresh insights.

The two writers echo each other's themes because they both rewrote and reevaluated gender roles, plantation settings, and historical events. The copresence between these two texts is clearly visible and demonstrable, but the current of ideas that connects them extends beyond them, as I will show. Hopkins's *Contending Forces* (1900) and French's *By Inheritance*, published twenty years after *Expiation*, demonstrate that two writers who were so unlike in background and reputation can and should be compared and contrasted for how they challenged and/or supported gender issues and addressed the reemergence of plantation ideals and the power of property rights. Although it is hardly surprising that a Black writer such as Hopkins debunked the plantation myth and defended a course of action that led to political and social equality and that a white writer such as French defended the racial hierarchies found on southern plantations and judged them to be desirable for the nation in general, it is less obvious that they responded to each other's beliefs, read the same books, and thought about the same issues. After introducing the two authors in relation to the topic of intertextuality, I will focus on two interrelated topics, one a comparison and the other a contrastive analysis. Based on two scenes that Hopkins appropriated in *Winona* from French's novel *Expiation*, I will explore the greatest common ground between the two writers: the portrayal of strong and resourceful women that runs like a thread between all of their novels. This comparison shows the direct and indirect intertextual links and will turn from questions of gender to a discussion of power and property. In *Expiation* French idealized the planter and his family beset by Gothic Civil War horrors and presented a strong and rebellious female heroine. In *Winona* Hopkins used passages from the earlier text to revise this idealization and tell a different story that is clearly meant to be an advancement over the past. While this section is comparative, the following section will contrast *Contending Forces* and *By Inheritance* in relation to a third text, Du Bois's *Souls of Black Folk* (1903).

Pauline Hopkins, Alice French, and Intertextuality

When all texts are related to other texts in the first place, we may go beyond the hunting for sources that has already been admirably done by a number of critics in the case of Hopkins and concentrate on the transformations that take place between and across texts. The relationship between French and Hopkins has become part of a recent literary discourse about appropriations, adaptations, direct quotations, indirect borrowings, and creative adaptation, with Hopkins as one of the key figures. Marilyn Randall, in *Pragmatic Plagiarism* (2001), Robert Macfarlane, in *Original Copy* (2007), and Geoffrey Sanborn in *Plagiarama!* (2016) provide useful overviews about and offer detailed discussions of the practices, pitfalls, advantages, and common practices related to plagiarism, one of the rather problematic forms of intertextuality. Pavletich, Sanborn, Richard Yarborough, Ira Dworkin, and Lauren Dembowitz have confronted the reader "with the need to revise our sense of exactly what kind of writer she [Hopkins] is and of exactly how she went about practicing her craft" (Yarborough e6). Critics have used multiple terms and metaphors to describe, understand, sanction, condone, and condemn intertextual practices: Robert S. Levine argues that William Wells Brown "kidnapped" texts in his novel *Clotel* (6–8); Holly Jackson writes about "textual atavism" when Hopkins manipulated an antebellum text such as *Clotel* in her novel *Hagar's Daughter* (132–52); Dworkin says that Hopkins paid an "ongoing tribute" to the many texts she used (introduction xxxvii); Pavletich writes about Hopkins's "muscular manipulation of texts as her own unique form of political conquest, with literature as her weapon and plagiarism as a strategy" ("'. . . We Are Going'" 115); Dembowitz emphasizes the "appropriations" and "adaptations" between Hopkins's *Hagar's Daughter* and "Two Women," a short story by Fanny Driscoll. This essay strives to pursue one of what Yarborough calls the "potentially quite fruitful directions" (e7) that originate from recent intertextual criticism.

Alice French also kidnapped earlier texts, manipulated them for her own political purposes, appropriated and adapted ideas from other writers, and directed us to question "exactly what kind of a writer" she was. French was quite frank about her writing strategies and even asked her readers for ideas. As her biographer George McMichael says, much of her fiction had "its genesis in anecdotes and newspaper stories" (112). He writes that she "had taken her plots where she found them, from folk tales, newspaper articles, from conventional ideas that were in the air, and from other writers" (189). She was certainly familiar with the fiction by Constance Fenimore Cooper, Thomas Nelson Page, Joel Chandler Harris, Thomas Dixon Jr., and others (188–89). She followed a common practice of "conscious borrowing" and "unconscious lending," as Brander Matthews argues in an essay entitled "The Ethics of Plagiarism" written in 1886 about his contemporary writers (623). Matthews wonders "not that there are so many parallel passages, but that there are so few" (626). French, Hopkins, and many other writers used all available material to signal the anxieties and repressions at work in the nation and to remember the past and envision the future.

Pauline E. Hopkins and Alice French are an unlikely pair. Hopkins was an eloquent advocate of Black women's rights, a writer of detective and historical fiction, an outspoken journalist associated with the *Colored American Magazine*. Writing for a mainly New England audience but also associated with the Atlanta-based *Voice of the Negro* and engaged with all national and international affairs, Hopkins led, for all that we know by now, an exciting life, produced an unusual set of novels, challenged the publishing industry by becoming an early African American editor and journalist, and contributed to most of the key debates of her time. French, originally from a prominent Massachusetts family, moved as a child to Davenport, Iowa, and later spent winters at a former plantation in Arkansas. She was a highly popular and successful writer of mainly local color fiction and was acclaimed as a "famous author" who could place her stories and novels in popular magazines and publishing houses with ease. She was a prolific writer, published widely on the labor question, and defended her privileged position against working-class agitation and people of color while also challenging contemporary notions of gender roles. She enjoyed a period of high popularity between the 1890s and the 1910s before she dropped into relative obscurity. However, while Hopkins has received a good deal of scholarly attention for some four decades now, French has received little recent recognition of her extensive writing.[1]

Despite all the differences in background, French and Hopkins share a number of quite striking similarities when we read George McMichael's 1965 biography *Journey to Obscurity: The Life of Octave Thanet* alongside both Lois Brown's 2008 *Pauline Elizabeth Hopkins: Black Daughter of the Revolution* and my own 2005 literary biography of Hopkins. There are obvious parallels, because they wrote during the same time period and often portrayed their char-

acters by using dialect, which situates them in terms of class and race.[2] Both
Hopkins and French were of the same generation, came from prominent Massachusetts families, began their public careers in the 1870s, and enjoyed the
public limelight, in Hopkins's case until she left the *Voice of the Negro* in 1905
and in French's case until the 1910s, when her writing began to sell less easily.
Both were avid readers and had access to a wide range of books. In addition,
they did not marry, French living a fashionable and genteel life with her girl-
hood friend Jane Allen Crawford, with whom she wintered in Crawford's Arkansas home near Clover Bend, named Thanford for their joint names, and
Hopkins living a very self-determined life that was shaped by her need to support herself. One main point of connection and disconnection between them is
French's living in a Boston marriage, a much more open demonstration of possible lesbianism than Hopkins's spinsterhood.[3]

Alice French's novel *Expiation* has been cited as one source for and influence on Hopkins's novel *Winona*. In 1890, from January to April, French published the historical romance *Expiation* in four installments in *Scribner's Magazine* and then as a book in May 1890 (McMichael 118). It is a turbulent story
set in the Arkansas swampland and backwoods near Clover Bend, the location
of the former plantation where French and Alice Crawford spent their winters. It is set in the last year of the Civil War and revolves around the adventures that Fairfax [Fair] Rutherford, the heir of the family's plantation, Montaigne, embarks on when he returns from overseas. His adventures involve a
secreted stash of money; a group of bandits who want to secure the money;
his lovely foster sibling, Adèle, who helps defend the money, the plantation,
and the young man; and some Gothic scenes of torture and dashing bravado.[4]
At some time between 1890 and 1902 Hopkins must have read French's novel.
There is evidence that she started to work on *Winona* in the late 1880s or early
1890s because there are records of an untitled play and sketch (Brown 367;
Wallinger 152–53). The novel *Winona: A Tale of Negro Life in the South and
Southwest* was published in six installments in the *Colored American Magazine*
between May and October 1902. The romantic and melodramatic content revolves around Warren Maxwell, an English lawyer who is looking for the heir
to the Carlingford estate; Winona, the eponymous heroine, who is reared on
a secluded island near Canada by her father, White Eagle, an honorary Indian
who turns out to be the real heir, Henry Carlingford; and Judas, Winona's foster brother and an escaped slave, who had been rescued by Winona's mulatta
mother.[5] There are a number of deliberate coincidences surrounding Bleeding
Kansas in 1856, when abolitionists and proslavery groups battled to turn Kansas into a slave or a free state. The most dramatic scenes involve the rangers

gathered around John Brown and their fight for the cause of freedom, as well as Warren's involvement in the action in the form of a near lynching and cruel imprisonment. Other dramatic scenes take place on the plantation of Colonel Titus, where Winona and Judah are enslaved.

Hopkins certainly felt inspired by some elements in French's novel, while at the same time she adapted them so that her historical novel exposes the plantation ideal as dangerously fraudulent and doomed to fail. Her historical novel, *Winona*, exposes the corrupt use of power to maintain actual property and challenges the hierarchies based on this property. The links between Hopkins's *Contending Forces* and French's *By Inheritance* are more indirect. *Contending Forces* follows the fate of the Montfort planter family in 1800 from Bermuda to North Carolina, where the family is either killed or enslaved. The plantation is sold to their descendants, the Smith family of Boston, and the novel describes their affairs in the contemporary world of politics and their social and personal struggles. The journey from the slaveholding South to the free North that is at the core of *Contending Forces* is reversed in French's *By Inheritance*, which follows the journey of elderly, white, and rich Agatha Danforth to Montaigne, the same plantation as in *Expiation*, and her experiences with her nephew, Giles, a member of the plantation-owning Montgomery family, whose fortunes need to be recovered, and her Black protégé, Sidney Danton, who has been promised some of her fortune for the establishment of a Black school. Through negotiations of the power politics relevant to occupying, owning, and inheriting land, all four novels feature gender constellations in which the brave and courageous women take care of, rescue, or motivate the masculinization of the male characters.

Transformations:
Expiation and *Winona*

Expiation provided Hopkins with a model for a man from England searching for an heir and desiring to prove his masculinity through battle experience, a stalwart parson, a ruthless villain, and pitched battle scenes. A look at two scenes will illustrate why *Expiation* served as one of the many sources for *Winona* and how the differences reveal a racialized and gendered understanding of history. This discussion addresses the method of how Hopkins wrote her novel and how the transformation originates in *Expiation* and reemerges in *Winona*: she used some passages from *Expiation*, inserted them into her own writing, and then revised them to serve her purposes.

In chapter 3 of *Expiation*, Fair rhapsodizes about Adèle's "white throat," "supple figure," "rapt young face," "sweet voice," and "dark eyes flashing" (59) as he begins to fall in love after he delivers the corpse of the man his father trusted with delivering the funds needed for the plantation. In French's novel these are highly acceptable and conventional words and emotions to represent what a romantically inclined and idealistic young man might feel toward his equal. Fair has known Adèle since childhood. She is young and pretty but also resilient, courageous, active, and resourceful. In one of the final scenes of *Expiation*, Adèle, who has always championed duty and honor and who is the shaping force behind Fair's change of attitude and gain of fortitude, is condemned to wait behind the lines and witness the battle against the bandits from a distance. But, significantly, she is no southern belle who needs to be protected from all unpleasant sights and kept out of harm's way. Fair wins the hand of Adèle, and she becomes the new mistress of the plantation after he has proven that he is a worthy future husband and master. The Rutherford property remains intact and preserved for future generations.

In chapter 9 of *Winona*, Hopkins uses the same words as above to describe the attachment that Warren begins to feel about the courageous and resourceful Winona: "Now and again across the confusion of his mind, images floated vaguely—a white throat tinted by the firelight, a supple figure, a rapt young face, a head held with all a princess' grace, and dark, flashing eyes" (359).[6] In the same chapter and after these words come to his mind, Warren is captured by the proslavery men and threatened with torture and death if he does not tell them where the slaves are. In a very effective manner, Hopkins turns Warren into a hero and changes French's story of bravado and adventure into a more fundamental reflection on the criminal system of slavery. Confronted with death and questioned by slaveholding Bill Thomson, Warren cannot give the secret away because it is not, as it is in *Expiation*, a stash of money that can be replaced but the lives of two foster siblings who would be sent back into slavery and become actual property when they are found. The men accuse Warren of being an "abolitionist an' a nigger thief, two crimes we never overlooks, bein' dangerous to our peace and principles" (367), and they prepare to burn him at the stake. There is an outspoken condemnation of the practice of lynching, one of Hopkins's main messages in this novel, in the sentence that uses a climactic structure to good effect: "It was not the voices of human beings, but more like the cries of wild animals, the screaming of enraged hyenas, the snarling of tigers, the angry, inarticulate cries of thousands of wild beasts in infuriated pursuit of their prey, yet with a something in it more sinister and blood curdling,

for they were men, and added a human ferocity" (367). Hopkins reused some
words and phrases from the earlier text because she wanted and needed to rewrite the sentiment behind them. She replaced the villain in *Expiation*, the torture of Fair, and his apparent cowardice with a scene that shows that there can
be no compromise in the case of slavery.

In addition, Warren's sentiments about Winona are exceptional because she
is definitely not the equal of an English aristocrat. Winona is of mixed-race origin, she is a slave, and she has witnessed unspeakable things at an age when
she should be living a sheltered life. Judah, who observes the growing affection of Warren toward Winona, is highly skeptical and wary because he "knew
the worth of a white man's love for a woman of mixed blood" (Hopkins, *Winona* 357). Both Adèle and Winona actively participate, rifles in their hands, in
a battle to rid a southern village of local bandits (Adèle) and in the abolitionist fight with John Brown (Winona). Winona relished the childhood freedom
that she experienced as the daughter of a father who let her roam wild (similar
to Adèle's childhood) but who protected her from the cruelties of life and who
gave her the stamina to withstand the horrors of slavery. Winona matures into
a likable and lovely young woman and turns into an efficient fighter who protects the camp when the men leave for battle. While she is allowed to take on a
more decisive action in the battle than Adèle is, she also serves as the moral and
humane influence that prevents her foster brother Judah from committing an
act of cold-blooded murder. Winona becomes the rightful heir to the Carlingford estate after Bill Thomson, whose murder she has just prevented and who
is modeled on the leader of the bandits in *Expiation*, confesses his wrongdoing
and confirms her identity. In this sense, Winona is rewarded for her strength
and moral superiority by being allowed to marry Warren, although, unlike
Adèle, the only property she will ever control is in England because of her African blood.

The second scene that Hopkins reused from French is the "patient-kissed-
by-a-nurse" moment. In *Expiation* this moment in the narrative emphasizes
a troubled father-son relationship and the handing over of power from one
planter generation to the next. Fair is nursed back to health under the tender
care of Adèle, but he is watched by his father, who cannot forgive him for his
earlier act of cowardice, when he betrayed the fact that he gave the money to
the parson. The old father would rather see his son dead than see him behave
in an unmanly and dishonest way. When Adèle leaves the room to get some
soup, however, the father shows his love: "The bed gave a little creak and rustle. The Colonel was leaning one elbow on the mattress and bending over him;
he felt a trembling light touch on his hair and a tear rolled down his cheek—a

tear not from his own eyes; his father had kissed him" (French, *Expiation* 114–15). There is no further display of emotion, a restraint that is explained as an "Anglo-Saxon" race trait (115). French's kiss of affection between father and son establishes the father as meeting his paternal responsibilities, which, the plantation myth holds, is at the core of national identity.[7] Eventually, it becomes clear, there will be a reconciliation between the father and a son who will soon have the chance to prove his manhood and bravery.

In *Expiation* Montaigne is an ordered and well-organized plantation despite the unsettling outcome of the war. It is depicted as containing the roots for survival and prosperity even after the end of the slave system because the father is benevolent and caring and the son and heir is capable of assuming control over the property. Winning the hand of Adèle, French emphasizes, is worth every effort and hardship because the future mistress guarantees survival and prosperity in postwar times. By setting the novel in the turbulent mid-1860s, French portrays a hierarchically ordered plantation. She sees the planter class, as Linda Rushton writes in her 1982 dissertation, as following chivalric codes and guiding the common white servants, often seen as violent, ignorant, and racist, and the dependent Black servants, often depicted as caricatures (see Rushton 195–99).[8] In *Expiation*, French does not reject the plantation ideal, but she criticizes its inherently patriarchal standards with the introduction of strong female characters and idealizes them with the prominent role she gives to Black characters.

In *Winona* the plantation myth is not only criticized but also reversed, and Black cultural difference is asserted. A comparative reading of the "patient-kissed-by-a-nurse" scene reveals that French uses it to establish the continuation of the plantation ideal and what it signifies into the next generation, while Hopkins provides the reader with a gendered and racialized view of a future that has interrupted plantation continuity. The attraction between Warren and Winona is more pronounced in the crucial chapters after Warren is captured by the proslavery men, headed by Bill Thomson, and nearly burned at the stake. He is taken to prison and sentenced to a one-year term before execution for aiding slaves to run away. Warren is seriously ill and recuperates very slowly. He gets better through "the tender care of his nurse" (Hopkins, *Winona* 386), who turns out to be Winona disguised as a young mulatto boy named Allen Pinks, also held in the slave pen. It is one of the many unlikely coincidences that Warren does not recognize Winona in her male attire but that he feels attracted to "the prettiest specimen of boyhood he had ever met" (388). He is forced to witness the cruelties and atrocities inflicted on the captives, including an indication of an especially shameful rape of a helpless Black man. When Warren faints, the perspective shifts to his nurse, the disguised Winona, who pities him and then bends over a sleeping but conscious Warren: "The cot gave a creak and a rustle. The nurse was leaning one hand on the edge of the miserable pallet bed bending over the sick man. There was a light touch on his hair; a tear fell on his cheek; the nurse had kissed the patient!" (387). This homoerotic scene— Warren attracted to an apparently male person—depicts Winona as the more capable and brave person. But only when contrasted with the earlier scene in *Expiation* does it open up a discourse on the nature of power and genealogy. When Winona nurses Warren and helps him escape from the prison, she is the capable and fearless daughter of a formidable father and braves imprisonment and slavery to take care of a white man. Warren, in turn, rewards her by ensuring her right of inheritance and title. It is a mutual give-and-take: Warren would not have survived on his own; Winona would not have gained any legal rights. Warren identifies and authorizes the records of marriage and birth, the ring with the family crest, and thus the complete chain of evidence (see 433) that ensures Winona's rightful status as a "noble woman" (435). Although Winona's slave condition makes her ineligible to own property in the United States and sets her outside the patriarchal system of property transmission, she is reinserted into the system once it becomes clear that she is the legal heiress of large wealth. Being the daughter of a noble and brave man, Winona is empowered and predestined to act bravely and nobly as well. Warren embodies the white English tradition of power and loves the beautiful and nearly white woman, who, of course, also insures his own future family's wealth and status. He can cross racial boundaries because, at least in England, wealth trumps race.

Adèle's right to earn the love of Fair and deserve the position of future plantation mistress is never doubted. Winona's legitimacy and right to win the hand of Warren are highly debatable. Hopkins, who was an avid reader, could have chosen any number of other and more obviously racist novels that portray a more standard view of the plantation myth to debunk. In *Expiation* she found the female role model, some characters, and, most important, an interpretation of history that constructs the plantation as the ideal model of a modern America.

In the following section, a contrastive examination of Hopkins's *Contending Forces* (1900) and French's *By Inheritance* (1910) reveals their references and appropriations of Du Bois's *Souls of Black Folk* (1903), which serves as a shared source for the public debates about the South, education, and the legacy of the past.

Evocations:
Contending Forces and *By Inheritance*

While the link between *Expiation* and *Winona* is the plantation narrative embedded in political and property matters, the link between *By Inheritance* and *Contending Forces* is the heated discussion about education in both northern and southern settings, with the plantation narrative as the main setting in French and as the historical backdrop to the action in Hopkins. The most explicit textual transformation in *By Inheritance* is the repeated reference to and evocation of Du Bois's *Souls of Black Folk*, which has to be seen as the hypotext that the later text rewrites. In this example the intertextual transformations run from two texts by different authors to Du Bois, but with no word-for-word similarity. While contemporary Black writers responded to the ideas of Du Bois and race leader Booker T. Washington in various ways (Sutton Griggs comes to mind in *The Hindered Hand*, Charles Chesnutt in *The Marrow of Tradition*, and George Marion McClellan in "Old Greenbottom Inn"), French's *By Inheritance* stands out as a remarkable and little-known evocation of Du Bois by a white female writer. In *Contending Forces* Hopkins anticipated the fight for leadership between Washington and Du Bois, but *By Inheritance* reacted to the same controversy by adding to it a southern white perspective.

For some Black and white Americans the first decade of the twentieth century was dominated by a controversy over race leadership between the accommodationist position of Booker T. Washington and his followers (called "Bookerites") and the more elitist and radical group around W. E. B. Du Bois. In *Contending Forces* both male and female characters are concerned with matters of education in these ways. Heroic and idealized Will Smith uses his excellent education and great intelligence to promote a dream of a Du Boisian school that will train future race leaders in higher fields of knowledge and culture. Ma Smith, her daughter, Dora, and the women's club leaders, especially Mrs. Willis, see it as their duty to "uplift the race" and educate less well privileged people by setting a good example; organizing meetings; providing, for example, educational lectures about the need to build up self-confidence, moral virtue, and good character; and attending public political meetings. In contrast, good-intentioned Dr. Arthur Lewis is an obviously Bookerite educator who is motivated by a desire to train his pupils in industrial crafts and to refrain as much as possible from political agitation. When Lewis argues that he and his fellow southern educators do not want social equality, he exhibits a Bookerite realism in his ambitions. He does not say that he would relinquish any claim for political equality, but he steers away from the great fear of southern white men that Black men would want to marry white men's daughters and sit down with whites at the dinner table.

When Hopkins published her novel, the controversy between the two race leaders was known but not yet widespread. By 1910, when French published *By Inheritance*, the antagonism between Washington and Du Bois that Hopkins previewed was public and well known. "Of Mr. Booker T. Washington and Others," a chapter in *The Souls of Black Folk*, left no doubt about his criticism of Washington's conciliatory politics.[9] When race tensions escalated during the 1906 Atlanta race riots, lynchings became more frequent throughout the South, and Washington's political influence began to be questioned more often, Washington's and Du Bois's positions were discussed in many journals and magazines. In *By Inheritance* the well-educated and idealistic Sidney Danton carries Du Bois's book with him as a kind of Bible and safeguard but is made to suffer and change his mind through the supposed guidance and benevolent influence of a paternalistic group of southerners.[10]

The white plot of the novel centers around the budding love relationship between Giles, Agatha's nephew and possible heir, and Lee, the hoydenish and energetic young granddaughter of General Montgomery, the owner of the plantation. Yet by far the more interesting relationship and one that begins to dominate the plot about halfway through is between Sidney Danton and Lily Pearl Rutherford, a Black descendant of the original white Rutherford family. She is a beautiful mixed-race woman, the offspring of what was most likely a master-slave relationship, and she has grown into a renowned cook and wise woman. Since much of the text refers to passages in Du Bois's book, it is likely that French was inspired by Du Bois's portrayal of Jenny, the sister whom northern educator John defends against rape in chapter 13, "Of the Coming of John." In her overall agenda of presenting strong women, French was certainly influenced by and drawn to Du Bois's defense of Black women, which, Nellie McKay argues, set him apart from many other contemporaries (264). French manipulated her references to this book into both a counternarrative in the figure of anti–Du Bois Sidney Danton and an acceptance of Du Bois's Black female figures as independent and important.

French's Du Boisian counternarrative develops via Lily Pearl, who understands that Sidney fancies a relationship with Matilda, Agatha's white servant. She cautions him not to address the subject directly with Matilda because she knows the possible results of a breach of the social etiquette that monitors the relationships between Black men and white women: "Mist' Danton, I see some things you don't, simply because your eyes are sealed by your dreams. That way out, the whites will kill us, rather'n let us try! They'll turn us all out of the country; you folks'll bring black trouble on us, bloodshed and misery" (French, *By Inheritance* 261–62). Sidney follows her advice and approaches the subject with Matilda only indirectly. In a central scene he tells her about his colored lawyer friend who killed himself after being rejected by a white woman. Matilda is outraged, because "no decent girl that has any respect for herself would allow a colored man to be hanging about her and courting her! Why, the idea is *awful!*" (280, emphasis in the original). This sharp and harsh reaction prompts Sidney to complain about the impossibility of social equality and the alienation he as an educated Black man feels toward the uneducated Black lower class. At this point Sidney exemplifies the common reproach of white people and Bookerites that education makes Black men unfit for life in the South.

By Inheritance weaves questions about social equality, accepted gender behavior, the value of education, and the threat of lynching into a chapter called "The Specter of the South." Sidney is wrongfully accused of attacking Matilda, killing her, and throwing her body into the river when in fact he rescued her from an attack by Lafe Meadows, the novel's villain and Lily Pearl's former husband. Sidney is caught with blood on his hands and immediately subjected to southern mob law. Ominously, bells ring and angry voices are heard. Lee immediately sets out to search near the river, because she thinks that Matilda might not have drowned. Agatha and Mrs. Phil, General Montgomery's daughter-in-law, are convinced that Sidney is not guilty, arm themselves in what is called "the grotesque combination of pistols and parasols," and descend upon the crowd of men assembled for a lynching (French, *By Inheritance* 300). Their serene presence has a dampening effect on the angry crowd, and they manage to defer action until Lee drives up with the living Matilda. The atmosphere is loaded with fury: "Here the air was penetrated by a strange sound, neither groan nor yell, but ominously like them both fused into one by that deadliest wrath of all, the fury of race hatred" (306). While a court proceeding is under way, Lily Pearl appears with drinks of lemonade. Agatha testifies for Sidney, relating the scene between Matilda and Sidney that she had overheard. Mrs. Phil condescendingly calls him a "nice, gentlemanly, respectful boy" (313). And to top this, Lily Pearl—in an African queen–like posture—says that he has asked for her hand (314). The force of old and young southern ladies, Black and white, speaks justice and prevents a lynching. Justice prevails, and the wrongdoer is exposed as Lafe, who, it turns out, is also responsible for an earlier murder. This is still a problematic turn of events when judged from today's point of view, because it puts the blame neatly at the Black door and exonerates all white people from guilt and blame. However, French's novel takes a different trajectory from the literary tradition of white-authored novels with the almost exclusive result of a dead Black man.[11] It turns out that the near-lynching scene serves different ends, namely, to shatter Sidney's illusions about social equality and to "kill" him intellectually and politically. I read this very problematic part of the novel as one of the solutions French proposes to the race problem: the threat of violence will silence the anti-Bookerites and cleanse the country of false claims about social and political equality.

The rightful transference of power between generations is threatened by Sidney in By Inheritance. First, the new plantation order depends on a proper hierarchy, with the planter family at the top of the social ladder, followed by the poorer farmers and landowners dependent on them, and ending with the former slaves as the much-needed workforce. Sidney, as an African American northern educator, jeopardizes this hierarchy because he does not fit in and upsets the established order. After his near-lynching experience Sidney comes to what we are asked to see as a more pragmatic assessment of southern race relations. Indirectly referring to the chapter about Alexander Crummell, the well-known African American Episcopal minister, educator, author, and activist in Du Bois's book, where Du Bois names hate, despair, and doubt as the three temptations besetting Crummell (French, By Inheritance 359; his name is misspelled in the novel as "Crummles"), Sidney says to Lily Pearl: "I'm spent, I'm cowed, if you like; the boys will think I'm a quitter; I know what they think, but I'm not Alexander Crummles; I can't fight a hopeless fight and fight my own doubts, too" (329). He knows that white people would rather kill Black people like him than let them have any chance. Sidney is demasculinized so that he conforms to racial stereotypes, although he is later granted a heroic moment of revenge when he tracks down and shoots Lafe Meadows, ridding the white community of the even more problematic Black man in the text. Sidney has learned his lesson. The day after the near lynching, Sidney surprises the General and Agatha by declining any kind of financial support: "I am afraid to take the responsibility. I think there are enough opportunities for the higher culture tempting my race, now" (341). He suggests that Agatha invest in industrial schools and the training of servants. The General interferes by saying that the so-called good white families would train their Black servants adequately (342). He also warns Sidney indirectly but clearly about the dangers of miscegenation, because the purity of the race has to be preserved (347). Although the lynching is prevented and the unruly mob restrained, the mere threat of violence serves the purpose of disabusing Sidney of supposedly wrong ambitions and attitudes. Agatha understands Sidney's change of mind as the result of the fear of lynching and his newly discovered and supposedly "authentic" racial childlike manner, while the General interprets it as a lesson teaching Sidney that a Black man can either rebel and be lynched or give up and accommodate. Rushton even quotes evidence that Booker T. Washington hoped for a sequel in which French would describe "the regeneration which is going on in the South, through the influence of just such schools as the hero of the story plans to establish" (231). Significantly, Sidney is sufficiently subdued to allow for the unimpeded transference of white property and, perhaps more important, white ideals for race relations.

Unexpectedly, however, the novel does not end only with the presentation of a chastened and defeated Sidney. Instead, it ends after the brutal murder of Lily Pearl by her former husband, Lafe. Lily Pearl dies because she is far more dangerous than Sidney. She is the respected, influential, successful, and wise member of the local population of upwardly mobile Black people. She fiercely defends her race, for example, when she urges Sidney to stand by his color (French, *By Inheritance* 136) and not to see himself as someone better because he has experienced some amount of social equality in the North. In addition and most important, Agatha sees Lily Pearl as far too attractive for her nephew, Giles. Agatha is suspicious when she watches Giles and "that quadroon woman" (120), although there is no evidence of a mutual attraction. In one of Agatha's letters to her friend Henrietta, she calls Lily Pearl's presence in the household "an Awful Problem," although Agatha values Lily Pearl's honesty and decency (106). In that sense, her death at the end serves several means: Sidney, although he is allowed his final moment of revenge against another Black man, is left embittered and silenced, and Giles is free of temptation. Furthermore, it almost seems that Agatha, clearly the writer's alter ego, is obsessed with Lily Pearl herself. The repeated references to her as a "dark lady" (40) and the many descriptions of her beauty, virtue, and skills are a tantalizing hint about Agatha's sexualized fascination with the mulatta who has to be placed out of temptation's way, both Giles's and Agatha's.

The novel is essentially about Agatha's education from old-stock abolitionist proponent of equal opportunities into a southern type of racist segregationist. When she moves South in the hope that her fantasy of race equality will be adequately met, she faces a reality check about supposedly proper race relations. Her kitchen romance with Lily Pearl is safe because it is based on an understood hierarchy and never-acknowledged attraction; her endorsement of Sidney, however, is dangerous. Agatha is converted to Giles's outspoken opinions on the impossibility of racial amalgamation and any other form of social equality by the notions of the era's racial science: the belief that the childlike state of the Black brain was due to an arrested development during puberty

(French, *By Inheritance* 239) and a peculiar atavism, the belief that the African strain will show even generations after the first mixture of bloods. Education will only produce "malcontents" (237). One can imagine Agatha as part of the white audience that is outraged at southern horrors and inspired by the spirit of antebellum abolitionism at the political meeting in Boston that Hopkins writes about in *Contending Forces*. But once Agatha is in the South, she is made to understand the need to monitor, guide, and restrict Black people.

Hopkins's novel *Contending Forces* offers an earlier reading of Du Bois that interprets him as the model race leader whose example should inspire his generation, while French's novel provides the counternarrative of a Du Boisian character come to grief. Sidney is not even allowed to live the happy and fulfilled life that Arthur Lewis, a Bookerite educator, does with Dora in Hopkins's novel. Dr. Lewis builds up a well-ordered school for Black people in New Orleans with beautiful buildings that are mostly built by the students, workshops, and lecture halls where "useful" industries can be taught. His brother-in-law, Will Smith, is not only given a reunion with the lovely Sappho but also granted the financial means by way of his lawful inheritance of the wealth his forefathers lost in slavery to found a school in Europe in which young African American students could stand on "equal terms with men of the highest culture" (Hopkins, *Contending Forces* 389). His dream carries the weight of a sense of doing justice, righting the past cruelties of slavery, and restoring property to its lawful owners.

As recent criticism has shown, *Winona* contains a number of intertextual links to other texts, and so do *Expiation*, *Contending Forces*, and *By Inheritance*. Future research will unearth many more appropriations and borrowings. I agree with Robert Macfarlane when he argues that "indebtedness, borrowedness, textual messiness and overlaps come more and more to be perceived not as qualities furtively to be hidden or disguised, but as distinguished features of a literary work, to be emphasized, explored, and in various ways commemorated" (9). As the discussion above has tried to show, the inspired borrowings and evocations do indeed lead to new insights about writerly practices and the ideologies behind them. Both Hopkins and French actively rearranged their era's discourses, overlapping and intersecting with each other. This comparative and contrastive discussion of two writers, well situated for comparison, positions them firmly as active participants in their contemporary discourses on gender, wealth, property, and hierarchy and, importantly, returns us to the slippery if intransigent ideologies of race and power.

NOTES

This has been a truly collaborative project, and I want to express my great thanks to editor JoAnn Pavletich and to John Cullen Gruesser for their suggestions and constructive criticism.

1. The main and most helpful sources about Alice French / Octave Thanet are McMichael; Tigges; Rushton; and "Iowa's American Gothic in Arkansas: The Plantation Fiction of Octave Thanet," in Kennedy-Nolle.

2. French and Hopkins used pen names, French first publishing as "Frances Essex" and then choosing "Octave Thanet," a masculine first name and a last name that she had apparently seen on a freight car (McMichael 43, 64). Pauline Hopkins published under her own name and that of Sarah A. Allen, her mother's maiden name, and J. Shirley Shadrach, a name consisting of a traditional female first name and most probably the name of Shadrach Minkins, one of many fugitive slaves (see Wallinger 60–62 for a discussion of pseudonyms). At some time all pseudonyms were known to the public, but there are no publications of Alice French signed with her real name.

3. Somerville sees Hopkins's narratives as "exploring historically specific structures of racialization, sexuality, and power" (141), including questions of homosexuality. Although it is not the focus of this essay, similar strategies of "shifting models of sexuality" (142) are apparent in French's set of fictive characters, especially her many tomboyish heroines.

4. In his assessment of the novel, McMichael writes: "The story was romantic, dashing, and melodramatic. And it clanked with such Victorian machinery as torch-light processions, solemn vows, wondrous coincidences, secret parleys in the swamp, horses galloping in all directions, and a villain so mean and low he was called 'Jew-Indian' by the poor white to indicate his worthlessness" (119).

5. Brown identifies the original source of the Carlingford heritage in the writing of Margaret Oliphant, a well-known Scottish novelist who began to publish the Chronicles of Carlingford in the 1860s (373–74).

6. For a complete list of the intertextual borrowing between *Winona* and other texts, see Pavletich, "Source Chart." Also see the section "'Inspired Borrowings'" on the Pauline E. Hopkins Society website.

7. My reading of the plantation tradition is influenced by Wells, who writes about the popularity of plantation literature in the decades following Reconstruction and argues that the plantation came to be seen as a "miniature version of present-day 'America'" (4), by which he means it is a "space, not unlike the western 'frontier,' that, though localized, nevertheless offered readers glimpses into much larger historical forces" (5). I am also influenced by Handley, who writes about the interdependency of plantation cultures in the Americas in the construction of divergent national identities.

8. In this interesting and helpful dissertation, Rushton analyzes French's Arkansas fiction in three novels: *Expiation; We All* (1891), a novel for and about children; and *By Inheritance*. Rushton also examines the short fiction collected by Dougan and Dougan.

9. When in 1908 French first sent a proposal for a new book to the *Saturday Evening Post*, *Scribner's*, *Harper's*, and *Collier's*, she sent along a description of the book as "the encounter . . . with the negro problem by a good New England gentlewoman of abolitionist stock" (qtd. in McMichael 179). She promised an analysis of the new southerner and "the mighty effort he is making" (179) and a glimpse of "what is under the surface" (180). The publishers were not interested until Bobbs-Merrill made her a very generous offer, welcome at a time when other publishers had started to reject her fiction (see McMichael 182). Bobbs-Merrill were, however, not happy with the first draft of the novel then called "The Long Way Out" and asked for substantial revisions of the epistolary form. French recorded in her diary that she came home in the evening and "went to work on my nigger lady" (qtd. in McMichael 185). The book was published shortly after her sixtieth birthday and became quite a public success. In an *Atlantic Monthly* review from 1910, Margaret Sherwood calls it "frankly polemical" because it is based on the thesis that the races must be kept distinct and because the portrayal of the young colored Harvard graduate is not entirely convincing. She gives credit to French, however, for knowing more "about the future of this unfortunate race" than others because she has lived with them (Sherwood 809). The book sold twenty thousand copies in 1910, but French was disappointed that the publisher did not promote it more vigorously (McMichael 191). At the end of the year, her biographer notes, she was disappointed and felt "the age was at fault, and the change in tastes was another aspect of the general weakening of old-time virtue, morality, and decency" (192–93).

10. Although the dominant reference to another text is to Du Bois's *Souls*, there are other carefully selected intertextual borrowings and references. Frequently, Frederick Douglass's marriage to a white woman is cited as an example of misguided intermarriage. In a conversation between Sidney and Giles, Giles heatedly defends a white supremacist stance by citing and referring to Harriet Beecher Stowe, Anna Dickinson, and Margaret Deland (Hopkins, *By Inheritance* 238–39). *What Answer?* by Anna Dickinson was published in 1869 and is the story of the infatuation of a well-to-do white youth with a woman who turns out to have a drop of Black blood but who is beautiful, rich, highly intelligent, and witty. They marry despite all hindrances. Similar to Stowe, whose *Uncle Tom's Cabin* certainly serves as another master text about slavery, Dickinson was a radical and outspoken advocate of abolitionism, a role model for women involved in the antislavery movement (see Anderson). In Margaret Deland's "A Black Drop" (1908), when a young man discovers that his beautiful beloved is colored, he recoils and abandons her. In the wide field of texts available to Alice French that contain scenes of miscegenation and interracialism, French chose two that give a nuanced picture of the issue, but she left out others that paint a much more dismal image. In both stories and in her own, the mulatta woman who loves a white man does not have to die tragically, succumb to illness, or even kill herself.

11. In the context of the many lynching scenes depicted in white-authored fiction of

that time, this part of the plot is indeed remarkable because it shows that Alice French selected her sources carefully. In most texts authored by white writers, a lynching scene shows the cruel Black rapist bent over a helpless white victim. Mob violence is often described as the rightful behavior of southerners, who defend their own. If Black people become part of a mob, they were seen as beasts out of the jungle. Before and after the Atlanta race riots, many newspapers reported that Black men were stealing, raping, and murdering. One obvious white supremacist reaction to the race riots is Thornwell Jacobs's *The Law of the White Circle*, published in 1908 when French started her work on the novel. Its plot involves two nearly indistinguishable beautiful half-sisters, one white, one colored, who become involved in the riots. The enraged reaction to the assumed attack of Black men on white women becomes a cry of race hatred: "Woman after woman, girl after girl, child after child, the jungle men assaulted; and even the babes were not exempt" (Jacobs 73). In addition, both *The Leopard's Spots* (1902) and *The Clansman* (1905) by best-selling racist writer Thomas Dixon feature scenes of beastlike Black men lusting after and attacking white women and Ku Klux Klan mobs revenging the attacks.

WORKS CITED

Anderson, Judith. "Anna Dickinson, Antislavery Radical." *Pennsylvania History*, vol. 3, no. 3, July 1936, pp. 147–63.

Brown, Lois. *Pauline Elizabeth Hopkins: Black Daughter of the Revolution*. University of North Carolina Press, 2008.

Deland, Margaret. "Black Drop." *R.J.'s Mother and Some Other People*. Harper and Brothers, 1908, pp. 219–76. Archive.org.

Dembowitz, Lauren. "Appropriating Tropes of Womanhood and Literary Passing in Pauline Hopkins's *Hagar's Daughter*." *American Literary History*, vol. 30, no. 4, Winter 2018, pp. e21–e30.

Dickinson, Ann. *What Answer?* 1st ed. Ticknor and Fields, 1868.

Dougan, Michael B., and Carol W. Dougan, editors. *By the Cypress Swamp: The Arkansas Stories of Octave Thanet*. Rose Publishing Company, 1980.

Du Bois, W. E. B. *The Souls of Black Folk*. 1903. *Three Negro Classics*. Avon Books, 1965, pp. 207–389.

Dworkin, Ira. "Black Livingstone: Pauline Hopkins, *Of One Blood*, and the Archives of Colonialism." *American Literary History*, vol. 30, no. 4, Winter 2018, pp. e14–e20.

———. Introduction. *Daughter of the Revolution: The Major Nonfiction Works of Pauline E. Hopkins*, edited by Ira Dworkin, Rutgers University Press, 2007, pp. xix–xliv.

Equiano, Olaudah. *The Interesting Narrative of the Life of Olaudah Equiano, or Gustavus Vassa, the African. Written by Himself*. http://docsouth.unc.edu/neh/equiano1/menu.html. Accessed 24 Oct. 2015.

French, Alice [Octave Thanet]. *By Inheritance*. Illustrated by Thomas Fogarty, Bobbs-Merrill, 1910.

———. *Expiation*. 1890. Illustrated by A. B. Frost, Charles Scribner's Sons, 1901.

Genette, Gérard. *Palimpsests: Literature in the Second Degree*. University of Nebraska Press, 1997.

Handley, George B. *Postslavery Literatures in the Americas: Family Portraits in Black and White*. University Press of Virginia, 2000.

Hopkins, Pauline Elizabeth. *Contending Forces: A Romance Illustrative of Negro Life North and South*. 1900. Schomburg Library of Nineteenth-Century Black Women Writers, Oxford University Press, 1988.

———. *Winona: A Tale of Negro Life in the South and Southwest*. 1902. *The Magazine Novels of Pauline Hopkins*, Schomburg Library of Nineteenth-Century Black Women Writers, Oxford University Press, 1988, pp. 285–437.

"'Inspired Borrowings': Pauline Hopkins's Literary Appropriations." Pauline Elizabeth Hopkins Society. http://www.paulinehopkinssociety.org/inspired-borrowings/. Accessed 1 Feb. 2022.

Jackson, Holly. *American Blood: The Ends of the Family in American Literature, 1850–1900*. Oxford University Press, 2014.

Jacobs, Thornwell. *The Law of the White Circle*. 1908. Edited by W. Fitzhugh Brundage, University of Georgia Press, 2006.

Kennedy-Nolle, Sharon D. *Writing Reconstruction: Race, Gender, and Citizenship in the Postwar South*. University of North Carolina Press, 2015.

Levine, Robert S. "Introduction: Cultural and Historical Background." *Clotel; or, The President's Daughter: A Narrative of Slave Life in the United States*, by William Wells Brown, edited by Robert S. Levine, Bedford / St. Martin's, 2011, pp. 3–27.

Macfarlane, Robert. *Original Copy: Plagiarism and Originality in Nineteenth-Century Literature*. Oxford University Press, 2007.

Matthews, Brander. "The Ethics of Plagiarism." *Longman's Magazine*, 1 Oct. 1886, pp. 621–34.

McKay, Nellie. "W. E. B. Du Bois: The Black Women in His Writings—Selected Fictional and Autobiographical Portraits." *The Souls of Black Folk*, by W. E. B. Du Bois, edited by Henry Louis Gates Jr. and Terri Hume Oliver, Norton, 1999, pp. 263–72.

McMichael, George. *Journey to Obscurity: The Life of Octave Thanet*. University of Nebraska Press, 1965.

Pavletich, JoAnn. "The Practice of Plagiarism in a Changing Context." *American Literary History*, vol. 30, no. 4, Winter 2018, pp. e9–e13.

———. "Source Chart and Bibliography for *Winona: A Tale of Negro Life in the South and Southwest*." Pauline Elizabeth Hopkins Society. http://www.paulinehopkinssociety.org/inspired-borrowings/.

———. "'. . . We Are Going to Take That Right': Power and Plagiarism in Pauline Hopkins's *Winona*." *CLA Journal*, vol. 59, no. 2, 2015, pp. 115–30.

Randall, Marilyn. *Pragmatic Plagiarism: Authorship, Profit, and Power*. University of Toronto Press, 2001.

Rushton, Linda Elizabeth. "The Arkansas Fiction of Alice French." 1982. University of Arkansas, PhD dissertation.

Sanborn, Geoffrey. *Plagiarama! William Wells Brown and the Aesthetic of Attractions*. Columbia University Press, 2016.

Sherwood, Margaret. "Lying Like Truth." *Atlantic Monthly*, Dec. 1910, pp. 806–17.

Somerville, Siobhan. "Passing through the Closet in Pauline E. Hopkins's *Contending Forces*." *American Literature*, vol. 69, no. 1, 1997, pp. 139–66.

Tigges, Sandra Ann Healey. "Alice French: A Noble Anachronism." 1981. PhD dissertation, University of Iowa.

Wallinger, Hanna. *Pauline E. Hopkins: A Literary Biography*. University of Georgia Press, 2005.

Wells, Jeremy. *Romances of the White Man's Burden: Race, Empire, and the Plantation in American Literature, 1880–1936*. Vanderbilt University Press, 2011.

Yarborough, Richard. Introduction. *American Literary History*, vol. 30, no. 4, Winter 2018, pp. e4–e8.

Pauline Elizabeth Hopkins

NINETEENTH-CENTURY AMERICA'S
CULTURAL STENOGRAPHER

Karin L. Hooks

Dissatisfied with the financial uncertainties of the theater, where she had worked for fifteen years as a singer, actor, and playwright, Pauline Elizabeth Hopkins trained and worked as a stenographer in the early 1890s. A field concentrated on transcribing the spoken word into print as precisely as possible, stenography would exert considerable influence on Hopkins's first novel, *Contending Forces*. Notably, in her preface to *Contending Forces*, Hopkins describes how she transcribed late nineteenth-century political speech into the novel: "I have used for the address of the Hon. Herbert Clapp the statements and accusations made against the Negro by ex-Governor Northen of Georgia, in his memorable address before the Congregational Club at Tremont Temple, Boston, Mass., May 22, 1899" (16). Lois Brown documents that Hopkins heard Northen's address firsthand and was so outraged by his "brazen disregard for African American rights and his willful manipulation of history" that she immediately began drafting *Contending Forces* (186). Though she fictionalized both the speaker and the occasion within the novel, Hopkins calls deliberate attention to her compositional strategies in her preface. In discussing how she put Northen's words into Clapp's mouth, Hopkins previews a pattern often noted by scholars: that she appropriated material from other sources into her fiction, often without acknowledging that she had done so.

Given the immediacy of her reuse of Northen's speech, it is likely that Hopkins recorded it verbatim in stenographic shorthand. Thus, by acknowledging that she relied on his words to craft her novel, Hopkins raised the specter of stenography's impact on her writing process. Her subsequent claim that she felt her "own deficiencies too strongly to attempt original composition" accurately indicates that she used other sources as well, and it is well documented that she incorporated material from published texts (Hopkins 16). In her preface to *Contending Forces*, Hopkins provides an explanation for quoting from others' texts within her work, indicating that she had a clear purpose for doing so. Because of what she presents as authorial inadequacy to what she saw as a moment of "crisis in the history of the Negro in the United States," she had, in chapter 15, made "Will Smith's argument in answer to the Hon. Herbert Clapp a combination of the best points made by well-known public speakers in the United States—white and black—in defense of the Negro" (16). Here, Hopkins also publicly calls attention to her own methodologies of writing, of borrowing freely from public discourses of the day. Hopkins's use of the term "combination" indicates some of the stenographic changes she made, combining the words of several orators to make Will a more effective spokesman for his race.

Despite her prefatory explanation, recent scholarship convincingly convicts Hopkins as a plagiarist who not only borrowed genre conventions but also systematically incorporated—often without the attribution she gives Northen—the words of others into both her fiction and nonfiction. For example, in *Plagiarama!* Geoffrey Sanborn identifies what he calls Hopkins's "process-oriented, plagiarism-friendly aesthetic," noting that she plagiarized approximately eighteen percent of her novel *Of One Blood* (22). The amount of plagiarism Sanborn documents might raise questions as to whether or not Hopkins knew there were nineteenth-century strictures against the practice. But as JoAnn Pavletich suggests in the December 2015 issue of *CLA Journal*, "As an editor, Hopkins was most certainly aware of the current critical perspectives on plagiarism; thus, it seems safe to assume that she employed this practice purposely and strategically as part of her larger mission of advancing African American lives and culture" (117). In other words, Hopkins was both a purveyor and a promotor of culture, tactically replicating sources in her own texts for her own purposes. Indeed, Hopkins made no secret of the fact that *Contending Forces* drew on sources beyond Northen and the other public speakers mentioned above. In her preface, Hopkins also references archival documents that prove that the "incidents portrayed in the early chapters of the book actually occurred" (14). The question, then, is not whether or not Hopkins reused material; instead, it is how we are to understand her practice and purpose.

This essay's investigation of the material practices of stenography allows us to push past investigations of plagiarism and to see Hopkins as a *cultural* stenographer who recorded and re-created the words of others to make new texts with new meanings for her readers. My term "cultural stenographer" builds on John Ernest's term "cultural editor" for the midcentury writer William Wells

Brown, another author vulnerable to charges of plagiarism. Brown established himself as a cultural editor, Ernest argues, by arranging "materials in a revealing demonstration of contradictoriness and tension" in his fiction to argue for Black agency during slavery (23). However, while Hopkins would go on to become the literal editor of the *Colored American Magazine*, Ernest's term "cultural editor" does not accurately describe her role in *Contending Forces*. My term gets at something distinct, that is, that the combination of shorthand and typing that Hopkins learned as a business stenographer showed her not only how to record and re-create the words of others but also how to infuse new meaning into existing texts by silently amending them in order to more forthrightly support her agenda of social reform.

Hopkins was both a recorder of and a participant in the post-Reconstruction debate about how best to combat the increasing U.S. tensions arising from racial prejudice, and her successful careers as a theatrical performer and as editor at the *Colored American Magazine* situated her as an authority on American and African American culture. Concomitantly, her experiences as a stenographer taught her that transcription could be both accurate and transformative. By assuming the mantle of cultural stenographer, Hopkins could actively mediate the historical record and contemporary political discourse in her fictional re-creation of both in the two separate but interconnected sections of *Contending Forces*, the first set during slavery and the second after Reconstruction. Understanding Hopkins's work as a cultural stenographer requires, first, an examination of the debate surrounding the rise of business stenography regarding the extent to which stenographers exercised creativity and of the impact stenography exerted on nineteenth-century American fiction. Looking next at the material practices of stenography, I will demonstrate how stenographers transform speech while ostensibly merely transcribing it. Finally, I will argue that Hopkins's role as cultural stenographer is best seen in her adept handling of the material that she incorporated into *Contending Forces* from Ralph Waldo Emerson. *Contending Forces* demonstrates that, with some skillful editing by Hopkins, Emerson's midcentury calls for the abolition of slavery could be just as effective in African Americans' turn-of-the-century demands for social equality and full citizenship.

The Rise of Business Stenography
and Its Entry into Fiction

Before the invention of recording machines, stenography offered the most effective means of capturing human speech. Stenography dates back to the Roman Empire; however, it was not widely used in the United States until Stephen Pearl Andrews was asked at the 1840 World Anti-Slavery Convention to introduce Sir Isaac Pitman's newly invented modern shorthand system to the American people. Inspired by stenography's power to capture speech, women quickly became the leading proponents of the trade, promoting and employing stenography in a wide range of social and political causes, including spelling reform, woman suffrage, and emancipation (Srole 89). By the 1890s, faster and more reliable typewriters made it possible to type more quickly than a person could write. The resulting field of business stenography offered stenographers unprecedented opportunities for employment, as more and more businesses relied on typewritten communications. In *Scripts, Grooves, and Writing Machines*, Lisa Gitelman notes that as technological advances increasingly impacted methods of writing, there "was an underlying conflict over how much intelligence the scribal technician had to supply, when and how much the head and the fingers worked, just how automatic stenographers, telegraphers, and other scribal technicians had to be" (203). In other words, the nature of the work of transcription and typing not only played a role in mechanizing and modernizing the business world but also raised new anxieties about how the transmission of information and the speed of production impacted authorial agency. As she copyrighted *Contending Forces* within three months of Northen's speech and published the novel within a year, Hopkins's stenographic skills must have enabled her to write quickly.[1] Motivated by her desire to counteract the racist rhetoric of Northen and his supporters and empowered toward efficiency by her training, Hopkins wrote a novel that has raised many scholarly anxieties about her compositional practices and her creative agency.

Ample evidence exists to support the typical view of stenography as uncreative labor, as nineteenth-century periodicals documented the rise of business stenography as a profession, one readily available to anyone willing to master its systematic procedures. There were advertisements for self-paced stenographic training courses, job postings for stenographers, and articles defining the differences between shorthand, stenography, and phonography, three closely related fields. Despite the growing number of stenographers, there were also articles decrying the dearth of well-qualified applicants, as too many newly trained stenographers evidenced signs of inattention to grammar and punctuation. As this evidence suggests, stenography offered enterprising men and women opportunities to gain the skills and credentials necessary to find employment in a field that relied on replicating the spoken word as precisely as possible, fulfilling, as one 1888 article puts it, "a constant and growing desire to find some way of representing the spoken language in an exact, concise, and rapid manner" (Andrews 68). Additionally, some believed that stenography impacted the writing of fiction, primarily in negative ways. For example, "Some Tendencies of Contemporary Fiction," from the December 2, 1899, issue of the *Living Age*, decries using stenography, the typewriter, and the phonograph to write fiction: "It has now become physically possible to produce a novel in about three weeks, and there are several writers whom the conscientious reviewer seems to meet in book form about once a month. This is not literature, it is simply manufacture" (589). Perhaps the most positive evidence of stenography's impact on literature comes from the type of notice paid to other stenographers turned writers, such as Charles Dickens, who fictionalized his own transformation from stenographer to author in *David Copperfield* and *The Pickwick Papers*, and Charles Chesnutt, whose fictional investigation of the "art" of stenography in *A Business Career* remained unpublished for over a century. Their work as stenographers was often mentioned alongside their literary aspirations or accomplishments.

It is not known if Hopkins was aware of Dickens's and Chesnutt's respective transformations from stenographer to author at the time when she decided to change careers. We do know that she joined a growing group of Boston stenographers whose numbers rose exponentially between 1885 and 1900, according to Carole Srole, going from 113 to 2,500 in less than two decades (90). In 1892, according to "Pauline E. Hopkins," an anonymous 1901 biographical sketch in the *Colored American Magazine*, Hopkins was stenographer for Republicans Henry Parkman and Alpheus Sanford, for whom she worked until she passed the civil service examination and found employment at the Massachusetts Bureau of Statistics of Labor. There, Hopkins worked on the 1895 Massachusetts decennial census, which tracked population rates, social statistics, manufacturers, agriculture, fisheries, and commerce according to the "distribution of the population by color and race" (*Census* 864). As Brown has thoroughly documented, Hopkins was a dedicated race woman who came of age in Boston's active and politically astute Black community, where she witnessed "sharply contrasting realities for African Americans" (162). At the bureau, she helped edit and tabulate information gathered by "more than 1000 enumerators, field agents, and inspectors" into reports that "would determine state legislative representation and provide details about state populations, economic stability, domestic arrangements, social service needs, and education" (166). From the banal mass of notes collected in the field, Hopkins and other stenographers compiled a range of materials, including the Massachusetts census, pamphlets, and annual reports to the state legislature, that were subsequently used to shape public life.

Because Massachusetts's population was 98.85 percent white and 1.06 percent Black, Hopkins's work at the bureau would have focused primarily on the lives of whites.[2] At the same time, her involvement in Boston's African American political community made her increasingly aware of racial oppression and injustice in both the South and the North. Brown documents that "Hopkins and fellow Bostonians routinely received shocking reports in the daily city papers about gruesome racial horrors of Southern mob rule and lynchings and widespread, almost routine instances of African American disenfranchisement, intimidation, and oppression" (162–63). Like Ida B. Wells, who had rewritten the narrative of lynching in *A Red Record*, a pamphlet compiled with data taken from white sources to expose the prevalence of lynching in the United States, Hopkins could readily see the efficacy of reshaping the words of others to fit her own purposes. As Ellen Gruber Garvey points out in her excellent analysis of American scrapbooks, *Writing with Scissors*, African American writers used a variety of printed materials to create alternate histories that rewrote the accounts provided by the white press. Garvey posits that scissoring words from printed sources and rearranging them to suit their own purposes allowed scrapbook makers, editors, historians, authors, and members of minority groups to speak back against the white press. Commenting on the impact such practices had on authorial agency, Garvey concludes, "Authorship was a practical task that entailed reshaping and recirculating existing writing" (77).

Not surprisingly, then, in chapter 12 of *Contending Forces*, Hopkins replicates an account of the lynching of "Jim Jones, a burly black Negro accused of the crime of rape against the person of a beautiful white woman" (223). Purportedly from *The Torchlight*, which Elizabeth Ammons identifies as a white newspaper, the piece describes Jones's death, as well as the hanging of three Black men "accused of hiding the guilty wretch from the justice of the populace" (Hopkins 223). Shortly afterward, Hopkins's narrator specifically acknowledges the distortion of justice not just in Boston but in all of Massachusetts, where the scales of justice "tip in favor of the white brother" despite the state's reputation for fair play toward its Black citizens (224). While Hopkins's only known scrapbook documents her theatrical days, it is not difficult to imagine her consulting a newspaper clipping while re-creating this account in order to build up to her novel's point about the more prevalent reality of the rape of Black women by white men. The inclusion of this newspaper article, whether historical or fictional, does not detract from Hopkins's originality, as it is her implied critique of its contents that propels her narrative forward.

The Material Practices of Stenography and
Unexpected Transformations of Meaning

Hopkins highlights different aspects of the material practices of stenography through her portrayal of two fictional stenographers. The first, a white male, works in the offices of John Langley, a villainous African American lawyer who agrees to quell Black anger about a recent lynching in return for Herbert Clapp's promise to support Langley's bid to fill the vacant city solicitor position. In the penultimate scene of chapter 12, Langley sits in his office and ponders how best to respond to the American Colored League's call for an outcry of public indignation regarding the lynching, with the sound of his white male stenographer "clicking away for dear life" ringing in his ears (Hopkins 225). Langley had deliberately hired a white stenographer, the narrator reveals, in order to make his political office seem more welcoming of white patrons, and he defended his choice when pressured by members of the American Colored League to hire a Black stenographer. By emphasizing the typist's race and Langley's reasons for hiring him, Hopkins highlights some of the racist hiring practices of the day, even among Black employers, and records her awareness of racial favoritism and its impact on employment practices. She also calls attention to some of the era's anxieties surrounding the impact of mechanized methods of writing on authorship. That white stenographer is, after all, transforming Langley's handwritten notes into their finished form. Hopkins seems to imply that, just as the white stenographer's presence reassures white visitors of their welcome, his influence ensures that Langley's text will meet with white approval. Tellingly, she placed the re-created white newspaper account of mob justice discussed above in the pages leading up to revelation of the existence of John Langley's white stenographer. Though Langley is not specifically said to have read the account, the paragraph discussing his stenographer begins with a sentence saying that news of the "horrible event had just reached the officers of the American Colored League" (225). Langley's adamant denial of prejudice toward men of his own race rings as hollow as the newspaper's claims that white vigilantism resulted in justice.

Hopkins's second stenographer, Sappho Clark, a beautiful, young, mysterious woman living in the Smith family's boardinghouse, exemplifies the material realities for many Black female stenographers. Unlike Langley's stenographer, Sappho works from home. She prefers working from her rented room, Sappho tells her friend Dora, because she had experienced multiple episodes of workplace prejudice and sexual harassment before being hired by her present employer. Isolated in her second-floor room, Sappho works largely independent of oversight: "She passed in and out each morning with a package of work in her hand; and all day long, from nine in the morning until late at night sometimes, the click of the typewriter could be heard" (Hopkins 97). Though she explains that she is prevented from teaching school because she does not have a college education, Sappho never details how, when, or why she trained to become a stenographer. By the time she reaches the Smith family's boardinghouse, she is in her early twenties and picking up "a good living at home" with her typewriter, transforming sheaths of notes into printed text (89). Through Sappho, Hopkins proposes that stenography requires far more than simply taking and transcribing dictation. For instance, when her friend Dora asks if stenographic work is difficult, Sappho replies that she likes it, even if the speaker "is obtuse, or long-winded, or thinks that the writer ought to do his thinking for him as well as the corrections" (99). Here, Hopkins implicitly suggests that a stenographer is a "writer" who must correct unintelligence, reduce wordiness, supply information, and correct mistakes, as Sappho edits her employer's obtuse dictation into a different—more useful—product. Sappho exemplifies that though it is typically considered clerical labor, stenography, like fiction writing, requires creativity.

Much has been written about Sappho and her transformative powers, though scholars have, to date, either ignored Sappho's stenographic labor or regarded it as uncreative. For instance, Ammons remarks on how Sappho's "artistic talent" shows up in "the literary name she has assumed, the way she beautifies her room, [and] her creation of a gorgeous son" before noting that Sappho's employment as a stenographer renders her writing "completely drained of creativity" (80). For Ammons, stenography may provide the means of economic self-sufficiency, but it drains rather than sustains artistic creativity. In *Contending Forces*, however, Sappho's creative and transformative powers are linked to her work. The transformation of her room in Mrs. Smith's Boston boardinghouse from functional to inviting involves not only making a few simple changes to the décor but also placing her typewriter in "the center of the room" (Hopkins 98). Her work on that typewriter as a self-employed stenographer sustains her own transformation from Mabelle Beaubean, the victim of rape, incest, prostitution, and unwed teenage motherhood, to Sappho Clark, a beautiful, untouched, self-sustaining career woman with aspirations of marrying Will Smith.

As Margery W. Davies argues in *Woman's Place Is at the Typewriter*, stenographers were more than transcribers. Using a phonetic note-taking system to record notes that only she could fully understand, a stenographer transformed the words of others into a text of her own making. Nineteenth-century stenographers relied on different phonetic systems to record and replicate the spoken word, depending on which school of stenography they learned. Various schools taught unique phonetic systems in which, according to Gerald S. Giauque, "special symbols represent and recall to the stenographer's mind the sounds of English" (353). In practice, each stenographer further complicated this process by adapting the system she learned to fit her own individual style. Thus, as Giauque posits, the effective stenographer must possess "imagination and the ability to derive meaning from contexts" to make "intelligent guesses about the meaning of the written symbols" (353). Unlike Herman Melville's infamous copyist, Bartleby, who laboriously replicates documents by hand and compares each copy to the original to ensure accuracy, Sappho instinctively rewrites, supplying any deficiencies and eradicating any inefficiencies.

It is through her fictional stenographers that Hopkins models Reconstruction's failure to enact lasting changes in the national social, economic, and legal landscapes. The white stenographer's noisy intrusion on the thought processes of John Langley keeps him aware of the white forces at work in his life. In return for the promise of more white clients, he refuses to hire Black men to work in his office, upholding the same type of discriminatory hiring practices as white employers. Though he tells Herbert Clapp that he wants "our men given something beside boot-blacking in the employment of the state" and "our girls given a chance as clerks," his own hiring practices belie his words (Hopkins 236).

Through Dora, Hopkins addresses the difficulty of Black women finding employment in white offices, having her question Sappho about having "always heard that it was very difficult for colored girls to find employment in offices" employing stenographers (Hopkins 127–28). In response, Sappho recalls how she was twice turned away from job opportunities because of her race. In this scene, Sappho addresses the issue of racial discrimination in the workplace, saying that working from home allowed her to remain unseen by the "other clerks" so that "the proprietor runs no risk of being bothered with complaints from them" (128). In In Freedom's Birthplace, John Daniels reflects the historical difficulties Black women faced finding employment, drawing on census data to show that only eight Black Boston women were working as stenographers in 1900, the year Hopkins wrote Contending Forces (345). Not only was it "ten to fifty times harder" for African Americans to find clerical work in the first decade of the twentieth century than it was for whites, but many African Americans with "literary or artistic" abilities were forced to temporarily or permanently accept lower-paying clerical jobs in order to make ends meet (321, 342). Admittedly, Sappho never makes the leap from clerical work to creative writing; yet, as we will see below, it is through her, the novel's most creative figure, that Hopkins envisions continuities between stenography and authorship.

Building Cultural Capital /
Becoming a Cultural Authority

It is through Sappho that Hopkins configures what it takes to become a cultural authority. In an imagined scene of social and cultural camaraderie and, notably, preceding a similar scene in W. E. B. Du Bois's *Souls of Black Folk* by three years, Hopkins pictures Sappho intermingling in white society in the library, enjoying access to public resources that had never been granted to her in the South:

> To this woman, denied association with the vast sources of information, which are heirlooms to the lowliest inhabitants of Boston, the noble piles, which represented the halls of learning, and the massive grandeur of the library, free to all, seemed to invite her to a full participation in their intellectual joys. She had seen nothing like them. Statuary, paintings, sculptures,— all appealed to her beauty loving nature. The hidden springs of spirituality were satisfied and at rest, claiming kinship with the great minds of the past, whose never-dying works breathed perennial life in the atmosphere of the quiet halls. (116)

Within the library, which Dora Smith has to convince Sappho she can enter without "fear of insult," Sappho finds she has free access to books, statues, paintings, and sculptures—items collectively representative of human intellectual and artistic achievement (Hopkins 116). In other words, living in Boston for the majority of her life gave Hopkins access to the rich cultural resources Sappho lacked. In the corresponding passage from *Souls*, Du Bois similarly situates himself as an African American male enjoying rich cultural interactions: "I sit with Shakespeare and he winces not. Across the color line I move arm in arm with Balzac and Dumas, where smiling men and women glide in gilded halls. From out the caves of evening that swing between the strong-limbed earth and the tracery of stars, I summon Aristotle and Aurelius and what soul I will, and they come all graciously with no scorn nor condescension. . . . Is this the life you grudge us, O knightly America?" (90).[3] Contained within a discussion of the difference between northern and southern social exclusionary practices, the passage from *Contending Forces*, like the one from *Souls*, points toward the ongoing exclusion of African Americans from most parts of white society by placing their inclusion within the idealized space of the library. Du

Bois's accusatory question points out his realization that white America be-
grudges him these kinds of diverse cultural experiences. Hopkins uses her vi-
gnette of Sappho enjoying cultural kinship at the library to establish her own
camaraderie with the literary greats whose words she appropriated and refash-
ioned within *Contending Forces*. Hopkins's representation of female "kinship
with the great minds of the past" is central to her situating herself as a cultural
authority. Walking the halls of the library, Sappho is not daunted but inspired
to discover the wealth of cultural resources at her disposal. By placing Sappho's
discovery on an imaginary plane, Hopkins lays claim to even more cultural authority than was actually possible for a Black woman, even in Boston. Like Du
Bois, she seems to be charging white Americans with only grudgingly allowing Black participation in American society. Yet the scene serves an important
function, as it helps Hopkins bridge the gap between her accurate recording of
the degrading effects of slavery in the first section of her novel and her transformative transcription of historical and contemporary political speech in the
second section. By arguing that a Black woman has "kinship" with the "never-
dying works" of the past, Hopkins takes a crucial step toward her revisioning of
Emerson to argue for African American equality and participatory citizenship.

Hopkins as Cultural Stenographer:
Reshaping Emerson

Though race literature took many forms, Hopkins chose the genre of fiction for
Contending Forces, viewing it as the forum through which she could best rene-
gotiate the historical record in order to effect future change. As she says in an
often-quoted passage from the preface to the novel, "Fiction is of great value to
any people as a preserver of manners and customs—religious, political, and social. It is a record of growth and development from generation to generation.
*No one will do this for us; we must ourselves develop the men and women who
will faithfully portray the inmost thoughts and feelings of the Negro with all the
fire and romance which lie dormant in our history*, and, as yet, unrecognized by
writers of the Anglo-Saxon race" (Hopkins 13–14, emphasis in original). Both
a lament for the dearth of African American fiction writers and a call to action,
Hopkins's statement underscores her awareness of the necessity of renegotiat-
ing the historical record, of more accurately reflecting African American contributions to American culture. Though she does not mention culture directly,
her listing of the individual components—manners, customs, religious beliefs,
political philosophies, and social capital—makes clear that it is the topic scru-
tinized in fiction. Even more clear is her willingness to accept the role of tran-

scribing a more accurate narrative—"a record of growth and development"—even if it runs counter to narratives about African Americans written by white writers. Here, Hopkins discusses the work of transcription, even though she is now self-employed, so to speak, in the arena of racial uplift rather than working for the Massachusetts Bureau of Statistics of Labor. Much as Sappho edited her employer's obtuseness as she shaped his words into useful products, Hopkins edits American history, especially in the second section of the novel, insisting that the trauma slavery imposed on its citizens must be revisited before the nation can be healed of its prejudiced and discriminatory practices. For instance, within the novel, Hopkins's revisionist history pushes past historical re-creation to rectify the unbalanced discussion of African American life that resulted when, as Brown documents, Northen exceeded his time limit and left his African American respondent, Bishop Benjamin Arnett Jr., only twenty minutes of his allotted hour (186–87).

In saying that Hopkins offers a "revisionist history" in *Contending Forces*, I refer to Gitelman's assertion that "before phonographs and televisions, making history was unquestionably done on paper by a variety of means" and that "legible inscriptions . . . like . . . stenographers' scripts, made history" (24). Hopkins understood and was responding to what Gitelman describes as "anxiety about the efficacy of memory, about experience slipping away, potential evidence squandered, and alien experience unaccounted for" (57) because in her preface she calls for writers who will document—in fiction—the hitherto unrecognized history of the "colored race" (Hopkins 13). Her training as a stenographer would have introduced her to shorthand manuals, which "offered themselves as solutions to these imagined problems—relegating experience by making it textual, running it down and pressing it onto the page" (Gitelman 57). Here, Gitelman envisions shorthand systems as integral to textualizing the history-making process or, in Hopkins's case, the history-remaking process. The racists Hopkins fights, whether historical like Northen or fictional like Clapp, have all manner of imagined problems that she textualizes, or inscribes on the page, in order to promote a more accurate understanding of slavery's impact on the nation. Hopkins, responding to her own call for writers of fiction to record African Americans' culture, to preserve their "manners and customs—religious, political, and social," recognizes the fallacy of leaving the historical record entirely within the domain of "writers of the Anglo-Saxon race" (13–14). Focusing her readers on fiction's power to fill in historical gaps, Hopkins situates herself—despite her protestations to the contrary—as one uniquely qualified to *right* the historical account by *writing* the events that occurred. She was, as Hazel V. Carby convincingly argues in *Reconstructing Womanhood*, responding to the rhetorical question raised in the novel's prospectus, "Of what use is fiction to the colored race at the present crisis in its history?" Seizing on the promise of stenography, Hopkins intervenes by rewriting that moment of crisis, imprinting her account within the pages of her novel.

As interesting as her revisionist history is, Hopkins's skills as a cultural stenographer are nowhere more evident than in her handling of the material she transcribes into *Contending Forces* from Ralph Waldo Emerson. She employs Emerson's 1844 adage, "The civility of no race can be perfect whilst another race is degraded," three times within the novel: as an epigraph on the title page, as part of the narrator's historical commentary in the opening chapter, and as a means of rewriting the dominant narrative of sexual promiscuity in African American women in chapter 8, "The Sewing Circle." As discussed below, Hopkins seems to have formed her fictional account of the events leading up to the emancipation of the West Indies, in the first chapter of *Contending Forces*, directly from Emerson's published lecture. She also silently assigns his ideology to her characters at several points within the novel, using Emerson to link nineteenth-century racism and sexism to chattel slavery and to urge her readers to action. As Ivy G. Wilson illustrates in *Specters of Democracy*, because they lived shadowy lives as second-class citizens, African Americans had to be "strategic about developing the means to engage with the political sphere" (5). Hopkins's strategic quoting (and misquoting) of Emerson situates him posthumously in the fight against racial injustice. By making small but significant changes to the contexts and content of Emerson's words, Hopkins appropriates Emersonian ideals about ending slavery to further her own fin de siècle argument for Black Americans' rights to full citizenship and social equality.

Hopkins took the adage, "The civility of no race can be perfect whilst another race is degraded," from Emerson's "Address on the Emancipation of the Negroes in the British West Indies" (1844), which he had delivered to the Women's Anti-Slavery Society of Concord on the tenth anniversary of Parliament's ratification of the bill that abolished slavery in all British colonies. Emerson's speech would have been readily available to Hopkins as she wrote *Contending Forces*, as it was published in pamphlet form shortly after he delivered it and republished twice in 1884 (posthumously, in the Riverside Edition of *Miscellanies* and the Little Classic Edition of *Miscellanies*). The address highlights and condemns the physical brutalities of chattel slavery, praises the British government for its bold stance against slavery, and argues that similar legislation needs to be enacted in America. Len Gougeon posits that the address marks Emerson's "transition from philosophical antislavery to active abolitionism" (xxx). This distinction would have meant little to Hopkins, who had yet to be born when Emerson made the speech that marked him as a member of the abolitionist community. From her vantage point, Emerson was a dedicated abolitionist of national renown whose ideals supported her agenda of social and political reform. The ready availability of Emerson's text, its concise summary of the British Empire's freeing of its slaves, its appeal to American sensibilities, and Emerson's reputation as an abolitionist made it an easily adaptable source for her fictional purposes.

Though separated by constraints of time, race, and gender, Hopkins shared with Emerson a New England heritage and an awareness of social injustice. As she frames her novel with his words, she shrewdly assumes the mantle of Emerson idealism to "raise the stigma of degradation from [her] race" (Hopkins 13). Though she does not mention Emerson here by name, his incorporation into her text marks him as one of the white "well-known public speakers" that she mentions in her preface. She mimics the dynamics between an employer and a stenographer, rhetorically situating Emerson as the voice of dictation within her text. By linking her text to his, she imagines a trajectory for American literature that moves it from midcentury concerns about slavery to late nineteenth-century issues regarding racial equality. Her references to his text provide a layer of authentication for her fictional narrative: a factual and familiar historical framework.

In chapter 1, "A Retrospect of the Past," Hopkins questions whether emancipation had a civilizing effect on the nation, since African Americans were still mistreated, murdered, and abused. To answer this question, Hopkins turns to the words from Emerson's address. Her retrospect opens in 1790 with a historical overview of the role of English humanitarians in abolishing slavery in the British Isles. The narrator recalls the efforts of British reformers that preceded emancipation, mentioning many of the same people and events Emerson cited in his speech. Like Emerson, the narrator mentions the efforts of the Quakers to alleviate the horrific conditions of slavery in the West Indies and to discourage the slave trade on the African coast. Both Emerson and the narrator detail Thomas Clarkson's confirmation of the immorality of slavery after he wrote an essay on the topic while a student at Cambridge; both mention the efforts of Mr. Pitt, Mr. Fox, Mr. Wilberforce, Granville Sharpe, and Lord Stanley; and both detail the conditions of the bill advocating gradual emancipation and mention the bill's ten defeats over a sixteen-year span. In addition to relating the same names and general details as Emerson, Hopkins quotes directly from his text at least three times: "[T]he air of England is too pure for any slave to breathe" (Hopkins 17; Emerson 11); "providence had never made that to be wise that was immoral; and that the slave trade was as impolitic as it was un-just" (Hopkins 18; Emerson 12); and "[t]hese conditions were that prædials should owe three-fourths of the profits to their masters for six years, and the non-prædials for four years. The other fourth of the apprentice's time was to be his own, which he might sell to his master or to other persons; and at the end of the term of years fixed, he should be free" (Hopkins 20; Emerson 14).[4] Here, Hopkins also repeats the words from Emerson's adage, saying that Great Brit-ain's emancipation of its slaves demonstrates the civility spoken of by Emerson. Propelled by the increasingly negative northern rhetoric regarding Black par-ticipation in society, Hopkins does what her stenographic training had taught her to do: to recirculate the words of others. Her appropriation of Emerson's text is a deliberate stenographic strategy that allows her to quickly and effi-ciently get her finished product into circulation.

In chapter 14, Luke Sawyer's speech to the American Colored League im-mediately follows that of Dr. Arthur Lewis, the novel's fictional characteriza-tion of Booker T. Washington. Dr. Lewis proposes that African Americans should be "patient, docile, [and] harmless" if they wish to achieve prosperity. In rebuttal, Sawyer charges that Dr. Lewis's "conservatism, lack of brotherly affiliation, [and] lack of energy for the right" are "the forces which are ruin-ing the Negro in this country" (Hopkins 256). After Sawyer sits down, Will Smith takes the podium and advocates a policy of agitation, saying, "We must *agitate*. As the anti-slavery apostles went everywhere, preaching the word fifty years before emancipation, *so must we do to-day*" (272, emphasis in original). The audience reacts positively to Will's speech, though they remain divided as to how best to achieve social, economic, and educational progress. Then, in chapter 17, "The Canterbury Club Dinner," Will argues with an unnamed character known simply as the Southerner about the extent of racial progress. The Southerner proposes that individual progress does not result in change for "the race as a whole" (295). In response, Will says, "If men are rude and fool-ish, down they must go. When at last in any race a new principle appears, an idea, *that conserves* it. Ideas only save races. If the black man is feeble and im-potent, unimportant to the existing races—not on a parity with the best races, the black man must serve and be exterminated. *But*, if he carries within his bo-som the element of a new and coming civilization, he will survive and play his part" (295, emphasis in original). Will's words regarding racial parity have been adapted from Emerson's address. To understand the significance of Will's re-sponse, we must compare his statement to the original passage by Emerson.

The changes, though slight, have a decided impact on the passage. Emerson writes:

> If they are rude and foolish, down they must go. When at last in a race, a new principle appears, an idea—*that* conserves it; ideas only save races. If the black man is feeble, and not important to the existing races not on a parity with the best race, the black man must serve and be exterminated. But if the black man carries in his bosom an indispensable element of a new and coming civilization, for the sake of that element, no wrong, nor strength, nor circumstance, can hurt him: he will survive and play his part. (31, emphasis in original)

Hopkins changes Emerson's "they" to "men," making an important intervention in the nineteenth-century debates that questioned African Americans' status as "human" and removing the third-person pronoun that allows Emerson to rhetorically distance himself from Black men. Additionally, "a race" becomes "any race," making racial issues in America larger than the Black community. The dash is omitted, punctuation is changed to separate one sentence into two, words are altered, and additional words are inserted; these changes, though slight, impact the reading of the text to strengthen Hopkins's call for racial unity by transforming the passage rather than merely transcribing it. The words "feeble, and not important" become "feeble and impotent, unimportant," implying that mere feebleness alone does not render one unimportant. Emphasis is placed on the "but," and the words "for the sake . . . hurt him" are silently omitted, a clear instance of Hopkins following her own suggestion, discussed above, that stenographers are to silently correct mistakes (in this case, a mistake in emphasis) and eliminate wordiness. Hopkins also adds an *s* to the word "race," which changes the implication of the sentence from the suggestion of there being one "best race" to multiple "best races." This last change effectively erases the notion of white supremacy from Emerson's address, an ideological construction that Hopkins's novel resists. Through her revision of Emersonian ideals, Hopkins restores his (white) voice to the fight for African Americans' rights. Not only does she situate Emerson as the abolitionist he was during his lifetime, but she also configures him as a posthumous collaborator in the fight against the incivility of late nineteenth-century racism.

As Edward Jones Kilduff observed in 1924, stenographers often worked without instruction from their employers: "[T]hese stenographers soon picked up many bits of information concerning their employers' business, their methods and policies, and their activities. . . . The more information they secured, the better able they became to decide upon matters that came up when the chiefs were busy or were away" (qtd. in Davies 130). In Emerson's "absence," Hopkins transforms the meaning of his words by making slight but significant changes. Like Sappho, whom Alisha Knight calls a "self-employed stenographer," since "she cannot work in her employer's office," Hopkins works under her own direction (85). Nor does she stop here. As we will see, she makes an even more significant change when she uses the same Emerson adage to criticize white rapists and defend their victims as nonculpable participants in what she describes as the late nineteenth-century parallel to slavery's system of "concubinage."

The third instance of Emerson's adage about civility occurs in chapter 8, "The Sewing Circle," where a group of Black women discuss the importance of race and the implications of miscegenation. The women meet in the home of Mrs. Smith, which, in addition to being the site of Sappho's intertwined transformations, provides the stage for much of the characters' cultural interaction. The Smiths' friends and neighbors come to their house for "literary and musical" occasions and stay to discuss issues of race: menial labor, poor wages, the lack of educational opportunities, and means of racial uplift. Here, Hopkins records representations of Black community members as engaged, concerned, and culturally vibrant citizens. These same issues are subsequently discussed in later chapters in larger, communal venues—at a church fair, at a women's club meeting, and at a "gigantic public meeting" of the American Colored League (Hopkins 421). Mrs. Smith's ties to the community connect her to various social events where the affairs of the African American community are discussed and debated. For instance, in her capacity as chairman of her church's "board of stewardesses," Mrs. Smith "inaugurat[ed] a fair" and held sewing circles and "parlor entertainments" in order to pay off the eight-thousand-dollar balance on the church mortgage (141). One of these sewing events, held in Mrs. Smith's parlor, provides the instance for the novel's third repetition of Emerson's words regarding civility.

As they sew, the women listen to Mrs. Willis, a widow who supports herself by lecturing on "the advancement of the colored woman" (Hopkins 147). On this occasion Mrs. Willis has chosen the topic of the "place which the virtuous woman occupies in upbuilding a race" (148). She urges the women to "refute the charges brought against us as to our moral irresponsibility" (148). Sappho asks Mrs. Willis if she thinks "Negro women" can refute charges of sexual "irresponsibility" (149). Will they, Sappho questions, be held "responsible for the *illegitimacy* with which our race has been obliged, as it were, to flood the world?" (149, emphasis in original). Sappho's question speaks directly to the late nineteenth-century discourse that situated African American women as unchaste and hypersexual. As Brown notes in her discussion of the novel, "[M]yriad problematic and racially intolerant nineteenth-century anthropological reports about the supposed lack, not abundance, of chastity and sexual interest in African women" persisted at the turn of the century, despite the end of American slavery and its often-accompanying system of concubinage (Brown 205). By this point in the novel, readers know Sappho's history as a rape victim and as the mother of a child born out of that rape, though Mrs. Willis remains unaware on both counts. In her answer to Sappho, Mrs. Willis soundly refutes the idea of African American women's inherent "moral irresponsibility," arguing, "[W]e shall not be held responsible for wrongs which we have *unconsciously* committed, or which we have committed under *compulsion*" (Hopkins 149, emphasis in original). She charges responsibility for sexual misconduct not to African American women but to their sexual oppressors, citing as support for her argument Emerson's "truism that 'the civility of no race is perfect whilst another is degraded'" (150).

In "The Sewing Circle," Hopkins pushes far beyond mere repetition to revoice Emerson's words through the character of Mrs. Willis, an outspoken African American woman who denounces nineteenth-century society's definition of virtue. With this move, she uses Emerson's words to offer a counternarrative to the often-postulated myth of the sexual misconduct of African American women. Whether Emerson would have endorsed this argument is immaterial, though doubtful. As Anne E. Boyd notes in *Writing for Immortality* (2004), questions about Emerson's support of the woman's movement have existed since the nineteenth century, both before and after his 1855 lecture to the Women's Rights Convention.[5] However, as she concludes, women writers tailored their view of Emerson's ideals to suit their own purposes: "Certainly, Emerson's thinking about women's rights is important to any discussion of his influence on women writers, but if we take our cues from the writers themselves, we see little concern with Emerson's position on the issue" (20). In "Publishing the Cause of Suffrage," Todd H. Richardson concludes much the same thing in his examination of how the *Woman's Journal* read Emerson as more supportive of woman suffrage than he actually was: "Eager to win converts and to increase the cultural legitimacy of their campaign, the suffragists pressed the Concord Sage into service. But . . . the icon they fashioned was refracted through their own progressive reform agenda" (580). Just as the journal identified Emerson as a suffragist, Hopkins employed him as a spokesman on behalf of African American women charged with a lack of virtue for acts "committed under *compulsion*" (149, emphasis in original). By using Emerson's words as the "truism" that establishes that Black women are not responsible for forced sexual relationships with white men, Hopkins effectively joined an established tradition of effective misrepresentations to rewrite contemporary social constructions that say otherwise.

In her role as cultural stenographer, Hopkins goes far beyond simply promoting a white authorial presence in her novel with her thrice-repeated incorporation of Emerson's words regarding civility. She calls on Emerson to rebuke the attenuating humanitarian efforts on the part of white activists and challenges her late nineteenth-century readers to agitate just as fiercely for social, political, and economic justice as the midcentury abolitionists. Finally, she recontextualizes Emerson's words about civility to resist dominant social mores concerning Black female sexuality. By reshaping the circumstances in which we read the words Emerson spoke against slavery to argue, instead, for social equality and full citizenship, Hopkins resists the "contending forces" that threaten to trap African Americans in an oppressive social system. Moreover, she makes a bold move when she recontextualizes Emerson's words about the evils of slavery to intervene in conversations regarding miscegenation resulting from the rape of African American women. She has assumed the mantle of Emersonian idealism, leaving her intellectual and conscientious readers no choice but to act with "civility"—to conduct themselves in such a way as to propel the Black race and, with them, the country to their highest potential.

If Hopkins explored the role of cultural stenographer in *Contending Forces*, she perfected it during her editorship at the *Colored American Magazine*, where she worked on a larger scale, writing under her own name as well as pseudonyms (Sarah A. Allen and J. Shirley Shadrach) to conceal just how much her voice informed the periodical.[6] As editor, she continued her practice of literary borrowing, treating editing and authorship much like stenography inasmuch as it meant taking the words of others and turning them into texts arguing for social justice. Between 1900 and 1904 Hopkins published prodigiously. Her work on behalf of Black Americans led R. S. Elliott, a white supporter of the *Colored American Magazine*, to call for "a few more Pauline Hopkins to help forward the brighter and better day for the race" (47). Working for herself and on behalf of her race, she dedicated herself to collating, combining, and editing existing sources, creating new frameworks and suggesting new interpretations. Ultimately, her reprisal of the past demonstrates that African Americans are both consumers and creators of American culture.

Yet despite her success at the magazine, Hopkins was "forced to resign" after Booker T. Washington orchestrated a hostile takeover.[7] She slowly slipped from public view after the failure of the *New Era*, a short-lived periodical that she cofounded with Walter Wallace after leaving the *Colored American Magazine*. As Brown documents, after 1916 "Hopkins began to live a version of the itinerant life she had created for Sappho Clark" (527). Hopkins lived in rented rooms, again turning to stenography, but only as a means of making a living. By the time of her tragic death in 1930 from burns suffered in a fire she accidentally caused, her role as cultural stenographer had been lost. It would be more than fifty years before she was rediscovered in the twentieth century.

Ever since the full-scale recovery of Hopkins began in the 1980s, scholars have been trying to define her place in late nineteenth-century American literature. While Hopkins filled many roles—dramatist, actress, novelist, editor, historian, biographer, and critic—only the term "cultural stenographer" seems inclusive enough to adequately describe her. Within the pages of *Contending Forces*, her transcription of late nineteenth-century American culture still stands, though like her fictional counterpart Sappho, Hopkins ultimately found herself shut out from "full participation" in the rich cultural association she had imagined within the pages of her novel.

NOTES

1. As Keep documents, speed was a major factor in stenography's appeal. Keep notes that stenographers "could take two hundred words a minute from dictation" (153).

2. The percentages come from the census, which enumerates 2,471,418 white citizens and 26,540 Black citizens (vol. 1, p. 864).

3. Hopkins's novel predates both *Souls* and "Of the Training of Black Men," the chapter from which this quotation is taken, which appeared in the *Atlantic Monthly*, vol. 90, Sept. 1902, pp. 289–97. See Lewis 278, 642n31.

4. In his "Address on the Emancipation," Emerson encloses these words in quotation marks, referencing Lord Mansfield, a.k.a. William Murray (1705–93), and his decision in the case of George Somerset, a slave whose master had him transported to Jamaica to be sold. Mansfield, who served as lord chief justice on the King's Bench of Great Britain from 1756 to 1788, ruled that slave owners could not forcibly remove their slaves from England, a decision that—contrary to popular opinion—did not end slavery on British soil.

5. Despite his speech to the convention, Emerson's commitment to the cause remains a matter of debate. According to Richardson, Len Gougeon and other scholars argue that Emerson was "engaged in the cause of woman suffrage," while Phillis Cole and others maintain that "Emerson remained aloof and ethereal on the 'woman question'" (579).

6. Brown suggests that Hopkins may have also written as Gardner Goldsby and J. I. Morehead. Brown posits that the work of Goldsby (known to be a pen name) and Morehead closely resembles Hopkins's in style and content (469–70, 513).

7. Hopkins to W. M. Trotter, 16 Apr. 1905, reprinted in Brown 546–54, 552. According to Du Bois, Hopkins was asked to resign because "her attitude was not conciliatory

enough." See [W. E. B. Du Bois], "The Colored Magazine in America," *Crisis*, vol. 5, Nov. 1912, pp. 33. For an alternate explanation of Hopkins's resignation, see Bergman.

WORKS CITED

Ammons, Elizabeth. *Conflicting Stories: American Women Writers at the Turn into the Twentieth Century*. Oxford University Press, 1992.

Andrews, Alfred. "Shorthand, Stenography, Phonography." *Phrenological Journal and Science of Health (1870–1911)*, vol. 88, no. 2, 1888, pp. 67–69. *ProQuest*, https://www -proquest-com.proxy.ohiolink.edu:9100/scholarly-journals/shorthand-stenography -phonography/docview/137895219/se-2?accountid=12953.

Bergman, Jill. "'Everything We Hoped She'd Be': Contending Forces in Hopkins Scholarship." *African American Review*, vol. 38, no. 2, 2004, pp. 181–99, https://doi.org /10.2307/1512285.

Boyd, Anne E. *Writing for Immortality: Women Writers and the Emergence of High Literary Culture in America*. Johns Hopkins University Press, 2004.

Brown, Lois. *Pauline Elizabeth Hopkins: Black Daughter of the Revolution*. University of North Carolina Press, 2008.

Carby, Hazel V. *Reconstructing Womanhood: The Emergence of the Afro-American Woman Novelist*. Oxford University Press, 1989.

Census of the Commonwealth of Massachusetts: 1895. Wright & Potter Printing, 1896. *Internet Archive*, 13 Apr. 2012. https://archive.org/details/censusofcommonwe189501 mass/page/n3/mode/2up.

Daniels, John. *In Freedom's Birthplace: A Study of the Boston Negroes*. 1914. Basic Afro--American Reprint Library. Johnson Reprint Corporation, 1968.

Davies, Margery W. *Woman's Place Is at the Typewriter: Office Work and Office Workers 1870–1930*. Temple University Press, 1982.

Du Bois, W. E. B. *The Souls of Black Folk*. 1903. Penguin Books, 1989.

Elliott, R. S. "The Story of Our Magazine." *Colored American Magazine*, vol. 3, no. 1, 1901, pp. 42–77. *Hathi Trust*, 19 Nov. 2011. https://babel.hathitrust.org/cgi/pt?id=uc1 .b3793661&view=1up&seq=53.

Emerson, Ralph Waldo. "An Address on the Emancipation of the Negroes in the British West Indies." 1844. *Emerson's Antislavery Writings*, edited by Len Gougeon and Joel Myerson, Yale University Press, 1995, pp. 7–38.

Ernest, John. *Resistance and Reformation in Nineteenth-Century African-American Literature*. University Press of Mississippi, 1995.

Garvey, Ellen Gruber. *Writing with Scissors: American Scrapbooks from the Civil War to the Harlem Renaissance*. Oxford University Press, 2013.

Giauque, Gerald S. "Conversational Ability through Stenography." *Modern Language Journal*, vol. 60, no. 7, 1976, pp. 353–56. *JSTOR*, 16 Dec. 2011. http://www.jstor.org /stable/324411.

Gitelman, Lisa. *Scripts, Grooves, and Writing Machines: Representing Technology in the Edison Era*. Stanford University Press, 1999.

Gougeon, Len. "Historical Background." *Emerson's Antislavery Writings*, edited by Len Gougeon and Joel Myerson, Yale University Press, 1995, pp. xi–lvi.

Hopkins, Pauline E. *Contending Forces: A Romance Illustrative of Negro Life North and South.* 1900. Schomburg Library of Nineteenth-Century Black Women Writers, edited by Henry Louis Gates Jr., Oxford University Press, 1988.

Keep, Christopher. "Blinded by the Type: Gender and Information Technology at the Turn of the Century." *Nineteenth-Century Contexts*, vol. 23, no. 1, June 2001, p. 149. EBSCOhost, https://doi.org/10.1080/08905490108583536.

Kilduff, Edward Jones. *The Private Secretary: The Duties and Opportunities of His Position.* Century, 1924.

Knight, Alisha R. *Pauline Hopkins and the American Dream: An African American Writer's (Re)Visionary Gospel of Success.* University of Tennessee Press, 2012.

Lewis, David Levering. *W. E. B. Du Bois: Biography of a Race, 1868–1919.* Henry Holt, 1993.

"Pauline E. Hopkins, Author of 'Contending Forces,' 'Talma Gordon,' 'General Washington,' etc." *Colored American Magazine*, vol. 2, no. 3, Jan. 1901, p. 218. *Hathi Trust*, 19 Nov. 2011. https://babel.hathitrust.org/cgi/pt?id=uc1.31970005429730&view=1up &seq=574&skin=2021&q1=talma%20gordon.

Pavletich, JoAnn. "'. . . We Are Going to Take That Right': Power and Plagiarism in Pauline Hopkins's *Winona*." *CLA Journal*, vol. 59, no. 2, Dec. 2015, pp. 115–30. *EBSCOhost*, lorainccc.ohionet.org/login?url=http://search.ebscohost.com/login.aspx ?direct=true&db=brb&AN=119466764&site=eds-live.

"Prospectus." *Colored American Magazine*, vol. 1, no. 4, Sept. 1900, p. 195. *Hathi Trust*. https://babel.hathitrust.org/cgi/pt?id=uc1.b3793660&view=1up&seq=207&skin=2021 &q1=prospectus.

Richardson, Todd H. "Publishing the Cause of Suffrage: The *Woman's Journal*'s Appropriation of Ralph Waldo Emerson in Postbellum America." *New England Quarterly*, vol. 79, no. 4, 2006, pp. 578–608.

Sanborn, Geoffrey. *Plagiarama! William Wells Brown and the Aesthetic of Attractions.* Columbia University Press, 2016.

"Some Tendencies of Contemporary Fiction." *Living Age*, 2 Dec. 1899, pp. 587–90. https://s9100-search-proquest-com-proxy-ohiolink-edu.lorainccc.ohionet.org/docview /90179248?accountid=12953.

Srole, Carole. "'A Blessing to Mankind, and Especially to Womankind': The Typewriter and the Feminization of Clerical Work, Boston, 1860–1920." *Women, Work, and Technology*, edited by Barbara Drygulski Wright et al., University of Michigan Press, 1987, pp. 84–100.

Wilson, Ivy G. *Specters of Democracy: Blackness and the Aesthetics of Politics in the Antebellum U.S.* Oxford University Press, 2011.

"It's This Cursed Slavery That's to Blame"

NINETEENTH-CENTURY DISCOURSE
ON SLAVERY AND PAULINE HOPKINS'S
HISTORIOGRAPHIC COUNTERNARRATIVES

Sabine Isabell Engwer

"The old virus of slavery . . . still exists," Pauline Hopkins wrote in the *Colored American Magazine* in 1901, "in spite of . . . [the Negro's] plea thrown to the white citizen: 'The people of this country are all alike. They are all Americans'" (Hopkins, "Robert Brown Elliott" 46). The latter part of the author's statement acknowledges the unfulfilled promise that lay dormant in the Thirteenth through Fifteenth Amendments to the Constitution. Their ratifications had—at least briefly—allowed people of color the hope that in the United States, all men were indeed created equal. Despite the fact that prejudice and southern Jim Crow laws created harsh and precarious living conditions for people of color in post-Reconstruction America, the amendments presented textual anchors that were ready to be invoked, cited, and appealed to in a fight for full citizenship and equality, as Hopkins does in these lines. It is the first part of Hopkins's lament, however, that emphasizes the fact that these letters of law were not the only texts contributing to the discursive universe that addressed slavery. The passage points the reader to a central concern and recurring theme in her work. In public discourse, the "old virus of slavery"—in spite of its legal abolishment—not only "still exist[ed]" but was positively thriving. White supremacist voices promoted a revisionism that categorically denied an acknowledgment of slavery's horrors, replacing them instead with nostalgia for the "Old South." This glorification of plantation life was harmful to the Black community, as it went hand in hand with claims of "Black degeneracy" and a worsening of race relations after emancipation. Its implications were that racial harmony could only be achieved by reinstating firm racial hierarchies and curtailing Black rights. American discourse on slavery—particularly in its literary representations—was thus simultaneously anchored in a glorified past and attuned to a postbellum present.

Hopkins was well aware that the literary was very much the political in post-Reconstruction America and countered the dominating revisionist accounts of the "peculiar institution" in her own writings. By examining Hopkins's portrayal of slavery in her journalistic writings and her novels, I intend to reveal the strategies she pursued in responding to dominant discourse on the American antebellum past. I propose that Hopkins shores up portrayals of Black suffering under slavery against a romanticizing revisionism and that her novels show a continuity where a culturally dominant nostalgia implied a rupture with an unattainable antebellum past. In discussing the linkage she achieves between present and past, I argue that Hopkins's narrative strategies, as well as her intertextual practice, were means of gaining access to a discourse that deemed America's slavery past untouchable and that categorically excluded Black voices. I focus on ways in which Hopkins's novels counter the arguments and conventions of plantation literature, which had been a prime site for the American discourse on race throughout the nineteenth century and a successful and highly popular vehicle for proslavery ideology. I will show that Hopkins's use of intertextuality in *Contending Forces* likewise facilitated a critical engagement with American discourse on slavery—affirming some texts while undermining others—by "presentifying" them, that is, forcing them into dialogue with her own text.[1] Remarkably, some of her borrowings stemmed from a group of texts whose ideology Hopkins so fervently contested: the plantation genre.

Characteristics of a Genre

A tradition of literature on the plantation goes back to earlier decades of the nineteenth century, John Pendleton Kennedy's *Swallow Barn* (1832) being considered the founding text of the genre (Jordan-Lake 1; Cowan 68; Gaines 18). From its inception, the plantation genre was a site for the ideological dispute between slavery's opponents and its apologists. Rising and falling in popularity with the intensity of the conflict between North and South, the genre was popular during the years leading up to the Civil War and would soar again, this time even dominating the national literary landscape (Hale 51; Gaines 73) at the pinnacle of Hopkins's literary activity, when conflicts between Black and white reached new heights during the American Nadir.

The genre typically presented the plantation as a place populated by sim-
pleminded, happy slaves with ample leisure and their benevolent masters, who
felt deeply for their slaves and thought of them as children in need of a strong,
guiding hand (Wells 3; Hale 51). Likewise, slaves were portrayed as deeply loyal
to the plantation owners. African American poet and literary critic Sterling
Brown, in one of the early critical discussions of the plantation tradition, sum-
marized its characteristics as follows: "[T]he grown-up slaves were contented,
the pickaninnies were frolicking . . . , God was in heaven, and all was right in
the world" (18).

Postbellum plantation literature differed in some aspects from its antebellum origins.[2] For one, it looked back on the plantation as a place that no longer
was and perceived of it as part of a self-contained past, denying the many connections and continuities between the two eras—a stance that, as I will show,
Hopkins countered in all of her novels. In those postbellum texts that included
plotlines playing out after the war, former slaves mourned the loss of this unattainable past or the passing of former masters and yearned to be back "home"
on the plantation (Wells 3). Fugitive slaves, if they appeared at all, did not find
happiness in their freedom, eventually "steal[ing] back to the South" (Brown
28). According to southern social conventions, miscegenation, which was freely
practiced but never addressed, remained conspicuously absent from these writings (28). In the hands of white authors, the common denominator remained a
deep-seated desire to gain interpretative authority over the experience of slavery for Blacks and whites alike. At the height of Hopkins's literary production,
America's romance with its slavery past was as powerful as ever. At the end of a
century that had seen bitter discord between North and South and the near destruction of the Union over the very issue of slavery, the plantation genre had
successfully moved from the margins to the national mainstream.[3] Once representative of merely one side in the argument over slavery, it was now a cultural
unifier, dominating American popular culture.[4]

These national narratives overwrote historical and historiographical accounts of slavery. They were bound by fewer limits because the number of firsthand witnesses of the antebellum plantation was ever shrinking. The way the
genre discursively engaged with America's slavery past can be aptly described as
an act of "pastification," a term that I take from Aleida Assmann's work on cultural memory and that she, in turn, borrows from systemic therapy.[5] Pastification is a cultural strategy that presents the past, or a period of it, as something
that is closed off and therefore "exempt from inspection and scrutiny" (Assmann 3, all translations mine). "Whatever is transferred to this realm is deemed

untouchable and sacrosanct" (3). Dominant post-Reconstruction discourse on slavery, as exemplified by the plantation genre, pastified the plantation because it presented it in terms of an idyllic and self-contained past—a racially harmonious space irretrievably lost to those living in a postbellum world and, therefore, "untouchable." Aided by the writings of the plantation tradition, this revisionism effectively silenced the historical truth of slavery as a cruel, inhumane system. It categorically excluded people of color from discursive participation, thus preventing a broad engagement with alternative accounts and the trauma of slavery while further harming the African American community through the promotion of a racist ideology that inflicted new communal trauma in Hopkins's post-Reconstruction present.

Plantation literature is often described in terms of simple nostalgia; however, it far surpassed a romanticized longing for what once had been, or rather was thought to have been, and was now irretrievably gone: it actively challenged the postemancipatory status of Black individuals in America. The texts' ideological power lay in the comparisons they evoked between their fantasies of an antebellum past and a purportedly dire present, on the one hand, and North and South, on the other. The argumentative mechanism of the genre was twofold. First, the idyllic, pastoral depiction of slavery served as justification of the South's past. It retroactively challenged the narrative of the North fighting and winning a just war that liberated a suppressed people.[6] Second, a revisionist account of the past was instrumentalized in order to defend racist policies such as segregation, Jim Crow legislation, and the law's leniency toward racially motivated vigilantism in the present. This enabled the genre, while being narratively dedicated to a closed-off past, the pastified plantation, to engage with the dominant discourse on race that targeted the African American community at the turn of the century. The plantation genre's display of alleged "law and order" and peaceful race relations under slavery meshed with discourses such as Darwinism and eugenics, which promoted myths of Black degeneracy as a direct result of emancipation and claimed that crime and disease were on the rise in the Black community.[7] The assumptions put forth by the genre were particularly damaging, as many white readers thought of this tradition as categorically authentic and as providing them with "unprecedented glimpses . . . into 'negro' thought and culture" (Wells 75). Due to the texts' sprawling influence, even racially progressive readers absorbed the misleading images of African American culture, rife with stereotypes of primitivity, innate musicality, and a wealth of folktales. The dominance of this cultural revisionism constituted a veritable threat to people of color, making their deconstruction a central concern of the authorial projects of Hopkins and other writers of color.

Challenging (Re)Vision

If plantation literature pastified American slavery, that is, presented it as "exempt from . . . scrutiny" (Assmann 3), Hopkins's writings do just the opposite: they closely examine the horrors of the peculiar institution. Hopkins's journalistic work challenges the romanticized image of the "many-headed monster" (Hopkins, "Toussaint L'Ouverture" 12) of slavery through its strong historiographic focus. It holds the North equally historically accountable, reminding readers "of all the horrors of Northern servitude" and calling slavery "a sin of both North and South" (Hopkins, "Sojourner Truth" 124). Countering the plantation tradition's claims of the slaveholders' benevolent paternalism, Hopkins asks: "If the slaveholders ever cared for the crippled, the old, the sick, under slavery, still the question arises: Where was the glory to them in this act?" (Hopkins, "Robert Brown Elliott" 46). Liberty and proper payment, she argues, would have rendered these acts superfluous, freeing their alleged recipients from "the aid of that charity" (46) and elevating them to the status of self-reliant individuals. In writings such as her portrait of Harriet Tubman, published in her Famous Women of the Negro Race series in 1902, Hopkins highlights the precariousness of the Black body under slavery, presenting the marks of physical violence it bears as undeniable proof of the cruelties of slavery, conveniently omitted by writings of the plantation genre. Writing of Tubman, she argues that "[h]er back and shoulders . . . marked by the biting lash . . . bear witness to the inhumanity of the institution from which she fled" (Hopkins, "Harriet Tubman" 134).

In spite of these genuine and straightforward journalistic efforts to shore up a historiography that acknowledges the horrors of slavery against the prevailing literary revisionism, Hopkins had one assumption in common with the plantation genre: she, too, believed that the plantation was the site "where the true romance of American life and customs is to be found" ("John Mercer Langston" 77). Hopkins, however, saw "the romance of American history" best realized in "the fate of the Negro . . . , in the thrilling incidents and escapes and sufferings of the fugitives" ("Charles Winter Wood" 261). Knowing full well that the traditional plantation romance allowed no room for alternative accounts of slavery and counterhegemonic depictions of people of color, Hopkins called upon the African American community to *"faithfully portray the inmost thoughts and feelings of the Negro with all the fire and romance which lie dormant in our history"* because *"[n]o one will do this for us"* (*Contending Forces* 14, emphasis in original).

In her novels, Hopkins rejects both the glorification of a southern aristocracy and the denial of its system of bondage and exploitation. She hails heroes and heroines who have suffered at the hands of whites but have taken matters into their own hands to become the central agents of their own liberation; it is the former slave who has risen above this suppression, not the slaveholder who has caused such suffering, that she places at the core of her narratives. Here, Hopkins locates the literary material for a "future Walter Scott of America" ("Charles Winter Wood" 262), placing herself firmly in the literary tradition of the historical romance novel. From this setting "will come the freshest laurels of American literature" (262), a bold suggestion in a debate, still very much occupying her contemporaries, over what was to be the essence of a national literature. To stipulate that it be African Americans and a portrayal of their trials and tribulations entailed moving people of color from the margins to the literary center; in promoting the "other" side of the plantation narrative, Hopkins makes an audacious call for a straightforward engagement with the traumatic and shameful aspects of America's race relations. It is thus in her novels that Hopkins counters the plantation tradition's revisionism most effectively and in like form: the historical romance genre.

Tales of Continuity

It is also here that Hopkins's strategy of countering the pastifying tendencies of plantation literature comes to full fruition. Hopkins challenges the romanticization of the plantation in all of her novels; with storylines at least partially set in antebellum times, she presents her readers with alternative accounts of slavery. She counters the effects of the cultural dominance of revisionist discourses of the past by creating works of both fiction and historiography that mediate "incidents . . . [that] actually occurred," as Hopkins proclaims in *Contending Forces* (14). Where Hopkins's journalistic writings examine and highlight the horrors of slavery, her novels likewise depict Black suffering under slavery. They also, however, effectively attack another ideological pillar of the genre: by demonstrating a historical and causal continuity where plantation literature implies a rupture—with the plantation portrayed as a pastoral site of alleged racial harmony forever lost to those living in a purportedly dismal present—the author proves the causal ties between slavery past and post-Reconstruction present and thus presentifies this seemingly untouchable period of the American past.

Hopkins's novels achieve this in part due to their narrative structure: they tend to consist of a dual plot, with one part set before the war and the other after emancipation. The texts trail a family's history, with one generation dominating the antebellum plot and the following one the postbellum action, enabling Hopkins to not only convincingly demonstrate the horrors of slavery but also show how these reverberated in the African American experience in her turn-of-the-century present. The effect can be aptly described as one of presentification. Whereas dominant discourse on the peculiar institution in Hopkins's time pastified slavery, that is, relegated it to the realm of the untouchable by elevating the plantation to an ideal, Hopkins, through her demonstration of a historical continuum with strong causal ties between antebellum and postbellum times, breaks open the rigid culturally authorized boundaries between present and past.[8] This narrative transference of an earlier traumatic event, the experience of slavery, into the present makes it discursively accessible: thus, in the act of presentification, change can be "therapeutically induced" (Assmann 3), and future healing is made possible. As I will demonstrate through close examination of Hopkins's novels, the texts intervene in the dominating revisionist and pastifying discourse and narratively presentify America's antebellum past by illustrating slavery's lasting effects on a post-Reconstruction present. They thus achieve said "therapeutically induced change" (3)—a change that, through the nineteenth-century conjunction of literature and politics, was intended to move beyond intracommunal healing and mere discursive deviation to affect the political reality of Hopkins's Black readership.

Hagar's Daughter, Hopkins's first serialized novel, follows such a dual plot formula. The first section of its two-tiered plot is set in the antebellum South, where Hagar Enson, the mistress of a plantation, faces the loss of her property, status, and freedom, becoming a slave on her own plantation when her mixed-race identity is revealed. In the second section of the text, the "accursed system of slavery" (Hopkins, *Hagar's Daughter* 238) still claims victims in a postslavery society: young heiress Jewel Bowen, who is revealed to be Hagar's daughter and thus racially mixed herself, is, like her mother before her, confronted with her own prejudices (281) and simultaneously a white audience with their racism and the unsettling observation that "black blood is everywhere . . . [even in] the most exclusive families" (160). Racial identity is shown as a highly unstable category, unreliable even to the characters themselves. The ramifications of this instability are all the more profound, as the narrative revolves around the planter aristocracy, so fervently idolized by plantation literature in its pastifying efforts. It consequently also subverts one of the genre's narrative strategies: the promotion of racist claims of a dichotomy between Black and white that places supposedly noble, virtuous, and attractive white slaveholders in juxtaposition to depictions of Black slaves often caricatured as grotesque-looking, animalistic, and overall physically and mentally inferior (Boeckmann 52). It is also the planter aristocracy that the novel's central villain, St. Clair Enson, hails from, further aiding Hopkins's narrative intervention. In the character of Isaac Johnson, however, the loyal servant of the text's primary villain, Hopkins follows the logic of the plantation genre to the extreme: a "faithful servant and ex-slave," he is unwavering "in his devotion to his employer's interests" (*Hagar's Daughter* 263). Isaac is trapped in the behavioral patterns of his slave past, and, "knowing no law save the will of his former owner" (263), his story is a cautionary tale of the effects of the idealization of the peculiar institution. Isaac's blind loyalty makes him an accomplice to numerous crimes—from perjury, to abduction, to murder—eventually landing him in jail in his master's stead. Hopkins stakes the laws of the country, which forbid all of these crimes, against the "laws" that Isaac knows and that have been instilled in him through the system of slavery, making the stereotype of the loyal slave, hailed by plantation literature, fundamentally irreconcilable with American values and laws. Thus, here too the repercussions of slavery carry on into a post-Reconstruction present.

Hopkins's *Winona* follows the novel's eponymous racially mixed heroine from an idyllic childhood in a racially diverse community in Buffalo into slavery after her abduction by the former owner of her mother and his overseer.[9] Here Hopkins reverses the plantation tradition's conventions by contrasting the interracial harmony of Winona's free upbringing in an Indigenous environment with the cruelties she and her adopted brother, Judah, experience under slavery on the southern plantation. Hopkins employs the theme of active resistance against slavery and fulfills her didactic objectives by familiarizing her readers with an alternative historiography of slavery that includes armed resistance. Although the entirety of the action in *Winona* takes place before emancipation, Hopkins once again demonstrates continuity in the form of slavery's impact beyond enslavement by tracing her protagonists' development before, during, and after captivity and establishing how profoundly the experience of slavery still affects them in freedom. Thus, Judah exclaims that he feels "sorry" for them all, even after their flight from the plantation, explaining, "It's this cursed slavery that's to blame" (Hopkins, *Winona* 378).

Even *Of One Blood*, Hopkins's last completed novel, whose plot is entirely set in an unspecified post-Reconstruction present and contains a plethora of phantasmagoric elements, includes critically important components that reference a slavery past and the looming shadow it casts on the present, thus presentifying the traumatic African American experience of enslavement.[10] The specter of slavery appears in the form of a spirit, Mira, who is always silent but reveals her secrets in writing and stands as testament to Hopkins's convictions of the singular power of the pen in effecting change. She is, as the reader learns in the closing chapters of the novel, the mother of Dianthe, Reuel, and Aubrey, making the central characters of the narrative literally "of one blood." Mira represents the archetypical female slave, who had no choice but to tolerate her master's sexual advances, resulting in the birth of the novel's main protagonists. In Mira's story, Hopkins counters the plantation genre's categorical omission of miscegenation in its depiction of life on the plantation (Brown 28): similarly to *Hagar's Daughter*, tragedy unfolds only because none of the siblings are aware of their true origins—a circumstance entirely owed to the historical denial of this nonconsensual practice in the antebellum South, which was mirrored in dominant discourse. A central concern of Hopkins is the precarious status of Black women under slavery and beyond, the "years of foulest wrongs heaped upon the innocent and defenseless women of a race" (*Of One Blood* 594). History repeats itself in the three generations of Black women featured in the novel, underscoring the presentifying continuity Hopkins seeks to establish in her work: Aunt Hannah's sexual abuse by her master is followed by her daughter's through her master and eventually by Dianthe's suffering at the hands of her "white" brother, Aubrey. Hopkins's literary endeavor to rectify plantation literature's harmful revisionism focuses on the Black woman, who continues to be vulnerable to sexual abuse in a postbellum world. What follows from her precarious status is a fractured Black family, as exemplified by the three siblings and by Hannah's and Mira's separation from their children, respectively. Hopkins's assault on a plantation revisionism is all the more effective, as Aubrey, the character most representative of a planter aristocracy, is also the novel's central villain, thus embodying the largest threat to white supremacist notions promoted by plantation literature.

It is, however, *Contending Forces* that deserves particular attention and that I want to focus on for the remainder of this essay. In *Contending Forces*, Hopkins's first novel, the author is already invested in examining the causal ties and continuities between post-Reconstruction present and slavery past. Following a dual plot structure, the novel takes the reader from an antebellum past to a postbellum present where slavery's shadow still looms, threatening the future of the lovers, Sappho Clark and Will Smith. In this novel, as in her later work, it is the precarious status of women under slavery and beyond that the author illuminates. Much like *Hagar's Daughter*, the novel begins with a slave-owning family who, through the evil scheming of one of the novel's villains, is relegated into slavery on their own plantation. The owner, Charles Montfort, is murdered; his wife, Grace, who is both physically and sexually assaulted, is driven to suicide.[11] The second part of the narrative is likewise invested in highlighting the precariousness of Black women's bodies and lives. Through Sappho, the second plot's heroine, not only does history repeat itself, but Hopkins once again shows its continuity: the racist ideology that sustained slavery still perseveres in post-Reconstruction America and conceives of women of color as sexualized objects, excluding them from the Victorian ideal of true womanhood, pervasive in U.S. culture at the time.[12] Continuous is also its circular logic: because women of color, it was argued, had been victims of sexual abuse, they must be licentious, and because they are licentious, it is justifiable to continue to sexually abuse them. Thus, transgressions against them in the American past justified those in the present and future. This twisted logic entitles Sappho's white uncle, who is the white half-brother of her Black father, to abuse her, leave her in a brothel, and then, when confronted with his crime, boldly ask: "[W]hat does a woman of mixed blood, or any Negress, for that matter, know of virtue?" (Hopkins, *Contending Forces* 261). Further proof of slavery's enduring ideological existence is delivered by the uncle's offer "to pay" Sappho's father for the young woman (260) as retribution for his crimes, representative of a larger and lasting cultural perception of women of color as property. Sappho is brought to a convent, where she eventually delivers a child who is raised as a foundling by her aunt, while Sappho—whose original name was Mabelle Beaubean—assumes a new name and identity. It is this child, material proof of her abuse, that years later makes the heroine vulnerable to the intimidations of John Langley, the central villain of the second plot and a distant relative of the planter class who tries to force her into a sexual liaison with him by threatening to divulge her secret and inform her fiancé, Will. Sappho, fearing that the "[d]isgrace" (329) connected with her secret would hurt Will's reputation, decides to flee from Boston and return to the convent in New Orleans. Hopkins, however, exonerates her heroine and other Black victims of similar crimes by proxy. "We are virtuous or non-virtuous only when we have a *choice* under temptation" (149, emphasis in original), she has Mrs. Willis, a prominent clubwoman and community leader, explain to Sappho. The observation that choice is an integral element of culpability refutes white supremacist notions of an alleged inherent licentiousness as justification for the sexual abuse of Black women. While this momentous message is delivered toward the middle of the narrative, the reader has to hold out hope for Sappho until the end, where Hopkins reunites Sappho with her lover, who respects the heroine while fully aware of the secrets of her past.

The raw portrayal of the crime perpetrated against Sappho presented a post--Reconstruction audience with a counterhegemonic depiction of interracial gender relations, reversing the claim, prominent in public discourse at the time, that it was white women who had to fear sexual violence from Black perpetrators.[13] Much like *Of One Blood* and *Hagar's Daughter*, *Contending Forces* realizes Hopkins's intersectional agenda by highlighting the twofold discrimination Black women experienced due to both their gender and the color of their skin. Sappho's eventual ability to move beyond the status of victimhood and achieve romantic and societal acceptance—Will marries her and adopts her child—is notably in keeping with Hopkins's call for a literature that depicts African American suffering and Black self-empowered liberation in order to reap "the freshest laurels of American literature" ("Charles Winter Wood" 262) while still conforming to established romantic conventions put forth by genres such as the plantation novel.

Borrowed Affirmations

In *Contending Forces*, not only are the culturally endorsed revisionism and glorification of the plantation that dominated turn-of-the-century discourse on slavery challenged on the plot level, but Hopkins's use of intertextuality underscores her narrative argument of exposing the evils and cruelties of the peculiar institution and, as I will show, ultimately also follows a strategy of presentification, one geared toward a cultural kind of healing by achieving access to discourses that otherwise excluded the voices of people of color.

The publication form of this text, fundamentally different from her other novels, appears to have played a role in her choice and thus warrants closer observation. *Contending Forces* remained the only novel published in book form during her lifetime. Here, unlike with any of her other novels, Hopkins was free from the pressures and conventions that the serial format entailed. Serialized novels had to work toward memorability within each published segment, having to provide their readers with a quick succession of narrative climaxes and cliff-hangers. In *Contending Forces*, however, the author was able to rely on the unity of the text: readers would likely consume this novel within a short time frame, be more aware of details, and therefore be able to situate them within the overarching theme of the novel. Hopkins made use of this circumstance by frequently incorporating intertextual elements in a very straightforward manner, prominently placed and thus calling attention to their intertextual character, much more so than in her other novels. Each chapter of the novel opens with a quote. Some of these passages specify their authors, while others appear anonymously. The entire novel is also preceded by an epigraph, which is repeated twice more throughout the narrative.

This epigraph, Emerson's observation that "the civility of no race can be perfect whilst another race is degraded," already situates us within the context of American abolitionism. Taken from Emerson's address "Emancipation in the British West Indies" (856) and delivered in Concord in 1854 on the ten-year anniversary of the abolition of slavery in the British colony, it stresses the universality of freedom, which it calls the message of "the voice of the universe" (857). The subject matter is both relevant to the novel's slavery beginnings and Sappho's figurative bondage, caused by the stronghold of the past on her current life. In keeping with the logic of the novel and mirroring its argument, Emerson's words reflect that both Blacks and whites are negatively affected by the wrongs of slavery and that the degradation effected through this system, as well as through its enduring racist ideology, must fall back on the perpetrators, not the victims. Fittingly, Emerson's line reappears in the text when Hopkins gives an overview of the historical events prefiguring the abolition of slavery in the British colonies. Hopkins employs Emerson's lines once more; in the second part of the two-tiered plot, they provide an intertextual reinforcement of Hopkins's argument for a causal and structural continuity between slavery past and postbellum present. Mrs. Willis presents the quote at a pivotal moment in the text: while discussing the significance of choice regarding Black female virtue and personal guilt, she unknowingly corroborates Sappho's innocence by placing blame with white perpetrators, who, "*consciously* false to . . . [their] *knowledge* of right" (150, emphasis in original), commit a crime, thus degrading society at large, as Emerson's lines imply.[14]

Hopkins stays within the context of abolitionism with much of the other instances of intertextuality in *Contending Forces*, opening a dialogue between the abolitionist epigraphs and their source texts and the content of the chapters that follow them. Intertextual quotes thematizing freedom and slavery appear in the first part of the plot, which addresses antebellum times and the fate of the Montforts, thus refuting revisionist portrayals of slavery as a system beneficial to Blacks and whites alike. Intertextual borrowings then move to the theme of romantic love, mirroring the developments of Sappho and Will's romance, only to return to the prior theme in chapters 13 through 15, which discuss slavery's ideological legacy in the form of sexual violence toward women of color and lynchings. Intertextual quotations are frequently slightly altered by Hopkins. These minor variations, often merely omissions or changes in punctuation, give credence to the theory that Hopkins may have simply quoted some sources from memory.

The first chapter of the novel opens with lines from John Greenleaf Whittier's "Ein feste Burg ist unser Gott," published in the poet's *"In War Time" and Other Poems* (1864).[15] The poem's entire first stanza introduces the chapter. It reads:

> We wait beneath the furnace-blast
> The pangs of transformation;
> Not painlessly doth God recast and mould anew the nation.
> Hot burns the fire
> Where wrongs expire;
> Nor spares the hand
> That from the land
> Uproots the ancient evil. (17)

The chapter that follows provides the reader with an overview of the historical events preceding the abolition of slavery in the British West Indies, leading Charles Montfort to move his slaves and family to the American South, where tragedy awaits them. Whittier's lines frame the Montforts' fate as part and parcel of the "pangs of transformation" that come with the elimination of "the ancient evil" of slavery. It is, after all, Montfort's plan to free his slaves that leads to his murder and the enslavement of his family. The rest of the narrative, however, sees "wrongs [indeed] expire" and preconceptions transformed: Sappho will be happily reunited with her lover, who, by accepting her fully aware of her abuse, places blame solely with the perpetrator, thus reestablishing a defaced womanhood, the initial violation of which was Grace Montfort's abuse in the beginning of the novel. Poetic justice is served when John Langley, the central villain of the second plot, freezes to death, the last surviving member of an expedition to the "Klondike gold-fields" (Hopkins, *Contending Forces* 398), at last receiving punishment for his greed and lack of morals and those of his great-grandfather. The intertextual quote can accordingly be also read as commentary on the entire plot that follows.

Hopkins returns to Whittier repeatedly, introducing four of the novel's chapters by lines penned by the abolitionist poet. Among others, she cites from his "Stanzas for the Times" and "Lines, Written on Reading the Spirited and

Manly Remarks of Gov. Ritner, of Pennsylvania, in His Message of 1836, on the Subject of Slavery" (sometimes abbreviated as "Ritner"), both included in Whittier's collection of antislavery poems, *Voices of Freedom* (1846). "Ritner" was written in commemoration of a speech given by the governor "denouncing the demands and the threats from the South in its promotions of slavery" (Rogal 151). The poem's quoted lines, which praise Ritner for his brave independence in making his argument (Hopkins, *Contending Forces* 263), are mirrored in the chapter that follows it, "Will Smith's Defense of His Race" (263–73), which sees Will likewise dismiss opportunism and address inconvenient truths. In a speech given at a meeting of the American Colored League, Will speaks out against southern claims of the "crime of rape" (269) being perpetrated by Black men against white women—a circumstance he identifies as the "Irony of ironies" (271) by pointing to the *"men who created the mulatto race . . . by the very means which they invoked lynch law to suppress"* (271, emphasis in original). Will further makes a bold and unambiguous call for equality, full rights of citizenship, and broad access to higher education and positions himself in direct opposition to the accommodationist propositions of several previous speakers.

Chapter 2 of *Contending Forces* opens with lines from William Cullen Bryant's "The Antiquity of Freedom" (1842), a poem that Hopkins employs to establish freedom as an ancient and universal principle. The excerpt she chooses ends with the observation that "Thy [freedom's] birthright was not given by human hands: / Thou wert twinborn with man" (Hopkins, *Contending Forces* 32), establishing at once that freedom cannot be legitimately granted or taken by others, it is not a privilege that needs to be earned, and it cannot be achieved by membership in an allegedly "superior" race; instead, it is a feature of human nature itself. Hopkins's logic also argues that the infringement upon others' freedom—as happens repeatedly in the plot of the novel, which is representative on a macrocosmic level of like wrongs perpetrated in the interracial history of the United States as sanctioned by dominant racial ideology—cannot be legitimized by custom or societal norms. If an understanding of and desire for freedom is elemental to all humans, then the logic of a historical revisionism that points to the customs of "different times," which this logic portrays as "untouchable and sacrosanct" (Assmann 3), implying, once again, a rupture where Hopkins points to a continuity, must fall short.

English poet William Cowper's work constitutes another intertextual source from the context of antislavery writings. Hopkins opens two chapters with excerpts from *The Time-Piece*, the second volume of his six-volume poem *The Task* (1785).[16] The section that Hopkins cites from in both instances is titled

"Slavery" and is straightforward in addressing and condemning the wrongs of the peculiar institution. The chapter that sees tragedy for the Montforts unfold begins with Cowper's lament that

> [M]an . . . destroys . . . [his brother];
> And worse than all, and most to be deplored
> Chains him, and tasks him and exacts his sweat
> With stripes that Mercy, with a bleeding heart,
> Weeps when she sees inflicted on a beast. (65)

The lines both reference Charles Montfort's murder (i.e., his destruction) and foreshadow the brutal whipping of his wife, Grace, by prefiguring the "stripes" it will leave on her body. They also, however, evoke a previous conversation between Anson Pollock's overseer, Bill Sampson, and his friend Hank Davis, both of whom, along with Pollock, will be instrumental in the crimes that are about to unfold. Davis, as he recounts to his friend, went to prison because he "[s]hot at a free nigger an' killed Brady's dog Pete. Ef it'd been the nigger I'd happened ter kill, hit would 'a' been all right, but bein' 'twas a bluded hound . . . it wuz another question" (Hopkins, *Contending Forces* 38). Their exchange illustrates the truth of Cowper's words and exposes the hypocrisy of a legal system that protects the life of an animal but not that of a fellow human being.

Hopkins's decision to include these borrowings, all hailing from the context of antislavery writings, bears significance not only due to their subject matter. Her intertextual employment of the texts notably enables the author to bring her sources into the present, ensure their endurance, and effectively alter and widen their discursive amplitude by linking them with the specific post-Reconstruction plights of people of color. Hopkins's intertextual practice, however, also allows her to inscribe her own voice in a discourse that, while being invested in instituting and defending a right to freedom for individuals of color, is rather uninterested in acknowledging their voices outside of a narrow path of expression.[17] Thus, intertextuality presents a means to achieve access to an excluding discourse and affirm its purpose while diversifying it through the addition of her own voice. In this respect, Hopkins also presentifies: her texts take up these abolitionist voices—untouchable insofar as they belong to a discourse concluded in the past and rejecting full African American participation—and engage in conversation with them.

Intertextual Discontents

It is worth noting that instances of intertextuality in *Contending Forces* are not all equally accessible to readers of the novel. Some of the borrowings are quasi "buried" in the flow of the texts.[18] Others are plainly exposed, calling attention to themselves and their character as quotations by being placed separately, in most cases as epigraphs preceding the different chapters. Among these, however, is a quantifiable difference: the vast majority of the twenty-two chapter epigraphs are accredited by specification of either title or author, while four appear anonymously. Two of these unaccredited epigraphs stem from the same author, even the same text, the nature of which allows for the assumption that Hopkins's choice in including, yet not crediting, the lines was deliberate.[19] They are taken from William J. Grayson's epic poem "The Hireling and the Slave." This instance of intertextuality, thus far unaddressed by Hopkins scholarship, is profoundly different from other literary borrowings in *Contending Forces*, and the author's choice is a noteworthy one. The lines are easily overlooked for their inconspicuousness, yet their intertextual character is what imparts them with subversive potential and political significance. Grayson's "Hireling and the Slave," first published in the 1850s, is notably a proslavery poem that is highly devoted to romanticizing life on the plantation. It thus falls into the very literary tradition whose assumptions Hopkins was invested in refuting.

Grayson's poem is an anti-Tom text, a direct response to Stowe's famous novel, which had fueled a plethora of literary responses within the tradition of plantation writing. The poem includes several pages on Stowe, describing her as a writer who "with prostituted pen, assails / One half her country in malignant tales" (Grayson 40). Stowe's protagonists, in many ways similar to Hopkins's protagonists, are described by Grayson as "[c]haste quadroon virgins," "[m]ulatto cavaliers," and "[d]emoniac masters" (41), as well as "distorted" and "[c]reatures in fancy, not in nature found" (41), begging the question why Hopkins would choose to include such a text—contrary in so many ways to her own convictions—in a narrative invested in highlighting slavery's horrors and its harmful legacy.[20]

While Grayson's text was popular at the time of its publication, critical interest in his work is almost nonexistent today, a fact likely owed to its openly racist content and agenda and a general lack of formal or aesthetic innovation.[21] It is primarily remembered for coining the term "master-race" (see "Master, n.1 and adj." in the online *Oxford English Dictionary*). The argument Grayson makes in "The Hireling and the Slave" is a predominantly linguistic one, hinging upon

the definition of "slavery," a word that was in fact often avoided by those in favor of slavery, many of whom preferred the vague and seemingly more neutral
"peculiar institution" (Phan 2). In his poem, Grayson makes the claim that the
"state of the hireling and the slave [are] the same substantially . . . [the difference being that] the hireling does not always obtain the reward . . . [namely,]
subsistence" (18).[22] His comparative approach is, of course, based on a logical
fallacy, which Sterling Brown aptly characterizes as follows: "[I]t isn't true that
slavery is a bad system, it is really a fine thing—no worse than the northern
and English system of wage-slavery, which is terrible" (29). Grayson's text was,
nonetheless, well-received, quickly going through three editions (Jarrett 487,
490). Particularly, the idyllic depictions of slave life, in keeping with the conventions of the plantation genre, appear to have been very popular, as Grayson
continued to add to them over the years (Jarrett 490).[23]

It is a section from this setting of his poem that Hopkins chose to intertex-
tually employ in her own commentary on America's race relations and its slavery past. Chapters 10 and 11, "The Fair" and "The Fair.—Concluded," open
with quotations from the same segment of "The Hireling and the Slave" that
describes a supposedly carefree life for slaves on the plantation. The choice of
the excerpt appears to be carefully crafted from the source text: Hopkins omitted several couplets, with the effect that the lines opening chapter 10 bracket
those that open chapter 11 in Grayson's original, further emphasizing the unity
of the chapters Hopkins already indicated through the wording of their respective titles. The consecutive chapters present a climax in the narrative. Chapter 10 depicts the preparations for a fair that is organized by Ma Smith and
other members of her Boston community and geared toward raising money
for their church, an institution that not only houses their religious activities
but also provides a vital locale for Black political activism. Chapter 11 follows
the actual festivities. It is at this fair that the villainous Langley makes his romantic interest in Sappho known to her. After being reprimanded by the young
woman, he confronts her with the stunning resemblance between her and her
unacknowledged child, foreshadowing the crisis that his knowledge of her secret will eventually cause.

"The Fair" opens with Grayson's characterization of the alleged gaiety in
the slave quarters of the plantation:
Boisterous jest and humor unrefined,

> That leave, though rough, no painful sting behind;
> Warm social joys surround the Negro's cot.
> No ennui clouds, no coming cares annoy,

> Nor wants nor sorrow check the Negro's joy.
> (Hopkins, *Contending Forces* 183; Grayson 51–53)

At first glance, the lines are a seemingly apt fit for the context of the festivities of the fair. The epigraph to "The Fair.—Concluded" provides an even closer connection to this setting in regard to its content. It reads: "In feasts maturing busy hands appear, / And jest and laugh assail the ready ear" (Hopkins, *Contending Forces* 197; Grayson 52).

A closer look, however, provides a different picture and lays open Hopkins's strategy in employing this quote. The events of the chapters thoroughly contradict the light-hearted tone of Grayson's lines, exposing Hopkins's cutting irony in her intertextual employment of them. While the fair in itself is a delightful occasion, no "jest and laugh assail the ready ear," as Sappho is deeply plagued by "coming cares" and "sorrow," which do indeed "check . . . [her] joy." The "painful sting," contrary to Grayson's assertion, left behind by Langley's advances simultaneously also foreshadows the coming events that will lead to Will and Sappho's separation.

In addition to these "coming cares" that cast their shadows on Sappho, the event itself couldn't be further from the characterization provided by the epigraphs. The fundraiser, an elaborate and distinguished Black middle-class affair, stands in stark contrast to Grayson's depiction of Black festivities as "rough" and marked by "[b]oisterous jest and humor unrefined." What's more, Grayson's suggestion of an inherent Black laziness, to be remedied only by the promise of some festive celebration that is implied in the second excerpt, as well as its surrounding text in the original—the line preceding it has Grayson refer to the "loiterers" (52) on the plantation—is contradicted by the purpose of the fair: here is an occasion that is entirely motivated by altruistic intentions and whose central reason for existence lies in the lasting benefits it will provide to the community. Hopkins underscores this point, even on an individual level, by having the winner of a competition that rewards the person who raises the most funds at the fair give up the monetary prize she receives in order to buy a new suit for the congregation's pastor.

Where Grayson's stereotyping of people of color is challenged, his assumptions about their white counterparts do not fare better. Hopkins repeatedly stresses that it is Langley's white blood, his inheritance from those whom Grayson describes as a "master-race" and characterizes as fit to instruct "the black savage" in "forms of law" and to "refine" "his moral sense" (74), that leads to the villain's moral corruption.[24]

In a battle between abolitionists and southern apologists, Grayson's work was singled out by southerners not only for its perceived argumentative value but also as an artwork of aesthetic value intended to also counter abolitionism on a metadiscursive level. In an age characterized by the conjunction of literature and politics, Grayson's work was touted as disproving the "charge of the opponents of slavery—that the tendency of . . . [the southern] institutions is to depress literary effort and to stifle the promptings of the Muse" (Jarrett 493). The alleged literary value of Grayson's poem was thus seen as discrediting "the abolitionist contention that slavery dehumanized both the slave and the slave owner" (Wells 53), meaning that Hopkins's intertextual employment of this text, one that disproved and ridiculed its simplistic logic while simultaneously resisting to fully acknowledge it by omitting author and title, not only targeted Grayson but also challenged the entire side of the argument he represented—and, by extension, the literary tradition of plantation writing his text was claimed to aptly epitomize.

Hopkins's choice to withhold the quotations' source was likely not motivated only by a desire to avoid unnecessary publicity, as the citation's anonymity also points to the disconcerting universality of Grayson's racist assumptions. They, indeed, were his words, penned in the American South of the antebellum era; their underlying sentiment, however, remained valid in Hopkins's post-Reconstruction present, having even gained new currency through the revival and popularity of plantation literature, thus making his words potential utterances of a majority of the American population.

With Grayson, much like her abolitionist sources, Hopkins achieves through her practice of intertextuality what her novels already enact on the plot level: she presentifies "The Hireling and the Slave," a text that, by the time of her literary activity, firmly belonged in the canon of a revisionist tradition of writings on the plantation. In this borrowing we encounter Hopkins's boldest assertion of access to a discourse yet. Where she merely adds her voice to an existing conversation in her employment of abolitionist sources, she dominates and subverts Grayson's text and, by extension, the genre he belongs to, denying both equal footing. Unlike her abolitionist borrowings, Hopkins is not invested in achieving discursive endurance for this source. The transferal that results from her appropriation enables her to turn the tables on a text deeply engrained in a racist discourse, to merge it with her own writing and deny it textual autonomy. Detached from author and work, her intertextual employment of the text allows Hopkins to alter a seemingly fixed entity, the permanence of which appeared to have been achieved upon completion of its original composition and the subsequent reception by dominant white culture.

Hopkins consistently contradicts Grayson's assumptions, exposing and ridiculing the unsophisticated argument of his text. It is incorporated in a narrative that centrally addresses and contests racial prejudice and inequality, revealing the horrors of slavery and its lasting legacy in a postbellum world. Thus linked with the contents of a distinct race literature, Grayson's proslavery poem is defamiliarized, recoded, and diversified; it becomes a building block in a narrative invested in exposing the evils of the institution it so fervently defends and is forced to be complicit in its own deconstruction. Hopkins takes the right to contribute to a discourse that categorically excluded her as a person of color yet claimed representative authority over her. In her intertextual practice, she finds a viable strategy for intervening in this discourse's portrayal of the American past as "untouchable" and "exempt from scrutiny" (Assmann 3). "The Hireling and the Slave" and with it the myth of the idyllic, peaceful plantation purported by the plantation tradition are forced into the light of Hopkins's present moment. Thus presentified, they become available for critical engagement and close scrutiny. Together with her narrative investment in demonstrating the historical and causal continuity that connected antebellum and post-Reconstruction America, it is Hopkins's use of intertextuality that enables her to challenge the harmful pastification of slavery so prominent in her day, effect both "therapeutically induced change" (3) and healing within her community, and prove to her readers that it was indeed "this cursed slavery that's to blame."

NOTES

1. In this chapter I employ an understanding of intertextuality as the relationship of texts with other texts, an understanding that goes beyond the term's original, poststructuralist meaning. Intertextuality, as coined by Kristeva in her 1966 essay "Word, Dialogue, and Novel" and expanded on in "The Bounded Text," is conceived of in poststructuralist theory as an utterly pervasive phenomenon at work in all texts and at all times. Lachmann suggests a distinction between the text-ontological and the text-descriptive aspects of writing, meaning that which is an intrinsic dimension of any given text versus specific forms of textual production of meaning through the dialogue with other texts (8). It is the latter, specific, text-descriptive forms of intertextuality that I am exploring here, seeking to establish clear lines of influence and conscious authorial decisions.

2. What Kinney has termed the "rebirth of the Plantation Tradition" began in the 1870s and 1880s, particularly aided by the publication of Joel Chandler Harris's widely popular Uncle Remus stories, and continued its success well into the twentieth century. Thomas Dixon, whose novel The Clansman (1905) would later be adapted to the equally popular and deeply racist silent film The Birth of a Nation (1915), was another author whose work was prominently associated with the revival of the genre.

3. The fact that the abolition of slavery had been followed by mass migrations to the

North, which made Black and white workers competitors and lastingly affected its labor market, might help explain why the romanticization of the plantation and the depiction of slavery as a "good" system under which both Blacks and whites had thrived held some appeal for a northern audience, as it narratively reinstated an antebellum status quo that had preceded the incisive societal changes that this region experienced.

4. A case in point is the fact that popular plantation author Joel Chandler Harris's work "was celebrated not only as a great work of local color fiction but also as a national contribution to world literature" (Wells 28). The genre's authors were also no longer only natives of the South but now hailed from the entire nation (Gaines 82).

5. Heavily influenced by systems theory, systemic therapy, also known as systems therapy, is a psychotherapeutic school of thought that shifts analytical focus from the individual to the overarching systemic contexts of her environment and relationships. Its employment within a cultural studies framework allows Assmann, whose work focuses on cultural memory, to highlight the junction between oppressive ideologies and communal trauma and healing.

6. Part of this approach was the Lost Cause ideology, which reinterpreted the Civil War as having been justly fought by an honorable Confederacy to combat northern attacks on southern sovereignty and lifestyle (DeCleene 182). Idealized depictions of the South were often pitted against a gloomy picture of the North. The happy slave was contrasted with portrayals of the freedman as a "poor [and] unemployed wretch" (Brown 28). Thus, the tradition denied an understanding of slavery as a rational economic system that had provided the South with a large and inexpensive workforce. Instead, it singled out the North as the sole domain of a ruthless capitalism in America. By pointing toward the alleged kind paternalism of the slaveholders, the tradition promoted the argument that receiving no wages in the South was somehow more desirable than earning low wages in the North.

7. Page made the logic of the genre's comparative approach quite explicit when contrasting claims that "the old-time Negroes were industrious . . . and . . . well-behaved" with descriptions of Blacks in post-Reconstruction America as "lazy, thriftless, intemperate . . . [and] dishonest," even warning his audience of a pending "reversion to barbarism" (80).

8. Note that although narrativization generally engages us with the past—whether because it looks toward past events or because it was written in the past—and thus performs an act of presentification, Assmann stresses that it is specifically those events that are "supposedly inaccessible" that "presentifying" brings into the "availability of the present" (4). The underlying logic of presentification hinges on the observation that "all problems are at all times problems of the present" (4), irrespective of when they originated—a logic that Hopkins's narratives promote as well through her strategy of transporting readers back to an antebellum past and tracing its lingering harmful effects to her post-Reconstruction present.

9. For *Winona*, Hopkins borrowed extensively from Octave Thanet's *Expiation* (see Pavletich), a source that holds particular significance in the context of turn-of-the-century discourse on slavery. The 1890s text is an exemplary plantation romance that is emblematic in its deeply racist promotion of an idyllic antebellum South that is con-

trasted with disorder and lawlessness shortly after the end of the war. Pavletich makes a convincing argument for a multilayered employment of this and similarly problematic source texts when Hopkins embraces their specific strengths—in *Expiation,* for example, the heroine's marked agency and courage—while condemning their racism. My analysis of Hopkins's intertextual practice, which focuses on *Contending Forces,* however, examines instances of borrowings where Hopkins either wholly embraces source texts or categorically dismisses them. I agree, however, with Pavletich's observation that intertextuality provided Hopkins with a safe avenue to "publically critique such texts" and that it provided her with the means "to conquer white discourse for anti-racist ends" (122). I echo this observation in my reading of Hopkins's practice as effecting forms of "presentification," thus allowing her participation in an otherwise closed-off discourse.

10. This narrative also follows a dual plot structure, though one of a geographical nature: an American narrative and an African one.

11. Although Grace Montfort appears to be white, Hopkins alludes to her racially ambiguous features, which the perpetrators use to legitimize their assault, thus countering plantation literature's omission of this subject matter in its idealized portrayal of antebellum life.

12. White supremacist ideology perceived of Black women as either asexual and mannish, exemplified by the mammy stereotype, a staple in much plantation writing, or as lascivious creatures, inherently promiscuous and ruled by strong sexual urges, best exemplified by the Jezebel stereotype. The stereotype that also frequently appeared in plantation literature was instrumentalized to help justify sexual transgressions against Black women in both antebellum and postbellum America.

13. Hopkins's contemporary Ida B. Wells documented the repeated, unsubstantiated use of this claim as legitimization of lynchings throughout the South.

14. Willis indicates that the words are not her own but fails to specify the quote's author and simply refers to it as a "truism" (150), further emphasizing the universality Hopkins attributed to them.

15. The poem is sometimes also titled "We Wait Beneath the Furnace Blast" and "Furnace Blast," respectively. It continued to hold significance for Hopkins, who penned an essay series called Furnace Blasts for the *Colored American Magazine* in 1903. The series addressed controversial issues such as miscegenation and prostitution and may well have contributed to Hopkins's ousting from the staff of the magazine; it was abruptly discontinued after two installments, and Hopkins was warned to eliminate "anything which may create offense . . . [and] stop talking about wrongs and a proscribed race" (Hopkins, "Letter" 243).

16. The second Cowper quote opens chapter 14, introducing the speech of Luke Sawyer, who, upon speaking at a meeting of the Colored American League, tells of his father's brutal lynching and Mabelle Beaubean's / Sappho Clark's abduction and rape (Hopkins, *Contending Forces* 254). The excerpt, originating from the same source as the earlier one, is likewise direct in its condemnation of slavery and racial prejudice, condemning white supremacism to find "his fellow guilty of a skin / *Not colored like his own*" (254, emphasis in original).

17. Literary critic Dwight McBride convincingly argues that abolitionist discourse

shaped and limited the ways in which people of color could express themselves vis-à-vis a white audience of their time—predominantly, of course, in the form of the highly formulaic slave narrative—and that this discourse, while attacking "the institution of slavery . . . supports . . . the idea that the slave, if not subhuman, is certainly not of the same class of people as free Europeans" and white Americans (7).

18. Mrs. Willis's aforementioned usage of Emerson's words presents a good example of such a "buried" quote. Willis does not present them as her own but also doesn't specify their author or even indicate their literary character.

19. The other two instances are a Bible quotation, which would have been easily identifiable as such to Hopkins's readership, and an excerpt taken from William Cullen Bryant's "The Antiquity of Freedom." The latter's anonymous publication is somewhat puzzling and likely constitutes a simple oversight, as there appears to be no reasonable difference, in regard to author and text, that would explain Hopkins's divergent treatment of this epigraph from others in the novel.

20. An early review of Hopkins's *Contending Forces*, in fact, noted the similarities between Stowe's and Hopkins's protagonists, suggesting that Hopkins "would be to the Anti Lynching cause what Harriet Beecher Stowe's 'Uncle Tom's Cabin' had been to the Anti Slavery Cause" (Jewell 558).

21. The scarcity of secondary material on "The Hireling and the Slave" forced me to turn to sources that were often dated themselves and sometimes ideologically dubious to be able to collect what little information there was on its author and the circumstances of its creation. I did so carefully, weighing the respective limitations and biases of these texts. For a discussion of Grayson's stylistic choices, see Jarrett 494.

22. Grayson used the term "hireling" to refer not only to free laborers in the industrial North but also to workers in England, a country that he sought to attack due to ongoing English philanthropic campaigns for the abolition of slavery in the United States.

23. These idyllic depictions were decidedly not based on firsthand observations. While Grayson lived in the South for most of his life, it was not until the very year that he wrote "The Hireling and the Slave" that he, already in his sixties, became the owner of a plantation—in accordance with his views, fittingly named Fair Lawn (Wilson 337, 339).

24. Hopkins describes Langley as having inherited "the worst features of a dominant race," namely, a "revengeful . . . character . . . , a carefully concealed strain of sensuality in his nature, . . . [and a] love of money" (*Contending Forces* 91).

WORKS CITED

Assmann, Aleida. *Zeit und Tradition: Kulturelle Strategien der Dauer*. Böhlau, 1999.

Boeckmann, Cathy. *A Question of Character: Scientific Racism and the Genres of American Fiction, 1892–1912*. University of Alabama Press, 2000.

Brown, Sterling. *The Negro in American Fiction*. 1937. Kennikat Press, 1968.

Bryant, William Cullen. "The Antiquity of Freedom." *Poetical Works of William Cullen Bryant*. D. Appleton, 1899, pp. 198–99.

Cowan, William Tynes. *The Slave in the Swamp: Disrupting the Plantation Narrative*. Routledge, 2005.

Cowper, William. *The Task, a Poem.* 1785. James Nisbet and Co. Berners Street, 1855.

DeCleene, Christine. "Civil War Films." *Race in American Film: Voices and Visions That Shaped a Nation*, edited by Daniel Bernardi and Michael Green, Greenwood, 2017, pp. 181–85.

Emerson, Ralph Waldo. "Emancipation in the British West Indies." *The Complete Essays and Other Writings of Ralph Waldo Emerson*, edited by Brooks Atkinson, Modern Library, 1940, pp. 831–60.

Gaines, Francis Pendleton. *The Southern Plantation: A Study in the Development and the Accuracy of a Tradition.* 1924. Smith, 1962.

Grayson, William J. *"The Hireling and the Slave," "Chicora," and Other Poems.* McCarter & Co., 1856.

Hale, Grace Elizabeth. *Making Whiteness: The Culture of Segregation in the South, 1890–1940.* Vintage Books, 1999.

Hopkins, Pauline Elizabeth. *Contending Forces: A Romance Illustrative of Negro Life North and South.* 1900. Oxford University Press, 1988.

———. "Famous Men of the Negro Race. I. Toussaint L'Ouverture." *Daughter of the Revolution: The Major Nonfiction Works of Pauline E. Hopkins*, edited by Ira Dworkin, Rutgers University Press, 2007, pp. 11–22.

———. "Famous Men of the Negro Race. IV. Robert Brown Elliott." *Daughter of the Revolution: The Major Nonfiction Works of Pauline E. Hopkins*, edited by Ira Dworkin, Rutgers University Press, 2007, pp. 40–48.

———. "Famous Men of the Negro Race. IX. John Mercer Langston." *Daughter of the Revolution: The Major Nonfiction Works of Pauline E. Hopkins*, edited by Ira Dworkin, Rutgers University Press, 2007, pp. 77–86.

———. "Famous Women of the Negro Race. II. Sojourner Truth." *Daughter of the Revolution: The Major Nonfiction Works of Pauline E. Hopkins*, edited by Ira Dworkin, Rutgers University Press, 2007, pp. 113–31.

———. "Famous Women of the Negro Race. III. Harriet Tubman." *Daughter of the Revolution: The Major Nonfiction Works of Pauline E. Hopkins*, edited by Ira Dworkin, Rutgers University Press, 2007, pp. 132–39.

———. *Hagar's Daughter: A Story of Southern Caste Prejudice.* 1901–02. *The Magazine Novels of Pauline Hopkins.* Oxford University Press, 1988, pp. 1–284.

———. "Letter to William Monroe Trotter, April 16, 1905." *Daughter of the Revolution: The Major Nonfiction Works of Pauline E. Hopkins*, edited by Ira Dworkin, Rutgers University Press, 2007, pp. 238–48.

———. *Of One Blood; or, The Hidden Self.* 1902–03. *The Magazine Novels of Pauline Hopkins.* Oxford University Press, 1988, pp. 439–621.

———. *Winona: A Tale of Negro Life in the South and Southwest.* 1902. *The Magazine Novels of Pauline Hopkins.* Oxford University Press, 1988, pp. 285–437.

Jarrett, Thomas D. "The Literary Significance of William J. Grayson's 'The Hireling and the Slave.'" *Georgia Review*, vol. 5, no. 4, Winter 1951, pp. 487–94.

Jewell, Addie Hamilton. "Appendix 3: Review by Addie Hamilton Jewell of *Contending Forces*, 5 December 1899." *Pauline Elizabeth Hopkins: Black Daughter of the Revolution*, by Lois Brown, University of North Carolina Press, 2008, pp. 558–61.

Jordan-Lake, Joy. *Whitewashing Uncle Tom's Cabin: Nineteenth-Century Women Novelists Respond to Stowe*. Vanderbilt University Press, 2005.

Kinney, James. *Amalgamation: Race, Sex, and Rhetoric in the Nineteenth Century American Novel*. Greenwood, 1985.

Knight, Alisha R. *Pauline Hopkins and the American Dream: An African American Writer's (Re)Visionary Gospel of Success*. University of Tennessee Press, 2012.

Kristeva, Julia. "The Bounded Text." *Desire in Language: A Semiotic Approach to Literature and Art*, edited by Leon S. Roudiez, Columbia University Press, 1980, pp. 64–91.

———. "Word, Dialogue, and Novel." *Desire in Language: A Semiotic Approach to Literature and Art*, edited by Leon S. Roudiez, Columbia University Press, 1980, pp. 36–63.

Lachmann, Renate. „Vorwort." *Dialogizität*, edited by Renate Lachmann, Wilhelm Fink Verlag, 1982, pp. 8–10.

McBride, Dwight. *Impossible Witnesses: Truth, Abolitionism, and Slave Testimony*. New York University Press, 2001.

Page, Thomas Nelson. *The Negro: The Southerner's Problem*. Charles Scribner's Sons, 1904.

Pavletich, JoAnn. "'. . . We Are Going To Take That Right': Power and Plagiarism in Pauline Hopkins's *Winona*." *CLA Journal*, vol. 59, no. 2, 2016, pp. 115–30.

Phan, Hoang Gia. *Bonds of Citizenship: Law and the Labors of Emancipation*. New York University Press, 2013.

Rogal, Samuel J. *Congregational Hymns from the Poetry of John Greenleaf Whittier: A Comparative Study of the Sources and Final Works, with a Bibliographic Catalog of Hymns*. McFarland and Company, 2010.

Shadrach, J. Shirley (*see also* Hopkins, Pauline Elizabeth). "Charles Winter Wood; or, From Bootblack to Professor." *Daughter of the Revolution: The Major Nonfiction Works of Pauline E. Hopkins*, edited by Ira Dworkin, Rutgers University Press, 2007, pp. 259–62.

———. "Furnace Blasts: The Growth of the Social Evil among All Classes and Races in America." *Daughter of the Revolution: The Major Nonfiction Works of Pauline E. Hopkins*, edited by Ira Dworkin, Rutgers University Press, 2007, pp. 201–07.

Wells, Jeremy. *Romances of the White Man's Burden: Race, Empire, and the Plantation in American Literature, 1880–1936*. Vanderbilt University Press, 2011.

Whittier, John Greenleaf. "Ein feste Burg ist unser Gott (Luther's Hymn)." *"In War Time" and Other Poems*. Ticknor and Fields, 1864, pp. 14–18.

———. "Lines, Written on Reading the Spirited and Manly Remarks of Gov. Ritner, of Pennsylvania, in His Message of 1836, on the Subject of Slavery." *Voices of Freedom*. Thomas S. Cavender, 1846, pp. 57–59.

———. "Stanzas for the Times." *Voices of Freedom*. Thomas S. Cavender, 1846, pp. 121–25.

Wilson, Edmund. *Patriotic Gore: Studies in the Literature of the American Civil War*. Oxford University Press, 1966.

"Gazing Hopelessly into the Future"

UTOPIA AND THE RACIAL POLITICS OF GENRE IN *OF ONE BLOOD; OR, THE HIDDEN SELF*

Courtney L. Novosat

> Fiction is of great value to any people as a preserver of manners
> and customs—religious, political, and social. It is a record of
> growth and development from generation to generation.
>
> —PAULINE HOPKINS, preface to *Contending Forces*

> As he sat beside his friend, his mind was far away in America looking
> with brooding eyes into the past and gazing hopelessly into the future.
>
> —PAULINE HOPKINS, *Of One Blood*

In the preface to her first novel, *Contending Forces* (1900), editor, author, performer, and activist Pauline E. Hopkins lauds the "great value" of fiction, calling it a "preserver of manners and customs" that marks the "growth and development" of a people across generations. Regardless of her enthusiastic support for literature, the editor of the *Colored American Magazine* essentially stopped writing fiction to consciously cultivate a "more directly political nonfiction voice" (Dworkin, *Daughter* 215).[1] As scholar and Hopkins biographer Lois Brown has advanced, Hopkins may have felt that her "stints as a public performer . . . competed with her efforts to craft a more reserved . . . reputation of intellectual and political awareness" (19), which may have further encouraged her to distance herself from writing fiction. Nevertheless, as much scholarship notes, Hopkins's novels *are* forceful iterations of Black feminist politics rendered in genres as varied as musical plays and historical fiction, detective stories and utopia. Yet despite marked discussion of Hopkins's politics and some attentive discussion of her use of various genres, few have explored her choice of utopia, an overtly political genre, for her final novel, *Of One Blood; or, The Hidden Self* (1903).[2] As a genre vested in the act of remaking society, the utopia is a literary form cum political act that consciously reimagines the future. Given Hopkins's own attentiveness to genre throughout her career, one must consider the political possibilities utopian conventions offered a "race woman" "who endeavored to uplift the race" (Brown 190), an avenue of inquiry this essay pursues.

In this chapter, I first explore Hopkins's *Of One Blood* in the context of Edward Bellamy's *Looking Backward* (1889), the utopia credited with generating the genre's late nineteenth-century boom and rearticulating the form's conventions for the era, as well as other potentially influential predecessors among early Black intellectuals exploring utopian ideation. By enumerating the utopian conventions of Bellamy's prominent novel, one is better able to consider how Hopkins adopts the genre in order to subvert its conventions. With an eye toward Hopkins's tactics, I argue that the literary utopia allowed her to both examine America's past with "brooding eyes" and refuse to gaze "hopelessly" (*Of One Blood* 163) toward an uncertain future for African Americans. The utopia's conventional intertextuality, which ranges from allusion to appropriation, offered Hopkins a means to intercede in the discourse of the present by revising the past and speculating about the future. Further, the genre's intertextuality, visible in Bellamy's work and across the more than "one hundred and twenty" (Pfaelzer 50) utopian novels *Looking Backward* inspired, offers another partial explanation for Hopkins's well-documented "plagiarism" in *Of One Blood*.[3] Although this essay cannot account for all of the novel's "plagiarized" passages, it will argue that such replication and intertextuality is often *conventional* and offered Hopkins a means to disrupt white-authored notions of Black identity across a host of disciplines. Distinct from other genres, utopia's intertextual, hybrid, and multidisciplinary conventions allowed Hopkins an inroad for disrupting the mechanisms supporting race and gender prejudice, particularly the racialized discourses of science and history, which, like utopia, were dominated by white male voices in the late nineteenth and early twentieth centuries.[4]

In the chapter's third section, I contend that scholarship must place *Of One Blood* amid a continuum of understudied African American utopias from the late nineteenth century. Collectively, works such as Frances Harper's *Iola Leroy; or, Shadows Uplifted* (1892), Sutton E. Griggs's *Imperium in Imperio* (1899), and Hopkins's *Of One Blood* subvert traditional utopian conventions as they recognize that the genre and its attendant philosophies have long supported race prejudice. Reading *Of One Blood* as a "critical utopia," a work penned to "evoke and criticize the white-dominated utopian tradition" (Veselá 285), alongside Harper's *Iola Leroy* and Griggs's *Imperium in Imperio* highlights their influence on Hopkins's work. Such a comparative reading also reveals an emerging pattern for subverting white utopian conventions that often actively excludes Black Americans, a pattern that modern scholarship on Afrofuturism, a popular term for contemporary Black speculative fiction, has yet to fully explore. Even André M. Carrington's *Speculative Blackness: The Future of Race in Science Fiction* (2016) only mentions Griggs (but neither Harper nor Hopkins) in passing. Importantly, he asserts that more work remains to be done in terms of "rethinking" how "Blackness and speculative fiction . . . occlude knowledge from the watchful eye of White supremacist governance, to fictionalize scientific racism, and to question our destiny" (241), characteristics that, I argue, are central to early African American utopian novels.

Further, a collective consideration of these early Black literary utopias may help us to map two trends that emerged in later Black speculative fiction. First, these early works attentively criticize the white nationalism shaping traditional imaginings of a (white) utopian future. Second, they reimagine utopian conventions such as point of view, intertextuality, and the concept of travel in ways that appear to be distinct to early African American utopias. With all of this in mind, the utopian form as a fiction that depends on "objects and structures that already exist in the real world" and "cannot defy logic" (Vieira 8) allowed Hopkins to advocate beyond the confines of the novel to assert a critical—and feminist—Black voice in the present that can articulate a Black future absent from traditional utopias. Through these lines of inquiry, I argue that Hopkins's utopia refuses to "continue gazing hopelessly into the future" (*Of One Blood* 163). Instead, the genre allowed her to imagine a "blueprint" for a more "ideal polity" (Sargisson 8) and to carve a space for Black feminist thought. By generating a space for the era's participatory reader swayed by literature's "transformative powers" (Roemer 84), Hopkins challenged the mechanisms of prejudice generated by the actual polity of white male voices that strove to define not only Blackness but also the nation's past, present, and future.

Utopia and Its "Negro Problem"

Although contemporary scholarship has considered the ways in which the fin de siècle utopia was a "potentially dangerous diversion" (Pfaelzer 4) from the work of social reform, to readers in Hopkins's time the unprecedented popularity of Bellamy's *Looking Backward* bespoke the genre's efficacy as a form. That novel led to Bellamy's publication of the *New Nation* magazine and to the creation of "at least 165 'Nationalist Clubs'" advocating for various reforms (Roemer 9). It also led to the formation of the People's Party, a short-lived political party that nevertheless invigorated nativist Populism at the close of the nineteenth century (Lipow 31). Given the lasting fervor of Bellamy's novel, the political awareness of Hopkins's writing, and her recently published homage to Frances Harper, a foremother of the African American utopian novel, Hopkins's choice to explore the utopian form in her final novel becomes less surprising.[5] However, to map Hopkins's political subversion of typical utopian convention, one must first consider the conventions of the traditional utopian form, its popularity in fin de siècle America, and how it has—and has not—been studied.

While the idea of a utopia, the hope for a more desirable world than our own, is ingrained across cultures and epochs in our very mythos of origin and destination, the word "utopia" and its early conventions trace to Sir Thomas More's sui generis *Utopia* (1516). More's *Utopia*, "scarcely ever out of print" (Davis 29), forged a politically invested, hybrid genre whose wryly ambiguous name, a pun on the Greek phrases for "good place" (*eutopia*) and "no place" (*outopia*), heralds the form's inherent contradiction. Nevertheless, blending travelogue with romance and satire with political tract, More's political critique of exploitive monarchies played "a crucial role in the constitution of the nation-state as an original spatial, social, and cultural form" (Wegner xvi). Grounded in reimagining a new nation governed by its people, More generated both a generic form and a didactic political "program" for nation building (Jameson 3).[6] Thus, from its inception utopia was a rule-bound literary and political act that offered a means to critically appraise the ideas and practices of the present in order to consciously rescript society for the future.

Given the racialized political tumult of fin de siècle America, it is unsurprising that a literary form offering a means to rewrite our national narrative would gain popularity among white writers and readers. Many white Americans likely found solace in utopian messages of future (racial) stability. Concerned by the growing din of nativist rhetoric, many perceived the nation's present as "plagued" by the so-called Negro problem and immigrant problem. And such rhetoric was far from hollow.

Throughout the nineteenth century, an authoritative class of white professionals in science and politics grappled with the so-called Negro problem by advancing a specious "race science" that later scholars would come to more accurately term "scientific racism." By midcentury, the American school of ethnology dominated lectureship, publication, and theories of race in the United States to advance a belief in polygenesis, that is, of distinctly different creations by racial group. Aided by the sweeping craniological mapping and comparative (mis)measurement of Caucasian, African, and Indigenous American skulls in Samuel George Morton's *Crania Americana* (1839) and *Crania Aegyptiaca* (1844), renowned physicians such as Josiah C. Nott and George Gliddon could graft such racially biased measurement to the theory of polygenesis to argue in *Types of Mankind* (1854) that the races were clearly different species. Thus, for Nott and Gliddon and ethnologists trained by their works, the natural variation among human skulls scientifically "confirmed" their white biases: nonwhites were a distinct and inferior species.[7] Though by 1871 English naturalist Charles Darwin's *The Descent of Man* would volubly refute polygenism and the idea that the races were separate species, the American school of ethnology had already trained countless scientists and physicians in its wake, ensuring its ideological legacy.[8] Rooted in such "science," anti-Black racism, prejudicial colorism, and notions of a "variegated whiteness" (Jacobson 41) codified for the nation a racial caste system, a system wherein the races were *not* of one blood well into the twentieth century.

Despite the centrality of the "race question" to scientific discourse for the better part of the century, the damning rhetoric of what Dr. J. R. Hayes dubbed "negrophobia" among whites by 1869 (Frederickson 188), and waves of xenophobic press in response to the rise in immigration at the century's end, scholarship on the literary utopia rarely comments on how the desire to preserve whiteness shaped the utopian imagination or the futures imagined within the utopian novel. While modern scholarship on the nineteenth-century utopia cites overtly racialized histories—the Civil War and abolition, unprecedented immigration and labor strikes, professionalizing and migrating Black Americans—as a catalyst for the form's fin de siècle boom, it remains silent about how the predominantly white utopian works published in the era were shaped by considerations of the "racial other" or by their own racism, a consideration that a race-conscious reader such as Hopkins may have noted. Indeed, I would argue that through her study of the utopian genre, probable Black ancestors engaging with the form, and the noticeably whitened futures among the genre's predominant works, Hopkins offered a strategy for considering how whiteness influences the racial character and program of "reform" within the traditional utopia—and perhaps even our own adoption of the term "plagiarism" with regard to her work.

As a writer and editor acutely aware of both her industry and her activism, Hopkins would have known the utopian works of fellow Bostonians Nancy Prince (Hopkins's "maternal ancestor" in social activism) and Edward Bellamy, as well as that of Martin Delaney. Although Prince was not a utopian novelist, Hopkins knew Prince's travel writing and Bellamy's wildly popular utopia, *Looking Backward*, before penning *Of One Blood* (Brown 172). As a Boston race woman, researcher, and biographer of select Black American notables, Hopkins was likely to have encountered Prince's *Narrative of the Life and Travels of Mrs. Nancy Prince* (1853), in which Prince actively sought in her travels "an egalitarian, colorblind Christian society," that is, a *utopia* accessible to Black Americans in an era rife with "utopian communitarian activity" (Foster 345, 332). As Amber Foster convincingly argues in "Nancy Prince's Utopias: Reimagining the African American Utopian Tradition" (2013), given the constraints of midcentury readership and (white) tastes for personal narratives by writers of color, "it is not surprising that Nancy Prince opted to incorporate utopian conventions into a personal narrative, rather than writing a novel" (333). Nevertheless, Prince's work likely recorded for Hopkins both "African American women's 'engagement in utopian dreaming' considerably prior to the emergence of the African American utopian novel" (333) and an early perception that the conventions of the utopian form were mutable rather than fixed.

Like Prince, Martin Delany, too, may have inspired the character of Hopkins's utopian dreaming. As Mandy Reid argues in "Utopia Is in the Blood: The Bodily Utopias of Martin R. Delany and Pauline Hopkins" (2011), not only does *Principia of Ethnology* (1879) suggest some degree of Delany's influence on Hopkins's racial theories, but both "employ the discourse of racial science" to generate their "own racial utopias" (92). Notably, Hopkins was familiar with the work of this scientist, activist, and physician, mentioning Delany as early as 1900 in her year-long series, Famous Men of the Negro Race, for the *Colored American Magazine*. In 1905, however, she reverently cited *Principia* at length in The Dark Races of the Twentieth Century, a series penned for *Voice of the Negro*, calling it an "eminent work" and positioning it as the representative of "scientific opinion" in her own writing (Hopkins, "Oceanica" 307). However, what may be more significant in terms of Delany's influence on Hopkins's work is the rhetorical character of his argument. From the first pages of *Principia*, Delany forthrightly "discards" the polygenism of "Champollion, Nott, Gliddon and others" to "be refuted in the general deductions" of his work (2). In this way, not only does Delany position his argument in dialogue with the polygenists of the era, but he does so by savvily highlighting their blasphemy (and, thus, their questionable science), "making no apology" for his "liberal use of Creation as learned from the Bible" (10). Though modern readers might immediately bristle at the use of biblical authority to justify the monogenesis of a singular human species, Delany's rhetoric clearly recognizes the tactical advantage of highlighting the flaws of his white predecessors' assumptions. By highlighting how their assumptions balk at the biblical authority accepted in the era, Delany encourages his readers to question, just as Hopkins does, the integrity of white scientific interpretation that would go to such lengths to justify and maintain the inferiority of Black Americans. In this way, utopia "enables both Delaney and Hopkins [not only] to refute contemporary scientific claim" and "use the discourse of science to establish the utopian past (and, Hopkins argues, the future) of Ethiopia" (Reid 92) but also to refute the flaws of a scientific process blinded by racist assumptions about color and intervene in its discourse.

Despite the intellectual ancestry Hopkins might have traced to Prince's and Delany's work, however, Bellamy's *Looking Backward* might have been her most direct literary interlocutor, given its popularity, numerous literary progeny, and anxious erasure of the nonwhite other. A shrewd observer of racial inequity, Hopkins likely recognized the hasty demise of the novel's single character of color, as well as the influence Bellamy's self-termed "Nationalism" had on the growth of a nativist—and increasingly racist—populism. Set in Boston, Bellamy's novel tells the story of protagonist Julian West's century-long mesmeric sleep and awakening in a seemingly egalitarian society in the year 2000. In this idyllic new world, West finds that men and women both labor in the "Industrial Army," pay is equal across professions, and housing and goods are managed by the state. Yet much about this new world was less than idyllic. In social organization, the future mirrored the white middle-class patriarchy of the present. In its private homes, utopia's gender hierarchy ensured that women also retained domestic duties and worked shorter hours to compensate for their fragility. Further, the utopia's conspicuous consumption, caste-based segregation, and Aryan-featured populace assured its white nineteenth-century readers that the creature comforts of middle-class capitalism, social mores, and expected racial segregation remained in the future. With this verisimilitude in mind, it is little wonder that some scholars of utopia have even considered the genre a diversionary surrogate. As one critic has put it, utopia could sate the desire for change while becoming a "diversion from the difficult task of forging a new society" (Pfaelzer 40), enacting what we might term the "theater of reform," one that ultimately benefited the (white, male, and middle-class) status quo.

However, *Looking Backward*'s theater of reform does not disguise the fact that the mechanisms by which West advances to the future are marked by racial prejudice. Notably, West's mesmeric sleep is precipitated by a fire caused by immigrant labor, those "anarchists" of an encroaching "alien race" (Bellamy 12), and begins on Decoration Day, shortly after the protagonist has whitewashed the postbellum holiday started by Black Americans. Bellamy simply characterizes the day as commemorating the "war for the preservation of the union" (12) and sidesteps any mention of slavery as its central cause.[9] More concretely, as if an act of retributive justice, the novel noticeably eliminates the "Negro question" by leaving its only identifiably Black character, West's "faithful colored man . . . Sawyer," to perish in flames in the nineteenth century (13). Nevertheless, Bellamy insisted that "Nationalists are color-blind" when responding to a letter to the *New Nation* dated October 3, 1891, that questioned the place of "the negro" in the future. However, by 1898 in the ironically titled *Equality* (1898), the sequel to *Looking Backward*, Bellamy clearly endorsed a white-topped racial hierarchy and championed segregation. In *Equality* he affirmed that labor and neighborhood segregation would remain to the satisfaction of "the most bigoted local prejudices" (qtd. in Peyser 56). The assertion may have begrudgingly pandered to Bellamy's increasingly Populist fanbase, whose nativism, as many Black Americans noted at the time, often harbored racism as well, but it certainly affirmed a racial dystopia.[10] Considering Hopkins's investment in Black politics and the press, she may have been aware of the double-edged sword that Bellamy's Nationalism was helping to forge—and of *Equality*'s overt segregating of *Looking Backward*'s utopia.

Given politics and popularity, *Looking Backward* would have been an impossible utopia for Hopkins to ignore. Bellamy's work was the epicenter of the utopia's late-century boom and direct inspiration to more than one hundred other utopian novels. It also rearticulated the formal conventions of the utopian genre for the era. Formally, Bellamy's novel and its literary progeny rely on the conventional utopian device of a white male traveler who, by some mystical means, is relocated to a more desirable (utopian) or less desirable (negative utopia / dystopia) future. Once he is discovered, convention dictates that he meets a white male guide, who becomes his primary interlocutor. The two then engage in an ongoing tête-à-tête and variety of tours, through which the traveler learns the history, philosophy, and social customs of his new society. However, these lessons are formally imparted through various types of conventional intertextuality as well. This little-discussed "conventional borrowing," which ranges from intertextual nods to other published works to the *uncredited, verbatim recitation* of passages from known texts, helps to define the genre's hybridity and generates the societal engagement that endows utopia's political program with an air of authority. For readers, then, the utopian novel becomes an active discourse on the sociopolitical questions and preoccupations of the era in part *through* its literary borrowings.

Looking Backward was the novel that rearticulated utopian convention for the late nineteenth century, and Bellamy's borrowings in it reshaped the genre, making *standard* the informal intertextual nods in the hundred literary utopias it inspired. In *Looking Backward*, Bellamy alludes to Caligula and Dickens, overtly directs readers to the recent histories of the Haymarket Strike of 1886 and the financial Panic of 1873, and employs the genres of the sermon and the daily news. However, the fact that both early readers and later critics recognized plagiarism in *Looking Backward* is significant to understanding Hopkins's "plagiarism" in *Of One Blood*, as it reaffirms that some variety of borrowing is a convention of the genre—at least post-Bellamy. Indeed, as early as May 25, 1890, one reader of Bellamy's novel recounted many similarities between a section of the novel titled "Mr. Barton's Sermon" and T. L. Harris's poem "The Great Republic" (1867), including at least one line transcribed verbatim. More significantly, in *Plagiarism in Utopia: A Study of the Utopian Tradition with Special Reference to Edward Bellamy's "Looking Backward"* (1944), Arthur E. Morgan notes the "remarkable likenesses" *Looking Backward* shares with John Macnie's *The Diothas* (1883), a utopia that predates Bellamy's work by five years. Morgan, who contends that Bellamy may have appropriated Macnie's heroine's name (Edith) and borrowed the "device of hypnotism" to facilitate time travel, also recounts the "striking similarities" of the future each text imagines (15). Yet perhaps the clearest instance of "plagiarism" within Bellamy's text is his uncredited replication of two stanzas of Alfred, Lord Tennyson's "Locksley Hall." Though current editions note and cite the poem's use, the original publication contains no citation, signifying not only that Bellamy saw the replication of two stanzas as "fair use" within an open genre but also the possibility that the form's white privilege has kept more recent critics from exploring such "conventional" borrowings as plagiarism.[11]

The corpus of literary utopias written in direct response to *Looking Backward* that use Bellamy's setting, employ his machinations of an imagined future, and even develop the lives of his characters further supports viewing intertextuality and uncited borrowing as a post-Bellamy convention of the genre.[12] In other words, early writers responding to Bellamy's novel felt called to engage with the work. They perceived the utopia as a participatory literary form, an open forum that they could share in—perhaps as they would a utopian community itself. In *Utopian Audiences: How Readers Locate Nowhere* (2003), a book-length study of utopian readership past and present, Kenneth Roemer documents the "significant number of striking examples demonstrating that readers [of utopian literature from More to the present] can not only create but act out their interpretations" (34) of utopian works and the imaginary cultures within them, a relationship to the form that challenges readers' perception of what constitutes "plagiarism" in a utopian work. Encouraged by the genre's hybridity, these post-Bellamy writers arguably perceived utopia as a performative genre calling them to participate as much in its theater of reform as in its writing. Given this tacit understanding, it is unsurprising that few critics have examined Bellamy's uncited appropriation of stanzas from Tennyson's "Locksley Hall." Although treating intertextuality and uncited borrowings as conventional to the utopian form cannot explain the "plagiarism" scholars have documented in Hopkins's other novels, it offers a way to reconsider her act of "plagiarism" in *Of One Blood*. Reconsidering her "plagiarism" as a conventional borrowing, too, allows us to refocus on how her skillful manipulation of these conventions seeks to lay bare and, ultimately, disrupt the genre's inherent race prejudices.

"Plagiarism," Utopian Convention, and the Disruption of Racial Discourse

To this point, I have offered a brief sketch of the politics of the utopian form that *Looking Backward* made familiar to readers and writers of Hopkins's era and those politics that have been overlooked by modern scholars. In this section, I propose that Hopkins used the utopian form in *Of One Blood* because it both "invite[d] . . . readers [to] give meaning to the texts" (Roemer 4) and allowed her to subvert the politics of race and generic convention. For the African American writer, whose works articulate "a long history of political and cultural resistance" (Fabi 45), utopia offered a way to participate in imagining an ideal polity that notably excluded Blacks. As "a narrative tradition that has characteristically thrived on subversive revision[s] of popular literary modes" (Fabi 45), utopia offered Hopkins another way to intervene in the "racialist" discourse of white writers. With this tactical impulse in mind, this section reconsiders portions of the novel's "plagiarism" that Geoffrey Sanborn meticulously documents in "The Wind of Words: Plagiarism and Intertextuality in *Of One Blood*" (2015). Observing that nearly one-third of the sources he notes are histories, philosophies, or travelogues, I argue that Hopkins's "plagiarism" is in part guided by a strategic use of utopian convention to disrupt prejudicial white discourses of Black identity. As a participatory and interventionist form, utopia not only traditionally borrows from other works but also enables Hopkins to disrupt the genre's own mechanisms for supporting race prejudice.

One of Hopkins's most studied works, *Of One Blood* tells the story of Reuel Briggs, a gifted but melancholic Black medical student who passes as white to advance his education at Harvard University. Finding that rumors about his race prevent him from earning a living suitable to marry Dianthe Lusk (later revealed to be his sister) and support a family, Reuel agrees to join an expedition

to Africa. Reuel leaves with the aid of a traitorous friend named Aubrey Livingston (later revealed to be his brother), who attempts to prearrange Reuel's "ac-
cidental" death so Aubrey can marry Dianthe himself. However, amid a melancholic episode, Reuel wanders off from the camp and discovers Telassar, a lost
city and Afrotopia. Upon his arrival, its leader immediately recognizes Reuel
as the nation's prophesied king returned to "restore . . . the Ethiopian race to
its ancient glory" (Hopkins, *Of One Blood* 114). After learning about Telassar
through a series of conventional utopian tête-à-têtes with Ai, the city's prime
minister, Reuel, renamed King Ergamenes, embraces his destiny to rule the nation. After learning of his familial bond to both Aubrey and Dianthe, whom
Aubrey poisons after murdering his own fiancée, Molly Vance, Reuel / King
Ergamenes is united with Queen Candace. Remaining in Telassar, he vows to
teach the nation's people about modern American racial history and awaits the
inevitable "advance of mighty nations penetrating . . . his native land" (193).
Significantly, at the novel's close Reuel is positioned within Telassar to formally
disrupt both narrative and nation, an echo of the epistemological disruption
that Reuel's character encourages among readers from the outset of the novel.

Fittingly named to challenge the rules of convention and discourse alike,
Hopkins's Reuel is rendered as an exceptional figure, a member of what W. E.
B. Du Bois would call by 1903 the "talented tenth" ("Talented" 209). Reuel is
"blessed . . . with superior physical endowments" (Hopkins, *Of One Blood* 3)
and is "a genius in his scientific studies" (4); further, he has been gifted with
mesmeric powers. To the prevailing discourses of scientific racism, a Black man
like Reuel was a "science fiction fantasy" (Posnock 65). For Hopkins, however,
Reuel was an embodied challenge to conventional scientific racism. Given his
status as an anomaly, it is unsurprising that Hopkins focused on the effect such
"otherness" had on him. Feeling as though "no alternative . . . [could] be conceived as possible" (James 361), Reuel not only *performs* (i.e., *passes*) as white
to avoid suffering "the woes of unfortunates" (Hopkins, *Of One Blood* 9) but
also contemplates suicide.

Considering the isolation of Reuel's exceptionalism and the anxieties of
choosing to pass as white, Hopkins may have positioned suicidal ideation as a
rational response to an irrational science of race. According to the "best" race
science of the time, Black Americans were continually perceived as the "missing link" between human and animal; they were routinely "denied a rank among
the human race and . . . degraded into a species of talking baboons" (Hopkins,
Of One Blood 105). It is unsurprising, then, that Black intellectuals would recognize both the anti-Black racism and the "capacious and flexible . . . definition
of science" (Rusert 5) during the nineteenth century and work consciously to

intervene in it. This conscious intervention by Black Americans into white scientific discourse is what Britt Rusert terms "fugitive science" (5) in *Fugitive Science: Empiricism and Freedom in Early African American Culture* (2017). As Rusert explains, "[E]arly African American practitioners repeatedly questioned the very definition of science, radically expanding its borders," while many "were [also] interested in building evidence and crafting arguments against race science" (7). Notably, Rusert mentions *Of One Blood* as exploring "black ethnology" through a "speculative kinship forged through actual ancestry as well as . . . mesmerism and parapsychology" (181). Though the scope of Rusert's project inhibits further exploration of Hopkins's work, Rusert clearly recognizes Hopkins's extension of a "fugitive" intervention into white race science into the twentieth century. Even at the level of characterization, Reuel is a work of resistance. To that end, I would suggest that Hopkins drew him as a composite of Black intellectuals (including Du Bois) to map the ways in which racism codified shocking inaccuracies and irrationality as scientific discourse and compelled light-skinned Black Americans—despite the damage to their psyches—to pass.

However, to further disrupt the inaccuracies of white science, I argue that Hopkins made use of utopia's conventional intertextuality. The malleability and scope of this generic form—one that reimagines a world and its worldviews—allowed her to intervene in scientific discourse, most concretely through Reuel's recitation of William James's "The Hidden Self" (1890), which Hopkins retitles "The Unclassified Residuum" in the novel's first chapter. As Reid has argued, through "the genre of utopian writing," Hopkins "refute[d] contemporary scientific claims" and "contest[ed] the epistemology of contemporary racial science" advancing anti-Black racism (92).

I would suggest that Hopkins's use of James's "The Hidden Self," more than simple refutation, offers a philosophical framework for dismantling white epistemologies of Black identity by showing their insufficiency. At the outset of the novel, Reuel's thoughts are consumed by "new discoveries in psychology" (Hopkins, *Of One Blood* 2) found in the works of cognitive scientists William James and Alfred Binet. As Sanborn importantly documents, sixteen words in this chapter are "plagiarized" from James's work, words that "could easily have been normalized by the presence of a candle or little afternoon light" to signify that they were read (75). However, given that Hopkins does attribute the work to an author (though mistakenly to Binet rather than James), this instance of "plagiarism" falls under the aegis of conventional borrowings similar to Bellamy's replication of Tennyson. It is also important to note that Hopkins "plagiarized" James through the dialogue of another man of science. As a medical professional, Reuel is equipped to engage with and challenge the ideas James raises. Reinforcing Hopkins's ideological engagement with James's work, she borrowed her novel's own subtitle from the actual title of James's essay. However, she also keenly associated Reuel with James's notion of "unclassified residuum" by retitling James's work as "Unclassified Residuum" in her narrative (James 361). As Reuel forcefully declares, "I have the power, I know the truth . . . of all M. Binet asserts" (Hopkins, *Of One Blood* 3), he identifies himself as part of the inexplicable "phenomena . . . lying broadcast over the surface of history" (James 361). More fundamentally, Reuel is part of the phenomenon of exceptional Black Americans whom science has "legislated . . . outside the realm of normal existence" (Posnock 65). Through these tactical borrowings, Hopkins highlights an epistemological space within white thought for Black Americans, a space of possibility white scientific understanding has misused to maintain its racist view of Black peoples as "talking baboons" (Hopkins, *Of One Blood* 105).

Hopkins's strategic use of James's work also directs readers to consider the limitations of white scientific knowledge and effectively positions Reuel as a disruption to scientific discourse. Importantly, James's "The Hidden Self" (1890) offered Hopkins a philosophy of scientific practice that pointed to the field's limitations. From the outset of the essay, James criticizes the scientific community's preoccupation with "a closed and complete system of truth" that problematically characterizes the "unclassifiable" as "paradoxical absurdities" (361). Rather than persist in our "contemptuous scientific disregard" when these "irregular phenomena" become more routine, James urges the scientist to "renovate his science" (361). In this way, Hopkins's appropriation seems strategic; she borrowed from a field-defining scientist who critiqued the very limitation of the scientific method Hopkins encouraged her readers to question. James's criticism allowed Hopkins to highlight gaps in scientific knowledge and to confirm that individual bias may amplify those gaps. While James refocused the essay on qualms about "the mystical," namely, extrasensory perception and the phenomena that accompany hysteria, Hopkins used James's assertion as a philosophical frame for explaining Western epistemology's inability to account for the realities of Black lives. Whether Hopkins believed in "the mystical" per se is of little consequence here; the point is that she recognized the tactical advantage of drawing a critical framework from William James—not unlike Delany did before her.

One might also consider Hopkins's misattribution of James's work a retributive criticism. Although borrowing may be a convention of the utopian form, her misattribution deliberately writes James out of focus. From this perspective, her erasure of James arguably mirrors the way Black accomplishments have been deliberately silenced throughout history, a topic that she explores in greater detail when Professor Stone confirms to the shock of many that Ethiopia had "a prehistoric existence of magnificence" (Hopkins, *Of One Blood* 99). Through this frame, Hopkins highlighted the fallibility of a scientific epistemology codified by racial bias and carved out a space within the residuum for the "Black intellectual."

Science was not the only paradigm that Hopkins suggested needed shifting. Through Reuel's relocation to Africa, Hopkins again strategically "plagiarized" from other texts to advance underdiscussed historical narratives. Rather than treat Black intellectuals as a "paradoxical absurdity" (James 361) inexplicable to science, Hopkins reaffirmed the "naturalness" of their origin through her use of travelogue and history. Like Reuel, whose authority partially authorizes his engagement with James's and Binet's words, Professor Stone, the leader of the African expedition, becomes the authority figure charged with the telling of African history, relayed verbatim from George Rawlinson's *The Five Great Monarchies of the Ancient Eastern World* (1862) and Mary Elsie Thalheimer's *A Manual of Ancient History* (1872) (Sanborn 83). As a didactic figure and field expert, Stone allows Hopkins to authoritatively resituate the origin of human advancement. As Stone explains, although humanity is indebted to the development of "three thousand years [of] Romans, Greeks, Hebrews, Germans, and Anglo-Saxons" (Hopkins, *Of One Blood* 98), he confirms that "it was *otherwise* in the first years" (98, emphasis added). In those years, Ethiopia and Babylon, led by "descendants of Ham" (98), were the "pioneers of mankind in untrodden fields of knowledge" (98) and "the first abode of civilization" (100) that Rawlinson's and Thalheimer's histories record.

It is also significant to note that slightly more than one-third of the sources from which Sanborn finds that Hopkins has "plagiarized" are travelogues, philosophies, or histories, works that are often an amalgamation of voices meant to inform the reader and the very genres Sir Thomas More's borrowed in his sui generis *Utopia* (1516). As More scholar J. C. Davis confirms, it is likely that More drew from Amerigo Vespucci's "sensational accounts of his adventures" and Pietro Martire d'Anghiera's travel compendium *De Orbe Novo* (1511) (34). Unsurprisingly, Davis stresses influence rather than "plagiarism." He also argues that "*Utopia* was emphatically a collaborative work" (34) among a group of "lay intellectuals" (36) despite being credited to More, further normalizing the genre's hybrid, polyvocal origins, echoed in the later utopian works of Bellamy and Hopkins. Established as precedents by More's work, this collaboration and hybridity offer a fitting genre for a writer who "conceptualized her

writing practice in collective terms" (Dworkin, introduction xx), a conceptualization that inherently assumes writing is an intertextual practice.

Given the utopian form's precedent of borrowing, at least some portion of
Hopkins's "plagiarism" is arguably an anticipatable convention used to critique
the systems of the present. Just as the science she borrows questions the limitations of scientific epistemology, through her use of Professor Stone and choice
of history, Hopkins encouraged readers to question the narratives told and the
ownership of history's telling. Like Reuel, Professor Stone performs as a didactic textual authority. Importantly, Hopkins aligned the two characters as authorities intended to disrupt prejudice with fact: "You and I, Briggs, know that
the theories of prejudice are swept away by the great tide of facts" (*Of One
Blood* 87). Mirroring Reuel's ability to authoritatively engage with scientific
discourse, Professor Stone decisively confirms in the novel's twelfth and thirteenth chapters that Africa, with its architectural "grandeur" (99) and "popu-
lous cities" (99), is the origin of human civilization. By reciting a "tide of facts"
(87) rather than a dialogue driven by theory or speculation, Stone disrupts
long-coveted white narratives of the ilk Samuel McKenney advances in *Slavery: Indispensable to the Civilization of Africa* (1855). There McKenney charges
that the "negro race" was "in a state of the lowest mental and moral degradation" and could be brought to God and civilization only through enslavement (8). Bespeaking the idea's popularity, McKenney's work was issued in
four editions—and this is merely one work of the type. Working against these
dominant white narratives, Hopkins's "plagiarism" may be more usefully understood not only as a convention but also as a tactical intervention.

By replicating two history texts as the dialogue of a learned white authority figure, Hopkins attempted to silence more dominant prejudicial histories
and beliefs with fact, a censure the text wryly performs. Listening to Professor Stone, aghast southern expeditioner Charlie Vance is dumbstruck with
"horror" (Hopkins, *Of One Blood* 99) that "all this was done by *niggers*" (99).
Stone meets Charlie's response with a bemused smile and the recitation of more
than three hundred lines drawn verbatim from Thalheimer's and Rawlinson's
works, lines that are presented simply as "*the* story of ancient Ethiopia" (98,
emphasis added).[13] Using the definite article "the" to characterize the story encourages readers to question what it means to tell history and perhaps what it
meant for Hopkins to tell *the* story of Ethiopia. Further, she allows the history's most skeptical critic, Charlie Vance, to be moved by "the inspiration of the
moment" (106). After Professor Stone's stirring—and uncredited—recitation
of an 1842 poem by *Liberian Herald* editor Hilary Teage that calls for Africa
to "arise" and "retake [its] fame," Charlie, too, recites history (106).[14] Citing

Napoleon (though not the published travelogue from which the quotation is taken), Vance exclaims: "From the heights of yonder Pyramids forty centuries are contemplating you" (106). Notably, Charlie's words record a self-reflexive shift in perspective and agency because he moves from the one who contemplates to the object being contemplated, which may signal an openness to a changed perspective. Given his "inspiration" (106) in the moment, the novel suggests that he begins to form a new worldview about Africa.

Throughout this recitation of history, Hopkins recognized that to advance "the great tide of facts" (*Of One Blood* 87), one must necessarily repeat facts. To that end, she used the form's conventional borrowing to replicate little-- discussed African histories and to question how we conceive of telling history. This tactic also tacitly raises the question of what it means to "plagiarize" as well. If history is a great tide of facts that demands repeating, how do we know to whom the narrative belongs? This pattern of thinking further raises much more troubled questions of the systemic pervasiveness of the white ownership of knowledge and knowledge-making. I would suggest that Hopkins may have pondered such questions herself when she turned to two histories that openly acknowledged the collaborative nature of their work. In fact, in the preface to *A Manual of Ancient History* Thalheimer notes that her work is merely an "outline of the results of the labors of Niebuhr, Bunsen, Arnold, Mommsen, Rawlinson and others" (iv). Similarly, the title page of Rawlinson's *Five Great Monarchies* notes that the work is "collected and illustrated from ancient and modern sources" (n.p.). Whether by intention or happenstance, Hopkins borrowed from history texts that openly acknowledged the work of history as a collaborative endeavor, blurring the lines of "ownership." In this way she both reinforced her own conceptualization of writing as a collective practice and used the conventions of the utopian genre to disrupt the two dominant discourses advancing race prejudice: science and history.

Hopkins's choice to render "plagiarized" passages of science, history, and travelogue as the dialogue of authority figures enabled her to reject the mechanisms of race prejudice that guide scientific and historical narrative and remind readers that knowledge, too, is a white political production. By reminding readers that science faces limits to its understanding of the world and that lesser told histories confirm how prejudice shapes the stories American culture has privileged, Hopkins used utopian conventions to claim ontological space for the Black intellectual. Through this framework, when Reuel finally arrives at the utopian Telassar midnovel, his intelligence is no longer a "paradoxical absurdity" inexplicable to science (James 361). Rather, readers see Reuel as part of a lost past; he is scientifically unclassifiable within a skewed contemporary system and, historically, the continuation of an ancient African civilization, a replica of the lost continent's original inhabitants. To that end, for the partici-patory utopian reader's burgeoning epistemology, Reuel's arrival at Telassar re-futes prejudicial race science, reclaims an oft-ignored history, and reasserts a Black-defined ontology. His arrival literalizes readers' awareness that the Black intellectual is not "an alien life form" (Posnock 65), but rather the fount of all human civilization. From this vantage point, the novel's hidden self is not sim-ply a metaphor for a Black individual passing in white society, it is a metonymy for a once great Black civilization suppressed through fictive constructions of race and prejudicial repression of long-hidden truths.

Performing Disruption:
Intertextuality, African American Utopia,
and Rethinking Utopian Convention

While Hopkins's choice of genre may partially explain her tactical "plagiarism," the utopian form itself, long "a playground for the racialist, eugenicist, and seg-regationist discourse of white writers" (Fabi 45), becomes a site of critique and subversion within her novel. As a hybrid and speculative literary form, utopia afforded African American authors an opportunity to critically engage with the past and present while consciously rescripting a more desirable nation of the fu-ture. Through utopia, the African American novelist could participate in a "lit-erary exercise" intent on "founding a whole new society" (Jameson 3); how-ever, that exercise meant necessarily revising the form, too, given its investment in racialist discourse.

Moving beyond a consideration of Hopkins's "plagiarism" to a discussion of her intertextuality and revision of form, this section argues that Hopkins, likely influenced by Frances Harper and Sutton Griggs, defied utopian convention to subvert the white racial character and program of traditional "reform." African American utopists "adapted in important ways the prescriptive pattern of the utopian genre" to focus on "the process of individual and collective ideologi-cal change that would lead to utopia" (Fabi 46), a utopia wherein the "Negro" wasn't chiefly conceived of as a "problem." While some conventional utopian borrowings may have enabled Hopkins to disrupt racist epistemologies, she, like her predecessors, also necessarily reformulated utopian conventions to sub-vert the mechanisms of a genre that had long supported race prejudice.

Well before readers arrive in Telassar, Hopkins subverted the utopian form by reformulating utopia's traditional first-person narration. Perhaps recalling the "collective terms" through which she envisioned her own literary practice

(Dworkin, introduction xx), Hopkins rejected the utopia's traditional first-person narration traceable to More's work and instead employed a third-person limited narration that directs readers' perspective. Eschewing the limit of first-person narration, which offers little interiority and a singular surrogate for the utopian experience, Hopkins's narration is multiperspectival; it offers intimate, reliable access to several characters' interior development. Hopkins further fostered this readerly intimacy by occasionally giving way to a collective first-person viewpoint, wryly ensnaring the reader in the narrator's fold. Building rapport and ideological perspective at the start of the novel's fifth chapter, for example, the narrator soliloquizes on how "we" come to learn about nature through scientific study (Hopkins, *Of One Blood* 37). The narration even asks a rhetorical question, calling readers to participate in the novel's intellectual project and to wonder about the "revelations of science" they're encountering (37). Further, the novel's final paragraph reaffirms the reader's role within the tale's intellectual project by speaking of "*our* human intelligence" (193). Beyond establishing a participatory reader aligned with the text, Hopkins's changed point of view wages a subversive challenge to the implied white exclusivity of the traditional utopia. While first-person narration offers a surrogate experience of utopia, it is a limited and exclusive one. Readers are given access to a white traveler's tale, a whiteness routinely reinforced by the reader's subvocalization of the first-person "I." By contrast, Hopkins's shift in point of view invites a participatory "we," implicating the reader within an interracial reading collective. Just as Telassar's Afrocentrism challenges our image of a traditional white utopia, Hopkins challenges the way utopia is told by subverting its racial exclusivity.

Hopkins may have drawn inspiration for her subversive adaptations of the utopian form from Griggs's *Imperium in Imperio* and Harper's *Iola Leroy*, pointing to another facet of *Of One Blood*'s intertextuality. For instance, although Griggs names his narrator, Hopkins employs the same third-person limited narration, which gives way to a first-person collective viewpoint.[15] Hopkins's and her predecessors' utopias are characterized by their adaptation of the form's conventions and their criticism of the genre. More importantly, they're also characterized by their re-presentation of history, criticism of scientific epistemologies of Blackness, and relocation of utopia to "the author's present or . . . recent past" (Fabi 47). In *Passing and the Rise of the African American Novel* (2004), M. Giulia Fabi theorizes that rather than displacing utopia to a "future never-never land," African American utopias are vested in a "radical *this*-worldliness," a term Fabi borrows from Hortense Spillers and recasts in her application to utopias (47). Through this radical shift in point of view, time, and place, African American utopias invest in imagining an America that might operate "otherwise" with respect to its Black population, a population that white America has long cast as "a nation within the nation."

For Griggs, imagining an America that might function "otherwise" involved literalizing a nation within the nation. As the Latinate title suggests, *Imperium in Imperio* tells the story of a state within a state. Led by Belton Piedmont and Bernard Belgrave, a secret Black shadow government, the Imperium, covertly operates within America. Despite the significance of imagining a utopian haven for Black readers, however, for the first two-thirds of the novel Griggs, like Hopkins, subverts traditional convention. The work delays an arrival at utopia in order to interrogate, as Hopkins does, the manifold ways in which anti-Black racism and systemic white supremacy were socially and legally codified. Hopkins may also have drawn on Griggs's rhetorical approach, as he, too, replicated history as a means to critique official white discourses of Blackness. Using his novel as an "intervention into official [white] history" (Ernest 188), Griggs juxtaposes the forthcoming trial for the brutal lynching of Postmaster Frazier Baker (novelized as Felix Cook) and his family to the bombing of the U.S.S. *Maine* overshadowing it and relays details from news accounts in each instance.[16] Further, a pivotal plot point that precipitates the "discovery" of the utopian Imperium—a female character's suicide—hinges on the misinformation masquerading as science advanced by John H. Van Evrie's *White Supremacy and Negro Subordination* (1868). Convinced of the truth of this specious work, Belton's betrothed, Viola Martin, summarizes Evrie's text in a suicide note. As she explains, she takes her own life to avoid "impairing the vital force of our race and exterminating it" by marrying a mulatto man, which, according to the work, would lead to sterility (Griggs 84). In other words, Griggs adapted the literary form to highlight the influence of white racial discourse on the Black psyche. By highlighting the extent to which white scientific racism limits Black American agency and self-conception, Griggs used the utopian form's conventional intertextuality to subvert the genre's temporal convention and refocus readers' attention on the mechanisms generating prejudice in the present.

In another intertextual nod to *Imperium in Imperio* (beyond temporal shift, narrative point of view, and Hopkins's curious choice of "Briggs" as her protagonist's last name), *Of One Blood* begins with Reuel's contemplation of suicide.[17] Like Griggs's Viola, who would rather die than contribute to the extinction of her race, Hopkins's Reuel contemplates suicide with "tormenting persistency" (*Of One Blood* 1) as he continues to live in a world where his Blackness and the threat of its discovery determine his potential. Lamenting the "loneliness of his position" (1), that is, the imperiled position of passing as white in a society whose science views a Black genius as an impossibility, Reuel questions the point of toiling "for a place in the world" (1) when "fate had done her worst" (3) by him. Rather than unquestioningly internalizing the specious scientific racism as Violet did, Hopkins uses Reuel's contemplation of suicide and the form's conventional intertextuality to offer readers an alternative epistemology of Blackness. Reuel does not commit suicide; instead, he recites from James's "The Hidden Self." Through this recitation Hopkins provides readers with a critical framework and vocabulary of "new discoveries" that allow them, in application, to question—and even reject—the scientific racism that dooms Viola. In this way, Hopkins offers hope; she offers a science that rejects the "mere dismissal" (Hopkins, *Of One Blood* 2) of "phenomena . . . lying broadcast over the surface of history" (James 361), phenomena that include the Black intellectual.

Through Reuel's contemplation of suicide, Hopkins also makes an intertextual gesture to *Hamlet* that further highlights the insufficiency of contemporary science to account for the psyche of the Black intellectual. Rather than simply lament Reuel's lot or allow him to acquiesce to the weight of racial fictions, as Griggs's Viola does, Hopkins forges Reuel's kinship with one of literature's most psychologically complex characters: Hamlet. As Reuel contemplates whether to be, or not to be, in the novel's opening scene, Hopkins characterizes him as a figure who, arguably, "assumed madness" by passing as white. She thus renders Reuel as a modern Black Hamlet, replete with royal lineage, ever the contemplative "dissimulator" (Vining 48). Further reinforcing this textual allusion, Hopkins scripts Reuel's actions as stage directions "[P]resently Briggs threw the book down, and, rising from his chair began pacing up and down the bare room," only to comment a few lines later that Reuel spoke "aloud" (*Of One Blood* 3) and even that he "soliloquized" (4) about the madness of science. Aside from his physical and intellectual superiority, Reuel has a "passionate, nervous temperament" (3) and acts against gender type as a "benign mother" (4) to his fellow students, solidifying the extent of his existential otherness and kinship to Hamlet.

Unsurprisingly, the character of Hamlet was beset by contentious scholarly debates rooted in equally biased scientific beliefs. Scholarship tended to valorize the Danish prince's "deep humanity" (Vining 61) while castigating his "essentially feminine" (54) temperament and likewise questioning whether his madness was genuine or feigned. Through this "feminine" nervousness, passion, and potential mental illness, Hamlet and Reuel both literalize James's discussion of the "hysteric woman" in "The Hidden Self," as she is a woman who "abandons part of her consciousness because she is too weak nervously to hold it all together" (371). Yet Hopkins, like Shakespeare, faults not the "feminine" character but society's—and science's—proscribed and limited understandings of personhood. Moreover, the allusion allowed her to assert the complexity of Black character denied by white discourses of Black identity. In this way, Hopkins's inspired allusion and the interiority fostered by third-person narration carved a space for Black agency that waxed feminist. Arguably, she imagined an intersectional space that need not see feminine as synonymous with weak or Black as synonymous with bestial.

Imperium in Imperio is not the only African American utopia from which Hopkins may have drawn inspiration to use the form as a meditation on Black agency and the psychological experience of passing. Harper's *Iola Leroy*, the first known African American utopian novel, helped redefine convention for both Griggs and Harper by recasting utopian "space travel" as "race travel" (Fabi 47). Rejecting the futuristic displacement of the traditional utopia and presenting readers with a heroic mulatta, *Iola Leroy* is the eponymous story of an apparently white female traveler who is transported not by time or space travel but by *race travel*. When a scheming white relative reveals the "cross [of Blackness] in her blood" (Harper 85) in order to claim Iola's inheritance as his own after her father's sudden death, Iola is transported from the utopia of genteel southern whiteness to a dystopian Black enslavement. Although Iola is soon freed and relocates to a near-utopian Black community in North Carolina by the novel's close, the story's more crucial travel narrative is that of Iola's passage into Blackness. Though most scholars who characterize *Iola Leroy* as a utopia point to the novel's closing chapter, Fabi argues that the novel wholly recasts the form's conventional traveler trope.[18] Rather than a journey to a different time and space, Harper centralizes the journey of passing, as Iola's "new subject position as a Black woman is at once the cause and the result of the journeys she embarks on after her fall from whiteness" (Fabi 58). In other words, Harper introduces the experience of passing as a device of utopian travel that is clearly dystopian in character. This device not only revises convention but also critically highlights race as both a construction and a performance, ideas that I would argue Hopkins also explored in *Of One Blood*.

Although Harper's contemplative Iola, who wrestles with and rejects the opportunity to pass, may at first glance find kinship with Hopkins's melancholic Reuel Briggs, who wrestles with the torment of passing, I would argue that Harper's attention to the female voice, as well as to the construction and performance of race, may have inspired Hopkins's subversive use of mesmerism and hysteria in her own novel. While Mira, the "sad Negress" (Hopkins, *Of One Blood* 51) (and mother of Reuel, Aubrey, and Dianthe), and Dianthe, Reuel's sister and betrothed, are typically read as tragic characters, by considering Harper's influence on Hopkins the characters develop a degree of feminist agency within their mesmeric/hysteric trances. Rather than viewing hysteria as a "secondary self, or selves, coexist[ing] with the primary one" or "the trance personalities with the normal one" (James 373), I suggest that Hopkins, like Harper, recast hysteria as a subversive performance in response to a dysfunctional culture. By conflating mesmeric and hysteric trances and conceiving of them as performances rather than as part of the "irregular phenomena" (James 361) of science explored in "The Hidden Self," Hopkins denied the centrality of the white male pathological gaze in determining Black women inside—and outside—the text.

In her rendering of both Mira and Dianthe, Hopkins anticipated Du Bois's later theoretical understanding of hysterical behavior as a response to "the experience of racism and its effects on the psyche" (Showalter 334). In *Dusk of Dawn* (1940), Du Bois explains the phenomenon of racism in a segregated white America; he metaphorizes Black Americans as "prisoners" coming to realize that "the [white] passing throng does not hear" their cries of injustice and even "laugh[s] and pass[es] on," leading Black Americans to "become hysterical" in response (66). Significantly, "Mira, the Negress" (Hopkins, *Of One Blood* 51) is one such prisoner; she is an enslaved woman whose name bids readers "to look" as she enters a mesmeric "trance-state" (51) at the command of Dr. Livingston, whose rape of Mira resulted in Aubrey's birth. Hopkins also twice reinforces that Mira's trance is a performance orchestrated by Dr. Livingston. In a public display of his power, he often called upon her "to come and amuse the guests" (51). After he "made the necessary passes" (51), the mild-mannered "Mira changed to a gay, noisy, restless woman, full of irony and sharp jesting" (51). In her changed guise and during what would become her final performance, she foretold the coming peril of the Civil War, and "the dinner-party broke up in a panic" (51). As Hopkins explains, the performance hastened Livingston Sr.'s choice to sell her, since he "could not abide the girl" thereafter, a detail that also hints at their collusion (51). By reading the act as collusion and Mira's trance as a master-demanded performance, the scene becomes a witting defiance of her master and Mira's assertion of her own agency. Cast another way, Mira's performance mends the "twoness" of "double-consciousness" that Du Bois argues characterizes Black Americans' experience of the world ("Strivings" 68). In the moment of her performance she is her primary self; her hidden self is able to express her desire for freedom and retribution upon her captors. She is the loud woman "full of irony and sharp jesting" whose antics make the white throng hear and ultimately call the reader to reconsider the origin of hysteria.

Characterized as both a mesmeric subject and a hysteric, Dianthe, like Mira, asserts feminist agency in her performances. Although Dianthe remains a tragic mulatta, scholarly readings overlook the agency of her mesmeric and hysteric trances, agency perhaps only highlighted when accounting for the novel's ideological nod to Harper's exploration of race travel and performance in *Iola Leroy*.[19] While one scholar rightly points out that Dianthe's "dissociated states imitate accounts of hysteria given in . . . James's own work" (Horvitz 248), she also overlooks that Dianthe, without any prior revelation of magnetic talent, was also a mesmeric subject. As the novel explains, Dianthe left the Fisk University singers, a group that marked her Blackness, "to enter the service of a traveling magnetic physician—a woman—for a large salary" (Hopkins, *Of One Blood* 38), a detail readers are called to reconsider when they learn of the trances of her mother, Mira. Given the typical master/slave, male/female dynamic of "physician" and performer, it is noteworthy that Dianthe worked with a female physician, traveled, and earned "a large salary" (38), details that subvert gender roles, allow her to pass as white, and suggest a profitable collusion. Further, Hopkins's verb choice and syntax emphasize Dianthe's agency in her employment, for Dianthe "*left* the troupe" (38), "*remained*" with the physician for "three weeks" (38), and then "mysteriously *disappeared*" (39, emphasis added). One must also recognize that it was an accident, not an act of agency, that reintroduced Dianthe to Reuel. Curiously, a train accident, the same method of conveyance that precipitates Iola's "race travel" in Harper's *Iola Leroy*, marks Dianthe's passage into a new, white life through a performance that enables her to discard her old one. As Hopkins explains, Dianthe is unrecognized by "the men that admired the colored artist . . . a few weeks before" (39). Hopkins adds that "*her incognito* was complete" (39, emphasis added), a phrase that suggests Dianthe willfully assumes a guise rather than passively succumbing to hysteria.

Further indicative of Dianthe's hysteric agency, her "trance" performance in the hospital echoes that of a mesmeric Veiled Lady and gestures toward Nathaniel Hawthorne's *The Scarlet Letter* (1850) and the utopia *The Blithedale Romance* (1852), two works marked by contrived performances. Just after Dianthe's hysteric/mesmeric performance, Aubrey alludes to a passage in *The Scarlet Letter* about concealed identity that privileges reason over mystery and wryly suggests that most mysteries are contrivances.[20] Dianthe's hospital "trance" is arguably just such a contrivance; it even arouses Aubrey's "keen artistic sense" (Hopkins, *Of One Blood* 42), as if to confirm it is a performance, a performance also marked by amnesia that enables her to continue passing as white. However, for the witting reader the first chapter of *The Blithedale Romance* (1852) explains that the Veiled Lady, a "phenomenon in the mesmeric line," was an "old humbug" that relied on "skillfully contrived . . . stage effect," or, more plainly, a hoax dependent on the skill of the performer (Hawthorne 6). With this context in mind, Dianthe's performance of a trance state from "behind the veil" (Hopkins, *Of One Blood* 40) might also be read as a satirical confession. In her "trance," Dianthe confesses to Reuel and Aubrey that she sees "powers and influences behind the Veil" (she had experienced such power as a mesmeric performer) (40), admits that for "some time the full power will be [hers]" (she overtly controls her performances) (38), and ultimately predicts (or, rather, plans) her own waking and wellness in seven months' time. In her hysteric "trance," which mirrors a mesmeric performance, Dianthe does little more than recapitulate her experience and announce her time frame for waking. Wittily, Hopkins may even have proposed that performance is an underexplored pathway of Black female intellectual agency—for Dianthe does outwit the "genius" Reuel with her hysteric performance, an assertion that may carry an air of personal truth for Hopkins, who was once an actress and singer (*Of One Blood* 3). Nevertheless, reading Dianthe's hysteria as a performance of race travel gives the Black female character feminist agency and subverts the utopian convention of the white male traveler.

As this section has argued, *Of One Blood* belongs within a tradition of fin de siècle African American utopias that adapt utopian conventions to subvert the mechanisms of a genre long supporting race prejudice. Challenging utopia's role as a "playground" for the "segregationist discourse of white writers" (Fabi 45), Hopkins's altered narrative point of view, revised temporal setting, and conceptual exploration of race travel defy utopian convention to subvert the white program of traditional "reform" and to reconceptualize hysteria as a rational response to race and gender oppression. From Reuel's own hysterical antics—pacing, gesticulating, and soliloquizing—to Mira's and Dianthe's performances, Hopkins rejected the notion that hysteria was "a disease only affecting white middle-class women" (Horvitz 256). Instead, Hopkins seems to anticipate feminist scholar Dianne Hunter's definition of hysteria as "feminism lacking a social network in the outer world," as a term reserved for women who defy patriarchal convention (485). More than that, Hopkins predates Du Bois in recognizing hysteria as a logical response to an oppressive culture by using it as a trope to disrupt the white utopia's theater of reform.

Conclusion:
Rethinking the Politics of Black Utopia—
the Prehistory of Afrofuturism

Pauline E. Hopkins's *Of One Blood; or, The Hidden Self* is one of several early Black-authored utopias that collectively subvert the conventions of the traditional white utopia. Recognizing that the traditional utopia (re)actively rejects racial diversity, works such as *Of One Blood*, Frances Harper's *Iola Leroy*, and Sutton E. Griggs's *Imperium in Imperio* subvert the traditional utopian form to critique the genre and to intervene in the systemic white nationalism the form has long helped to preserve. As I have argued throughout this essay, Hopkins's intertextuality and "plagiarism" in *Of One Blood* both participate in generic conventions and constitute a political act of generic remaking. Ultimately, the novel recasts the theater of reform central to white-authored works as a performance of disruption. As a didactic genre straddling the boundary between fact and fiction, politics and literature, the utopian form allowed Black intellectuals such as Hopkins to instruct their readers in the mechanisms of prejudice central to both novel and nation. Indeed, it is only by considering the politics of genre and the novel's place among African American utopias that *Of One Blood* becomes more than a singular political act. Placed among these utopias, the novel becomes a collective decree of Black self-determination, a collective "talking back" (hooks 5) to the fantasy of an American utopia predicated on whiteness.

However, it is not enough to reconsider *Of One Blood* simply in opposition to the traditional utopia or in concert with African American utopias of its period; it must be placed amid the growing study of Afrofuturism, that is, of speculative fiction by writers of color considering the relationship between genre and the politics of race.[21] While volumes such as Reynaldo Anderson and Charles E. Jones's *Afrofuturism 2.0: The Rise of Astro-Blackness* (2015) and Carrington's *Speculative Blackness* map the scope and shape of Black speculative work, Hopkins goes unmentioned. Future historiographies must recognize that these early utopias offer a bridge to later Black speculative fiction and map historic trends of resistance. These early works highlight a critical attention to how white nationalism shaped the traditional utopia form and forge formal innovations in point of view, intertextuality, and the concept of travel distinct to African American utopian novels. As a whole, these Black utopias collectively refuse to "continue gazing hopelessly into the future" (Hopkins, *Of One Blood* 163). Instead, the genre allowed Hopkins, like Griggs and Harper before her, to imagine a more ideal America, one that could challenge the mechanisms of prejudice generated by a nation full of white male voices, recover an intentionally suppressed African past, and conceive of an Afrofuturism.

NOTES

1. Hopkins published only three stories, "Bro'r Abr'm Jimson's Wedding" (1904), "Topsy Templeton" (1916), and "The Test of Manhood, a Christmas Story" (1906) (pseudonymously as Sarah A. Allen), after *Of One Blood* (1903).

2. Only Reid and Fabi consider in any detail Hopkins's use of utopia.

3. For a detailed list of sources "plagiarized" in the novel, see Sanborn. I use the term "plagiarize" with regard to Hopkins's work in scare quotes throughout this essay to highlight the censure attached to the term. I also suggest that racial politics may influence its use in Hopkins's case—and its avoidance when characterizing white utopian novelists. Overall, I want to recast the idea of "plagiarism" as a convention of the utopian genre better characterized as "borrowing," given the systemic criticism inherent in the form, and as a "tactical intervention."

4. See Roemer, especially chapter 1, for a demography of utopian writers.

5. In April 1902 Hopkins wrote about Harper in an installment of her "Famous Women of the Negro Race IV: Some Literary Workers," which was published in the *Colored American Magazine*.

6. In *Archaeologies of the Future*, Jameson calls utopia a "program" that has the formal political intention of "founding a whole new society" (3).

7. See Stanton for a thorough intellectual history of the scientific theories of and publications on race in this period.

8. See *The Descent of Man* (John Murray, 1871), chapter 19, "Secondary Sexual Characters of Man," where Darwin speaks singularly of the different races of man as a single species with varieties, not unlike the variety in color among primates (316–20).

9. In *Race and Reunion* Blight clarifies that "Black South Carolinians and their white Northern abolitionist allies were primarily responsible for the founding of Decoration Day" (65).

10. Bennet explains, "[M]any Populist leaders harbored nativist passions" and often "made derogatory references to 'negroes' and 'orientals' as inferior peoples" (178).

11. Digitized copies of the 1889 Houghton Mifflin edition of the novel include no citation of Tennyson's work.

12. See Sargent for a list of works that reimagine Bellamy's world and characters.

13. Calculated via Sanborn's "The Wind of Words," which documents Hopkins's plagiarism by word count.

14. This work is not documented in Sanborn's "The Wind of Words" or elsewhere. The poem, dated 1 December 1842, is published as "Liberian Poetry" in the *Maryland Colonization Journal*, vol. 2, no. 2, Aug. 1843, p. 32.

15. Griggs's *Imperium in Imperio*, narrated as Berl Trout's "dying declaration," shifts from first-person singular point of view to a first-person plural narration in chapter 1 (7).

16. Griggs uses precise numbers of U.S.S. *Maine* bombing casualties (266) and of the

inhabitants of the town (300) where Baker/Cook lived, likely drawn from the newspapers (99, 100).

17. Coleman argues that "in terms of literary productivity, Charles Chesnutt and Pauline Hopkins were [Griggs's] only rivals," suggesting the likelihood that Hopkins was familiar enough with Griggs's work to include him as part of her "composite" for Briggs (x).

18. See, for example, Kilcup; and Johns, a source that helps to define the modern study of utopia as a genre.

19. For an insightful treatment of the "tragic mulatta" trope in Hopkins's novels, see Pavletich; for a discussion of hysteria as a response to African American women's traumatic victimization, see Horvitz.

20. The line is spoken by Chillingworth, a character disguising himself, to Hester Prynne, who is concealing her lover's identity.

21. Anderson and Jones note that Afrofuturism originated in the early 1990s to characterize "speculative fiction that treats African-American themes and addresses African-American concerns in the context of twentieth-century technoculture" and spans a number of fields (viii).

WORKS CITED

Anderson, Reynaldo, and Charles E. Jones. *Afrofuturism 2.0: The Rise of Astro-Blackness*. Lexington Books, 2015.

Bellamy, Edward. *Looking Backward, 2000–1887*. 1889. Oxford University Press, 2007.

Bennet, David Henry. *The Party of Fear: From Nativist Movements to the New Right in American History*. Vintage, 1988.

Blight, David. *Race and Reunion: The Civil War in American Memory*. Belknap Press, 2001.

Brown, Lois. *Pauline Hopkins: Black Daughter of the Revolution*. University of North Carolina Press, 2008.

Carrington, André M. *Speculative Blackness: The Future of Race in Science Fiction*. University of Minnesota Press, 2016.

Coleman, Finnie D. *Sutton E. Griggs and the Struggle against White Supremacy*. University of Tennessee Press, 2007.

Davis, J. C. "Thomas More's *Utopia*: Sources, Legacy, and Interpretation." *The Cambridge Companion to Utopian Literature*, edited by Gregory Claeys, Cambridge University Press, 2011, pp. 28–50.

Delany, Martin R. *Principia of Ethnology: The Origin of Races and Color*. Harper & Brothers, 1880.

Du Bois, W. E. B. *Dusk of Dawn*. 1940. Oxford University Press, 2014.

———. "Strivings of the Negro People." 1897. *The Problem of the Color Line at the Turn of the Twentieth Century: The Essential Early Essays of W. E. B. Du Bois*, edited by Nahum Dimitri Chandler, Fordham University Press, 2015, pp. 67–76.

———. "The Talented Tenth." 1903. *The Problem of the Color Line at the Turn of the*

Twentieth Century: The Essential Early Essays of W. E. B. Du Bois, edited by Nahum Dimitri Chandler, Fordham University Press, 2015, pp. 209–42.

Dworkin, Ira, editor. *Daughter of the Revolution: The Major Nonfiction Works of Pauline Hopkins*. Rutgers University Press, 2007, pp. 215–48.

———. Introduction to *Daughter of the Revolution: The Major Nonfiction Works of Pauline Hopkins*, edited by Ira Dworkin, Rutgers University Press, 2007, pp. xix–xlii.

Ernest, John. "Harnessing the Niagara: Sutton E. Griggs's *The Hindered Hand*." *Jim Crow, Literature, and the Legacy of Sutton E. Griggs*, edited by Tess Chakkalalkal and Kenneth Warren, University of Georgia Press, 2013, pp. 186–213.

Fabi, M. Giulia. *Passing and the Rise of the African American Novel*. University of Illinois Press, 2001.

Foster, Amber. "Nancy Prince's Utopias: Reimagining the African American Utopian Tradition." *Utopian Studies*, vol. 24, no. 2, 2013, pp. 329–48.

Frederickson, George M. *Black Image in the White Mind: The Debate on Afro-American Character and Destiny, 1817–1914*. Harper, 1971.

Griggs, Sutton E. *Imperium in Imperio: A Study of the Negro Race*. 1899. Greenbook, 2010.

Harper, Frances. *Iola Leroy; or, Shadows Uplifted*. 1892. Dover, 2010.

Hawthorne, Nathaniel. *The Blithedale Romance*. 1853. W. W. Norton & Company, 2010.

———. *The Scarlet Letter*. 1850.

hooks, bell. *Talking Back: Thinking Feminist, Thinking Black*. South End, 1989.

Hopkins, Pauline. "Oceanica: The Dark-Hued Inhabitants of New Guinea, the Bismark Archipelago, New Hebrides, Solomon Islands, Fiji Islands, Polynesia, Samoa, and Hawaii." *Daughter of the Revolution: The Major Nonfiction Works of Pauline E. Hopkins*, edited by Ira Dworkin, Rutgers University Press, 2007, pp. 307–11. Originally published in *Voice of the Negro*, vol. 2, no. 2, Feb. 1905, pp. 108–15.

———. *Of One Blood; or, The Hidden Self*. 1903. Washington Square Press, 2004.

Horvitz, Deborah. "Trauma in Pauline Hopkins' *Of One Blood; or, the Hidden Self*." *African American Review*, vol. 33, no. 2, 1999, pp. 245–60.

Hunter, Dianne. "Hysteria, Psychoanalysis, and Feminism: The Case of Anna O." *Feminist Studies*, vol. 9, no. 3, 1983, pp. 464–88.

Jacobson, Matthew Frye. *Whiteness of a Different Color: European Immigrants and the Alchemy of Race*. Harvard University Press, 1998.

James, William. "The Hidden Self." *Scribner's*, Mar. 1890, pp. 361–73.

Jameson, Fredric. *Archaeologies of the Future: The Desire Called Utopia and Other Science Fictions*. Verso, 2005.

Johns, Alessa. "Feminism and Utopianism." *The Cambridge Companion to Utopian Literature*, edited by Gregory Claeys, Cambridge University Press, 2011, pp. 174–99.

Kilcup, Karen L. *Soft Cannons: American Women Writers*. University of Iowa Press, 1999.

Lipow, Arthur. *Authoritarian Socialism in America: Edward Bellamy & the Nationalist Movement*. University of California Press, 1982.

McDowell, Deborah. Introduction. *Of One Blood*, by Pauline Hopkins, 1903, Washington Square Press, 2004, pp. v–xxi.

McKenney, Samuel. *Slavery: Indispensable to the Civilization of Africa*. 3rd ed., John D. Toy, 1855.

Morgan, Arthur E. *Plagiarism in Utopia: A Study of the Utopian Tradition with Special Reference to Edward Bellamy's "Looking Backward."* Yellow Springs, 1944.

Pavletich, JoAnn. "Pauline Hopkins and the Death of the Tragic Mulatta." *Callaloo*, vol. 38, no. 3, 2015, pp. 647–63.

Peyser, Thomas. *Utopia and Cosmopolis: Globalization in the Era of American Literary Realism*. Duke University Press, 1998.

Pfaelzer, Jean. *The Utopian Novel in America 1886–1896: The Politics of Form*. University of Pittsburgh Press, 1984.

Posnock, Ross. *Color & Culture: Black Writers and the Making of the Modern Intellectual*. Harvard University Press, 1998.

Rawlinson, George. *The Five Great Monarchies of the Ancient Eastern World; or, The History, Geography, and Antiquities of Chaldea, Assyria, Babylon, Media, and Persia, Collected and Illustrated from Ancient and Modern Sources*. 2nd ed., John Murray, 1871.

Reid, Mandy A. "Utopia Is in the Blood: The Bodily Utopias of Martin Delany and Pauline Hopkins." *Utopian Studies*, vol. 22, no. 1, 2011, pp. 91–103.

Roemer, Kenneth. *Utopian Audiences: How Readers Locate Nowhere*. University of Massachusetts Press, 2003.

Rusert, Britt. *Fugitive Science: Empiricism and Freedom in Early African American Culture*. New York University Press, 2017.

Sanborn, Geoffrey. "The Wind of Words: Plagiarism and Intertextuality in *Of One Blood*." *J19*, vol. 3, no. 1, 2015, pp. 67–87.

Sargent, Lyman Tower. *British and American Utopian Literature, 1516–1985: An Annotated, Chronological Bibliography*. Garland, 1988.

Sargisson, Lucy. *Utopian Bodies and the Politics of Transgression*. Routledge, 2000.

Showalter, Elaine. "Hysteria, Feminism, and Gender." *Hysteria beyond Freud*, edited by Sander Gilman, University of California Press, 1993, pp. 286–344.

Thalheimer, Mary Elise. *A Manual of Ancient History*. Van Antwerp, Bragg, & Co., 1872.

Veselá, Pavla. "Neither Black nor White: The Critical Utopias of Sutton E. Griggs and George S. Schuyler." *Science Fiction Studies*, vol. 38, no. 2, 2011, pp. 270–87.

Vieira, Fatima. "The Concept of Utopia." *The Cambridge Companion to Utopian Literature*, edited by Gregory Claeys, Cambridge University Press, 2011, pp. 3–27.

Vining, Edward Payson. *The Mystery of Hamlet: An Attempt to Solve an Old Problem*. J. B. Lippincott & Co., 1881.

Wegner, Phillip E. *Imaginary Communities: Utopia, the Nation, and the Spatial Histories of Modernity*. University of California Press, 2002.

Stolen Words

LITERATURE AS A TOOL
FOR REVOLUTION

Colleen C. O'Brien

Elizabeth Ammons's 2010 monograph, *Brave New Words: How Literature Will Save the Planet*, made brilliant connections between Pauline Hopkins's serial novel *Winona: A Tale of Negro Life in the South and Southwest* and Hopkins's views of the relationship between the natural environment and racial justice. Contrasting the multiracial characters who form their own New World family to the characters of Shakespeare's *Tempest*—a white father who is a healer rather than a sorcerer, a missing mother, a Caliban marked by slavery who is emancipated rather than subjugated, and a virginal daughter who is biracial— Ammons says: "[T]he opening of Hopkins's novel argues that America must embrace its multiracial origins and ground the nation's values in indigenous ways of living with, not in opposition to, the earth" (73).

Intrigued, as was Ammons, by the multiple influences and sources from which Hopkins seems to have created her stories, I wrote in 2014 about Hopkins's borrowings from Henry Wadsworth Longfellow's *Song of Hiawatha* to revisit Seneca history in *Winona*. Carefully studying who could and could not adapt to the many natural environments featured in the novel, I contrasted the issues of encroachment and removal with stewardship, a way of "living with, not in opposition to, the earth" (Ammons 73). More specifically, Hopkins often voiced critical reactions to historical misappropriations of the natural world and misrepresentations of people of color in critical rewritings of or borrowings from various white authors.

In 2016 JoAnn Pavletich extended the critical conversation about Hopkins's "borrowings," illustrating how the turn-of-the-century author and editor plagiarized twenty-five percent of her third novel, *Winona*. Hopkins's generic borrowings, ranging from the western to the dime novel, were already part of the conversation, as was her reappropriation of texts such as *King Solomon's Mines*, an adventure novel by H. Rider Haggard, in her last novel. Pavletich invites us to think about how Hopkins manipulated her literary environment to make similarly political points. Whereas I wrote about the conquest of the landscape, Pavletich wrote about a literary conquest of sorts, claiming for Hopkins "the right to take provocative action to explode racist assumptions, promote justice for African Americans, and expand the possibilities for the representation of black female agency" (116) by conquering and colonizing white literature.

Stealing land and labor are one thing—as are violations of the physical body. Stealing words or literature, on the other hand, might be a strategy for liberation. While Hopkins's contemporaries such as William Dean Howells and Mark Twain would have characterized borrowing twenty-five percent of words from other people for one's novel as plagiarism, I agree with Pavletich that Hopkins was actually making a revolutionary literary move by conquering and appropriating the deracialized or sometimes racist prose of her popular contemporaries to further her radical political agenda. In this essay I make an even stronger case for Hopkins's attention to materialism and her strivings for revolution than I have in the past. The clear demarcation between the institutional practices of theft that she decries—slavery and territorial expansion, for example—and the theft of words for the purpose of telling the truth about the history of the United States suggest that only another revolution could "take that right" (Hopkins 432).

When we question Hopkins's use of plagiarism, I suggest that we view these acts of appropriation as reappropriations, or an attempt to reclaim the territory, both literary and geographic, stolen in four hundred years of colonial conquest. A case in point is Mary Hartwell Catherwood's novel *The White Islander* (1893), from which Hopkins copied many passages directly into the pages of *Winona*. Catherwood's novel takes place in the mid-eighteenth century, specifically, the Great Lakes during Pontiac's Rebellion, yet it does not paint Indigenous rebels as righteous or justified. In contrast, if Pontiac could try to reclaim his own geographic territory, which is the underlying yet unheralded historical impetus of the plot of *The White Islander*, Hopkins could try to reclaim the discursive terrain of savagery and civilization that Catherwood outlined by transposing Catherwood's passages into a story of righteous rebellion that culminates in John Brown's sacking of Kansas. Above and beyond the appropriation of passages, Hopkins intervened in the tone of Catherwood's novel by playing with variants of "civilize[d]" and "savage" (twelve total occurrences for Hopkins) to Catherwood's twenty-two instances of unproblematically dropping the racist terms "savage" and "savagery." Upturning dominant expectations of who is civilized and who is savage or who is a villain and who is a hero was part of Hopkins's practice of refining and refocusing the progressive agenda; this observation informs some of the best scholarship on Hopkins. Alisha Knight's book-length study of Hopkins, for example, argues quite convincingly that Hopkins intervened in conventional narratives to combat racism and sexism, thereby offering up a new version of a dominant narrative. This practice of rewriting dominant narratives mirrors the practice of what we might call plagiarism.

Like Pavletich, Ira Dworkin, and Lauren Dembowitz, I am interested in the historical context of Hopkins's appropriations and sources. Whereas Hopkins's British protagonists, Henry Carlingsford and Warren Maxwell, flee the tyranny of their own family members and of slaveholders, Catherwood's protagonist escapes the Chippewa rebellion at Fort Michilimackinac (June 2, 1763). Like Hopkins, Catherwood painted the British protagonist as a hero. Since the uprising at Michilimackinac was part of Pontiac's Rebellion, we might ask whether Hopkins likewise drew a parallel between Pontiac and the star rebel of *Winona*, John Brown. Certainly, both men were prophets and believers, each in his own form of divine justice.

The subtleties of her plagiaristic appropriations could have sounded a call to arms for contemporaries of Hopkins who had read both Catherwood's and Hopkins's novels; for example, Hopkins describes "squaws . . . with their gaudy blankets wrapped about them in spite of the heat" (288) as she depicts Buffalo, New York, and Grand Island in the 1850s. Language such as "squaws" troubles twenty-first-century readers such as Ammons, and it certainly troubled me until I considered what Hopkins is doing with Catherwood's sentence. Catherwood's opening 1763 scene in Michigan features "Chippewa squaws, huddling their blankets around them in spite of the heat" as well (2). Someone familiar with Catherwood would have noticed foreshadowing in Hopkins's appropriation, for in *The White Islander* only a few moments pass before "the squaws threw back their blankets, revealing the weapons they had carried into the inclosure" to slay the British (3). Hopkins's eponymous, Seneca-identified heroine becomes a warrior woman as well; with this seemingly "gaudy" and even derogatory reference to Indigenous women, Hopkins also marks them as warriors in whose image Winona can become a very different kind of "real woman," one who carries a weapon, as she does later in the novel.

In that light, to continue my discussion of Pauline Hopkins's *Winona* and its historical contexts, this essay first considers the image of Black womanhood, or the "true woman" whom Hopkins depicts in her revision of Catherwood. Second, it returns to the story of Pontiac's Rebellion, which provides a causal background for Catherwood's love story between two white cisgender heterosexuals and considers how that spirit of rebellion nudged Hopkins in an entirely different narrative direction.

Ecstasy or Rapture?
The Budding of a True Race Woman

Lauren Dembowitz registered similar contextual revisioning in *Hagar's Daughter*, particularly a rewriting of the "true woman" trope. The intersections of race and gender figure no less powerfully in *Winona*. In terms of the Indigenous women (by birth and ancestry, that is, not by chosen affiliation), the contrasts between Catherwood's grandmother figure, Noko, and Hopkins's Nokomis are telling. Catherwood took direction from Thomas Jefferson's *Notes on Virginia*, as she represented the Indigenous woman as a drudge. Noko provides some comic relief, instructing the "white islander" and Frenchwoman, Marie, who is betrothed to Noko's grandson, Wawatam. As Noko explains men's uselessness to Marie, she concludes that it would be impractical for people to "be old first, and when we have wisdom enough, grow young" because women "[n]ever would marry any man at all, then" (Catherwood 84). While she occasionally shares bits of folklore and wisdom, Noko primarily is "engaged in the slave work of an Indian woman" (58). We could read her critique of masculinity with a feminist edge; however, she is more of a comic character than a truth teller, as Ammons describes Hopkins's Nokomis (71).

Marie, on the other hand, sleeps on a raised bed rather than the floor and even prefers a "pillow . . . a thing Noko despised" (Catherwood 103). Due to her "Latin prejudices," Marie also prefers a bench to a mat on the ground for sitting (81). This eugenic gesture toward furniture preferences becomes even more pronounced in sexual preferences. Although Marie is supposed to marry Wawatam, she falls in love (and, I would say, lust) with Alexander Henry during their only day together.

In fact, the primary plot motivator of *The White Islander* is the love affair between Marie and the British fur trader, Alexander Henry, whom her fiancé, Wawatam, rescues from the massacre at Michilimackinac. Marie's preference for Henry is as natural as their beautiful natural surroundings on Mackinac Island. Much of Hopkins's borrowed description of nature actually originates in Catherwood's details of setting. Catherwood associates Marie directly with the Indian-pipes, also known as ghost flowers, which also appear in Hopkins's novel. While I have written previously on the significance of the Indian-pipes in Longfellow's *Song of Hiawatha* and their original legendary connection to disputes over land, Catherwood's ghost flowers blatantly signify Marie's sexual awakening and openness to the first Englishman she meets—Alexander Henry. Marie actually gives the flowers they find on the island to Henry, whereas Hopkins's Winona warns her stepbrother not to disturb them and leaves them in their sacred place, untouched.

> Marie beckoned to the new inhabitant of the island. She was sure there could be no rapture like the first finding of Indian-pipes. Her breath paused on her lips as she pushed dead leaves aside and showed the bunch. Their glistening white stems, on which the lucent scales were as delicate as gauze, stood in a family perhaps fifty strong, closely and affectionately holding their waxen heads together. Through some of them flushed a faint pink, but the majority palpitated with a spirit of lustrous whiteness in every part, strangely purified from color.
>
> "Look at them," said Marie, impressively. "They are my own flower."
>
> Henry knelt down and looked at them. He looked also at her face in its birch cap, her wide brows, the rounded chin and beautiful throat, and the braids hanging down over the swell of her young breasts. She lifted her eyelids, and shared the great pleasure of the Indian-pipes with him.
>
> "You may take these. But as soon as you touch them they will begin to change. Doesn't it seem impossible they can turn black?"
>
> "Do they turn black?"
>
> "Quite black, if they are handled. But left in the woods, they go away like spirits." (Catherwood 54–55)

Aside from Marie proclaiming that the Indian-pipes are "her own flower," Henry's shifting gaze (between the flowers and the "swell of [the girl's] young breasts") pretty clearly substitutes Marie's sexual awakening for the "rapture" of the flowers' "open cups" (Catherwood 54–55). In fact, the novel's focus on the rightness and beauty of Marie's love for Henry is just an extension of her love for European furnishings such as benches and pillows. Catherwood takes for granted that a white woman like Marie would fall for the first white man she meets, even though "when Marie sat down in the night camp she never had the degraded feeling of herding with barbarians" (103).

It might seem, at first glance, that Hopkins's heroine is equally problematic because she chooses a British man over her adopted black brother, who loves her in every way imaginable. Yet consider the logic of eugenics at the turn of the century. Whereas Catherwood implicitly argues for the naturalness of two white people preferring one another, Hopkins insists that a woman of color such as Winona has the right to choose a white man. I don't think it's because Winona finds her adopted black brother inferior—he's clearly a hero and an exemplary man. But Judah is Winona's brother and an American, and Winona's claim on justice might include her British inheritance—her land rights—as well as her right to choose a British husband.

As Winona and Judah encounter the Indian-pipes, Judah too looks over the young woman who admires the flowers. His gaze is a bit less lewd, although the "booming of the Niagara's distant flood" that they hear in the background suggests a rather tumescent response in the flow of corresponding human veins. Winona experiences "ecstacy" [sic] rather than rapture, but, more important, she leaves the flowers intact. Comparing this passage to Catherwood's, Winona seems like the "true woman" and Marie impetuous and permissive (if not promiscuous). Not only does Winona refuse to pluck the Indian-pipes, she honors the wishes of the Indigenous woman, Nokomis, who has warned her not to do so:

> A distant gleam among the grasses caught the girl's quick eye. She ran swiftly over the open and threaded her sinuous way among the bushes to drop upon her knees in silent ecstasy. In an instant Judah was beside her. They pushed the leaves aside together, revealing the faint pink stems of the delicate, gauzy Indian-pipes.
>
> "Look at them," cried Winona. "Oh, Judah, are they not beautiful?"
>
> The Negro had felt a strange sense of pleasure stir his young heart as he involuntarily glanced from the flowers to the childish face before him, aglow with enthusiasm; her wide brow, about which the hair clustered in rich dark rings, the beautifully chiselled features, the olive complexion with a hint of pink like that which suffused the fragile flowers before them, all gave his physical senses pleasure to contemplate. From afar came ever the regular booming of Niagara's stupendous flood.
>
> "But they turn black as soon as you touch them."
>
> "Yes, I know; but we will leave them here where they may go away like spirits; Old Nokomis told me."
>
> "Old Nokomis! She's only a silly old Indian squaw. You mustn't mind her stories."
>
> "But old Nokomis knows; she speaks truly," persisted the girl, while a stubborn look of determination grew about her rounded chin. (Hopkins 291–92)

A debate ensues between brother and sister about whether Nokomis knows what she is talking about and whether the nuns at the convent school, whom Winona professes to hate, have brainwashed Judah into believing in some sort of racial inferiority. This solidarity between women—one born Indigenous and the other born a slave—doesn't take the same shape in *The White Islander*. Marie, furthermore, never questions the nuns or priests who advise her.

What Dorri Beam reads as Winona's flowering desire in the Indian-pipes passage carries far more sexual innuendo in Catherwood's version. By comparison, Hopkins's passage seems to veer away from sexual metaphors and instead interrogate the value of Indigenous lore over the dominant culture's religious authority. This is just one way in which reading Hopkins against the "original" contexts of her influencers suggests that Hopkins's literary reappropriations point toward a reappropriation of that which was lost in colonial conquest.

By the end of the novel, Catherwood's Marie escapes her "barbarian" family and weds her Anglo-Saxon hero, providing comfort to the conscience of the Jesuit priest who marries them and who had "guarded her at all seasons in the semi-savage lot from which she sprung into beauty" (163). *Winona*, on the other hand, does not end in marriage. Rather, Hopkins explains, "they made no plans for the future. What necessity was there of making plans for the future? They knew what the future would be. They loved each other; they would marry sooner or later, after they reached England, with the sanction of her grandfather, old Lord George, that was certain. American caste prejudice could not touch them in their home beyond the sea" (435). In the next few paragraphs, at the very end of the novel, a Black woman comments on the irony that Winona could be enslaved in the United States but was a lady in the mother country, England. But it is the "black blood" to which Aunt Vinnie refers that endowed Winona with her righteous spirit and whose righteousness she heralds in the novel's final words as she sings: "De Lord has come to set us free, / O, send dem angels down" (437). Prophecy, this time, travels through the Black woman's voice, and with sights set on divine justice, Aunt Vinnie calls on God's soldiers to end slavery. As Ammons also points out, this is hope that "[j]ustice will come, one way or the other" (75).

Power, Righteousness, and Racial Admixture

Both the Delaware prophet who ultimately inspired Pontiac's Rebellion in 1763 and the Seneca prophets such as Handsome Lake who would reinvigorate Indigenous traditions in an effort to reclaim lost territory in the first half of the nineteenth century advocated a separation from white culture and white people in order to fortify and save Native American populations. Thus the Indigenous religious current behind the movement that incites the plot action in *The White Islander* (perhaps unbeknownst and irrelevant to Catherwood) and the conflict over Buffalo Creek in *Winona* grew from a belief that cross-racial contact endangers Indigenous people. As I wrote in 2014, Handsome Lake's "traditionalist" revivals in the early nineteenth century emphasized unity and the protection of land. When the Ogden Company took control of Buffalo Creek Reservation in 1842 (a historical instance mentioned in *Winona*), the old idea that Christian missionaries and land deals destroyed communities resurfaced.[1] As Matthew Dennis describes it, "[D]islocation . . . undermined traditions," which was also a "characteristic effect of witchcraft to members of the Six Nations" (27). I would go so far as to say that colonizing or land-grabbing practices in Hopkins's representation also epitomize a form of evil.

Seneca nationalism, however, lacked the militant spirit of Pontiac's Rebellion, and perhaps the fact that the Seneca did not reach beyond their own national boundaries (as Pontiac did when he urged the Three Fires Confederacy to attack Detroit) facilitated their removal from Buffalo Creek in 1842. By crossing racial and national boundaries, however, Hopkins's freedom fighters and prophets become a formidable force against white supremacy. Hopkins knew about the controversy over Buffalo Creek Reservation, but it is only the backstory to her more important transnational agenda. It seems that coalition building—the combination of Winona and Judah's history with the Seneca, who were dispossessed, with slavery and with John Brown's multiracial band of militants—provides the force required to stand up to Anglo nationalism. Hopkins appropriated the Seneca past to enter it into an equation, one that not only resists colonial conquest on a variety of levels but that also consolidates acts of resistance from different groups.

Catherwood's novel implicitly endorses white racial purity, albeit in a marriage between French and English characters. However flawed her attempt, Hopkins seemingly desired not only to amalgamate Black and Indigenous movements but also to acknowledge the often forced intermingling of white "blood" among these populations, for, as she says in the first paragraph of *Winona*, "the mischief is already done" (287). No clear line demarcates Winona's Black or Indigenous or Anglo-Saxon selves, just as Judah's horse-training skills emanate mysteriously from "Indian tribes of the West," although he spent his boyhood among the "savage tribes" of slaveholders (320). Hopkins celebrates this combining and commingling of blood and culture. However, while Catherwood permits her Anglo-Saxon hero to marry a French woman, there was no love lost between the French and English in the 1760s. On the other hand, in terms of rising up against the British, as Colin Calloway points out, "a dozen years before American colonists did it, American Indians [under Pontiac] did it" (34). Intrigued, perhaps, by Pontiac's ability to unite with other nations and engage the Three Fires Confederacy in war against their oppressors, Hop-

kins tried to rally a transnational effort against oppression in the early twentieth century. Anglo-Americans, not just English Anglo-Saxons, become the en-
emies in Hopkins's rendition.

In addition to constructing a true Black womanhood in contrast to Catherwood's inherent white womanhood, Hopkins's literary appropriations repeatedly weave transnational tales from nationalistic ones. Winona and Judah negotiate among Seneca, Anglo-American, and African American worldviews.
They also navigate Seneca, U.S., Canadian, and English territory quite successfully. John Brown, the rebel hero of *Winona*, was often compared to Haitian leader Toussaint L'Ouverture by Hopkins, as well as W. E. B. Du Bois.
Winona, for her ability to handle a rifle like a man, continues the path of Hopkins's "Famous Women" Sojourner Truth and Harriet Tubman, who worked
and "fought like a man," respectively (Dworkin, *Daughter* 123, 140).

Perhaps, for Hopkins, the novels and texts that she plagiarized were mere
historical objects that needed revision and recontextualization. The idea of the
individual author does not suit the project of revolutionary social change very
well, anyway. As Ashley Barnes argues in her comparison of Herman Melville's
Pierre and Hopkins's *Of One Blood*, "[T]ogether, the novels deconstruct and
abandon the figure of the author as lone visionary, replacing him with an author who ritually reenacts the truth for all to see. Both novels suggest that this
truly melodramatic author is more progressive than the would-be prophet who
turns his back on the past" (23). Whether Hopkins was reenacting the truth or,
more likely, reenacting to revise what she viewed as the lies of history, we cannot divorce Hopkins from her progressive agenda.

NOTE

1. For more background on the Ogden Company and the Seneca Nation, see Manley.

WORKS CITED

Ammons, Elizabeth. *Brave New Words: How Literature Will Save the Planet*. University
of Iowa Press, 2010.
Barnes, Ashley C. "Variations on a Melodrama: Imagining the Author in *Pierre* and *Of
One Blood*." *Arizona Quarterly*, vol. 73, no. 3, Autumn 2017, pp. 23–47.
Beam, Dorri. "The Flowering of Black Female Sexuality in Pauline Hopkins's *Winona*."
Recovering the Black Female Body: Self-Representation by African American Women,
edited by Michael Bennet, Vanessa Dickerson, and Carla Peterson, Rutgers Univer-
sity Press, 2001, pp. 71–96.
Calloway, Colin G. *The Shawnees and the War for America*. Penguin, 2007.
Catherwood, Mary Hartwell. *The White Islander*. Century Company, 1893.

Dembowitz, Lauren. "Appropriating Tropes of Womanhood and Literary Passing in Pauline Hopkins's *Hagar's Daughter*." "Rethinking Pauline Hopkins: Plagiarism, Appropriation, and African American Cultural Production," by Richard Yarborough, JoAnn Pavletich, Ira Dworkin, and Lauren Dembowitz. *American Literary History*, vol. 30, no. 4, Winter 2018, https://academic.oup.com/alh/article/30/4/e3/5099108?login=true.

Dennis, Matthew. *Seneca Possessed: Indians, Witchcraft, and Power in the Early Republic*. University of Pennsylvania Press, 2010.

Dworkin, Ira. "Black Livingstone: Pauline Hopkins, *Of One Blood*, and the Archives of Colonialism." "Rethinking Pauline Hopkins: Plagiarism, Appropriation, and African American Cultural Production," by Richard Yarborough, JoAnn Pavletich, Ira Dworkin, and Lauren Dembowitz. *American Literary History*, vol. 30, no. 4, Winter 2018, https://academic.oup.com/alh/article/30/4/e3/5099108?login=true.

———, editor. *Daughter of the Revolution: The Major Nonfiction Works of Pauline Hopkins*. Rutgers University Press, 2007.

Edwards, Lissa, "Deadly Lacrosse Game in Mackinac Straits at Fort Michilimackinac in 1763." MyNorth.com. 16 May 2010. https://mynorth.com/2010/05/deadly-lacrosse-game-in-mackinac-straits-at-fort-michilimackinac-in-1763/. Accessed 2 Jan. 2019.

Hopkins, Pauline. *Winona: A Tale of Negro Life in the South and Southwest. The Magazine Novels of Pauline Hopkins*. Oxford University Press, Schomburg Library of Nineteenth-Century Black Women Writers, 1988.

Knight, Alisha. *Pauline Hopkins and the American Dream: An African American Writer's (Re)Visionary Gospel of Success*. University of Tennessee Press, 2012.

Manley, James E. "History of Lein Park: Lot 329." Town of West Seneca. http://www.westseneca.net/about-west-seneca/history/history-lein-park#gsc.tab=0. Accessed 3 Mar. 2019.

O'Brien, Colleen C. "'All the Land Had Changed': Territorial Expansion and the Native American Past in Pauline Hopkins's *Winona*." *Studies in American Fiction*, vol. 41, no. 1, 2014, pp. 27–48.

Pavletich, JoAnn. "'. . . We Are Going to Take That Right': Power and Plagiarism in Pauline Hopkins's *Winona*." *CLA Journal*, vol. 59, no. 2, Spring 2016, pp. 115–30.

PART 3

Textual Practices

"Coming Unalone"

REFLECTIONS ON
TEACHING PAULINE HOPKINS

Geoffrey Sanborn

> All language comes from elsewhere. Few of us really create words of our
> own. . . . We are always trying to integrate new things we've heard from
> elsewhere that don't really fit our own historical language. So that's
> what our sign of ourself is . . . in picking up stuff and trying to fit it in.
>
> —ANNA DEAVERE SMITH

> [I]n the main, I feel like a brown bag of miscellany propped against a
> wall. Against a wall in company with other bags, white, red and yellow.
> Pour out the contents, and there is discovered a jumble of small things
> priceless and worthless. . . . [It is] so much like the jumble in the [other]
> bags, could they be emptied, that all might be dumped in a single heap
> and the bags refilled without altering the content of any greatly.
>
> —ZORA NEALE HURSTON

I've always found it hard to imagine that what I write is my own. Only by virtue of not being my own—of being, instead, no one's at all—can the words I
use be understood; if I were to invent my words, I would be an original writer,
certainly, but no one would have any idea of what I was trying to say. The idea
of owning a certain sequencing of those unoriginal words—this sentence, say,
or this dash-enclosed phrase—is no less strange to me. For one thing, the gram-
matical rules that determine word order cannot be mine for the same reason
that words cannot be mine; for another, I can never know that a chain of words
that I have constructed has in fact never been constructed before. I may *feel*
that what I am writing is emerging spontaneously from the extra-special depths
of my being and that it belongs to me more certainly and inalienably than just
about anything else, but when I subject that feeling to reality testing, it quickly

dissipates. What I write emerges from an interplay between consciousness and language, and it can never be mine alone.

I have, accordingly, a hard time believing what copyright law tells me to believe about the relationship between subjectivity and word order. Here, in one of the most influential passages in the history of copyright law, is what William Blackstone had to say in 1766 about that relationship:

> The identity of a literary composition consists intirely [*sic*] in the *sentiment* and the *language*; the same conceptions, cloathed [*sic*] in the same words, must necessarily be the same composition: and whatever method be taken of conveying that composition to the ear or the eye of another, by recital, by writing, or by printing, in any number of copies or at any period of time, it is always the identical work of the author which is so conveyed; and no other man can have a right to convey or transfer it without his consent, either tacitly or expressly given. (qtd in Rose 63)

"In Blackstone's thought," the critic Mark Rose observes, "the literary text has become an incorporeal entity that can be conveyed from owner to owner according to the same principles as a house or a cow" (64). A remarkable sleight of hand has been performed; the fact that every statement is in at least some infinitesimal way different from every other statement—the fact that "the same doctrines, the same opinions, never come from two persons, or even from the same person at different times, cloathed [*sic*] wholly in the same language," as the eighteenth-century jurist Francis Hargrave puts it—has been turned into the basis of commodification and ownership (qtd. in Rose 72). It's like saying that since you can never step into the same river twice, you must be the sole proprietor of the version of the river into which you have stepped.

A large part of the reason why we tend not to notice the strangeness of this doctrine is that we continue to exist in the culture of possessive individualism out of which the concept of copyright sprang. When that culture first achieved dominance in seventeenth-century Europe, the individual began to be conceived of, in C. B. Macpherson's words, as "the proprietor of his own person or capacities, owing nothing to society for them. . . . The relation of ownership, having become for more and more men the critically important relation determining their actual freedom and actual prospect of realizing their full potentialities, was read back into the nature of the individual. The individual, it was thought, is free inasmuch as he is proprietor of his person and capacities. The human essence is freedom from dependence on the wills of others, and freedom is a function of possession" (3). Only if one understands oneself in this decontextualized, proprietary, and agonistic way is it possible to claim the elements and contours of one's writing—the words that one selects and the order in which one presents them—as one's own personal property. Only in a culture of possessive individualism, where one is "the proprietor of [one's] person and capacities," is it possible to believe that certain small snatches of prose are one's own, to such a degree that their appearance in the midst of someone else's writing may be experienced as a seizure and violation of that which is most intimately related to one's self.

What I love most about the spirit of Pauline Hopkins's nonindividual compositional practices is that it makes it possible for us to dissolve, to at least some degree, the boundaries that have been established by the culture of possessive individualism.[1] "There is no such thing as a single human being, pure and simple, unmixed with other human beings," the psychoanalytic theorist Joan Riviere writes. "We are members one of another" (Riviere 317–18). Yet, Riviere goes on to say, "we cling to the fiction of our absolute individuality, our independence, as if we owed nothing to anyone and nothing in us had been begged, borrowed or stolen" (318). By putting pressure on the belief in the existence of "a single human being, pure and simple, unmixed with other human beings," Hopkins makes it possible to become, in Riviere's words, "deeply conscious of the extent to which our lives and our beings are interwoven with those of others" (318). Both at the level of characterization and at the level of composition, Hopkins contributes to what Dewey Dell, in William Faulkner's *As I Lay Dying*, calls "the process of coming unalone" (62).

In what follows, I want to offer an example of how a recognition of Hopkins's profoundly relational understanding of subjectivity can affect the way in which her works are experienced in the classroom. The example comes from a course called Race and Relationality that I taught at Amherst College in Spring 2017. One of the books on the syllabus—appearing after William Wells Brown's *Clotel*, Mark Twain's *Pudd'nhead Wilson*, and Charles Chesnutt's *The Marrow of Tradition*—was Hopkins's *Of One Blood*. The week that we spent on that book was a turning point in the semester insofar as the students began, it seemed to me, to sense the possibility of a shift in their understanding of the terrain on which one encounters another. With their permission, I have incorporated into the following account of that week some of the things that they posted to an online discussion forum in response to a series of prompts that I had provided. I have also provided excerpts from those prompts and from the handouts that I provided at the beginning of each class. In the spirit of Hopkins, I have tried here to evoke the way in which a chorus of voices emerged from a book that is itself a chorus of voices and to suggest, by those means, how an awareness of Hopkins's collage-like compositional practices can lead to a transformative opening up of relational possibilities.

On Saturday, March 4, 2017, I uploaded the following posting to the class's online forum:

Hi—
As always, you can respond to one of these prompts or write on a topic of your own.
   1) Pauline Hopkins published *Of One Blood; Or, The Hidden Self* over a series of months at the end of 1902 and the beginning of 1903 in *The Colored American Magazine*, a Boston-based periodical that primarily circulated among African-American readers. Where in the opening chapters of the novel does she seem to you to be writing with those readers distinctly in mind? What kind of relationship does she seem, at such moments, to be attempting to establish with those readers?
   2) We've been talking a lot recently about the preemptive denial of the possibility of relations, with Olivia's repeated turning-away from Janet in *The Marrow of Tradition* as the primary example. Where in the chapters so far are you most struck by the flow of relational energies (the current of the current moment)? What are the risks of that flow? What are the rewards?
   3) Intensity, the critic Brian Massumi writes, "is not exactly passivity, because it is filled with motion, vibratory motion, resonation. And it is not yet activity, because the motion is not of the kind that can be directed (if only symbolically) toward practical ends. . . . It resonates to the exact degree to which it is in excess of any narrative or functional line" (86). What are the moments of greatest intensity, in Massumi's sense of the word, in the opening chapters of *Of One Blood*? What kinds of relational possibilities—as opposed to "practical ends"— seem to emerge at such moments?
   4) Like Brown, Hopkins composed in a collage-like way, using fragments of other texts at will. As I've said before, I'm not only not troubled by this, I'm actively interested in it—interested, maybe most of all, in the way that it makes it possible to talk about the fact that language con-

sists of moveable parts belonging to no one in particular and that it operates on the basis of impersonal principles of organization. What, to
you, is most interesting about Hopkins's quoted and unquoted uses of
previously published texts? What exactly makes it interesting?

On Monday, students began uploading responses to my prompts. Here are
parts of a few of those responses:

Hopkins's text is useful in that it gets us thinking about the ways reading
might cause us to think that something emanated from deep inside of us, instead of strictly coming to us from an outside author. This is perhaps the
effect of Hopkins de-centralizing herself through this structural approach.
To me, this is the essence of the type of suspended listening and interaction
we've emphasized throughout the semester. If reading is truly a journey, and
if we are truly actively listening, we can engage in this type of conversation
with the text and the author, momentarily giving ourselves over to their possibilities and producing that relational third that stems out of the experience
of this interaction.

Mr. Livingston professes his love for the now Mrs. Briggs: "I love you better than all in the world. To possess you I am prepared to save you from the
fate that must be yours if ever Reuel learns your origin" (69). Setting aside
the messed-up language of possession, and the fact that he's straight up lying through his teeth this whole time, I found myself stuck on the word "origin." I think that finding the genesis of any object or phenomenon or person is really difficult. Our very being originates in a social structure because
we don't exist in solitude. We become who we are through engagement with
the established social, political, and cultural components that dictate dynamics within our communities. . . . The term "origin" is further complicated by
her lack of memory. She cannot tell her true story, so any attempt to define
her roots would still leave her origin hazy. . . . Finally, because white people
own history, any link between Mrs. Briggs and Africa or the slave trade are
unknown. She's not allowed to have an origin beyond that which is dictated
by the white man.

I thought the opening performance in chapter 2 was incredibly affectively
charged, but in a way you wouldn't expect. Propped up by the description
of Dianthe's transcendent voice—the passage oddly focuses on the anguish
that the audience comes to feel in response to something so lovely. The pre-

ceding hymn washes over the crowd, "sweeping the awed heart with ecstasy that was almost pain" and Dianthe's performance seems to drive the knife home by "[straining] the senses almost beyond endurance" (14, 15). However, the performance's ability to ubiquitously affect each person in the audience with the sheer weight of this anguish, this pain, creates a weird kind of pleasure for those in attendance as well as the reader. Almost like a kind of charged sympathetic affect. . . . It takes you right up to the brink of saturated sensation, but doesn't push you over. It's interesting to further consider that this energy flow is occurring between two sets of experiences; that of the performers and that of the audience. One emerges and is inextricably tied to a history of witnessing and undergoing oppression, and the other is devoid of this particular type of pain. Thus, to borrow a biology term, it might be a flowing of energies via affective "diffusion"; movement from a high to low emotional gradient.

"Reuel was carried out of himself; he leaned forward in eager contemplation of the artist; he grew cold with terror and fear" (15). . . . The New Englanders and Reuel lean in, bending nearer to the sound of those outside themselves, whose lives are speaking in melody to a world not their own— encouraging a bridge from the isolated rooms of mind they may occupy, to lead across to a space beyond their personal enclosures. . . . I recall similar moments in the scenes of the ghost story told on Hallow's Eve and Reuel's reanimation of Dianthe's body. During the ghost story, Reuel and his group sit together in the Vance estate: laughing and exchanging; agreeing and disagreeing; listening and changing with the rhythms of the conversation. Likewise, as Reuel reanimates Dianthe's body there is both skepticism and interest in the air. His confidence impresses the surrounding medical students who are in disbelief, revealing the possibility for their perspectives to change: "physicians and students, now eager listeners, gazed spell-bound upon him, straining their ears to catch every tone of the low voice and every change of the luminous eyes [of Reuel]" (33). Just as the listeners to the music were spell-bound, the crowd here is, too—leaning in to consider Reuel's process, open, though many are hesitant.[2]

On Tuesday, we met to discuss the first half of the novel. At the beginning of class, I gave them a handout on which I had assembled a series of quotations (this too was something that happened in every class). In addition to quotations from their postings, the handout contained passages from Hopkins's works that I hoped to refer to during our discussion and some excerpts from scholarly publications on Hopkins, including the following passages from works by Laura Doyle, Daphne Brooks, and Dorri Beam:

> [*Of One Blood* offers] a theory of association or "magnetism" between bodies that is neither hierarchical nor contractual, neither determined from above nor chosen from below. (Doyle 268)

> By "sweeping the awed heart" of listeners, the choir [in *Of One Blood*] establishes a theatre of movement built on a relational model of "contact." The passage recognizes the ways in which the connection between audience and performer is one of improvisation and interaction and one that is fundamentally constitutive of identity. (Brooks 301)

> [T]he "romantic flashes" in [Hopkins's *Winona*] are textual folds where Hopkins' suddenly sensual language employs a vocabulary of dreams, flowers, and spirits—delaying the action of the plot and lingering over seemingly superfluous nonevents. . . . [She thereby] open[s] an interim in which to sense . . . an alternative presence, not one that emanates from the force of Winona's character but rather is something to which she, more than any other actor in the story, has access. (Beam 172–73)

There are always a lot of voices in the room in a seminar-style literature class, but there were an unusually large number of voices in the room on that day. It wasn't just that most of the sixteen students in the room talked over the course of the eighty-minute period, although that was one of the most valuable parts of the experience, or that there were fragments of scholarly texts in circulation, although that too was valuable. It was that when we turned to the text, the passages to which we turned resonated in ways that exceeded Hopkins's author function, either because it could be shown that other people's writing entered into those passages or because it was at the very least possible that other people's writing entered into them. The generally high level of interest in *Of One Blood* led many of the students to want to anchor what they were saying in specific passages from the text, but what we found ourselves anchored to when those passages were read aloud—particularly the passages from chapter 2, in which Hopkins describes Dianthe's performance with the Fisk Jubilee Singers—were peculiarly unstable places, places that were defined neither by univocality nor by anonymity but by reverberations between multiple points of origin. When a student read the portion of chapter 2 in which the narrator describes Dianthe's singing as "sweeping the awed heart with ecstasy that was almost pain," for example, the words appeared in the room as though spoken in a nearly simultaneous unison by Hopkins and Sir Arthur Quiller-Couch, whose novel *Dead Man's Rock* (1887) had contained the same phrase (Hopkins, *Of One Blood*, 14; Quiller-Couch 255). They carried with them, as well, the specific tones of the student speaking them, not to mention the tones of the critic Daphne Brooks and a student on the online forum, each of whom had quoted them. They conjured up, moreover, the diegetic space of the auditorium, in which, over the course of the chapter's final paragraphs, the relationship between Dianthe's singing and the audience's reaction grows more and more charged.

In all these ways, the words evoked what we had become accustomed to calling "the relational matrix," a phrase derived from the work of the psychoanalytic theorist Stephen Mitchell. "From the earliest days of infancy," Mitchell writes in an essay that I had distributed during the first week of classes, "the individual is in continual interaction with others; his very experience is in fact built up out of these interactions. The representation of self which each of us forms is a secondary construction superimposed upon this more fundamental and fluid interactional reality" (19). We are all animated, Mitchell argues, by "a pervasive tendency to preserve the continuity, connections, familiarity of one's personal, interactional world," in which one is "associated with, positioned in terms of, [and] related to, a matrix of other people, in terms of actual transactions as well as internal presences" (33). What our discussion of Hopkins seemed to crystallize for many students was just how basic and mysterious that relational matrix is, as well as how impoverished one's understanding of race and racialization can become when it does not take that matrix into account. The moments of greatest intensity and excitement for them in the first half of *Of One Blood* were the moments in which a "representation of self" dissolves suddenly into a "more fundamental and fluid interactional reality," a reality in which one is not—in which one has never been—oneself alone.

The discussion turned, at that point, toward James Baldwin, whose work had been a major touchstone throughout the semester. Hopkins's repeated references to the ways in which white supremacism closes certain characters off from that fluid interactional reality called to mind, for several students, passages from Baldwin's works that we had previously discussed. Bits and pieces of those works reentered the room: "Each of us, helplessly and forever, contains the other—male in female, female in male, white in black and black in white. We are a part of each other. Many of my countrymen appear to find this fact exceedingly inconvenient and even unfair, and so, very often, do I. But none of us can do anything about it" (Baldwin 690). "To be sensual, I think, is to respect and rejoice in the force of life, of life itself, and to be present in all that one does, from the effort of loving to the breaking of bread. . . . Something very sinister happens to the people of a country when they begin to distrust their own reactions as deeply as they do here, and become as joyless as they have become" (350). Moving from Hopkins to Baldwin and back seemed to deepen and broaden the class's already-existing understanding of whiteness as a compulsively regenerated defensive structure whose reiterations desperately mask the degree to which we are a part of each other. At no point in our discussion of Hopkins did anyone regret the fact that she was not a heroically self-reliant author, a go-it-alone originator of texts. The idea that there could be anything valuable about that kind of authorship was very far removed from the regions of thought into which our discussions of the novel had taken us.

In my prompts for Thursday's class, I left things more open than I had in the first set of prompts, inviting students either to write on a topic of their own choosing or to pick three passages that stood out for them and write about what made them so distinctive. Several of their responses circled around the relationship between music and mystical experience, especially the following one:

> As a musician, I consider myself more aurally attuned and listening to music is a truly unique experience. I remember one time I was playing in a concert and I closed my eyes and felt my body and mind reacting to the swells and lulls of the music; I felt like the piece I was playing/hearing was taking me into an out-of-body state of being and I felt almost powerless. When I reflect on the power and impact of listening, I think it goes along with the mysticism present in *Of One Blood*. Mysticism as defined on the web is belief that union with or absorption into the Deity or the absolute, or the spiritual apprehension of knowledge inaccessible to the intellect, may be attained through contemplation and self-surrender. Listening to songs or recitations or just sounds has a penetrating effect on the soul and the force of it can cause this self-surrender.[3]

As a way of providing some grounding for our discussion of this topic, I included, on the handout, the following passages from an essay by the musicologist Alfred Schutz:

> [There are] certain forms of social intercourse which necessarily precede all communication. . . . [There is a] "mutual tuning-in relationship" upon which alone all communication is founded. It is precisely this mutual tuning-in relationship by which the "I" and the "Thou" are experienced by both participants as a "We" in vivid presence. (79)

[A] piece of music may be defined—very roughly and tentatively, indeed—as a meaningful arrangement of tones in inner time. . . . [The music listener] is led to refer what he actually hears to what he anticipates will follow and also to what he has just been hearing and what he has heard ever since this piece of music began. The hearer, therefore, listens to the ongoing flux of music, so to speak, not only in the direction from the first to the last bar but simultaneously in a reverse direction back to the first one. . . . While listening he lives in a dimension of time incomparable with that which can be subdivided into homogenous parts. The outer time is measurable; there are pieces of equal length; there are minutes and hours and the length of the groove to be traversed by the needle of the record player. There is no such yardstick for the dimension of inner time the listener lives in. (87–88)

Since . . . all performance as an act of communication is based upon a series of events in the outer world—in our case the flux of audible sounds—it can be said that the social relationship between performer and listener is founded upon the common experience of living simultaneously in several dimensions of time. (93–94)

After sending around the handout at the beginning of class, I played a You-Tube video of Mahalia Jackson singing "How I Got Over." As we talked about our separate experiences of the performance, we built up an increasingly strong awareness of how strange the temporal experience of a piece of music really is. At a certain point, it began to feel as though Schutz's description of "the dimension of inner time the listener lives in"—a time without subdivisions, in which one listens both forward in the direction of the last note and backward in the direction of the first note—was no longer abstract; it began to feel as though it was, instead, a quite clear-eyed way of describing the kind of time that we had all lived in together for the duration of Jackson's recorded performance.

By way of transition, I read aloud another one of the passages on the handout, from Ralph Ellison's "Living with Music": "Perhaps in the swift change of American society in which the meanings of one's origin are so quickly lost, one of the chief values of living with music lies in its power to give us an orientation in time. In doing so, it gives significance to all those indefinable aspects of experience which nevertheless help to make us what we are. In the swift whirl of time music is a constant, reminding us of what we were and of that toward which we aspire" (236). I then asked them to pursue Ellison's evocation of the historical and political implications of music's "power to give us an orientation in time." In what sense, I asked, does your temporal orientation while living with music remind you of what you were? In what sense does it remind you of that toward which you aspire? During the ensuing discussion, I reintroduced some passages I had given them earlier from the work of the psychoanalytic theorist Wilfred Bion:

[The analyst should be guided by] "faith"—faith that there is an ultimate reality and truth—the unknown, unknowable, "formless infinite." This must be believed of every object of which the personality can be aware: the evolution of ultimate reality (signified by O) has issued in objects of which the individual can be aware. (31)

[O] stands for the absolute truth in and of any object; it is assumed that this cannot be known by any human being; it can be known about, its presence can be recognized and felt, but it cannot be known. . . . That it exists is an essential postulate of science, but it cannot be scientifically discovered. (30)

If racism is, psychically speaking, a defensive structure, then maybe, I suggested, what it's defending against is "O"—the always partially withdrawn truth and reality of the other. I brought in another passage, this time from the psychoanalytic theorist Michael Eigen, who argues that "O" is, practically speaking, "the emotional truth of a session," or, in broader terms, the emotional truth of any interpersonal encounter. "In itself the emotional truth at stake may be unknown and unknowable," Eigen writes, "but nothing can be more important than learning to attend to it" (20–21).

Something remarkable happened at this point. The furniture in the classroom consisted of four identical tables positioned at right angles with one another, which meant that we were all sitting on the external perimeter of a square with an open center. Someone, I can't remember who, gestured toward that open space in the center of the tables and asked if that was where the "O" of our class was. This seemed to feel not just true but excitingly true to most of the people in the room. One of the central questions of the semester to that point had been, "Antiracism is pro-what?" From varying perspectives and with varying points of reference—the novel, our class, and experiences outside of class—we went on to say a series of things that explored the possibility that antiracism is, or can be, "pro-O." Many of the students of color in the classroom had already used the word "exhausting" on multiple occasions to describe the often-relentless experience of being forced to attend to racialization and racism. But perhaps, some of us suggested, there might be something nonexhausting, something positively replenishing, that antiracist activities can open up, something that might be described as "O," or an orientation toward "O," and might be located in the psychically charged spaces between oneself and others. Two sentences from Eigen on the handout seemed to resonate with special force at this point: "Our faith in something important happening when we reach out toward the unknowable sustains the attention that clears a working space for truth. . . . For better or worse, the individual who addresses this issue cannot be the same, in the long run, as one who does not" (21).

The class ended here, but our awareness of the musical/mystical dimension of experience, our collective reaching-out toward the unknowable, did not. In our discussions of the course's subsequent texts—especially Nella Larsen's *Passing*, Faulkner's *Light in August*, and Ellison's *Invisible Man*—the postu-late of "O" repeatedly helped to make it possible to resist the pull of the racial binary, the culturally powerful drag in the direction of a strictly white/Black world. That white/Black construct is, of course, as everyone in the class knew from the outset, socioculturally real, and we are all always already positioned in relation to it. But the postulate of "O" enabled us to position ourselves in relation to something else as well: the ultimately inaccessible reality of each of us, the never entirely knowable emotional truth of our encounters with one another, the always potentially open space between us. A huge part of what made that shift possible was Hopkins's remarkable willingness to plunge into mystical interpersonal territories, combined with her equally remarkable desire not to speak as herself alone. If we hadn't read *Of One Blood*, if we hadn't al-lowed ourselves to surrender, at least in part, to what Hopkins describes as "the spell of . . . mysterious forces," it may well never have happened (*Of One Blood*, 102).

"We feel that even when *all possible* scientific questions have been an-swered, the problems of life remain completely untouched," Ludwig Wittgen-stein writes. "Of course there are then no questions left, and this itself is the an-swer. . . . There are, indeed, things that cannot be put into words. They *make themselves manifest*. They are what is mystical" (Wittgenstein 149, 151, empha-sis in original). In the standard account of the novelistic tradition, there is only a peripheral place for existence as such, understood, in Wittgenstein's useful formulation, as that which would still subsist, inaccessibly, even after the last imaginable question about it had been answered. The novel, Nancy Armstrong writes, "was not made to think beyond the individual." But as Armstrong im-mediately goes on to say, "[N]either . . . was it made to reproduce the status quo." It is possible, she speculates, that there will come a time "when novels begin to think of a genuine alternative to the individual, one that does not in-spire phobia and yet is grounded in the world we now inhabit" (Armstrong 25). Teaching *Of One Blood* in ways that draw attention to Hopkins's reuse of other people's language is, or can be, a means of helping to usher in that time. We do not have to—and in fact I think we should not—characterize that reuse in ways that return us to the cult of the independent creator and culture of possessive individualism. We can, instead, think of Hopkins's importation of fragments of other texts as a series of efforts to undermine the separate solidity of her texts, to reground us in "O," to help us hear what she describes in *Winona*, in language drawn from elsewhere, as "the whisper of a secret that has lasted from the foundations of the world" (Hopkins, *Winona* 376; Catherwood 140).

NOTES

1. For accounts of those practices, see Pavletich; Sanborn, "Wind"; and Sanborn, "Pleasure."

2. I am grateful to the four students quoted anonymously here for allowing me to reproduce these excerpts from their postings.

3. I am grateful to the student quoted anonymously here for allowing me to reproduce this excerpt from the posting.

WORKS CITED

Armstrong, Nancy. *How Novels Think: The Limits of British Individualism from 1719–1900*. Columbia University Press, 2005.

Baldwin, James. *The Price of the Ticket: Collected Nonfiction, 1948–1985*. St. Martin's, 1985.

Beam, Dorri. *Style, Gender, and Fantasy in Nineteenth-Century American Women's Writing*. Cambridge University Press, 2010.

Bion, Wilfred. *Attention and Interpretation*. Rowman & Littlefield, 2004.

Brooks, Daphne. *Bodies in Dissent: Spectacular Performances of Race and Freedom, 1850–1910*. Duke University Press, 2006.

Catherwood, Mary Hartwell. "The White Islander." *Century Illustrated Monthly Magazine*, vol. 46, June 1893, pp. 222–30.

Doyle, Laura. *Freedom's Empire: Race and the Rise of the Novel in Atlantic Modernity, 1640–1940*. Duke University Press, 2008.

Eigen, Michael. "The Area of Faith in Winnicott, Lacan, and Bion." *Relational Psychoanalysis: The Emergence of a Tradition*, edited by Stephen A. Mitchell and Lewis Aron, Routledge, 1999, pp. 1–38.

Ellison, Ralph. "Living with Music." *The Collected Essays of Ralph Ellison*, edited by John F. Callahan, Modern Library, 1995, pp. 227–36.

Faulkner, William. *As I Lay Dying*. Vintage, 1990.

Hopkins, Pauline. *Of One Blood*. Washington Square, 2004.

———. *Winona*. Reprinted in *The Magazine Novels of Pauline Hopkins*, edited by Henry Louis Gates Jr., Oxford University Press, 1988, pp. 439–621.

Hurston, Zora Neale. "How It Feels to Be Colored Me." *Folklore, Memoirs, and Other Writing*. Library of America, 1995, pp. 826–29.

Macpherson, C. B. *The Political Theory of Possessive Individualism: Hobbes to Locke*. Clarendon, 1962.

Massumi, Brian. "The Autonomy of Affect." *Cultural Critique*, no. 31, Autumn 1995, pp. 83–109.

Mitchell, Stephen A. *Relational Concepts in Psychoanalysis: An Integration*. Harvard University Press, 1988.

Pavletich, JoAnn. "'. . . We Are Going to Take That Right': Power and Plagiarism in Pauline Hopkins's *Winona*." *CLA Journal*, vol. 59, no. 2, Dec. 2015, pp. 115–30.

Quiller-Couch, Arthur. *Dead Man's Rock: A Romance*. Cassell, 1887.

Riviere, Joan. "The Unconscious Phantasy of an Inner World Reflected in Examples from Literature." *The Inner World and Joan Riviere: Collected Papers, 1920–1958*. Karnac Books, 1991.

Rose, Mark. "The Author as Proprietor: *Donaldson v. Becket* and the Genealogy of Modern Authorship." *Representations*, vol. 23, Summer 1988, pp. 51–85.

Sanborn, Geoffrey. "The Pleasure of Its Company: *Of One Blood* and the Potentials of Plagiarism." *ALH* Online, vol. 32, 2020, pp. e1–e22.

———. "The Wind of Words: Plagiarism and Intertextuality in *Of One Blood*." *J19*, vol. 3, no. 1, Spring 2015, pp. 67–87.

Schutz, Alfred. "Making Music Together: A Study in Social Relationship." *Social Research*, vol. 18, Mar. 1951, pp. 76–97.

Smith, Anna Deavere. Interview with Thulani Davis. *Bomb*, no. 41, Fall 1992. Accessed 22 Mar. 2022.

Wittgenstein, Ludwig. *Tractatus Logico-philosophicus*. Translated by D. F. Pears and B. F. McGuinness, Routledge, 1961.

The Serial Pleasures of Reading
Pauline Elizabeth Hopkins

Cherene Sherrard-Johnson

Recent scholarship on Pauline E. Hopkins has focused on her tendency to engage in "inspired acts of borrowing" from contemporaneous fiction writers, including plotlines and dialogue that she recycled for her own purposes (Brown 385). This type of data mining has left her open to a spectrum of accusations ranging from outright plagiarism to narrative recycling. As I reread Hopkins's serial fiction available in various forms, from online periodical collections to the Schomburg's recovered, compact editions, it seems there's been a reversal of sorts. Current popular culture appears to be taking its cues from Hopkins's novels. Before Meghan Markle—formerly an actress who could easily have been cast as the heroine in a Lifetime movie adaptation of *Hagar's Daughter* and now H.R.H. the Duchess of Sussex—wed Prince Harry, Hopkins's mixed-race characters were finding "all the fire and romance" with their suitors along with freedom on British soil; before Wakanda, there was Telassar, a hidden city in the technologically advanced Black nation of Meroe; and before BlackLivesMatter was a hashtag and a movement, there was Hopkins's serialized anti-lynching campaigns, amplified by a conjunction of fictive and journalistic exemplars featured in the *Colored American Magazine*. A case in point: reading Hopkins's staging of Grace Montfort's figurative "rape" in *Contending Forces* as a lynching underscores what we know from the case of Sandra Bland: that gender does not exempt women from lynching's brutal exemplary logic. Conversely, today's headlines seemed "ripped" from Hopkins's novels, underscoring the resonance of her political and aesthetic concerns for twenty-first-century readers. This chapter reflects on the ways in which Hopkins's serial fiction, with its collation of art and activism, print culture and sensation, provides a source of unending pleasure and inspiration that we see reciprocated in contemporary cultural productions.

In considering how popular culture seems to have its recursive fingers on the pulse of Hopkins's literary imagination, several comparative options come to mind. Hopkins's fascinating fusion of political and aesthetic aims uses sensational plot trajectories and sentimental tropes to unsettle and galvanize, as well as entertain. We return to her serial fiction for complex revisionist histories, cliff-hanging chapters, and irresistible heroines. With the emergence of Afrofuturism, scholars and practitioners have identified *Of One Blood* as a generic forerunner of speculative fiction. As science fiction writer Nisi Shawl writes, "[D]eclaring the Martin Bernal–esque idea of Black civilization's primacy in audacious fullness, Hopkins has an official of this proto-Wakanda lecture American-born Reuel that from it came 'all the arts and cunning inventions that make your modern glory'" (1). Hopkins's fictive recovery of the lost city of Meroe becomes a way of filling in historical lacunae with an inspiring ancestral past, even if it runs the risk, as in the case of *Black Panther*'s Wakanda, of embracing a romanticized, "authentic" African past that overwrites and obscures contemporary Black achievements. Hopkins's Pan-Africanist, proto-Afrocentric vision is simultaneously Afrofuturistic and recursive. And while there are reasons to cheer the revelation of Telassar in *Of One Blood* as we do director Ryan Coogler's cinematic rendering of the technologically superior yet culturally intact Wakanda, the class/caste dynamics of dynastic inheritance remain uninterrogated in both settings. The intractability of social hierarchy as it manifests inter- and intraracially also underscores the otherwise celebratory atmosphere surrounding coverage of Meghan Markle's biracial identity, courtship, and nuptials.

Reading Markle as a twenty-first-century reboot of a Hopkins heroine, I explore how Hopkins makes room for Black women's audacious desires as they negotiate their relationship to labor and leisure in *Hagar's Daughter: A Story of Southern Caste Prejudice* (1901–02). As I watched the early morning televised royal wedding, I was struck by Reverend Curry's sermon about the resilient faith of enslaved Africans. Preaching about the hope for a "balm in Gilead" was an utterly appropriate preface to the marriage vows of an African American woman and an heir to British imperialism. I struggled, however, to process my conflicted response to a union that we are meant to celebrate as "historic" but that is also potentially a reinscription of the melodramatic tragic mulatta plot trajectory made familiar through Hopkins's many serial novels. The hoopla surrounding Markle's identity indicates that an undiminished appetite for sensational race melodrama, especially when combined with aspirational social climbing, remains a serial pleasure for American and British audiences. A significant difference: one hundred years after Hopkins's heroines took their last tragic leaps, another of "Hagar's beautiful daughters" finally got her fairytale ending (Wallinger v).

Within the matrix of Hopkins's intertextual recycling, the uncanny resonance of her themes, characterizations, and plotlines prompts transhistorical thinking about representations of Black labor and leisure across artistic genres. *Hagar's Daughter* is an evocative exemplar of both Hopkins's literary versatility and the urgency of identifying and privileging Black women's perspectives on their own labor. In light of the success of Kathryn Stockett's novel *The Help* (2009) and the mainstream accolades showered on the subsequent (2011) film adaptation about a white amanuensis who purports to reveal the corrosive side of southern aristocracy from the point of view of African American domestics, we remain in desperate need of richer, contextualized portrayals of Black women's labor and domestic work in the nineteenth century that invert the margin to center approach valorized in mainstream representations of racialized dissent. Mid-nineteenth-century writers such as Eliza Potter and Elizabeth Keckley penned "tell-alls" that were gleaned from their outsider-within positions and that achieved a measure of notoriety, if not popularity. The uniquely diasporic, transnational sensibilities expressed in Hopkins's serialized novels move representations of Black labor beyond the constraints of the politics of respectability. In the broadest sense, I'm interested in how returning to Hopkins and her nineteenth-century predecessors helps us reconsider our understanding of Black women's labor and leisure and explains the nostalgic traffic in works such as *The Help* that purport to explore the complex intimacy of the relationship between the white mistress and the Black servant/caregiver. Reading contemporary cinematic and popular culture with Hopkins's pioneering writing exposes and foregrounds Black women's audacious desires; however, such reading also reveals the ways in which, even as the historical context shifts, class/caste mobility continues to be tethered to unequal racial hierarchies and colorism. Such residual dynamics remain entrenched even as we celebrate seemingly progressive events such as Meghan Markle's wedding to Prince Harry.

Audacious Desires and Stolen Pleasures

Before delving into Hopkins's complexly racialized delineations of labor and leisure in *Hagar's Daughter*, I turn briefly to Valerie Martin's *Property* (2003) to identify what I mean by Black women's audacious desires. Audacious desires are Black women's aspirations for minor pleasures in the face of radical fights against racial and sexual violence. These often-suppressed yearnings to consume or experience pleasure are integral to individual self-realization and personal fulfillment. They can be overshadowed by the seemingly insurmountable injustices Black women have faced throughout their sojourn in the Americas. Hopkins's writing makes room for these lesser longings within her political advocacy for social and economic parity and racial justice. The following passage from Martin's *Property* illustrates how inconceivable these desires can be to white women who cannot see beyond the superficial stereotypes of enslaved domestic labor. *Property* is what Glenda Carpio calls a fiction of slavery, a more capacious category than the neo–slave narrative genre (32).[1] In the final scene of the novel, which takes place on a Louisiana plantation in 1828, the mistress has gone to great expense to have her housemaid, who escapes during an insurrection, remanded to slavery:

> Her eyes wandered away from me, to the plate on the table, the cup next to my hand. A strange inward-looking smile, as at a recollection, compressed her lips. "When you gets to the North," she said, "they invites you to the dining room, and they asks you to sit at the table. Then they offers you a cup of tea, and they asks, 'Does you want cream and sugar?'"
>
> I was dumbfounded. It was more than I had ever heard her say. My uncle was right, I thought. She had changed; she'd gone mad. I took a swallow of my coffee. "And this appealed to you?" I asked.
>
> "Yes," she said, raising her eyes very coolly to mine. "It appeal to me."
>
> I considered this image of Sarah. She was dressed in borrowed clothes, sitting stiffly at a bare wooden table while a colorless Yankee woman, her thin hair pulled into a tight bun, served her tea in a china cup. The righteous husband fetched a cushion to make their guest more comfortable. It struck me as perfectly ridiculous. What on earth did they think they were doing? (Martin 192)

The mistress's response to her servant's longing to be served and catered to, to have her individual preferences acknowledged, underscores how unimaginable Black leisure was for white slaveholders. The mistress/servant dynamic overwhelms and subordinates Black women's desires, which are read as uppity or absurd. But it is precisely this audacious yet minor desire for comfort and specificity that provokes confounding irritation on the part of the mistress and subsequently mobilizes extreme, suppressive action. Affect theory from Sianne Ngai to Sarah Ahmed has traced the impact of the sly undercurrent of emotions often hiding in the crevices of the overplots of late nineteenth-century and early twentieth-century fiction. Reading with a set of tools designed to probe the petty and pleasurable alongside the elevated and politically charged allows for a textual encounter that on the surface appears to be more organic to nineteenth-century rather than twenty-first-century reading. Such analysis remains pertinent because, as the textual and cinematic iterations of *The Help* indicate, Black women's desires continue to be illegible to mainstream reading/viewing audiences.

Revisiting nineteenth-century Black women's writing can unearth the multidimensional complexities of Black laboring women, thus contradicting popular, even sympathetic stereotypes of these women as childlike, asexual, or static. In *A Hairdresser's Experience in High Life* (1859), Hopkins's predecessor Eliza Potter explored the mistress/maid dialectic without the need for a white amanuensis to ventriloquize for Black domestic workers. In her preface Potter writes: "[N]owhere do hearts betray themselves more unguardedly than in the private boudoir, where the hair-dresser's mission makes her a daily attendant" (1). As Xiomara Santamarina describes, the "triangulated relationship between a Black working woman, her elite female clients and her Cincinnati readers illustrates how African American working women's authorship offered an even more contradictory and paradoxical space for racial social legitimacy than we have yet recognized" (xx). Potter, referred to by her clients as "Iangy," moves through some of the most fashionable leisure spaces of the mid-nineteenth century: Saratoga, Newport, Paris, and London. Similar to Elizabeth Keckley in *Behind the Scenes* (1868), a tell-all memoir of life in the White House during the Lincoln administration, Potter establishes herself as an authority on the genteel performance of ladyhood. She moves with surprising autonomy and mobility through interclass, interracial, transnational sites. Observations include "I supposed some of my readers would like to know what a clambake is" and "My ladies in New York: I am proud to say *my* ladies" (Potter 102, 104). Potter explicitly demonstrates that women cannot achieve or maintain their class status, respectability, and chicness without her specialized niche labor as a stylist. Similarly, in *Property*, one of the motivating factors the mistress has for chasing down her maid is that she can't find another as skilled in French hair designs.

Showcasing Black women's varied perspectives on labor and leisure, as Hopkins does in her fiction, is an antidote to the superficial and skewed representations of domestics in *The Help* and echoes the types of textured representations now appearing with more frequency in popular culture.[2] It's worth noting that Hopkins's attentiveness to Black women's desires also drew in what Laura Wexler calls "unintended readers" (102) along with the audiences she was hoping to simultaneously entertain and educate, thus provoking responses such as the one from a white reader of the *Colored American Magazine* who canceled her subscription. In a letter to the editor, the reader writes: "[T]he stories of these tragic mixed loves will not commend themselves to your white readers and will not elevate the colored readers." Hopkins retorts: "I am glad to receive this criticism for it shows more clearly than ever that white people don't understand what pleases Negroes" (*Colored American Magazine*, May 1903, 399). The idea that there might be a discordance or fracture between white and Black readerships is no surprise. Conversely, my position as a potentially unintended reader/viewer of *The Help* allows me to discern how untenable Stockett's white female housewives find minor expressions of Black female desire and how drastically it is disciplined. Hopkins was writing at a time of intense racial violence and precarity, yet she still imagined a readership with the leisure time to absorb "fire and romance" and gain multiple benefits from her fiction. Identifying the pleasurable aspects of Black artistic production is not merely self-congratulatory appeasement; instead, it can be an affirmation of a complex interior self and a respite in a climate of extreme anti-Black violence.

Hagar's Daughter features the first example of an African American female detective, as well as a cohort of intergenerational, mixed-race characters that can be collectively referred to as what Hanna Wallinger calls "Hagar's Beautiful Daughters" (v). Each segment of the serial propels an expansive multigenerational tale of romance and political intrigue. It's a challenge to tackle the entirety of the novel—Holly Jackson rightly calls the plot "byzantine" (195). Lois Brown's historicized exegesis reveals the novel as a "highly textured literary palimpsest" whose layers include "the Old Testament, British epic poetry, romantic tragedy" (326). What better way to transmit revisionist history, especially Civil War accounts, than through a dynamic, novelistic medium? Jackson argues that the novel is marked by a "disruptive narrative mode," featuring interruptions, false starts, and repetition that reinforce themes regarding "the failure of historical progress" (194). Hopkins's recursivity points to the failure of the progressive narrative of history at the turn into the twentieth century. Stories, for Hopkins, exist to be retold. Recent scholarship tracing her textual recycling, what JoAnn Pavletich and Lois Brown respectively call her "unacknowledged" (116) and/or "inspired" (385) borrowings and what Gregory Sanborn has termed her "plagiaristic aesthetic" (84) illustrates the breadth and diversity of her source material.[3] I agree with Jackson that, "[f]ar from unoriginality, this repetition marks an instance of intertextual suturing that contributed to the establishment of an African American literary tradition and typifies Hopkins's signature strategy as a writer of politically-engaged historical romance" (193). What I find most intriguing is the novel's exploration of "caste prejudice" as it intertwines race and class in a politically inflected romance that dabbles in true crime.

Through Venus Camilla Johnson, Hopkins offers both a class critique and an alternative heroine of the homespun variety. By embedding a detective narrative within her revisionist historiography, she highlights the relationship between the passing narrative and the detective genre. Passing stories are often about detecting or revealing the hidden or mysterious. Writing just as the passing narrative and detective story became marketable and prevalent genres, Hopkins fused the two emergent forms. Her source material includes several thrillers and mysteries published in periodicals such as *Frank Leslie's Popular Monthly*.[4] In Hopkins's racialized conscriptions, detectives confront inadvertent passers with their "true identities"; deliberate passing performances are revealed or disclosed, but it is in the second half of the novel that the first instance of a Black female detective takes center stage. Two working women, a laundress (Aunt Henny) and a lady's maid (Venus), serve as witnesses to a murder and function as secret agents who provide critical information leading to the temporary salvation of the heroine and hero of the text. Venus possesses an intuitive ability to discern facts veiled to the white detective enlisted in the case: what Stephen Soitos calls her "double-conscious deductive ability" (67). She not only uses her intuitive powers but also disguises herself as a Black male in order to infiltrate the plantation estate where one of the main protagonists, Jewel Bowen, and Aunt Henny have been sequestered. Through her plucky sensibility, she also provides a comic aspect to the historical melodrama: "I'll see if this one little black girl can't get the best of as mean a set of villains as was ever born" (Hopkins 221). The celebration of Venus's acumen, however, is somewhat tempered by how she is juxtaposed with the central female figures of the book. As Brown writes, "It is sobering, though, to see that no matter their perspicacity, the rewards and advances for African American women are always linked to labor" (322). Another sobering and perhaps unanticipated deduction is that in Hopkins's fiction, leisure, it seems, is only for the light-skinned.

Dark-Skinned Labor and
Venus Johnson's Perspicacity

What, if any, forms of leisure or respite from labor does Hopkins imagine for Hagar's daughters' dark-skinned servants? Is their destiny vastly different from the one recycled in the narrative and cinematic versions of Stockett's *The Help*?

Offering *Hagar's Daughter* as anodyne to the unsatisfying mammies and maids who populate *The Help* has its own perils. Kristina Brooks identifies in her reading of Hopkins's use of "racial pornography" "a new and undertheorized category of representation that conjoins the loaded issues of racial difference and sexuality" (120). Wallinger and Brown in their respective biographies do not engage Brooks's reading of the stock figures in *Hagar's Daughter* as racial pornography. The dark-skinned characters whose habitat is not Washington, D.C.'s drawing rooms and boudoirs but the space of the plantation and the field recall stock characters from the minstrel tradition in discomforting ways. They provide comic relief as "sideshow to the main act." Though I would argue that the escapades of the "miscegenating mulataroons," to borrow a term from Jennifer Brody (14), is comedic melodrama at its finest, Marthy, one of the plantation darkies, astutely comments, "Colored women wasn't made to take their comfit lak white ladies. They wasn't born fer nuthin' but ter wurk lak hosses or mules" (Hopkins 171). According to Marthy's logic, Black women's labor buttresses white women's comfort. Indeed, the various deaths and near deaths experienced by the trio of passing mixed-race characters suggest that when the privilege of a leisurely existence is threatened, they cannot tolerate the alternative. Dependence on white male benevolence and their darker sisters' work renders their type of heroism unsustainable.

Rather than the proliferating mulattas, Venus Johnson (the Black female detective prototype) is the *real* figure of mediation in *Hagar's Daughter*. Brooks puts her finger on Venus's "interpretative slipperiness" (148) and her vacillation between embodying a racial stereotype and crafting a uniquely inventive individualism. Venus moves back and forth across the regional divide of North and South and the spatial negotiation of plantation versus parlor, and she thwarts the notion of a fixed distinction between male and female gender roles. In contrast to the women who are ignorant of their one drop, Venus consciously performs her shifting identities. She code-switches her dialect, affirming, on the one hand, that "I ain't a bit slow, no'm, if I do say it, an' I jus' thought hard for a minute, an' then *it struck me!*" (Hopkins 240, emphasis in the original), and, on the other, that she "forgot her education in her earnestness, and fell into the Negro vernacular, talking and crying at the same time" (224). As the linchpin between the passing narrative and detective story with the ability to traverse class and gender lines, Venus emerges as an important mediator. If the mulatta serves alternately as a surrogate for white readers and a challenge to binary constructions of racial identity, then Venus audaciously speaks for the majority of Black women in the early 1900s for which labor remains a more recognizable activity than leisure.

In *Living In, Living Out: African American Domestics and the Great Migration,* Elizabeth Clark-Lewis draws upon the oral histories of domestic workers to illustrate the conflicts between the established African American communities whose social activities were religiously covered in the society columns of the *Washington Bee* and the discomfort their behavior and affect provoked in the southern migrant women they employed. Beulah Nelson recalls the inflections of her employers: "[T]hey sounded so different and nice to me . . . clear and sweet to hear, like music"; "And then I heard me just talking so bad. I didn't like to talk to them, never" (Hopkins 93). Venus Johnson shares Beulah's background and ancestry, but Hopkins shows how she has adapted her voice in a way that allows her to move across spaces proscribed by race and class. Described as "a treasure" (217), what's valuable about Venus is her intellect and independence, not just her labor and loyalty: "The brain of the little brown maid was busy. She had her own ideas about certain things" (217). Like the Washington, D.C., domestics featured in Clark-Lewis's study, Venus has a tight-knit and nourishing kinship network. When not with her passing mistress, she returns home for a visit described as "a festival" complete with "gumbo soup, chicken and rice and coffee of an amber hue" (218). As Venus and her brother digest the delicious meal "with gusto" her mother observes "I reckon you don' git nothin' like it up yonder with all the fixin's you has there" (218). In nearly every scene, Hopkins makes a point of referencing Venus's brownness alongside her "extreme intelligen[ce]" (223). Moreover, unlike the self-conscious Beulah, Venus "was not at all embarrassed by the novelty of her surroundings, but advanced toward the chief with a business-like air" (223).

The American fixation on the upstairs/downstairs motif (as evidenced by the exceptionally dramatized popularity of the Masterpiece theater series *Downton Abbey*) has a tendency to reify rather than to overturn class lines. In Venus Johnson, *Hagar's Daughter* offers a more palatable and complex mediator than central protagonists of *The Help*. To sum up simply, *The Help* is the story of a burgeoning writer (Skeeter) who finds her own voice and a career by ventriloquizing the stories of domestic workers of her hometown in a "tell-all" bestseller. As Skeeter gains the trust of her informants, the partnership should be mutually empowering, but both the novel and subsequent film were criticized for portraying caricatures and stereotypical Black female characters designed to appease and appeal to white audiences. A key critique was that these women required a young white interlocutor to "find" their voices and resist the perniciousness of Jim Crow. Octavia Spencer won a Best Supporting Actress Oscar for her portrayal of Minny, while Oscar nominee Viola Davis regretted her participation in the film: "'I just felt that at the end of the day that it wasn't the voices of the maids that were heard,' Davis said. 'I know Aibileen. I know Minny. They're my grandma. They're my mom. And I know that if you do a movie where the whole premise is, I want to know what it feels like to work for white people and to bring up children in 1963, I want to hear how you really feel about it. I never heard that in the course of the movie.'" Moreover, continuing to traffic in civil rights fantasies that subordinate Black women's desire in service of white women's self-actualization overshadows how immigration has impacted domestic labor in the twenty-first century. It's a bitter irony that *The Help* could achieve wide success at a moment when the domestic labor market is in fact a transnational space populated not by the descendants of formerly enslaved African Americans but by women from Central and South America and the Caribbean basin.

The Black maid / white lady binary is usefully deployed in civil rights stories that subscribe to a progressive narrative of history that privileges interracial partnerships and the role of white liberals (as abolitionists, fellow travelers, etc.) over the role of grassroots intraracial organizing. In order to preserve its benevolent white heroine, the cinematic adaptation excised the novel's more pernicious portraits of the white mistress's vindictiveness: "It'll be a knock on the door, late at night. It won't be the white lady at the door. She don't do that kind a thing herself. But while the nightmare's happening, the burning or the cutting or the beating, you realize something you known all your life: the white lady don't *ever* forget. And she ain't gone stop till you dead" (Stockett 188). Aibileen's chilling narrative of the toxic toolkit of white femininity echoes the grotesque dynamics assiduously chronicled in Harriet Jacobs's famously disturbing chapter "The Jealous Mistress" in *Incidents in the Life of a Slave Girl* (1861). At best, *The Help* offers readers a backstage pass to the downstairs perspective via its cultural informant while obscuring the more complex intimacy of such labor relations and the global implications of outsourcing and surrogacy.

While the space of this essay does not allow extensive, comparative delving into the novel or film versions of *The Help*, one distinct omission or revision speaks to the film industry's continued reluctance to reckon with the unsettling evidence of racial ambiguity and Black interiority. To maintain the status quo, the film excludes a storyline that echoes the very thematics that have driven the plots of many of Hopkins's racial melodramas. The amanuensis in the novel has her own evolving mammy story that she feels compelled to include in the book she's writing. Because her childhood caretaker, Constantine, is dead, Miss Skeeter has to piece together the reasons for her dismissal or absconding. She discovers that Constantine left because Miss Skeeter's mother had insulted and injured Constantine's daughter when the girl had the audacity to come to the

front door while Miss Skeeter's mother was entertaining a crowd of society ladies, members of the local chapter of the Daughters of the American Revolution. In the novel, Constantine becomes estranged from her daughter, Lulabelle, whom she is forced to send away because it was impossible to raise a child
who could pass: "Being Negro with white skin . . . in Mississippi; it's like you
don't belong to nobody" (Stockett 358). Lulabelle's appearance, "pale as snow"
with straight "hair the color a hay," is unsettling in the way that evidence of interracial sex is always disconcerting in an environment of interracial domestic
intimacy. Her possession of a white skin and her willingness to weaponize its
privilege invoke both the systematic rape of enslaved women and the complicated, incestuous genealogies of the master's enslaved or free(d) children. This
is the very dynamic that Hopkins identified as one of the "contending forces"
facing Black communities following Reconstruction. I want to underscore that
what is audacious about Lulabelle is not just her appearance but "acting white
when she was colored" and "help[ing] herself to another piece of cake" at a
DAR party. The book does not delve too deeply into this act of resistance, so
it is easily dispensed with in the on-screen translation. I linger on this incident
to illustrate that Lulabelle's unforgivable transgression is her audacious desire
to access the minor pleasures of the parlor over the labor of the kitchen. Like
the refusal of the mistress in *Property* to acknowledge her fugitive maid's desire
for tea, not only does leisure remain out of reach, but any expression of Black
women's yearning for it is perceived as mental derangement: "She'd gone mad."
If Lulabelle's whiteness emboldens her to transgress the color line between mistress and mammy, it is also tragic because it severs her from her mother and,
when her mother cannot forgive her employer, indirectly results in her death.
Although the film banished the mid-twentieth-century version of the tragic mulatta, presumably because contemporary audiences may have found her anach-
ronistic, the novelized trope uncannily resonates with the racial logic of *Hagar's
Daughter*: if leisure is only accessible to the light-skinned mixed-race inhabitants of a white skin, it extracts a high price.

Light-Skinned Leisure and
Meghan Markle's Controversial Ascent

Hopkins's depiction of Venus and her innovative use of the detective genre
make good on Fannie Barrier Williams's assertion in "The Colored Girl" (1905)
that although press and magazine readers "seldom think of this dark-skinned
girl," she is "the most interesting girl of this country" (402, 401). Hopkins's
portrayal of intersectional class dynamics and what and who she imagines have

access to leisure are questions that guide the remainder of this chapter. After Venus rescues the not-so-white Jewel Bowen through her cross-dressing and initiative, Jewel's husband rejects her once the same mechanisms that led to her freedom also reveal her African ancestry. In short, Hopkins's mulatta heroines have ambivalent, often ephemeral destinies. Similar to Edith Wharton's oft-married Undine Spragg in *The Custom of the Country* (1913), for example, Aurelia, another of Hopkins's phenotypically white protagonists, intends to use marriage to "shake off all her hideous past and become an honest matron" (Hopkins 92). She fits the mold of the ambitious social climber. Her ambition is in line with the American success narrative Alisha Knight identifies in Hopkins's fiction, but it is also the presumed destiny of the ambiguously raced women whose floral beauty foreshadows the iconography of the mulatta that would be repetitively scripted in the fiction of the New Negro era. As uncanny precursors to the melancholic, mixed-race heroines of the Harlem Renaissance, each of Hagar's biological or figurative daughters meets a tragic or mysterious fate: Aurelia vanishes, Jewel dies, and Hagar herself ostensibly commits suicide before being resurrected into whiteness as Estelle Bowen.

Hopkins's title recursively repurposes the Sarah/Hagar dynamic, a nineteenth-century abolitionist metaphor for the antebellum relationship between the white mistress and the Black slave, particularly in the way the trope marks white women's culpability and complicity in Black women's sexual exploitation. In the Judeo-Christian tradition, the biblical Hagar is Sarah's bondwoman; Sarah either entreats or forces Hagar to lie with Sarah's husband, Abraham, to conceive an heir, whom they name Ishmael. This act is a breach of faith. God has promised Sarah and Abraham a son, but in Sarah's impatience she initiates an act of interracial, intercultural sex that results in a child who, after his or her own miraculous conception, will challenge the rightful heir. In Genesis 21:10 Hagar and her son are then cast out into the wilderness: "Cast out the bondwoman and her son; for the son of the bondwoman shall not be heir with the son of the freedwoman." The Hagar story, which continues to resurface in new forms of media, such as Margaret Atwood's dystopic novel *The Handmaid's Tale* and subsequently adapted television series, encapsulates the victimization of the enslaved and quotidian abuses of the antebellum South. Both the textual and televised versions of *The Handmaid's Tale* feature a militarized patriarchy that regulates women into the distinct roles of breeder, wife, and domestic, a system clearly derived from the gendered hierarchy of the plantation. Atwood's primary referent for the sexual slavery of the handmaid is the biblical story of Rachel and Leah, whereas the Egyptian Hagar is a more generative trope for African American artists because of her status as an oppressed other among the Israelites whose son ultimately founds a new religion.

In "Some Afro-American Women of Mark" (1892), which might be considered a precursor to Hopkins's series Famous Women of the Negro Race, author Elizabeth Frazier includes a lengthy paragraph on Edmonia Lewis's statue *Hagar in the Wilderness*. She hails Lewis as the "greatest of her race in the art of sculpture" and names *Hagar* her most prominent sculpture (Frazier 386). Egyptian ancestry aside, many critics have commented on the whiteness of the statue. Lydia Maria Child commented that Hagar looked more like a "stout German woman, or English woman than a slim Egyptian, emaciated by wandering in the desert" (164 as qtd. in Nelson). Neoclassical sculpture valorized and aestheticized whiteness, but the sculpture is also marked as nonwhite in the tradition of other "white slave" sculptures such as William Story's *Cleopatra*. Her wavy hair, for instance, marks her as an "interracial body type" (Nelson 178), as does the creamy undertones of the marble.[5] Lewis excised the other actors from the biblical story, leaving Hagar alone, devout, absent her "masters" and her son, Ishmael, the evidence of her sexual exploitation. In *The Color of Stone*, Charmaine Nelson writes: "Lewis orchestrated the confluence of a complex of issues that affected Black female slaves within nineteenth-century transatlantic slavery in American and the diaspora."[6] Similarly, *Hagar's Daughter* offers a multiplicity of outcomes for light-skinned bondwomen's descendants who form romantic and sexual relationships with white men.[7]

Hopkins and Lewis drew upon a potent combination of features that comprise the iconography of the mulatta to emphasize the virtue of their heroines and to reclaim them from the potentially degrading circumstances of their condition through an ambivalent whiteness. The Victorian language of flowers effectively situates the counterposition of Aurelia and Jewel: "Aurelia was a gorgeous tropical flower; Jewel, a fair fragrant lily" (Hopkins 103).[8] In death, Hopkins memorializes Jewel Bowen as a statue by eliding her with her grave marker, "a fair, slender shaft of polished cream-white marble" (283). Hopkins added the racialized qualifier "polished cream" to a description that is otherwise identical to the description she took from Fanny Driscoll's text (567). Consider also her portrayal of the eponymous Hagar Sargeant, "the pure creamy skin, the curved crimson lips ready to smile—lips sweet and firm,— broad, low brow, and great, lustrous, long-lashed eyes of brilliant Black—soft as velvet, and full of light with the earnest, cloudless gaze of childhood; and there was heart and soul and mind in this countenance of a mere girl" (Hopkins 35). If Lewis sculpted waves into her statue's hair to denote her ethnicity, Hopkins located Hagar's Blackness in her eyes, which, to use a common platitude, are the windows to her innocent soul, and in the "cream" in her skin. Given their historical and cultural context, both Hopkins and Lewis deliberately worked with and against white material. Not content to rely on what Dorri Beam aptly calls Hopkins's "highly wrought florid language combined with racialization" (173), the *Colored American Magazine* included Alexander Skeete's illustration of Hagar's leap from the bridge. In this image, Hagar is a floating angel ascending rather than falling, her child securely in her arms. This aforementioned leap has many antecedents; it recalls Eliza's ice-bound escape in Harriet Beecher Stowe's *Uncle Tom's Cabin* and William Wells Brown's *Clotel*. As the novel progresses, Hopkins introduces more characters easily decipherable as mixed-race mulattas, and the subplots thicken according to her playful yet deliberately entangled narrative. Elise Bradford, a white southern woman who will shortly be murdered by her employer, who has compromised her as if she were mixed-race, provides a lengthy articulation of the condition of "white" Negro women:

> Beautiful almost beyond description, many of them educated and refined, with the best white blood of the South in their veins, they refuse to mate themselves with the ignorant of their own race. Socially, they are not recognized by the whites; they are often without money enough to but [*sic*] the barest necessities of life; honorably, they cannot procure sufficient means to gratify their luxurious tastes; their mothers were like themselves; their fathers they never knew; debauched white men are ever ready to take advantage of their destitution, and after living a short life of shame, they sink into early graves. Living, they were despised by whites and blacks alike; dead, they are mourned by none. (Hopkins 159)

Hopkins uses Elise, a fallen white woman, to extensively detail the genus and demise of the white mulatta. Yet the sheer multiplicity of mulatta characters in *Hagar's Daughter* (Hagar; her daughter, Jewel; and her nemesis, Aurelia) complicates the narrative script provided by Elise and the visual grammar of their bodies in a way that presages how Meghan Markle would later be motivated to assert her own mixed-race identity without denying her Blackness.

In Hopkins's novels, the revelation of Black maternity is often the impetus for setting in motion a series of tragic circumstances: Hagar's daughter "would have remained in this social sphere all her life, beloved and respected by her descendants, her blood mingling with the best blood of the country if untoward circumstances had not exposed her ancestry" (62). Sensationalized speculation about Markle's ethnicity abounded despite the fact that, prior to her royal ascent, she wrote openly and cogently about her experience growing up mixed-race in terms that would have been familiar to Hopkins's readers (see Markle). Because Markle's ambiguous appearance and acting ability enabled her to be cast in roles of various marked and unmarked ethnicities, the "revelation" of her identity, when the TV series *Suits* cast an African American man as her father, reinforces Elise Bradford's warning that "black blood is everywhere—in society and out, and in our families even; we cannot feel assured that it has not filtered into the most exclusive families. We try to stem the tide but I believe it is a hopeless task" (Hopkins 160). Strikingly, neither Markle's white father nor her half-white siblings attended her nuptials, leaving her dreadlocked brown mother to sit alone as her daughter wed Prince Harry wearing a classic white sheath dress and straightened hair. This irony went unnoticed or unappreciated, as Salamishah Tillet writes: "Interspersed among the crowd's gleeful cheers, there was a cacophony of Black women offering up another song—ululations recognized as congratulatory greetings throughout the African diaspora—to welcome Ms. Markle and her new husband home." This homecoming would be further underscored by secrecy surrounding the newlyweds' honeymoon destination: most guessed they would return to East Africa, as they had previously traveled in Botswana and Namibia; we can safely assume their honeymoon was spent in Wakanda in a convergence of fact, film, and fiction.

While probing beneath the pomp and circumstance surrounding the royal nuptials reveals some disconcerting truths about the endurance of caste prejudice, the aspirational depiction of Meghan and Harry's interracial "romance" fascinated Black female viewers swept up momentarily in #BlackAmerican PrincessMagic. Significantly, like Hagar's beautiful daughters, Markle's ascent can be attributed to her ability to capitalize on the phenotypic malleability of her racial identity; a distinct difference is that rather than keeping circumstances of her background in the shadows, the so-called open secret of miscegenation is central to her story. Alisha Knight reads Aurelia Madison in *Hagar's Daughter* as "an anti-Alger heroine" because she subverts the "conventions of the young woman's success novel" and "ventures into spheres that are inappropriate for 'true women'" (88). Unlike the fathers of the tragic mulatto characters that populate antebellum, Reconstruction, and Harlem Renaissance era fiction, Markle's father acknowledged and supported his daughter, despite his absence from the wedding. Rather than condemning her to share Aurelia's fate, Markle's racial identity is simply one of the several unconventional features, like her status as an outspoken actress and divorcée, that did not prevent her from marrying a scion of the British royal family. While the elements of biracial identity Markle explores in her article cannot be equated to the historical situations faced by Hopkins's mulattas, pseudoscientific perceptions of mixed-race identity remain remarkably durable, as evidenced by racist speculations about the color of her firstborn child, who was also inexplicably denied the title of prince.[9]

In an "Open Statement to Fans of *The Help*," the Association of Black Women Historians tried to police the appeal of the film and the book. They did what historians do best: they provided historical context. In particular, the statement protests the celebration of the book as a progressive story of racial justice that "distorts, ignores, and trivializes the experiences of Black domestic workers." Implicitly, the historians mark the omission of the disturbing history of sexual exploitation. The statement concludes with a suggested reading list of fiction that focuses on the sexually vulnerable position of domestic servants and slaves and includes plucky heroines such as Blanche, from Barbara Neeley's series about a Black female detective who could be a descendant of Hopkins's Venus Johnson.

What's missing from *The Help* and the open statement isn't just historical accuracy, it's any notion of leisure or pleasure. When Eliza Potter comments, "As if it were an impossibility for a working woman to have such a wardrobe" (57), she refutes the notion that a lady's maid can't be a lady herself. She articulates an audacious desire that contradicts the impossibility of imagining a leisurely existence as a valid aim for Black women, as an important minor emotion that nevertheless adds to the texture of what freedom can mean. In this way, Potter's contention is of a piece with the statement at the finale of *Incidents in the Life of a Slave Girl*. Even after achieving her freedom, Harriet Jacobs, writing as Linda Brent, lacks "a home of [her] own" (170) where she and her children can dwell in safety and comfort in the free but coldly segregated North. Her desire for an autonomous domestic space that she may occupy with her children affirms the desire for a home of one's own as an essential and far from frivolous yearning.

As a Black feminist scholar, I had no problem adding my signature to the open statement, which I subsequently circulated to the members of my book club, who were lobbying to read *The Help* as our next book for discussion. As a literary critic, however, I was struck by the historians' assessment of the book's true form or plot: "*The Help* is not a story about the millions of hardworking and dignified Black women who labored in white homes to support their families and communities. Rather it is a coming-of-age story of a white protagonist, who uses myths about the lives of Black women to make sense of her own." Which type of book did the author intend to write? Historical accuracy in historical fiction is a tricky subject. Pauline Hopkins was also a historical revisionist when it suited her. She often shifted or reimagined elements of the Civil War, for example, moving the time, location, and occasionally the outcomes of key skirmishes. The African American women historians voiced a strong objection to the inaccurate use of dialect in *The Help*, but what about the use of dialect in Black women's fiction? One could subject Hopkins's use of Black vernacular, which she reserved primarily for her working-class characters, to a similar critique. I'm not arguing that if you liked *The Help*, then you need to read *Hagar's Daughter*; rather, I'm suggesting that as scholars and critics of nineteenth-century Black women's writing we not only populate and popularize alternative voices through our teaching and pedagogy but also explore the audacious desires of domestic workers whose negotiation of class boundaries and strategic maneuvers provide textured conversation about the intimacy of the upstairs/downstairs relationship.

NOTES

These comments were expanded from notes presented in response to the panel "Pauline Hopkins' Activism" at the American Literature Association Conference in San Francisco in 2018. I wish to acknowledge the participants' generative papers: Rhone Fraser's "Pauline Hopkins and Advocacy Journalism," Amadi I. Ozier's "Racial Transmigration in Pauline Hopkins's *Of One Blood*," and John Cyril Barton's "Anti-Lynching Activism in Pauline E. Hopkins' *Contending Forces*." Tragically, the relevance of Barton's investigation in our current climate of anti-Blackness is chillingly familiar.

1. Carpio expands the genre of the neo–slave narrative to include novels, short stories, comedy sketches, and other visual media.

2. I'm thinking here of the many new television series centered on African American women, such as *How to Get Away with Murder*, *Scandal*, *Insecure*, *Queen Sugar*, and *Being Mary Jane*, to name just a few.

3. For a collation of source material used by Hopkins to craft *Hagar's Daughter*, see the lists assembled by Lauren Dembowitz at http://www.paulinehopkinssociety.org/sources-for-hagars-daughter-a-story-of-southern-prejudice/.

4. In addition to the character descriptions from Driscoll's "Two Women," Hopkins recycled diction from Garry Moss and Etta Pierce.

5. A white neoclassical Negro complete with "a very pretty waviness to the hair," which is how sculptor John Rogers described the only "distinguishing" mark of race (Nelson 124).

6. Nelson has a fascinating reading on specific types of shackles, chains, or manacles

carved in association with the sculptors as more than ornaments, as a way of referencing American chattel slavery in particular as opposed to biblical or Greco-Roman servitude (105).

7. See also the television series *Scandal* and Dolen Perkins Valdez's novel *Wench*.

8. For a more thorough analysis of Hopkins's use of flower language, see Beam. Hopkins borrowed this juxtaposition and other sections of *Hagar's Daughter* from Driscoll's "Two Women": "June was a magnificent cactus-blossom, scarlet and gold, and subtle; Mignon was a fair day-lily" (562).

9. Royal watchers and supporters of Harry and Meghan who anticipated that the televised wedding was an augur of social or political change have been sadly disappointed. In a 2021 CBS interview with Oprah Winfrey, Markle revealed personal and public trauma she experienced after becoming part of "the Firm" through marriage. The incidents of racism and allegations of discrimination within the royal establishment ultimately led the couple to step away from their formal status as senior royals and relocate to the United States.

WORKS CITED

Association of Black Women Historians. "An Open Statement to the Fans of *The Help*." 12 Aug. 2011. ABWH.org. http://abwh.org/2011/08/12/an-open-statement-to-the-fans -of-the-help/.

Beam, Dorri. *Style, Gender, and Fantasy in Nineteenth-Century American Women's Writing*. Cambridge University Press, 2010.

Brody, Jennifer. *Impossible Purities: Blackness, Femininity and Victorian Culture*. Duke University Press, 1998.

Brooks, Kristina. "Mammies, Bucks and Wenches: Racial Pornography and Racial Politics in Pauline Hopkins's *Hagar's Daughter*." *The Unruly Voice: Rediscovering Pauline Elizabeth Hopkins*, edited by John Gruesser, University of Illinois Press, 1996, pp. 119–57.

Brown, Lois. *Pauline Elizabeth Hopkins: Black Daughter of the Revolution*. University of North Carolina Press, 2008.

Buick, Kirsten Pai. *Child of the Fire: Mary Edmonia Lewis and the Problem of Art History's Black and Indian Subject*. Duke University Press, 2010.

Carpio, Glenda. *Laughing Fit to Kill: Black Humor and the Fictions of Slavery*. Oxford University Press, 2008.

Clark-Lewis, Elizabeth. *Living In, Living Out: African American Domestics and the Great Migration*. Smithsonian Books, 1996.

Driscoll, Fanny. "Two Women." *Frank Leslie's Popular Monthly,* May 1884, pp. 562–67.

Frazier, Elizabeth. "Some Afro-American Women of Mark." *African American Episcopal Church Review,* vol. 8, no. 4, Apr. 1892, pp. 373–86.

Hopkins, Pauline E. *Hagar's Daughter: A Story of Southern Caste Prejudice.* 1901–02. *The Magazine Novels of Pauline Hopkins*. Oxford University Press, 1988, pp. 1–284.

Jackson, Holly. "Another Long Bridge: Reproduction and Reversion in *Hagar's Daugh-*

ter." *Early African American Print Culture*, edited by Laura Cohen and Jordan Stein, University of Pennsylvania Press, 2012, pp. 192–202.

Jacobs, Harriet. *Incidents in the Life of a Slave Girl*. Norton, 2001.

Knight, Alisha. *Pauline Hopkins and the American Dream: An African American Writer's (Re)Visionary Gospel of Success*. University of Tennessee Press, 2012.

Lofton, Kathryn, and Laurie F. Maffly-Kipp. *Women's Work: An Anthology of African–American Women's Historical Writings from Antebellum America to the Harlem Renaissance*. Oxford University Press, 2010.

Markle, Meghan. "Meghan Markle: I'm More Than an Other." *Elle*, July 2015. https://www.elle.com/uk/life-and-culture/news/a26855/more-than-an-other/.

Martin, Valerie. *Property*. Nan Talese, 2003.

Moss, Gary. "The Mystery of the Hearth: A True Story of Official Life in Washington." *Frank Leslie's Popular Monthly*, May 1884, pp. 546–51.

Neeley, Barbara. *Blanche among the Talented Tenth*. Penguin, 1995.

Nelson, Charmaine. *The Color of Stone: Sculpting the Black Female Subject in Nineteenth Century America*. University of Minnesota Press, 2007.

Pavletich, JoAnn. "'. . . We Are Going to Take That Right': Power and Plagiarism in Pauline Hopkins's *Winona*." *CLA Journal*, vol. 59, no. 2, Dec. 2015, pp. 115–30.

Pierce, Etta. *A Dark Deed*. Published serially in *Frank Leslie's Popular Monthly*, Jan.–June 1884.

Potter, Eliza. *A Hairdresser's Experience in High Life*. 1859. Edited and with an introduction by Xiomara Santamarina, University of North Carolina Press, 2009.

Sanborn, Geoffrey. "The Wind of Words: Plagiarism and Intertextuality in *Of One Blood*." *J19: The Journal of Nineteenth-Century Americanists*, vol. 3, no. 1, Spring 2015, pp. 67–87.

Santamarina, Xiomara, editor. Introduction to *A Hairdresser's Experience in High Life*, by Eliza Potter. University of North Carolina, 2009, pp. xi–xxx.

Sharf, Zack. "Viola Davis Shares Regrets over Acting in 'The Help': The 'Voices of the Maids' Weren't Heard." *IndieWire*, 12 Sept. 2018, https://www.indiewire.com/2018/09/viola-davis-regrets-the-help-aibileen-maid-1202003002/.

Shawl, Nisi. "What Men Have Put Asunder: Pauline Hopkins *Of One Blood*." Tor.com, 4 June 2008, https://www.tor.com/2018/06/04/what-men-have-put-asunder-pauline-hopkins-of-one-blood/.

Sherrard-Johnson, Cherene. *Portraits of the New Negro Woman: Visual and Literary Culture in the Harlem Renaissance*. Rutgers University Press, 2012.

Soitos, Stephen. *The Blues Detective: A Study of African American Detective Fiction*. University of Massachusetts Press, 1996.

Stockett, Kathryn. *The Help*. Putnam, 2009.

Tillet, Salamishah. "Meghan Markle and the Bicultural Blackness of the Royal Wedding." *New York Times*, 20 May 2018, international ed., https://www.nytimes.com/2018/05/20/arts/television/meghan-markle-royal-wedding-Blackness.html.

Wallinger, Hanna. *Pauline E. Hopkins: A Literary Biography*. University of Georgia Press, 2005.

Wexler, Laura. *Tender Violence: Domestic Visions in an Age of U.S. Imperialism*. University of North Carolina Press, 2000.

Williams, Fannie Barrier. "The Colored Girl." 1905. *Voice of the Negro*, vol. 2, no. 6, 1905, pp. 400–03.

Yarborough, Richard, JoAnn Pavletich, Ira Dworkin, and Lauren Dembowitz. "Rethinking Pauline Hopkins: Plagiarism, Appropriation, and African American Cultural Production." *American Literary History*, vol. 30, no. 4, Winter 2018, pp. e3–e30, https://academic.oup.com/alh/article/30/4/e3/5099108?login=true.

AFTERWORD

"I Sing of the Wrongs of a Race"

PAULINE E. HOPKINS
AS EDITOR AND AUTHOR

Edlie L. Wong

Pauline E. Hopkins was one of the most influential, versatile, and prolific Black female writers at the turn of the twentieth century, the era that Charles Chesnutt later usefully designated as "Postbellum—Pre-Harlem" (543). Her dynamic career ranged from musical theater, oratory, and fiction and essay writing to magazine editing and publishing, yet she was all but forgotten until the late twentieth century. In the first wave of sustained scholarship in the 1990s, literary critics began to draw attention to Hopkins's literary modernism, highlighting the formal complexity, unruliness, and experimentation of her long fiction. In John Gruesser's early collection of literary critical essays, Elizabeth Ammons deemed Hopkins "a radical experimenter whose work will be read in the next century as a model of early modernist innovation and revolution in the United States" (211). *Yours for Humanity: New Essays on Pauline Elizabeth Hopkins* demonstrates the continuing salience of this statement.

Hazel Carby was the first among these scholars to insist that studies of Hopkins's literary experimentation should account for her editorial work at the *Colored American Magazine* (159–60). The recent HathiTrust digitization of the *CAM* and more recent corrective digitization projects such as Eurie Dahn and Brian Sweeney's *Digital Colored American Magazine* have expanded access to Hopkins's entire corpus in its original periodical format and facilitated new research on Hopkins's work as an editor. Such digital archives, in addition to the mass digitization of nineteenth-century books and periodicals and the development of keyword-based searching algorithms, have produced new ways of reading Hopkins in the twenty-first century, adding additional complexity to our understanding of Hopkins as an editor and author. Geoffrey Sanborn's use of these new digital research methods first revealed the extent of Hopkins's unacknowledged borrowings in her serial fiction, and these discoveries have redirected critical attention to Hopkins's strategic intertextual appropriations from the popular fiction of her era (68). As we continue to advance our understanding of Hopkins's aesthetic investments in citation and recontextualization, we have also begun to learn more about Hopkins's complex compositional practices and strategic content management as an editor.

Hopkins's editorial work may have helped shape and mask her literary production and racial politics in more ways than we yet realize. In 1947 William Stanley Braithwaite recollected in "Negro America's First Magazine" that it was Hopkins, "as editor of the magazine, [who] inaugurated the policy of paying for contributions" (119). According to Braithwaite, Hopkins "not only wanted the Negro author to feel that his work, if accepted and printed, was worthy of remuneration, but as an editor she felt it gave her an independence of action in making selections, and a dignity in soliciting manuscripts of the best" (119). Braithwaite recalled one "frequent contributor . . . an African, Prof. C. C. Hamedoe," among the magazine's better-known essayists and poets, including Benjamin Griffiths Brawley, James D. Corrothers, Olivia Ward Bush-Banks, Augustus M. Hodges, Daniel Webster Davis, and Cyrus Field Adams, in addition to serial fiction by Maitland Leroy Osborne and Sarah A. Allen (117–18). Braithwaite also offered fulsome praise of Hopkins's fiction writing, calling *Contending Forces: A Romance Illustrative of Negro Life North and South* (1900) an "outstanding contribution in this field" (118).[1] Clearly, he did not know that Sarah A. Allen was a Hopkins pen name, and he was likely not the only contemporaneous figure associated with the *CAM* who was unaware of this fact.[2] Hopkins was adept at masking her writerly presence in the magazine, and Braithwaite's error reveals the complex interdependence between Hopkins's work as an editor and author.

My research has led me to speculate on the possibility that Hopkins may have published under additional pen names during her tenure at the *CAM*. Hopkins was a prolific writer and editor who found herself often hard-pressed for copy. As Ira Dworkin notes, she contributed many unsigned editorials to the *CAM*, and these numerous anonymous publications suggest alternative practices of authorship (xli). Hopkins is also well known for her penchant for pen names. It was not unusual for issues to feature Hopkins's work alongside articles and fiction that she penned as Sarah A. Allen and J. Shirley Shadrach. The use of pen names helped prevent the impression that Hopkins's work dominated the magazine. In this regard, Hopkins anticipated a figure such as George Schuyler, who published serial fiction and nonfiction under various male and female pen names in the *Pittsburgh Courier*, the influential Black newspaper that he also edited. For Hopkins, pen names allowed her to "disguise her identity, publish more frequently, and avoid public criticism directed at herself," writes Hanna Wallinger (62). Alisha Knight contends that these publications tended to be even more outspoken in their viewpoints (48, 57). In my own research, I have uncovered some highly suggestive connections between Hopkins and another regular contributor who went by the name of S. E. F. C. C. Hamedoe, the "African" professor whom Braithwaite named. Hamedoe is almost certainly a pen name, and I have come to believe that it most likely belonged to Hopkins.

From 1900 to 1904, during Hopkins's editorial tenure, *CAM* published one short story and seventeen installments of Hamedoe's series mapping the political contours of the emerging Global South, from Afghanistan, Benin, Botswana, Cuba, Ethiopia, Ghana, Haiti, the Lesser Antilles, Madagascar, Thailand, and Zanzibar to the newly acquired U.S. territories of Hawai'i, Samoa, and the Philippines. His "Interesting History" spanned the entire runs of Hopkins's three serial novels, *Hagar's Daughter: A Story of Southern Caste Prejudice* (as Sarah A. Allen) (1901–02), *Winona: A Tale of Negro Life in the South and Southwest* (1902), and *Of One Blood; or, The Hidden Self* (1902–03), and two nonfiction series, Famous Men of the Negro Race (1900–01) and Famous Women of the Negro Race (1901–02). Unlike the other regular contributors, Hamedoe remains a largely unknown figure. Thus far, I have been unable to locate Hamedoe (also spelled Hammedoe) in U.S. census, immigration, and birth records or passenger lists. Searches through British and American periodical archives and commercial genealogical databases have also yielded no results for this enigmatic figure. What we know of Hamedoe comes from two sources: *CAM* advertisements and Hopkins's much-discussed 1905 letter to William Monroe Trotter, editor of the *Boston Guardian* and cofounder of the oppositional Niagara Movement. Hopkins's letter referred to Hamedoe as a "paid contributor" and lists him among other "true friends," including William Lloyd Garrison Jr., Edward A. Horton, and South African editor A. Kirkland Soga, who provided Hopkins with material when she was hard-pressed for new content ("To William Monroe Trotter" 550–51). Unlike Braithwaite, Hopkins did not identify Hamedoe as an African. She rather outlandishly described him as "a colored linguist who had mastered seven modern languages and thirteen Chinese dialects" and "a man well-versed in history, a traveler who had visited every corner of the globe" (551). Hamedoe's abrupt disappearance from print history in 1904 coincides with Hopkins's forced departure from the *CAM*.

Hopkins held a complex relationship with authorship. It is not too difficult to imagine the rebellious Hopkins experimenting with a male pen name, especially given that Walter Wallace, Harper Fortune, Walter Johnson, and Jesse W. Watkins, the magazine's four founders, envisioned her role there as limited to the "Women's Department" (Brown 274). "Professor" Hamedoe (with his lengthy list of unidentifiable academic abbreviations) and his chosen genre of "History and Biography" might have allowed Hopkins to challenge such heteropatriarchal assumptions and offer subversive commentary on the gendering of such knowledge production as masculine. Hamedoe's writings have often been cited as an example of Hopkins's editorial commitments to Black internationalism, and this line of speculation brings additional nuance to our understanding of Hopkins's anti-imperialism and global politics. Hamedoe was also paid regularly for his contributions, and this pseudonymous identity may have provided Hopkins with much-needed remuneration for work that the male leadership largely undervalued. As Gruesser notes, Hopkins faced the responsibility of supporting herself and a bedridden mother on a meager salary of seven dollars per week, which was later raised to eight dollars when she took on additional secretarial work (114). If indeed Hamedoe was a Hopkins pseudonym, we witness the extension of an authorial practice that navigated the politics of both race and gender and the magazine world not merely by reifying but also by multiplying forms of identity. Elsewhere, I have explored the intertextual relays and similarities between the nonfiction writings of Hopkins and Hamedoe (see Wong; Gilmore, Wong, and Cohen). Here, I examine some equally evocative links between their short fictions.

In addition to three serialized novels, Hopkins published at least seven known short fictions in the *CAM*: "The Mystery within Us" (May 1900), "Talma Gordon" (October 1900), "George Washington: A Christmas Story" (December 1900), "A Dash for Liberty" (August 1901), "Bro'r Abr'm Jimson's Wedding. A Christmas Story" (December 1901), "The Test of Manhood. A Christmas Story" as Sarah A. Allen (December 1902), and "'As the Lord Lives, He Is One of Our Mother's Children'" (November 1903). Like her long fiction, Hopkins's short stories utilize a range of popular genres such as local color, humor, sentimentalism, melodrama, and historical romance, although they tend to feature mostly male characters or male narrators.[3] Some of these tales also bear a more than passing resemblance to the ones collected in Chesnutt's popular *Conjure Woman* (1899) and *The Wife of His Youth and Other Stories of the Color-Line* (1899). For example, Hopkins's "Bro'r Abr'm Jimson's Wedding" offers a humorous retelling of Chesnutt's "Wife of His Youth," although Hopkins relocates her dialect-speaking Black characters from the post-Reconstruction South to New England. This tale even alludes to the eponymous character,

Jimson, having "done goophered" a beautiful young woman into marriage after abandoning his first wife and children (Hopkins, "Bro'r" 110).

"Plixixit, the Palenachendeskies Kikoo of Arthabasca" might be best described as a mixed-race Afro-Indigenous revenge fantasy, and it remains the only known fictional work that Hamedoe published. Appearing in the January 1904 issue of the *CAM*, "Plixixit" was one of two fictional offerings in an issue that featured no writings by Hopkins.[4] Reminiscent of Hopkins's recently serialized *Winona*, "Plixixit" is a transnational tale that crisscrosses the U.S.-Canada border and explores fictive kinship and Black and Indigenous cross-racial affiliations. It also shares some provocative similarities with Hopkins's other short fictions, including the framed narrative structure of "Talma Gordon." Like Hopkins's fictionalization of the 1841 Creole slave revolt in "A Dash for Liberty," Hamedoe's tale is a historical fiction that depicts a raced rebellion against white dominance. The publication date of "Plixixit" is also significant in light of Hopkins's timeline at *CAM*. In 1903 William H. Dupree, along with Jesse W. Watkins and William O. West, purchased the Colored Co-Operative Publishing Company and the magazine in an effort to keep the publication afloat. As Braithwaite noted, Hopkins "resented bitterly" the "veiled authority" and "literary incompetence" of the magazine's male leadership (120). By early 1904 Hopkins was well aware of the magazine's dire finances as she struggled to maintain her editorial autonomy. As the *CAM* came under new management, Hopkins's publication of "Plixixit" served as a bold statement of her race politics and aesthetic preferences.

Even without the added consideration that Hopkins may have authored "Plixixit," her editorial decision to print the tale offered a direct rebuttal to white benefactors and advisors such as John C. Freund, the editor of *Musical Trades*, who found the fiction that Hopkins wrote and published objectionable. As Elizabeth Cali argues in this collection, Hopkins often channeled her resistance into her fiction selections for the magazine, and this popular but increasingly marginalized location within the magazine served as a strategic site for Hopkins's politics. In a series of letters that Freund sent to Hopkins and Dupree between late January and April 1904, which was the last month Hopkins was listed as "Literary Editor," Freund expressed increasing dissatisfaction with Hopkins's editorship. He cautioned Hopkins against offending white readers and suggested that she reduce the literary selections included in the magazine. Hopkins's letter to Trotter quotes from Freund's threatening missives: "Either Miss Hopkins will follow our suggestions . . . eliminating anything which may create offense; stop talking about the wrongs and a proscribed race, or you must count me out absolutely" (550). Knight suggests that Hopkins entertained the ambition of transforming the *CAM* into a literary monthly for primarily Black readers, and "Plixixit" was exactly the type of literature that white readers such as Freund would have found offensive (50).

Freund was not alone in his criticisms. He echoed the recently expressed sentiments of other white readers such as Cornelia A. Condict, whose letter Hopkins reprinted in the March 1903 issue. Active in the Presbyterian Church's Women's Missionary Society, Condict drew upon her work as a former superintendent of a Sunday school "among a greatly mixed people, Indian, Negro, Spanish, and Anglo-Saxon," to explain the reasons for discontinuing her subscription (399).[5] "If I found it more helpful to Christian work among your people," Condict proclaimed, "I would continue to take it" (398). She disapproved of the magazine's serial stories of "tragic mixed loves," insisting that these tales neither "commend themselves to white readers" nor "elevate the colored readers" (399). In her published reply, Hopkins explicitly identified her fictions as race literature and amplified the literary philosophy she first outlined in the preface to *Contending Forces*.[6] "My stories," Hopkins asserted, "are definitely planned to show the obstacles persistently placed in our paths by a dominant race to subjugate us spiritually" (Condict 399). Hopkins limned the dilemma facing the Black author of such race literature: "If you please the author of this letter and your white clientele, you will lose your Negro patronage. If you cater to the *demands* of the Negro trade, away goes Mrs. ———" (400). Well before the heyday of the Harlem Renaissance, Hopkins confronted the "racial mountain" of "whiteness" and "American standardization" in Langston Hughes's famous formulation, fashioning herself as a "serious black artist" dedicated to the task of producing "racial art" (93). Hopkins wrote for Black readers, and she may have used Hamedoe as a pseudonym to publish one of the magazine's most radical race fictions.

Hamedoe's framed tale begins shortly after the Civil War and during the U.S. wars against the Plains Indians in 1867. Inside a tepee on a cold winter's night, an agent with the Hudson's Bay Company, a Métis or "halfbreed," and a Cree brave named Alexinawathinoa sit mesmerized as an old Cree chief unwinds the tale of Plixixit. The unidentified first-person narrator translates the tale as he first "heard it" in "the languages of the Cree Blackfeet and stony tongues" (Hamedoe, "Plixixit" 41). The story he tells is set in 1850 and centers on Joseph, "a black man of full blood" from Santo Domingo and a missionary who survives shipwreck. Similar to *Winona*'s White Eagle, Joseph is adopted by an Indigenous tribe called the Athabascaanians (perhaps based on the Alas-

kan Athabascans or Athabaskans), and he becomes their new leader after marrying the chief's daughter. The story romanticizes Indigenous difference in a
manner reminiscent of Hopkins's serial tale. Like Winona, Joseph claims an affinity between Black and Indigenous peoples who suffered the violence of racist exploitation. Joseph cites the "story of the first American invasion" and the
"founding of the New World" in the "cargoes of slaves that perished" and the
"thousands of Indians who had to work like slaves" as the source of his "in-
born hate for the Paleface" (42). Descended from Black Haitians who "would
not allow themselves to be servants of the Paleface, but equals," Joseph goes
to war against the company's white traders and agents and their allied Indigenous tribes, including the Cree (42). Joseph channels the rebellious spirit of the
Haitian Revolution and stands as a figure for the militant Black internationalism that Hopkins celebrated in "Toussaint L'Ouverture" (November 1900), the
first essay in Famous Men.

The remainder of Hamedoe's story shifts focus to Joseph's mixed-race Afro-
Indigenous son, Plixixit, who becomes chief after his father is killed in battle
with the Cree (Hamedoe, "Plixixit" 42). Long allied with European fur traders, the Crees had refused to join Joseph's race war. Determined to avenge his
father's wrongs, young Plixixit defies the tribal council and wages battle against
the "Paleface" with a "party of young braves" (43, 44). In "Plixixit," amalgamation serves as powerful representation of the distinct yet overlapping histories of Black and Indigenous dispossession. Hopkins also used amalgamation
as a useful structuring concept in her short fictions. For example, "Talma Gordon" offers an intertwined critique of race and empire through a framed tale of
interracial marriage and amalgamation. The story begins at a meeting of the exclusive Canterbury Club of Boston, whose members have gathered to discuss
the topic "Expansion: Its Effect upon the Future Development of the Anglo-
Saxon" (Hopkins, "Talma" 271). Not surprisingly, the white jurists, politicians,
and theologians numbering among the club's distinguished membership embrace the missionary opportunities and other "advantages to be gained by the
increase of wealth and the exalted position which expansion would give the
United States in the councils of the great governments of the world" (271-72).
The lone voice of dissent comes from Dr. William Thornton, the host for the
evening, who poses a counterproposition: "Did you ever think that in spite of
our prejudices against amalgamation, some of our descendants, indeed many of
them, will inevitably intermarry among those far-off tribes of dark-skinned peoples, if they become a part of this great Union?" (272). This facet of America's
new "expansion policy" is given form in Thornton's subsequent recounting of

the events surrounding the murder of Captain Jonathan Gordon and the ambiguously raced "East Indian" man, Simon Cameron, who commits the grisly crime (273, 289).[7]

We see a similar dynamic at work in Hamedoe's "Plixixit," which channels a critique of racial violence, empire, and settler colonialism in the Americas through the plot of retributive vengeance across generations. Like Hopkins's vengeful Cameron, Plixixit inherits a history of racial dispossession. Both of these characters take murderous revenge upon villainous white men who wronged their fathers and stand as figures for broader systemic injustices. Hopkins's Gordon is "a retired sea captain, formerly engaged in the East India trade," who had partnered with and then killed Cameron's father "to satisfy his lust for gold" ("Talma" 289). In Hamedoe's tale, the dishonest Hudson's Bay Company agent, Carl Schmeltzenhoff, had attacked Plixixit's father when he attempted to protect the tribe from predatory trade agreements ("Plixixit" 42). In "Plixixit" the most trenchant social commentary and analysis lie in its treatment of white missionaries and the expansionist discourse of Christian civilization embraced by Hopkins's fictional Canterbury Club. Joseph taught his son Plixixit that "all missionaries were bad," for they serve as the harbingers of settler colonialism and Indigenous degradation and dispossession: "First, missionary, then square-face, then Indian's land gone" (43).[8] As the new chief, Plixixit refuses to convert to Christianity, flaunting Condict's earlier criticism of the magazine's preference for immoral fictions. "The Great Spirit made us all, but he has given us different complexions and customs," declares Plixixit. "Since he has made such difference in other things between us, why may we not conclude that he has given us a different religion, according to our understanding?" (43). In advocating such religious pluralism, Plixixit rejects Christianity's coercive monotheism: "We will not turn aside from the religion of our forefathers, for it was given them by the Great Spirit, who always does right" (43).

Like Hopkins's other historical romances, Hamedoe's tale plays fast and loose with historical events, dates, and settings to advance the narrative, plot, and characterizations. As Colleen O'Brien notes, Hopkins's *Winona* appropriated the Seneca past in an attempt to amalgamate Black and Indigenous movements. "Native Americans," O'Brien argues, are as much part of Hopkins's "insurgent cosmopolitanism as African Americans because of their resistance to white 'civilization' in the Americas" (525). In a similar fashion, Hamedoe's tale mentions "Riel's rebellion," which names two uprisings by the Métis people led by Louis Riel in Manitoba and Saskatchewan that took place in 1869 and 1885 after the story begins. "Plixixit" also alludes to a range of earlier Indigenous leaders, including "Corn-Planter," the last war chief of the Senecas,

"Keokuk" of the Sauks, and "Osceola, the great Seminole," who was the subject of an admiring historical sketch by Hamedoe in the May 1901 *CAM*. Having "learned the lesson so dearly bought" by these Indigenous leaders, Plixixit urges his tribal council, "We must fight or be like the slaves of which your chief, my father spoke" (Hamedoe, "Plixixit" 43). When the council again refuses war, Plixixit journeys to the Lakota leader "Sitting Bull's camp, where they were in council, and learned from him many things that he has not heard before about the Paleface nation" (43). He later joins Sitting Bull in Canada and dies a "hero" battling against the "Indian police" and "Canadian authorities," who had declared them outlaws (45, 46). The heroic death of Plixixit, who embraces death rather than be captured alive, also aligns this tale with Hopkins's "'As the Lord Lives'" and "General Washington." These two stories end with the heroic deaths of their Black male protagonists, although as martyrs for the salvation of white benefactors.

Hamedoe's "Plixixit" is a searing fantasy of Black and Indigenous retributive justice. Hopkins's short fictions offered more muted expressions of racial anger, yet they did not shy away from exploring Black vengeance and retribution against white violence. "Every act of oppression is a weapon for the oppressed," reads the final lines from Hopkins's story "A Dash for Liberty" (247). In "Talma Gordon," Hopkins created a wrathful Black daughter whose parricidal plot to restore her Black mother's stolen legacy is prevented only when Cameron commits the gruesome triple homicide before she does. Significantly, Hopkins did not pathologize Jeanette's anger, which is both individual and collectively shared. Hopkins also explored dark themes and graphic violence in her last known published story, "'As the Lord Lives,'" which begins with the brutal lynching of an innocent Black man. Hopkins set the story in a western "gold-mining region," yet the anti-Black lynching violence she depicts is an outgrowth of failed southern Reconstruction. The tale directly positions Hopkins within the anti-lynching activism that John Cyril Barton examines in this collection. The 1898 Wilmington, North Carolina, massacre, in which white vigilantes terrorized Black residents and overthrew the lawfully elected multiracial city government, drives the plot of this western tale. Like the protagonist in Chesnutt's *Marrow of Tradition* (1901), Hopkins's protagonist, Jim, is a college-educated Black man who loses his wife and child "when the mob fired" their Wilmington home ("'As the Lord Lives'" 799). Jim and a childhood friend named Jones attempt to start anew in the West but are unable to escape this tragic past. A white Wilmington man named Jerry Mason begins a ruthless campaign of racial harassment against their mining claim, and the two Black men are later blamed for Mason's murder. Jones is lynched, while Jim manages to escape with the assistance of a white pastor. As Hamedoe did in "Plixixit," Hopkins braids historical events and details into short fictions that explore the range of Black emotional responses to loss, violence, and trauma.

New inquiries into Hopkins's complex compositional practices and strategic appropriations may help us learn even more about the intriguing yet still inconclusive relationship between Hopkins and Hamedoe. Is Hamedoe an as-yet-unattributed pen name for Hopkins or another as-yet-unidentified Black author whom Hopkins inspired to write fiction? Regardless of Hamedoe's identity, Hopkins boldly exercised her editorial power and acted upon her literary politics with the publication of "Plixixit." As Braithwaite recalls, Hopkins "regarded herself as a national figure, in the company of Charles W. Chesnutt and Paul Laurence Dunbar and as such felt free to impose her views and opinions upon her associates in the conduct of both the book and magazine publications" (120). "Plixixit" may have pleased the magazine's Black readers, but it most certainly displeased Bookerite supporters and white readers such as Freund who later took vitriolic aim at Hamedoe's April 1904 publication on José Rizal, the martyred Filipino nationalist hero best known for his anticolonial novels, *Noli Me Tangere* (1887) and *El Filibusterismo* (1891).[9] "Opposition is the life of an enterprise," Hopkins reminds us. "Criticism tells you that you are doing something" (Condict 400). The Rizal essay marks Hamedoe's final appearance in the *CAM*. It perhaps comes as no surprise that Bookerite Fred Randolph Moore eliminated the fiction section and Hopkins's editorship once he took control of the *CAM* in May 1904. If indeed Hamedoe was a Hopkins pseudonym, we see the radical expansion of Hopkins's early feminism and modernist innovations. Her experimental compositional practices and uses of authorship negotiated race and gender by multiplying forms of identity in the dynamic multimedia space of the early illustrated magazine.

In the twenty-first century, the ongoing digitization of nineteenth-century periodicals and books and the development of new digital research tools continue to open important avenues of research into Hopkins's elusive biography and literary work during and especially after her years with the *CAM*. These new technologies enable access to other contemporaneous Black-owned or Black-edited newspapers and magazines, including T. Thomas Fortune's *New York Globe* (subsequently *New York Freeman* and *New York Age*), William Monroe Trotter and George W. Forbes's *Boston Guardian*, and John W. E. Bowen Sr. and Jesse Max Barber's *Voice of the Negro*, among many others. Hopkins occupied multiple and overlapping roles within this vibrant and protean world of Black publishing and print culture. Her work after the *CAM* included journalism and a popular essay series, Dark Races of the Twentieth Century (1905), for the rival *Voice*. Hopkins also self-published an ethnological pamphlet entitled *A Primer of Facts Pertaining to the Early Greatness of the African Race and the Possibility of Restoration by Its Descendants—with Epilogue* (1905), the first imprint in the new Black Classics series by P. E. Hopkins & Co., Publishers. Hopkins's brief turn to self-publishing calls to mind Harriet Jacobs's similarly dogged efforts to self-publish her pseudonymous autobiography, *Incidents in the Life of a Slave Girl* (1861), after failing to secure an established publisher to put out her book. In expanding her work from an editor and author to publishing, Hopkins likely sought to emancipate herself from literary gatekeepers in an industry that was characterized by the imbalance between white publishers and Black authors and that favors male writers even today (Farr 152–53). With the advent of the short-lived *New Era Magazine* in 1916, Hopkins would make yet another attempt to materialize this "idea of a large Publishing House for the race, which will issue books, pamphlets, music and art works of our people at minimal cost" ("Editorial" 124).

The title of my afterword comes from Hopkins's pointed reply to Condict. "I sing of the wrongs of a race that ignorance of their pitiful condition may be changed to intelligence and must awaken compassion in the hearts of the just," proclaimed Hopkins in defense of her fiction (Condict 399). These words channeled the activist spirit of an earlier generation of Black abolitionists even as her explicit commitment to write for and to please Black readers anticipated the future orientation of the New Negro Movement, or Harlem Renaissance. Hopkins thus epitomized the dynamic tensions and contradictions of the "Post-Bellum—Pre-Harlem," which "looked back to antebellum years and forward to a future glimpsed but not yet codified by the term 'Harlem Renaissance,'" as Barbara McCaskill and Caroline Gebhard argue (1). This critical bifocality, the twofold movement of looking backward and forward simultaneously, remains essential to interpreting Hopkins's work as an editor, author, and publisher. The novelist who adapted antebellum sentimentalism to the task of postbellum Black uplift in *Contending Forces* also pioneered Black speculative fiction in *Of One Blood*, anticipating the shape of Afrofuturism to come.

Considering Hopkins within the entirety of her corpus further enhances and complexifies our understanding of her literary practice and politics. Is Hopkins a plagiarist or a modernist experimenter who challenged conventional notions of authorship? Do her writings, which include *Peculiar Sam; or, The Underground Railroad* (1879), the earliest extant play by a Black woman, mark the end of the long nineteenth century, or do they lay the intellectual foundations for the "New Negro" and Black internationalism of the twentieth century? As this collection amply shows, Hopkins remains a vital figure for literary and print culture studies because she is all of these things and more, eluding our best efforts to categorize her work or pin her down. We now know more about Hopkins than we did thirty years ago, yet new questions have arisen in the place of old ones. Invoking the words of *Topsy Templeton*, her unfinished final serial fiction, Hopkins herself persists as "a woman of mystery" (80), and her waywardness and willingness to take literary risks will continue to inspire new readers and the next generation of scholars to come.

NOTES

1. Braithwaite mistakenly numbers *Contending Forces* among the standout serial fiction published in the *CAM* (118).

2. Hopkins continued using the Sarah A. Allen pen name in the *New Era Magazine*, where she published "Converting Fanny," a humorous short tale written in dialect.

3. Wallinger usefully surveys Hopkins's tales in relation to the roughly fifty other short stories published in the *CAM* (240–76).

4. The other literary offerings in the January 1904 issue include the second installment of a serialized tale entitled "The Cedar Hill School; or, The Tribulations of a Country Pedagogue" (chapters 5–8) by "B. Square," Frederick S. Monroe's poem "The Princess," and Chas. M. White's poem "The New Year."

5. Condict's collected papers can be found at the Burke Library Archives, Columbia University Libraries, Union Theological Seminary, New York.

6. In the preface to *Contending Forces*, Hopkins famously proclaimed, "Fiction is of great value to any people as a preserver of manners and customs—religious, political, and social. It is a record of growth and development from generation to generation. *No one will do this for us; we must ourselves develop the men and women who will faithfully portray the inmost thoughts and feelings of the Negro with all the fire and romance which lie dormant in our history*, and as yet unrecognized by writers of the Anglo-Saxon race" (13–14, emphasis in original).

7. Gruesser's reading of "Talma Gordon" suggests that Cameron, who is East Indian yet publicly identifies as English, may have been the product of miscegenation, thus linking the imperial exploitation of the East India trade with Thornton's discussion of racial amalgamation (123).

8. "Plixixit" makes an earlier reference to "'square-face' gin." The term may have been a play upon the ethnic slur "squarehead," which referred to immigrants from Germany or Scandinavia (see the *Oxford English Dictionary*, https://www.oed-com.proxy-um .researchport.umd.edu/view/Entry/188200).

9. Hamedoe based his account of Rizal on the first abridged English translation of *Noli Me Tangere*, which was originally published in Spanish. The anonymous translator entitled the English translation *An Eagle Flight* (1901), and the book numbers among the

historical acquisitions of the Boston Public Library, an institution that Hopkins likely patronized (*Annual List* 84).

WORKS CITED

Ammons, Elizabeth. "Afterword: *Winona*, Bakhtin, and Hopkins in the Twenty-First Century." *The Unruly Voice: Rediscovering Pauline Elizabeth Hopkins*, edited by John Cullen Gruesser, University of Illinois Press, 1996, pp. 211–19.

Annual List of New and Important Books Added to the Public Library of the City of Boston. Selected from the Monthly Bulletins. 1900–1901. Trustees, 1902.

Braithwaite, William Stanley. "Negro America's First Magazine." *The William Stanley Braithwaite Reader*, edited by Philip Butcher, University of Michigan Press, 1972, pp. 114–21.

Brown, Lois. *Pauline Elizabeth Hopkins: Black Daughter of the Revolution.* University of North Carolina Press, 2008.

Carby, Hazel V. *Reconstructing Womanhood: The Emergence of the Afro-American Woman Novelist.* Oxford University Press, 1989.

Chesnutt, Charles. *Conjure Woman.* Houghton, Mifflin and Company, 1899.

———. "Post-Bellum—Pre-Harlem." 1931. *Charles W. Chesnutt: Essays and Speeches*, edited by Joseph R. McElrath Jr., Robert C. Leitz III, and Jesse C. Crisler, Stanford University Press, 1999, pp. 543–49.

———. *The Wife of His Youth and Other Stories of the Color-Line.* Houghton, Mifflin and Company, 1900.

The Colored American Magazine. Negro Universities Press, 1969. HathiTrust Digital Library, https://catalog.hathitrust.org/Record/012294418.

Condict, Cornelia A. Letter to *Colored American Magazine* and Reply from Pauline Hopkins. *Colored American Magazine*, Mar. 1903, pp. 398–400.

Dahn, Eurie, and Brian Sweeney, project directors. *The Digital Colored American Magazine.* http://coloredamerican.org.

Dworkin, Ira, editor. Introduction. *Daughter of the Revolution: The Major Nonfiction Works of Pauline E. Hopkins.* Rutgers University Press, 2007, pp. xix–xliv.

Farr, Cecilia Konchar. "The Canonical Apple Cart: Reloaded." *J19*, vol. 4, no. 1, 2016, pp. 150–55.

Gilmore, Samantha, Edlie Wong, and Matt Cohen. "The Hopkins-Hamedoe Identity." *American Periodicals*, vol. 31, no. 1, 2021, pp. 54–67.

Gruesser, John. *The Empire Abroad and the Empire at Home: African American Literature and the Era of Overseas Expansion.* University of Georgia Press, 2012.

Hamedoe, S. E. F. C. C. "Osceola, the Great Seminole." *Colored American Magazine*, May 1901, pp. 39–42.

———. "Plixixit, the Palenachendeskies Kikoo of Arthabasca." *Colored American Magazine*, Jan. 1904, pp. 41–46.

Hopkins, Pauline. "'As the Lord Lives, He Is One of Our Mother's Children.'" *Colored American Magazine*, Nov. 1903, pp. 795–801.

———. "Bro'r Abr'm Jimson's Wedding. A Christmas Story." *Colored American Magazine*, Dec. 1901, pp. 103–12.

———. *Contending Forces: A Romance Illustrative of Negro Life North and South.* Colored Co-Operative Publishing Company, 1900.

———. "Converting Fanny." *New Era Magazine*, Feb. 1916, pp. 33–34.

———. "A Dash for Liberty." *Colored American Magazine*, Aug. 1901, pp. 243–47.

———. "Editorial and Publisher's Announcements." *New Era Magazine*, Mar. 1916, p. 124.

———. "General Washington. A Christmas Story." *Colored American Magazine*, Dec. 1900, pp. 95–104.

———. "The Mystery within Us." *Colored American Magazine*, May 1900, pp. 14–18.

———. "Talma Gordon." *Colored American Magazine*, Oct. 1900, pp. 271–90.

———. "The Test of Manhood. A Christmas Story." *Colored American Magazine*, Dec. 1902, pp. 113–19.

———. *Topsy Templeton. New Era Magazine*, Mar. 1916, pp. 75–84.

———. "Toussaint L'Ouverture." *Colored American Magazine*, Nov. 1900, pp. 9–24.

———. "To William Monroe Trotter." 16 Apr. 1905. *Pauline Elizabeth Hopkins: Black Daughter of the Revolution*, edited by Lois Brown, University of North Carolina Press, 2008, pp. 546–54.

———. *Winona: A Tale of Negro Life in the South and Southwest in the Magazine Novels of Pauline Hopkins*. Oxford University Press, 1988, pp. 285–437.

Hughes, Langston. "The Negro Artist and the Racial Mountain." 1926. *The Portable Harlem Renaissance Reader*, edited by David Levering Lewis, Penguin Books, 1995, pp. 91–93.

Knight, Alisha. *Pauline Hopkins and the American Dream: An African American Writer's (Re)Visionary Gospel of Success*. University of Tennessee Press, 2012.

McCaskill, Barbara, and Caroline Gebhard, editors. Introduction. *Post-bellum, Pre-Harlem: African American Literature and Culture, 1877–1919*. New York University Press, 2006, pp. 1–12.

O'Brien, Colleen C. "'Blacks in All Quarters of the Globe': Anti-imperialism, Insurgent Cosmopolitanism, and International Labor in Pauline Hopkins's Literary Journalism." *American Quarterly*, vol. 61, no. 2, June 2009, pp. 245–70.

Sanborn, Geoffrey. "The Wind of Words: Plagiarism and Intertextuality in *Of One Blood*." *J19: The Journal of Nineteenth-Century Americanists*, vol. 3, no. 1, Spring 2015, pp. 67–87.

Wallinger, Hanna. *Pauline E. Hopkins: A Literary Biography*. University of Georgia Press, 2005.

Wong, Edlie. "An Unexpected Direction: Pauline Hopkins, S. E. F. C. C. Hamedoe, and 'The Dark Races of the Twentieth Century.'" *American Literary History*, vol. 32, no. 4, Winter 2020, pp. 723–54.

CONTRIBUTORS

John Cyril Barton is associate professor of English at the University of Missouri, Kansas City. He is coeditor of *Transatlantic Sensations* (Routledge) and author of *Literary Executions: Capital Punishment and American Culture, 1820–1925* (Johns Hopkins University Press), chapter 5 of which won the Hennig Cohen Award for best scholarship on Herman Melville. Dr. Barton is currently writing a book on African American literature and anti-lynching legislation. His essays appear in journals such as *Nineteenth-Century Literature*, *Arizona Quarterly*, *Studies in American Fiction*, *Law & Literature*, *REAL: Research in English and American Literature*, and *Critical Horizons*.

Elizabeth J. Cali is an associate professor of English at Southern Illinois University Edwardsville, where she teaches courses on African American and Black diaspora literature, Black women's writings, and Black print culture. Cali is a specialist in African American literature, print culture studies, and editorship. She is the author of essays on Mary Ann Shadd Cary and Frances E. W. Harper, and she is currently writing a book on Pauline Hopkins's editorship of the *Colored American Magazine*.

Sabine Isabell Engwer is a PhD candidate at Freie Universität Berlin, currently finishing a dissertation on Pauline Hopkins that focuses on instances of intertextuality and interdiscursivity in the author's oeuvre. She holds a master's degree in comparative literature and North American studies from the Freie Universität Berlin. She has been a participant in Yale University's Teaching Fellow Program, attended CUNY's Institute for Research on the African Diaspora in the Americas and the Caribbean (IRADAC) as a visiting researcher, and received the Freie Universität Berlin's Junior Researchers Travel Grant. She has also been the recipient of a DFG dissertation scholarship.

John Cullen Gruesser, senior research scholar at Sam Houston State University and former president and longtime historian of the Pauline Elizabeth Hopkins Society, is the author most recently of *A Literary Life of Sutton E. Griggs: The Man on the Firing Line* (Oxford University Press, 2022) and the coeditor (with Alisha Knight) of the Broadview Edition of Pauline Hopkins's *Hagar's Daughter* (2021). A quarter of a century ago, he edited *The Unruly Voice: Rediscovering Pauline Elizabeth Hopkins* (University of Illinois Press, 1996), a collection of scholarly essays with an introduction by Nellie Y. McKay and an afterword by Elizabeth Ammons, which was the first book exclusively devoted to Hopkins.

Karin L. Hooks is associate professor of English at Lorain County Community College in Elyria, Ohio, where she teaches American literature, African American literature, and composition. Her research areas include American literary history, periodical studies, and women's fiction. She has previously published in *Legacy: A Journal of American Women Writers* and *Tulsa Studies in Women's Literature*; her recent article on Sarah Piatt can be found in *American Literary History and the Turn toward Modernity*.

Courtney L. Novosat earned her PhD in English at West Virginia University and is presently visiting lecturer of English in the Writing and Communication Program at Carnegie Mellon University. Her research explores how critical analyses of the rhetoric of race inform and reshape our understanding of nineteenth- and early twentieth-century speculative fiction. In addition to coauthoring several teaching resource guides for Bedford / St. Martin's Press, she has published essays in *MOSF: Journal of Science Fiction, Poe Studies*, and the collection *The Hallmark Channel: Essays on Faith, Race and Feminism* (2020).

Colleen C. O'Brien earned her PhD in the joint English and Women's Studies Program at the University of Michigan, Ann Arbor. She has been awarded two Fulbright grants, the most recent a research chair at the University of Western Ontario in 2012. She published her first book, *Race, Romance, and Rebellion: Literatures of the Americas in the Nineteenth Century*, in 2013 and received honorable mention for it from the British Association for American Studies. She won the Bank of America Award for scholarship in 2014 and currently teaches courses in African American studies, women's studies, and English.

JoAnn Pavletich is associate professor at the University of Houston–Downtown. She has published recent essays on Pauline Hopkins in *American Literary History, CLA Journal,* and *Callaloo*. She was the recipient of a Fulbright Scholarship and Department of State grantee for a two-year post at the University of Antananarivo, Madagascar. Prior, she served as director of composition at UHD from 2001 to 2006. Her teaching has focused on the lower-division writing classroom and upper-division American literature courses.

Geoffrey Sanborn is the Henry S. Poler '59 Presidential Teaching Professor of English at Amherst College. He is the author of *The Value of Herman Melville* (Cambridge University Press, 2018), *Plagiarama! William Wells Brown and the Aesthetic of Attractions* (Columbia University Press, 2016), *Whipscars and Tattoos: "The Last of the Mohicans," "Moby-Dick," and the Maori* (Oxford University Press, 2011), and *The Sign of the Cannibal: Melville and the Making of a Postcolonial Reader* (Duke University Press, 1998).

Cherene Sherrard-Johnson is a professor of English at Pomona College. She is the author of *Portraits of the New Negro Woman: Visual and Literary Culture in the Harlem Renaissance* (2007) and *Dorothy West's Paradise: A Biography of Class and Color* (2011) and the editor of *A Companion to the Harlem Renaissance* (2015). She is the author of two full-length poetry collections, *Vixen* (2017) and *Grimoire* (2020). Her creative nonfiction and poetry have been published in *The Rumpus, Plume,* the *New York Times Magazine, Verse, Daily, The Journal, Terrain.org, Blackbird, Water-Stone Review, Prairie Schooner,* and numerous other journals.

Valerie Sirenko received her PhD in English from the University of Texas at Austin in 2019. Her research specializes in nineteenth-century U.S. literature and culture, law and literature, critical race theory, and African American and multiethnic U.S. literature. Her current book project, *Fictions of Agency: Property, Personhood, and the Fragility of Legal Documents in American Literature,* examines how U.S. writers have critiqued law's structures of power using literary representations of destroyed documents. Her work has appeared in *ESQ, Western American Literature,* and *Early American Literature.* She currently teaches rhetoric and writing at Seattle Pacific University.

Hanna Wallinger is retired associate professor of American studies at Salzburg University in Austria. Among other publications in African American literature, her main field of research, she is the author of *Pauline E. Hopkins: A Literary Biography* (2005), editor of *Transitions: Race, Culture, and the Dynamics of Race* (2006), coeditor (with John Cullen Gruesser) of *Loopholes and Retreats: African American Writers and the Nineteenth Century* (2009), and coeditor (with John Cullen Gruesser) of a scholarly edition of Sutton E. Griggs's novel *The Hindered Hand* (2017). She is the past president of the Austrian Association for American Studies, a long-term member of the Collegium for African American Research, and a founding member of the Pauline Hopkins Society.

Edlie L. Wong is professor of English at the University of Maryland, College Park, and the author of *Racial Reconstruction: Black Inclusion, Chinese Exclusion, and the Fictions of Citizenship* (NYU Press, 2015) and *Neither Fugitive nor Free: Atlantic Slavery, Freedom Suits, and the Legal Culture of Travel* (NYU Press, 2009) and the coeditor of George Lippard's *The Killers* (University of Pennsylvania Press, 2014). Her work has also appeared in journals, including *PMLA, American Literary History, Social Text, American Literature, African American Review,* and *American Periodicals.* She is the recipient of fellowships from the NEH and Mellon Foundation and serves as the president of *C19: The Society of Nineteenth-Century Americanists* (2020–22).

INDEX